The Rogers Book

by Rob Cook

ISBN 978-1-888408-04-1

Copyright © 1999 Rebeats Publications
Second edition © 2004 Rebeats Publications

All rights for publication and distribution are reserved. No part of this book may be reproduced in any form or by any means including information storage and retrieval systems without the written consent of the publisher.

Cover photo by Mark Hamon of London, Ontario

Dedicated to Ben Strauss

1911–1998

Acknowledgements

This book would be little more than a shadow of the way it actually turned out had it not been for the gracious contributions and cooperation of a great many Rogers devotees:

Dave Simms

Dave Simms lives in St Marys, Ohio, near Covington. Although neither a drummer nor a historian, Dave recognized the importance of recording Rogers history before it was lost forever, and began to collect information on Rogers in about 1992. He went to great lengths and personal expense in tracking down former employees, even taking out ads in local papers and paying for interviews. Dave compiled the list of Covington-era employees found in the Covington section of the book, and supplied numerous photos, anecdotes, and leads.

Dave is shown at right with Patricia Miller Barker (local poet; see page 9) and at left at the top of the hill behind the old Rogers factory with the prizes he and Rob Cook unearthed with the aid of the metal detector; drum shells and hoops, a fire extinguisher, etc. On this day a good amount of sweat and discomfort went into the project; it was brutally hot, and the mosquitoes were relentless!

photo courtesy Dave Simms

Other sources of information, consultants and advisors;

John Aldridge, Jerry Ayles, Joyce Bashore, Louis Bernstein, Barbara Besecker (Kate O'Roark's sister), Ray Bungay, Roy Burns, Don Canedy, Robert Carone, John Cermenaro, Bob Chiasson, Jon Cohan, Dan Coluccio, Charlie Costello, Bill Crowden, **DAVE DREW**, Bruce Felter, Deborah Gillaspie, Dave Gordon, Phil Gorman, Terry Green, Bill and Jerry Hauer, Kirk Higgins, Bonnie Jenkins (Authority on pre-band instruments, pre-band teacher in Covington area), Craig Krampf, Lynn Lindemuth, William F. Ludwig II, John Maher, Don Martin, Steve Maxwell, Gary Minadeo, Joe Montineri, Gary Nelson, Jim Petty, Kate O'Roark (Covington area newspaper collector), Louis Porsi, Kelly Smith, Matthew Spitzer, Ben Strauss, Donald Tracey, Jerry Willford.

Sincerest apologies to those I've omitted!

Table Of Contents

Early Days of Rogers, Family	1
Rogers Calf Skin Heads	7
The Covington Era	9
Henry Grossman	12
Joe Thompson	13
Grossman Buys Rogers	19
Ben Strauss	20
Covington Factory Building	24
Rogers Personnel, Covington Era	26
George Way and Rogers	32
Roland "Peewee" Davidson	34
English Rogers	35
Arbiter Autotune Drums	38
Grossman sells Rogers to CBS	40
Covington Fire of 1967	41
CBS Moves Rogers From Covington	42
CBS-Era Rogers	43
Memriloc Hardware	46
Rogers Rack System	47
Rogers Snare Machine	48
R&D Projects, 1980s	53
Craig Krampf	54
Rogers Factory Moves 1952–1984	56
Roy Burns	57
Dave Gordon and John Cermenaro	61
Post-CBS Rogers	64
Rogers Endorsees	65
Craig Krampf	79
Dating interview with Bobby Chiasson	84
Rogers Catalogs	85
Colors	89
Steve Maxwell Collection	95
Gary Nelson Collection	97
Bruce Felter Collection	99
Ray Bungay collection	101
Bobby Chiasson Rogers photos	102
Brook Mays Music Rogers	107
Dating Guide	

Shells	117	Lugs	119
Strainers	123	Spurs	126
Badges	127	Bass Drum Logos	129
Cymbal Stands	131	High Hat Stands	134
Snare Stands	137	Pedals	140
Tom Holders	143	Hoops	148
Snare Drums	149	Outfits	157
Malletron	172	Timpani	173
Budget, Import Outfits	176		

Dyna-Sonic Snare Drum	179
Skinny Drum	195
Swivomatic Hardware	197
Parts	198
Index	225

Early Days of Rogers

Joseph H. Rogers learned his trade as a boy in the parchment yards of Dublin, Ireland. He immigrated to the United States in 1840, and in 1849 established what is reputed to be the country's first drum head factory. The most reliable sources available indicate that the first Rogers calfskin head facility was set up in Brewster's Station, New York, moving later to Danbury, Connecticut, and finally to Highview, New York. It was here that Rogers began to establish an international reputation as a supplier of top quality calfskin drum heads. Up until this time nearly all banjo heads had been made from sheepskin, which was easier to treat in terms of equipment, materials, and knowledge. Sheepskins, because they contain very little natural glue, wear more quickly and lose their tone from the constant pounding of the drum sticks. Although the prices of Rogers calf heads were higher, customers gladly paid extra to get the superior performance.

Joseph H. Rogers

Joseph H. Rogers Sr. won a blue ribbon, a bronze medal, and a citation at the World's Columbian Exposition in Chicago in 1893.

When Joseph Rogers died he left the operation to his son Joseph H. Rogers Junior (born in 1856) who maintained a tannery in Highview but moved his base of operations and opened a second tannery in Farmingdale, New Jersey in 1909. (Actually the facility was about a mile outside of downtown Farmingdale, "West of the center of town on the road to Ardena.") The standards of excellence established by Joseph Rogers Sr. were maintained by the family. By the early 1920s, Rogers heads were shipped as standard equipment on all of the finest banjos made by Gibson, Vega, George B. Stone, Walberg & Auge, Odell, M. Chapman, Wm. L. Lange (Paramount,) Weymann & Son, Bacon, and dozens of others. Rogers heads were not the cheapest, but were without question the finest. Even drum companies that eventually opened their own tanneries continued to catalogue Rogers drum heads as a premium option.

The banjo (and drum) head business was very lucrative for the Rogers family, particularly the first two generations. The fact that their heads were priced higher did not indicate that they were making more profit per head, since they had to spend more for premium skins to process. They sold far more heads than any of their competitors. The firm produced leather products in addition to drum heads; leather coverings for heavy books, as well as coverings for artificial arms and legs. Though the firm employed only about eight employees, they processed up to 500 skins per day. (One fair-sized skin could yield up to 8 heads.) Employees of the 1940s (when production was tapering off) remember that the Pennsylvania Railroad was still a major transporter of the skins. Large tractor-trailors would pull in weekly, and literally tons of skins would be unloaded into huge vats directly below the main head processing building in Farmingdale.

Joseph H. Rogers Junior left the business to two sons, Joseph B. Rogers and Cleveland S. Rogers.

Joseph H. Rogers Junior

The blue ribbon and bronze medal awarded to Joseph H. Rogers at the 1883 Colombian Exposition in Chicago.

The site of the Rogers tannery in Highview, New York. A secluded spring-fed pond.

The former home of Joseph B. Rogers, a few hundred yards from the former tannery site. When the author knocked at the door to inquire as to whether the current resident was aware of the Rogers connection, he met 91-year-old Helen Jervis who once knew Joseph B. Rogers. He built this house, she related, in 1924 and frequently shopped for groceries at her family's shop in a nearby village. As a young girl she visited the tannery with classmates on a field trip.

When his father died in 1929 Cleveland assumed control of the Farmingdale operation, while Joseph B. operated the Highview tannery. Surviving relatives remember "Uncle Cleve" as an affable man with a ready wit. Cleve was a member of the Iroquis Hunting and Fishing Club (private) in White Lake, New York, and went there nearly every weekend. He frequently took along employees on a rotating basis so everyone had a chance to enjoy the rustic setting. He nearly always was in the company of his faithful dog who had run of the factory in Farmingdale. Cleve was a crack shot who often had employees throw clay pigeons for him during the lunch break. According to a former employee, a visitor once taunted Cleve, "If you're such a good shot, Mr. Rogers," he said as he threw his hat high in the air, "let's see you hit that!" The words were barely out of his mouth before there was a crack of gunfire, and the hat settled to earth with the middle blown out.

Cleveland and Joseph B. had two sisters, Grace and Ethel. Ethel married Clayton Jones who worked for Cleveland in Farmingdale, doing all of the paint work on drums as well as some skin work. Clayton was very skilled at lacquering drums, using a lazy-susan to spin the drum as he quickly and evenly applied the paint. Relatives remember Ethel sitting at home in the evenings putting stitching on mallets that Rogers produced. Clayton's son Roger Jones also worked in the factory, in the head department just after World War II until Cleveland died in 1951 and the operation was sold to Grossman.

By the time Cleveland and Joseph B. inherited the family business, the winds of change were beginning to blow a death knell. Competitive pressures were the first factor, as Leedy, Slingerland, and Ludwig all started up their own tanneries. Although these firms catalogued Rogers heads as a premium option, the higher prices of Rogers heads slowed the demand for them when the nation's economy crashed.

The decline of popularity of the banjo played a major role in not only the Rogers family fortunes, but also those of all three of the major drum companies of the late 1920s; Leedy, Ludwig, and Slingerland. Slingerland had been a manufacturer of stringed instruments including banjos since the early 1920s. When Slingerland learned that Ludwig was responding to a government bid request for banjos, it prompted them to retaliate by beginning drum production. Both Leedy and Ludwig began to gear up for banjo production at the worst possible time. It was terribly expensive, the banjo's popularity began to plunge, and neither company could afford that kind of loss.

Cleveland S. Rogers served in the Expeditionary Forces in World War I; he joined the family business when he returned in 1922

Cleve and his dog at the factory

This was tremendously stressful for U.G. Leedy, who was already ill. He sold his entire operation to the Conn Company in Elkhart and died a year later. Soon after that, economic woes magnified by the banjo investment forced the Ludwig family to also sell their business to Conn.

Joseph B. Rogers decided to close his tannery and retire, while his brother Cleveland sensed an opportunity and decided to begin manufacturing drums– something that had undoubtedly been in the back of his mind ever since the drum companies began to operate their own tanneries. Many instruments, accessories, and hardware that Rogers sold was purchased from other manufacturers such as Zildjian, Gretsch, and Walberg & Auge. They did, however, steambend their own shells, apply the pearl coverings or lacquer, sew mallets, etc.

By the time Cleveland Rogers died, his company was producing over 150 items for percussion instruments and banjos. Additionally, he had diversified his operation beyond the music business. By the late 1930s, Cleve was forced to dip into his personal savings to keep the company in the black and could see that he would have to diversify to restore profitability.

Cleve hired a man named Miller from Philadelphia to design and install a full machine shop. There were five lathes, three or four punch presses, and drilling machines. This equipment was used to produce items as varied as tape measures, ladders for military trucks, and bolts for bolt-action guns. Much of the business was done on a sub-contracting basis for larger firms holding big government supply contracts.

During the 1940s the firm occupied four buildings; the largest was for processing calfskin heads, one of the smaller buildings was for painting drum shells, the other two housed the machine shop, drum assembly, and shipping.

Cleveland S. Rogers with Grand-niece Lynn Fenton, 1944

photo by Ray Bungay

The house (50 Academy St., Farmingdale) as it looked in 1998.

Cleveland Rogers and wife Ethyl in front of their home at 50 Academy St. in Farmingdale, New Jersey

The number of workers usually totalled 8 or less. This was pretty much a "family shop." Cleveland's brother-in-law Clayton worked with Mr. Megill in the wood shop. Mr. Megill's son Joe worked as a bookkeeper for a while in 1942, and his brother-in-law Jeff Smith worked as a scraper. Head finisher Jesse Smith worked there for 20 years. Head quality remained high and although the demand had dropped markedly, they coninued to ship heads all over the world. Jay Russell (a machinist from 1943–1945) and G. Donald Conrow (bookkeeper, salesman, truck driver in 1941) remember shipping heads to Africa, China, and many other destinations.

Photo by Ray Bungay

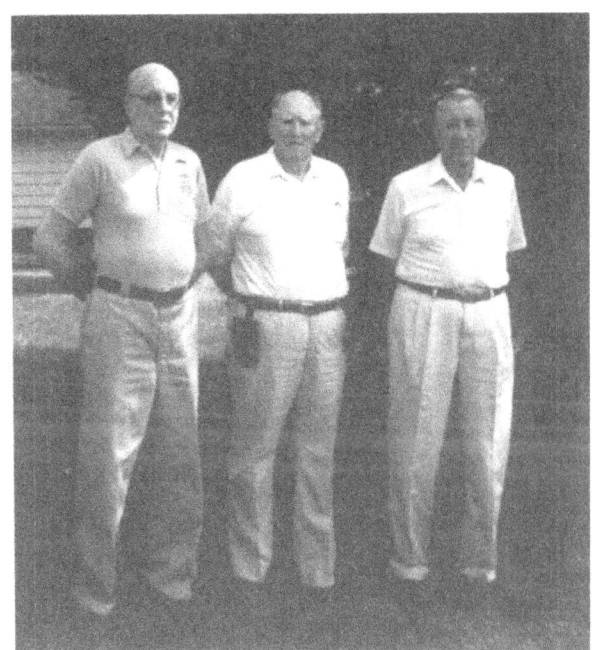

1998 photo of Rogers employees of the 1940s.
(l to r) Jay Russell, Joe Megill, and Donald Conrow

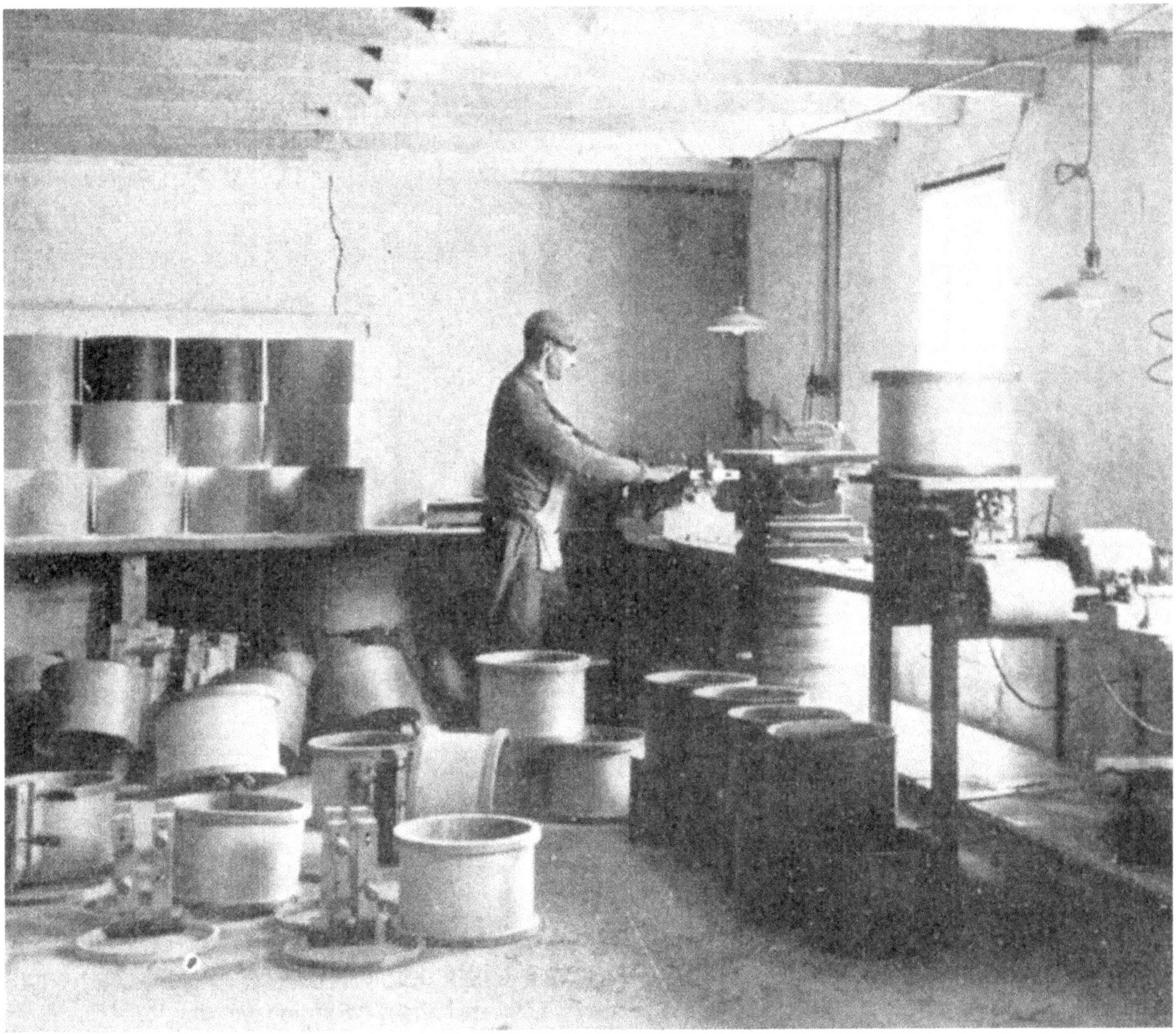

Drum manufacturing in Farmingdale, mid 1930s

Photo courtesy Dave Drew

Cleveland S. Rogers
Born 1890, died Saturday, May 17, 1952. First buried in Evergreen Cemetary, Farmingdale, New Jersey, and later moved at the insistence of family members to the family plot in a rural cemetary in Bloomingberg, New York.

Donald Tracey (nephew of Joseph B. Rogers and grandson of Joseph H. Rogers Junior) visits the family plot in Bloomingburg, a rural New York cemetary. The cemetary is located about 1.5 miles from the site of the Highview tannery.

ROGERS CALF SKIN HEADS

There were two basic reasons why Rogers skin heads were superior to any competition. They were made from the very finest materials available, and the processes & workmanship of the manufacturing process were unparalleled. As the Rogers catalogs of the 1930s pointed out, there were many skin heads on the market to choose from. These included:

Sheep skin Rogers cautioned their customers that some of their competitors made their heads from sheep skin and represented them as calf skin. These hides contained little or no glue and wore out quickly.

Goat skin Another inferior hide which, according to Rogers, was often sold as genuine calf skin. Like sheep skin, this material was inferior in quality to calfskin.

Veal calf The highest grade of calf skin, veal calf came from cattle which were fed only milk from the cow. This type of feeding provided the calf with "an excellent and healthy constitution thereby eliminating imperfections usually attendant in calves fed by other means." These hides were plump and tight-fibered. Rogers applied their name only to heads made from veal calf hides.

Patent feed calf Slightly inferior in quality to the veal calf hides, these hides came from calves that were fed by the farmer; patented feeds, skim milk, or buttermilk.

Pasture calf The lowest grade of hide, from calves allowed to graze in the pastures.

Grades of Rogers Heads, 1938

Three Star Brand, Superior Brand The "ultimate" head; the very best that Rogers was capable of producing. Three Star Brand heads were from Farmingdale, Superior Brand were from Highview.

Union Brand, First Quality Brand The next step down from Three Star and Superior. Rogers described these heads as "superior in every respect to competitive makes" and warranted them to be free from flaws and defects. First Quality Brand heads were from Farmingdale, Union Brand heads were from Highview.

Daisy Brand These heads were slightly off in color (the heads above were all guarenteed to be all white) or bearing some other slight defect which was "not detrimental to either wearing qualities or tone value."

Soo Brand These heads were not stamped with the Rogers name or bleached white; a budget head, though still made from veal calfskin.

Earliest known Rogers catalog; head booklet, mid 1920s

Highview, NY tannery stamp

Farmingdale, NJ tannery stamp

Processing the skins

The truckloads of skins were received pretty much free of flesh, but with hair. The heads were unloaded from the trucks directly into large soaking vats, where they soaked for two days.

When the skins came out of their initial soaking bath, they were put on a barrel-like board where the remaining flesh was removed and the rough edges were trimmed. They were next put into the "secret chemical bath," perfected by Rogers, for two weeks. This conditioned the skin and removed a lot of the hair. Now the skins were ready to be stretched onto drying frames.

Stretching skin onto drying rack

As soon as the skins were mounted on the drying frames, they were placed in the drying room for 24 hours. Former employees remember that they had to walk through the drying room to get to the office, and that the temperature there was kept over 80 degrees Farenheit year-round.

Shaving the skin

When the skins were removed from the drying room after 24 hours, they were scraped again. By this point, the procedures were done only by qualified and experienced workmen. One of the main "skin scrapers" for many years was William E. Gravatt. Cleveland Rogers' niece Marylyn loved to visit the factory because the Gravatts lived right across the road and had a daughter Marjorie's age she could play with. This daughter always fascinated Marylyn because she had an extra thumb. Gravatt's son Robert W. Gravatt also worked for Rogers for a few years.

Drying the skins outdoors

After the skins left the drying room and were scraped, they were taken outside to the drying field. Rogers prided themselves on the fact that the sun and open air bleached their heads, while other companies resorted to chemicals. This procedure took longer and was more costly, but this was part of the reason Rogers heads were more durable.

The dried heads were now ready for a final scraping. This final scraping was the most delicate stage of the entire process. Skilled workmen used 14-pound half-moon shaving knives with razor-sharp feather-edge blades to scrape the skins to a uniform thickness. It took workers at least three years to reach this level of skill which paid the top salary in the factory. This scraping was done in a clean room where the white shavings were carefully preserved and sold for use as gelatin stock.

Finally the scraped skins were removed from the racks and sent to the cutting bench where workers could produce over 400 heads per day.

It is unclear whether competitors did not know how to produce white heads using natural processes the way Rogers did or whether they found it neccessary to speed the process up. For whatever reason, they used chemicals in the whitening stage– usually sulfuric acid and hydrogen or sodium peroxide. (The more delicate "slunk" heads made from the hides of unborn calves and used for the snare side heads of snare drums were placed in a room with burning sulfer for less than an hour.) These processes resulted in heads of lesser quality than Rogers.

The Covington Era

The Covington era is what "put Rogers on the map" as a major drum manufacturer. It was while the company was in Ohio that it grew into one of the largest and most reputable drum companies in the United States. The first three years after the move from Ohio to California saw a temporary setback and a roaring resurgence to the third largest drum company in the country before a total collapse, but we're getting ahead of our story.

There were four basic factors in the Rogers Covington-era success story. The first was the man from Cleveland who bought the company and moved it to Ohio, Henry Grossman. The second was the man to became, to most endorsers and dealers, "Mr. Rogers;" Ben Strauss, whose job can best be described as sales and marketing manager. The third was Henry Grossman's good friend and business associate Joe Thompson. Thompson lived in Covington, the small Ohio town about 25 miles north of Dayton (approximately 225 miles from Cleveland.) The fourth was the Covington community itself, epitomizing the heroic notions of small town America. Without any one of these four factors, it's difficult to imagine Rogers gaining a shadow of the success it enjoyed.

COVINGTON

Simple lives,
Yet, complex in minor ways.
Families born to live and to die here,
within numbered, counted dates.
"A friendly town,"
I've heard many people say.
It has a lingering wave of
homespun passion throughout.
We'll live here–
We'll die here.
That's what Covington is all about.
People here seem "dubbed"
in hometown laughter, unlike big city ways.
It's a town united whenever sorrow invades.
There is sometimes a sting of loneliness
in the air... It's quiet, tame.
Neighbors have a way of blending,
A way of coping, good or bad.
But that's what Covington is all about.
Simple, yet complex in minor ways.
            Patricia Miller Barker

SMALLTOWN HARMONY

It grows on you...
Living in a small town.
All is familiar:
Even the curves in the road
can be driven blindfolded by those who live here.

It grows on you...
living here.
Everyone knows your name.
Your life is an open book
for all to read.

It grows on you...
The small town shops–
window displays from locals.
Here, your name is your honor.

It grows on you...
It traps your soul
Once you stay here past the leaving
time limit,
you must stay forever.

Our kids have grown up here.
They have their roots secured,
All made from home spun Harmony
Welcome to our small town...
            Patricia Miller Barker

Covington, Ohio, Corporation Limit

The flutophone was an instrument that Thompson invented long before Rogers came to Covington. (See page 15.) The Norman Rockwellian cover photo for the Flutophone instruction book was taken in a Covington school classroom on a Sunday morning after church by Paul Cromer who operated a photo shop in Covington.

Top row, back of room to front: Barbara O'Roark, Dick Shuff, Maxine Carey, Marilyn Davis
Second row from top: Emily Fessler, Howard Anderson, Elaine Arendall, Lewis Deeter, Richard Roberts
Third row from top: Diedre Wells, Dick Weer, Deanne Gish, Bettyann Davidson (niece of Joe Thompson)
Lower left: Janet Idle

Rogers donates drums to Covington High School

On Memorial Day (May 30th), 1961, the Covington High School Buccaneers were given a new set of Rogers marching drums. Participating in the presentation were (from left) : Joe Thompson, an unknown member of A.B. Cole Post #80 of the American Legion, F.V. Miller (also representing the Post,) "Biddy" Etter, School Superintendant C.S. Phillips, and Band Director Larry Hickman. (Photos courtesy of Ray & Edith Parks, former Rogers employees, via Dave Simms.) The band member standing behind the bass drum is Ron Parks, son of Ray and Edith. At this writing, Ron still owns his double-bass Rogers outfit.

HENRY GROSSMAN

Henry Grossman was born in Latvia in 1898. He emigrated to the United States as a child, growing up in Baltimore. As a young man he planned to become a physician and followed that dream to the point of enrolling in pre-med studies at Johns Hopkins University. His family could not afford the financial burden of this education and he reluctantly withdrew from classes in 1917 to take a job as a road salesman for a Baltimore music wholesaler.

Grossman was not a musician but had a deep appreciation for music and soon became the firm's top salesman because of his willingness to go to great lengths to satisfy his customers quickly. When the wholesaler expanded into the midwest a few years later, he was given a larger territory including Ohio, Indiana, and western Pennsylvania. At that point he moved to Cleveland which would be his hometown for over 70 years. In 1923 he left the sales position to found his own wholesale music supplier, Grossman Music.

Grossman was not content to be just another wholesale distributor of products made by other companies; his success was greatly enhanced by a number of proprietary products he helped develop such as Joe Thompson's mouthpiece puller, the Flutophone, Rogers drums, Grover banjo and guitar tuners, and other items.

Grossman did not marry until the age of 89, but he is remembered by most who knew him as a family man. Many former Covington Rogers employees interviewed still refer to him as Uncle Henry. His nephew, the late Joseph Berger, joined Grossman Music in the late 1940s and eventually became president. His great-nephew Richard Berger is currently head of the firm which is now known as Grover/Trophy Music Products.

Henry Grossman was committed to industry service; he was active in trade associations, serving as president of the National Association of Musical Merchandise Wholesalers from 1946 to 1950. In 1977 that group honored him as the first recipient of their "Industry Leadership Award." He was a founding member of another trade organization, the American Music Conference, in 1947. He headed that group's finance committee for over 20 years. Grossman was elected to the American Music Conference Hall of Fame in 1981 after having served on the board of directors for 34 consecutive years.

It would be difficult to overstate the impact that Henry Grossman had on music education and enjoyment in 20th century America. In one 35-year period (1946–1981) he sold nearly 20 million Flutophones throughout school systems in the United States. He was at one time the nation's largest wholesaler of sheet music, stocking over 75,000 titles. Grossman did business out of a six-story building in the warehouse district of Cleveland. The ground floor was used for shipping and receiving, the second floor was where the sheet music press was located, the third floor was for guitar and drum assembly, and the top three floors housed offices. Henry liked to point out to visitors that from his office window he could watch the Cleveland Indians baseball games.

Grossman was a 40+ year Mason who supported civic causes, giving generously to nearly all of Cleveland's cultural institutions. He swam daily and watched his diet, two habits to which he attributed his longevity and generally robust health. He received a number of awards from the Cleveland YMCA for the distances he regularly covered in the swimming pool.

Though he cut back on the time he spent in the office, Henry Grossman never really retired. He continued to go to the office at least one day a week well into his 90s. He died in his sleep on October, 1995, at the age of 97. A memorial fund was established in his name, in care of the music industry's largest trade organization, the National Association of Music Merchants.

Henry Grossman   1898–1995

Joe Thompson

Josephus Brown Thompson was born in Newton Township, Miami County, Ohio, on November 5, 1897 to George W. And Cora Brown Thompson. As a young man, Joe played drums and saxophone with various musical groups of the area. He had natural talent for things musical and mechanical; he was fascinated with the workings of musical instruments and enjoyed repairing instruments– especially antiques. One of the first instruments Joe owned was a boxwood clarinet he inherited from his great-grandfather. That instrument had gone out of production in 1825 when it was replaced by the Albert System clarinet which was in the early 1900s succeeded by the present day Boehm system. (Joe had all of these instruments in his collection.)

In 1924 Thompson went into partnership with his longtime friend G.F. "Biddy" Etter in the Piqua Music Shop located at Wayne and Water streets in Piqua– about eight miles east of Covington. Etter had just returned from a short stint with the Wylie Orchestra in Cleveland. The rest of Etter's music career pretty much paralleled Thompson's; he was the same age and had also performed locally since the age of 13. For years he was a member of local orchestras led by Harold Greenameyer and Les

Shepard. The Piqua Music Shop was only in business until the Great Crash of 1929. During the 1930s and 1940s Etter taught private music lessons. During the school year of 1944-1945 when teachers were in short supply he directed the Covington High School band in the interest of keeping it going.

During the great depression Joe repaired instruments at his father's farm several miles south of Covington and augmented his income by playing in a six-man dance band in one-night stands. Between them, the band played a total of 27 different instruments.

As he began to accumulate vintage musical instruments (eventually amassing a serious collection,) Thompson developed a long-term dream that in his retirement he would tour with a group of musicians who all played

photo courtesty Edith Whitenack

instruments dating back through the last century. Hoping to format the presentations so they would illustrate the progress of music history since the Civil War, Thompson collected and refurbished instruments for over 40 years and planned to use each one to play music popular in the era in which it was made. He was delighted to make finds such as the cavalry horn (named for the ease with which it could be played by a mounted horseman) he found hanging in the window of a little shop near Cleveland. The horn, which he got for $20.00, was similar to what is today known as the baritone horn.

Other instruments in his collection Thompson prized: A Civil War drum with rope Joe believed to be original, prompting him to leave the broken drum unrepaired since he did not want to destroy it's antiquity. An experimental sliding saxophone (which more closely resembled a toy than an instrument) made in 1915 of extra narrow tubing. A flute made of unstained grenadilla; a tropical hardwood with both light and dark grain. Modern clarinets are often also made of grenadilla but are nearly always stained black. An old tenor horn played over the left shoulder with the sound projecting backwards– quite similar to today's tuba but with a reverse bell. Joe used to comment about that instrument, "You heard the band after it passed in those days, whereas now you hear it coming."

Thompson's repair business grew until he once again partnered with Biddy Etter in 1939, working out of a two-story brick building behind his house. From there they moved to High Street in Covington as the Thompson-Etter Music store. Both men's wives, Helen Thompson and Ruth Etter, were involved in the family business. (That shop continued in business until Etter's retirement in April of 1967 after a 50-year career in the music business.)

Biddy Etter

photo courtesy of Roland Davidson

Helen and Joe Thompson cutting the cake at their 29th wedding anniversary party on November 23, 1967

Joe Thompson was first married on March 1, 1916. He divorced on the day after his 21st anniversary, on March 2, 1938. While he was at the courthouse getting his divorce finalized, he met second wife Helen and married her a few months later, on November 23, 1938.

Joe Thompson was a small wiry man with a quick wit and unpretentious style. A gold tooth flashed when he smiled, and he often wore a felt hat cocked to one side. He has been described as eccentric, and as a genius. He was outgoing and personable, but in a work environment was demanding and sometimes seemed to lack a strong sense of direction. This prompted one Rogers shop foreman to resign in frustration. Most friends and associates of Joe Thompson describe him as the world's nicest person. On his last birthday (1968,) a party was given for him at Don Canedy's home during which birthday greetings were phoned in from none other than Buddy Rich, who had not publicly played Rogers drums for two years.

Though he technically was making his living repairing instruments at his music store, Thompson continued his experiments at home. There was a large brick building he referred to as "the laboratory" as well as a smaller brick building known as "the model shop" which was used only by Thompson. Joe preferred to work here on his inventions late at night when there were few interruptions.

Perhaps Thompson's most significant invention was a "mouthpiece puller;" a device which enabled the user to remove a mouthpiece from a horn even when it seemed hopelessly jammed. The device is still available and in wide use today. What is probably even more significant about this invention is that it brought Joe into contact with henry Grossman. One of Grossman's sales reps, Ralph Staup of Tip City, Ohio, saw Joe's mouthpiece puller and asked Joe if it was the only one in existence. Joe said no, he had made two of them. Staub asked if he could borrow one to show to his boss in Cleveland. Thompson declined, expressing his reluctancce to get involved with "city slickers." Staup was persistent, however, and finally talked Thompson into loaning him one of the two mouthpiece pullers. The device was just the type of proprietary product that Henry Grossman was on the lookout for, and he immediately contacted Thompson to see if he could make more. Joe replied that it would be no problem to rig up a casting to produce the devices, and the relationship was established.

The next invention Thompson provided Grossman was the Flutophone. This was such a significant development in Thompson's career that one is engraved on his tombstone!

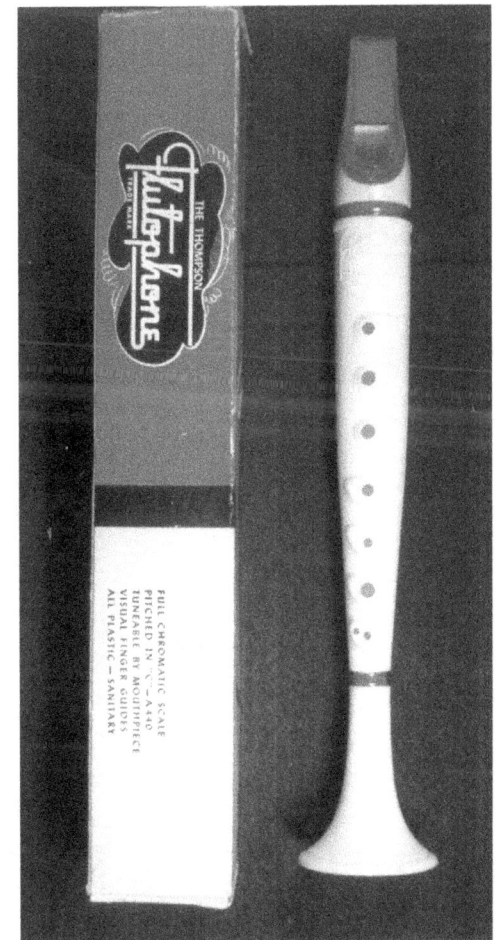

flutophone property of Mr. & Mrs. Richard Thompson, photo by Dave Simms

Joe Thompson was somewhat frustrated with the intonation problems of pre-band instruments such as the saxette and tonette– the two instruments in widest school use in the 1940s. With the help of Maurice Eidemiller he designed the holes of the flutophone. Thompson then contacted Trophy products, a plastic molding firm in Eleryia, Ohio, for the actual molding and production. The Cambridge recorder was also developed by Thompson and remains a popular pre-band instrument. The back of Thompson's tombstone is engraved with the flutophone, the Cambridge recorder, and a Dyna-Sonic snare drum.

The Flutophone was a huge success, which encouraged Thompson to make other plastic instruments, sales of which ran into the millions. There was the Skylark kazoo whistle, the "Hum-a-zoo," the Dixie and Piper fifes, the Sax-o-fun (sponsored by Spike Jones and modeled after the saxophone) andthe Hezzle, a junior slide whistle.

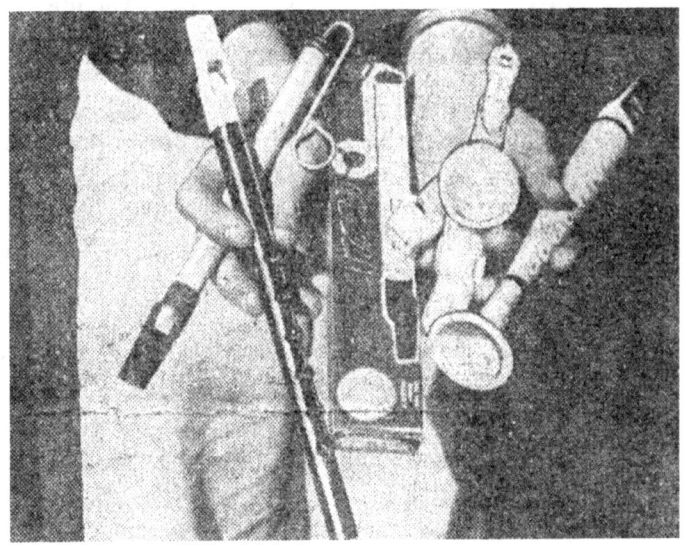

Thompson's plastic instruments

photos courtesy
Phyllis Graham Tucker

Another device invented by Thompson; a metal tenon joint expander. Pinching a sax neck or similar object between the two rollers and rotating the handle stretches the metal.

(Thanks to Dave Simms & Dean Schweizer for identifying this tool.)

phoho by Dave Simms

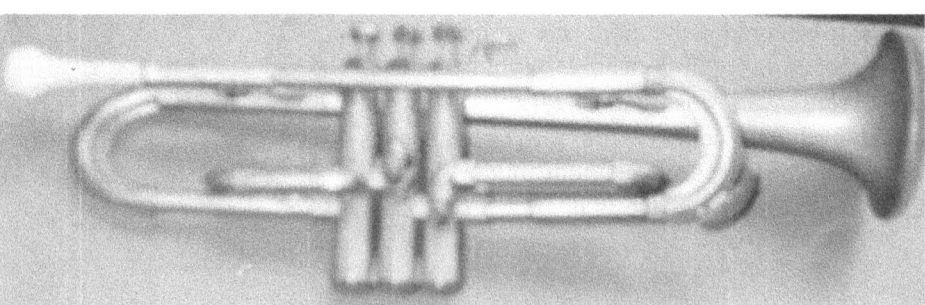

Thompson's plastic trumpet; only a couple prototypes were produced.

Peewee Davidson (see page 34) feels that one of Thompson's inventions with the greatest potential was one that never made it to market, a plastic trumpet. Davidson said Thompson spent a great deal of time perfecting the instrument, and was quite excited about the working prototypes he made. Thompson invisioned high schools ordering the instrument molded of plastic in school colors. Davidson still owns a couple of the prototype horns and speculates that the brass instrument makers were able to keep it off the market. Thompson never said why he abruptly dropped the project.

Dave Simms provides an interesting account of his visit to Peewee Davidson. "We were sitting in Peewee's kitchen one day when he mentioned the trumpet. My first thoughts were that this was somewhat interesting and probably worth noting. As he spoke more about it, I began to get the feeling that he was not referring to a toy instrument. He noticed that I was interested in hearing all the details of the trumpet, so he asked me if I wanted to see it. I'm a trumpet man, so I jumped at the chance. He went to his basement to retrieve it, which I could tell was not easy for this old man anymore. I about died when I saw it. Remarkable! I asked him what it sounded like. He said he'd never played any instrument, but that I was welcome to try it out. I tried to avoid looking too eager, but could hardly keep myself from snatching the instrument from his hands. I played some scales up and down, then just held the thing out where I could get a good look at it and stared. I was mildly shocked. I could not believe the tonal quality, projection, tone, tune, resonance, and playability! I *still* can't believe that an all-plastic (except springs) trumpet could sound *that* good. Peewee said that this was just the second prototype of the three that were made."

Like many inventors, Thompson often spent inordinate amounts of time inventing or improving devices which had marginal promise of monetary return. Ben Strauss at one point had to point out to him that some of the ideas Thompson was working on at the request of Louis Bellson were too experimental– even if Louis loved the prototype, the instrument stood no chance of commercial success. Thompson responded that he would work on Bellson's ideas on his own time; this was work he was doing more for self-gratification than for Rogers profitibility.

Thompson made an agreement with Henry Grossman that if Grossman bought Rogers, he would run it for him. Thompson bought stock in Rogers, and was given the title of plant superintendant. He continued to operate his music shop in partnership with Biddy Etter until May of 1967 when Etter retired and the store was dissolved. Thompson died less than a year later.

Dave Simms had heard that Joe Thompson died in the shower, and heard a few months later that he died in the hospital. It turns out that both accounts were accurate– he died in the shower at the hospital!

Joe's wife Helen lived on in their home until 1982. When she died, there was an "everything must go" estate auction. Over 175 vehicles were parked along the road. Most of the instruments, parts, and tools sold quickly, to the 200+ bidders in attendance. Household items were sold seperately, on the second day of the auction. Family members, unaware of the significance of Thompson's letters, photos, and drawings, burned or trashed everything that did not sell at the auction.

Even the Thompson family's heirloom photos were nearly lost. Covington's Marcella Poe, a book collector, had successfully bid on a box of old books on the second day of the auction. When she sorted out her purchases, she found a Bible dated 1867 at the bottom of the box. Inside it were Thompson family records of births, marriages, and deaths from 1802 through 1922. Between the pages of the Bible were family photos. Poe's husband Craig was touched by the treasure she brought home. As he told the newspaper reporter who came to look over the documents, Joe Thompson gave him his first job.

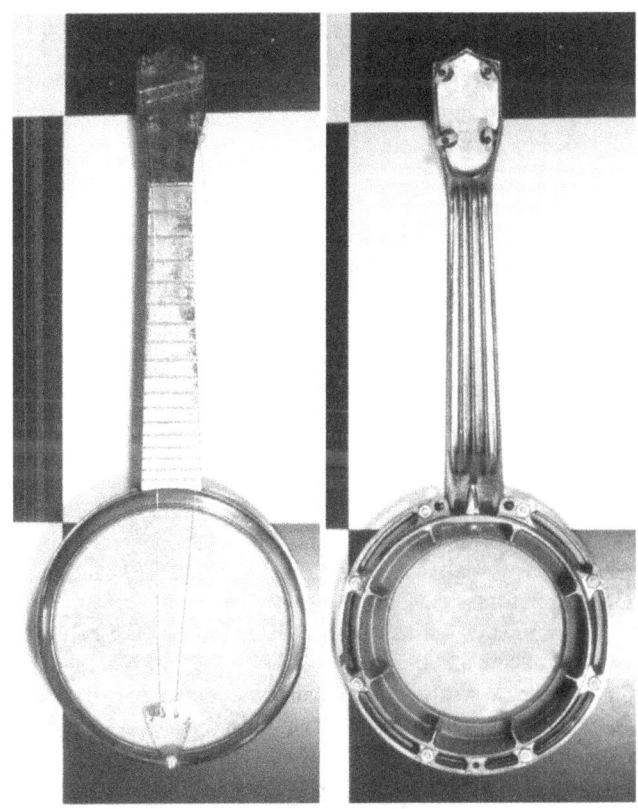

Prototype die-cast "Dixie" banjo that hung in Joe's lab for years.
photo by Dave Simms

Joe Thompson's grave, Covington, Ohio. (He died on March 8, 1968, after a three-week illness.) The inscription below the carved Flutophone: *Creative genius, extraordinaire* (sic) *human being in the finest sense, outstanding contributor to the world of music and all those sincerely associated with it.*

JOE THOMPSON EULOGY

Delivered by Henry Grossman on the occasion of Joe Thompson's funeral, March 11, 1968, in Covington, Ohio. Transcript provided by Dave Simms.

Dear Friends;

Reverend Eddy Henry asked me to give the eulogy for our departed friend, Joe Thompson. Though I knew that this would be the most difficult assignment I had ever undertaken, nevertheless, I accepted it with the hope that my emotions would hold out long enough to permit me to express what is in my heart.

Last November 5th, here in Covington, at the home of our gracious hosts, Evelyn and Don Canedy, through the thoughtfulness of Rogers' executives, we had the pleasure of celebrating Joe Thompson's 70th birthday. Who at that gathering could imagine the curcumstances under which we are assembled here today? Who, indeed, even remotely suspected that the honored guest of that evening would so soon be claimed as an honored guest by the Great Architect of the Universe?

The Scriptures tell us: "Man's life upon this earth is like the flower in the field, it bloometh in the morning and is cut down in the evening." With his prolific mind, his agile body and his cheerful spirit, Joe was still like a blooming flower. Alas, it is much too cruel to have him cut down so soon and so abruptly.

I met Joe Thompson 30 years ago, through our Ohio representative, Ralph Staup, of Tipp City. The relationship between us through all those years has been ideal. It was like the friendship of Damon and Pythias. Except for his beloved wife Helen, his partner, Bitty Etter, and his confidante Kermit Stade, I spent more days and nights with Joe than any other person now alive.

In our ventures, we lived through some mighty rough times together. Constantly by his side, all through our trials and tribulations, Joe had implicit confidence in our ultimate success. To me, he was both a source of inspiration and a tower of strength. And now, having achieved a measure of success, he has to forego the fruits of his hard labors.

The Lord bestowed upon Joe Thompson a spark of genious. He was an inexhaustable fountain of ideas. The creations of his mind have brought enjoyment and happiness to people of all ages. His Flutophone, his Recorder, and his other educational musical instrumentshave contributed to the cultural and educational development of countless thousands of children. They have started untold numbers toward successful musical careers. This in itself, Joe would often tell me, was a tremendous reward to him.

During the various Drum-O-Ramas conducted by Ben Strauss on Rogers drums, Joe would always tell me that such events gave him the thrill of his life. The fact that the world's top artists chose the instruments of his creation filled his heart to the brim with joy.

The highest tribute Joe Thompson could pay me was his declaration that I had inspired him to greater achievements. Actually, though, Joe had influenced the careers of Ben Strauss, Don Canedy, and manyothers.

Joe Thompson;s heart was made of gold. He never turned down an opportunity to do a favor for a friend, a neighbor, or even a stranger who needed help, neither asking nor expecting compensation. For example, one year ago, in Europe he met a manufacturer– a total stranger– who had production difficulties. Upon sizing up the situation, Joe advised him how to overcome them. When I again saw this man at the Frankfurt International Music Fair last week, he was exuberant. By following Joe's advice, he not only improved his product but nearly doubled production. He asked for Joe's address so he could send him a gift. No doubt the gift is enroute now.

Some years ago I read an essay entitled "How do you measure men?" Elaborating on this theme, the author asks: "Do you measure men by the amount of worldly goods they acquire? By the number of servants they employ? By the amount of charity they give? By the extent of the reputation they build up? No," says the author, "men are measured by the amount of service they render to their fellow men. As long as I knew him, that was Joe Thompson's creed. He detested foul play, and never understood the meaning of intolerance, much less practiced it.

Joe's philosophy on life was as deep as the ocean. During our discussions on the road, day after day, night after night, he would astound me with his rationalizations on government, education, economics, religion, science, and technoloy. His simple, homespun approach in these matters reminds me more of Abraham Lincoln than any man I have ever known or read about. Though not deeply religious, Joe acknowledged that a Supernatural Power had to exist to control the universe.

In patent applications, and in later descriptive text, we would often grope for the proper word or the exact technical phrase to define his inventions. While he never studied philology, it was he who often came up with the precise word which fitted like a silver picture in a golden frame.

Joe Thompson was a product of your native soil. Born on a farm close by, he was as much a part of Covington as Covington was a part of him. He loved the hill, the trees, the flowers, the brook, and his dog. However, the music shop was his true environment. It was here where he delighted to work and to experiment day after day, night after night. It was here where his best creations were developed and perfected. He was happy as a lark, after we acquired Rogers in 1952, that we decided to move the plant to Covington instead of Cleveland. This is indicative of the strong civic spirit he harbored. Today, he is a revered citizen of the music world, beloved for the legacy he left behind.

Joe Thompson's name will live long after all of us are gone, for his signature appears on many documents in the archives of the patent office in Washington. These will survive as long as there is a United States of America.

And now, I am addressing myself to you, dear Joe. You were not only a devoted friend and pal to me, you were a teacher, a guide, a counseler, a source of inspiration and, in my darkest hours, indeed a tower of strength. You were always confident that we would come out on top. You may be gone in the flesh, but your spirit will live on with me forever.

May the memory of your sterling personality prove to be an everlasting source of consolation to your beloved Helen, to your brother Louis, to your neighbors, friends, and admirers not only in Covington, but elsewhere in the world. We can never forget you Joe, and never will.

May your soul rest in peace.

GROSSMAN BUYS ROGERS

Grossman Distributing Company was a "jobber;" this means that the company sold only to music stores on a wholesale basis– they did not do business directly with the general public. For many years Grossman bought Ludwig drums from the Conn company and sold them to retail music stores. Conn had purchased Ludwig from the Ludwig family in 1930, moving production facilities from Chicago to Elkhart, Indiana. Wm. F. Ludwig Sr. moved from Chicago to Elkhart to work for Conn, but found the arrangement unacceptable and moved back to Chicago where Conn still had offices. In 1937 he formed his own drum company which he named the Wm. L. Ludwig Drum Company. Conn's lawyers protested, and the name was changed to the WFL Drum Company.

Conn had also purchased the Leedy Company, about a year before they bought Ludwig. Up until 1951 they made both Ludwig and Leedy drums in Elkhart, in the same facility. In 1951 the divisions were combined, and the drums produced were "Leedy & Ludwig" brand drums.

Henry Grossman could see the handwriting on the wall spelling out changes in the way drums were being distributed. In the early 1950s Conn began to consider getting out of the drum business altogether. They did just that in 1955, selling the Ludwig name back to the Ludwig family, and the Leedy name to Slingerland. The manufacturing equipment was split between Ludwig and Slingerland. The Ludwig company did not at this time have a sales force, so most of their drums were sold to jobbers such as Grossman. (A few music stores did buy directly from Ludwig.) Ludwig began to cut off the jobbers and concentrate on selling directly to the retail stores. This was not a sudden move; the jobbers were cut off one at a time and each one was a battle according to William F. Ludwig II.

Henry Grossman could see that he would need to somehow fill the gap that would be left when Ludwig drums would no longer be available to him as a jobber. He had already been buying drums from the Joseph Rogers Company of Farmingdale, New York, as well as calfskin drum heads. Rogers had been selling to not only Grossman but to other jobbers around the country. Knowing that Cleveland Rogers was in failing health and considering selling the business, Henry Grossman went to visit him. It was just the kind of situation that Grossman relished; the opportunity to buy a rather shaky small company and build it up. Grossman had no intention of becoming a major competitor in the drum manufacturing business; he just wanted to continue to be able to supply his dealers with a few drums in the interest of being a "full-service jobber."

Since Joe Thompson had been designing some drums, Henry Grossman told him that if he'd run Rogers, Henry would buy it.

It was unthinkable for Thompson to leave Covington. He took great pride in his family heritage there, once showing Henry Grossman an original copy of the land-grant deed by which President James Madison conveyed ownership of the property to the Thompson family. The decision was made to center the operation there. The local papers referred to the activity on Thompson's property as "Covington's best-kept secret." The factory building, which was built in 1952, could not be seen from the road and Henry Grossman would not issue any kind of statement until production had actually started. He later explained that the music industry was so highly competitive that it would have been damaging to announce his plans before they were implemented. Thompson built a tannery in Covington and they began head and hoop production there in 1954. The first public announcement of the establishment of Joseph Rogers Inc. in Covington was on May 5th, 1955, along with an announcement that work to double the size of the plant was about to begin. In 1956 they moved the rest of the factory from Farmingdale to Covington.

It should be made clear that the Rogers Drum Company was owned by Henry Grossman but did business as the Rogers Drum Company, selling to jobbers including the Grossman Company.

BEN STRAUSS

Ben Strauss was born April 4, 1911 in Kane, Pennsylvania (125 miles North of Pittsburgh). He took up the trumpet at 17, and started a little band with a seasoned saxophone player from the Nelson Maples Band who tutored the musicians in the band. The group was a 6-piece jazz-pop ensemble that primarily gigged in roadhouses. While he was on the road with the band his family moved to Cleveland, so when he came off the road to settle down he joined them there. He successfully auditioned for a spot in a radio station band, played there for a year or so, then went on the road again for a year. In 1937 he married and went to work at a music store, Shubert Music House of Cleveland. Strauss worked at the music store for 13 years before going to work for Grossman in 1950.

Ben Strauss (second from left) and His Cheerleaders; Kane, Ohio, 1931

photo courtesy Mark Garris

(l to r) Henry Grossman, Buddy Rich, daughter Elaine Strauss, Ben Strauss c. 1962

RC: What did you do at Grossman when you first went to work there?
Ben: I was in charge of shipping and receiving in the warehouse.
RC: How did you make the shift to Rogers?
Ben: I was familiar with drums from my years in retail as well as my experience with Grossman. Since all the shipping was done from Cleveland, I saw the drums coming in from Covington and I wasn't too happy with some of the things I saw. Not that there were terrible things happening... I just pointed things out to Henry when I felt something could be done better. Henry called Joe and told him that I would be talking to him about some of the changes I felt should be made.
RC: These weren't really professional drums at first?
Ben: No, but we did feel we were making good quality drums we could be proud of. A specific event comes to mind that prompted us to really get serious about making professional drums. We were exhibiting at a NAMM (National Association of Music Merchants) convention in Chicago in about 1957. Joe and Henry and I were all there in the room where the Grossman display included some of our new Rogers drums. One of our competitors came in. He didn't say much– he looked the drums over for a few minutes. Then he commented "not bad, for a bunch of toys...", and left. Henry came over to me and asked me if I had heard that. He was furious. He told Joe and I that we were going to really get serious about the drum business. That was what prompted Joe to start working on developing the Swiv-o-matic hardware.
RC: And your job became full time with the Rogers division of Grossman?
Ben: Yes.

The next nine years really witnessed the birth and growth of the Rogers Drum Company as a major force in the professional drum business. The three key figures were Henry Grossman, Ben Strauss, and Joe Thompson, and they had a very unique working relationship. The three did not have formal titles and job descriptions but managed to make drum history in the way they worked together. To define their roles in today's terms, Grossman was President and CEO. Strauss acted as the Marketing and Sales Manager as well as head of Artist Relations. Thompson was Chief Engineer and Designer.

Ben Strauss   c. 1967

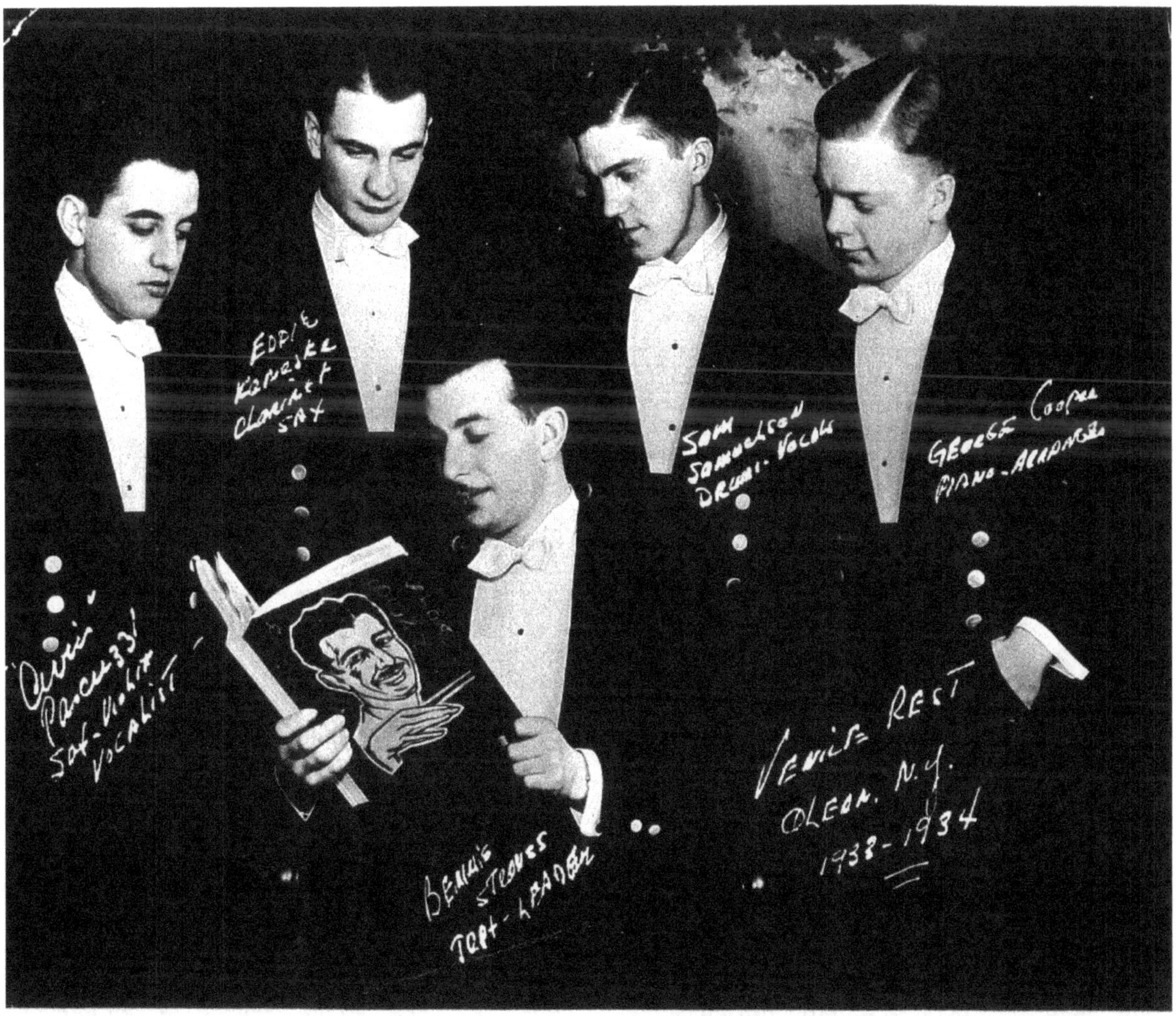

photo courtesy Mark Garris

Bandleader Ben Strauss with his orchestra at the Venice Restaurant in Olean, New York, 1933

photo courtesy Kirk Higgins

Ben Strauss

born April 11, 1911

10 years professional musician
13 years retail
26 years with Grossman/Rogers
22 years of retirement

died August 7, 1998

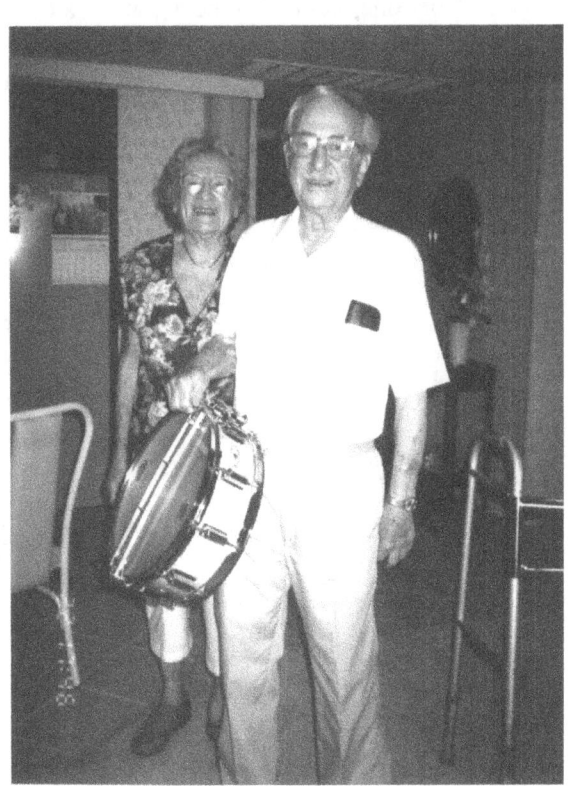

One of the last photos taken of Ben Strauss, taken by Kirk Higgins. Wife Julia looks on; Ben is holding a prized possession; the Dyna-sonic snare drum which was a gift from drum historian and author Harry Cangany.

THE COVINGTON FACTORY BUILDING

**The large letters and drum on the roof (circled) were evidently liberties taken by an artist–
former employees are sure they never existed.**

The concrete block building that was put up on Joe Thompson's property (only a stone's throw from his house) was built in a number of stages.

Joe did a lot of the construction himself, and personally supervised most of the rest. Although he was a very unique and talented man, he was not infallible, as some of his construction methods demonstrated. Joe and his helpers once poured a concrete floor for an expansion, which set up before they could level and smooth it. The floor had to be broken up and removed so it could be poured again. Russ Bunker (a supplier from Dayton) was making a call to the factory one day and was fascinated by the way Joe was going about constructing a wall for one of the plant's expansions. Only one section had been put up, a cement block wall. Joe dropped a load of fill with the scoop, then started to water it down with the hose. Russ warned him that the wall would fall down if he back-filled before he put in any joists of the other walls. Joe responded, "Oh, it's not going to fall!" and got back on the tractor to go get another bucket of fill. When he returned, he raised up out of the seat a couple inches so he could look over the scoop to see where the wall was in order to get his bearings on where to dump the fill. He had to raise a few more inches. Then he stood up all the way, to see that the wall was no longer there– it had fallen, just as Russ had predicted.

Still, Joe continued to do things his own way and at his own speed. For the fourth addition, he hired two men not known for their haste. One was a blind man who would pace off the distance to the sand pile from the cement mixer. Once he had the distance locked in his head he could toss whole shovel-fulls of sand from the sand pile to the mixer with great accuracy. This same man once won a weightlifting contest with two Rogers employees. The first lifted six concrete blocks at once, the second lifted five, then the blind man lifted seven.

photo by Dave Simms

This warehouse on Thompson Street in Covington was shared by Rogers and others in the 1960s. Rogers generally used it for storage of inventory, though it was used to store equipment during the fire cleanup.

This photo appeared in the Dayton Daily News in June of 1955. The accompanying story went into a detailed history of the Rogers company, explaining how Joseph Rogers had developed secret tanning processes which resulted in his renowned drum heads. The thrust of the story was that the new facility in Covington was now carrying on with the traditional manufacturing processes. The photo, however, illustrates that there was now a rather significant departure from the traditional procedures. All skins processed in Highview, New York, and Farmingdale, New Jersey, were scraped and shaved by hand. Some of the last employees of the Farmington facility have expressed the view that it was all the manual labor that had contributed to the demise of the Rogers drum and banjo head business. They point out that their competitors had all switched over to the use of machines such as the one in the photo, while Rogers continued to produce heads by hand. The additional labor expense priced Rogers heads out of the market.

Photo courtesy Kate O'Roark

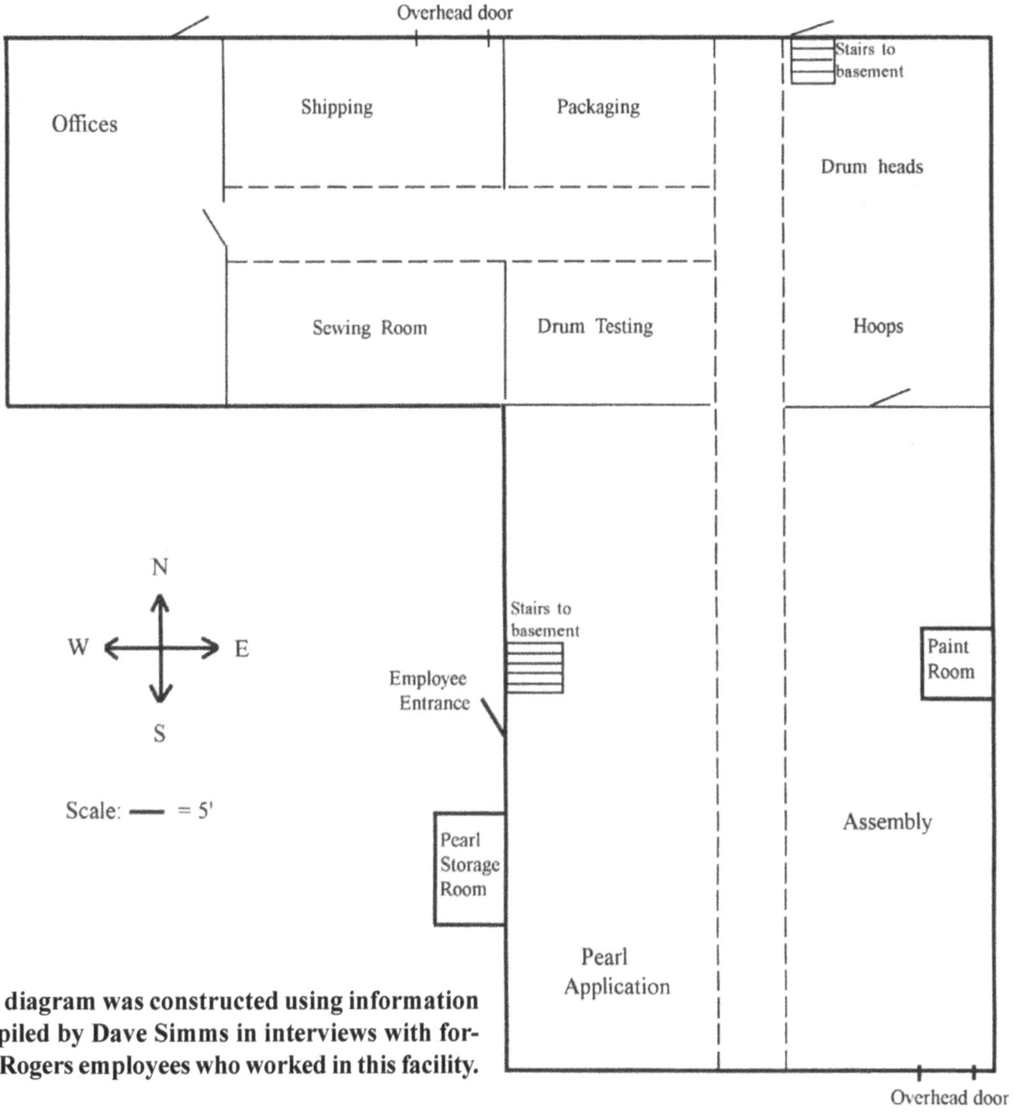

This diagram was constructed using information compiled by Dave Simms in interviews with former Rogers employees who worked in this facility.

ROGERS PERSONNEL, COVINGTON ERA

In the mid 1990s First Lady Hillary Clinton utilized the African slogan "it takes a village to raise a child" in her efforts to point out communal responsibility for the well-being of our children. In much the same spirit, the good folks of the village of Covington (population slightly over 2000,) along with some neighboring villages, shared responsibility for the well-being of the Rogers Drum Company. Although the company was not locally owned, the guy who was in charge was also responsible for having brought it to Covington: Joe Thompson was a beloved and integral part of the community. And although not a local, the owner was treated as such. Many Rogers staffers called Mr. Grossman "Uncle Henry" or simply "HS," and some continued to receive Christmas gifts from him long after Rogers had moved out of the area! Grossman endeared himself to the staff by expressing personal interest in them– he would occasionally put his hand on a shoulder and ask how life was treating you. Henry Grossman valued the concept of family members working together, and fostered the sense of family among his staff. There were annual picnics, a bowling team, and other get-togethers. Some of the Rogers "family" were indeed blood relatives. Probably the best example is Don Martin and his family. Don was the fifth employee to be hired at the Covington facility, just out of high school. (He was also one of the few to make the move with Rogers when it left the area.) Although Don's wife never worked for Rogers, most of the rest of his immediate family did:

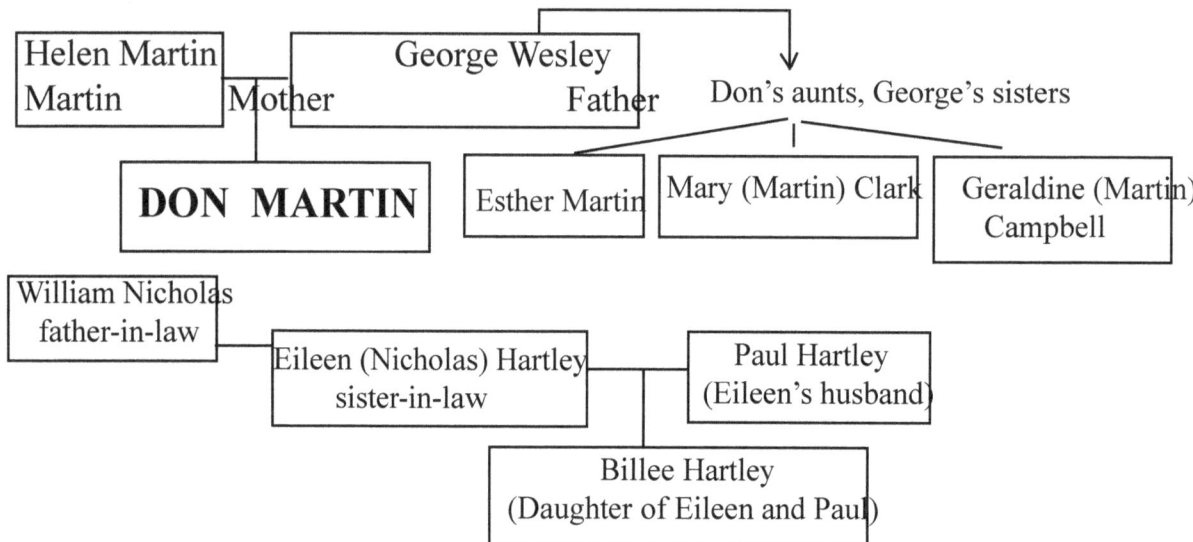

The first payroll of the Rogers Drum Company in Covington (1954) listed five employees. The number grew to twelve in 1955, 60 in 1965, and 110 in 1966. By 1967 CBS employed 120 workers in Covington and 45 in Dayton. The workforce was downsized by CBS beginning in 1968 when they first moved all operations to Dayton, then (1969) moved to California.

Adams, Pearl	Assembly
Alexander, Gladys	Joe Thompson's niece
Ashman, Carl	Hardware assembly
Barker, Jim	Painter
Bashore, Joyce	Supervisor; Covington, Dayton, Fullerton
Beireis, Helen	Assembly (member of the Rogers bowling team)
Bennett, Martha	Original employee
Black, Jeannie	Assembly
Blankenship, Bob	2nd shift machine shop foreman
Bowers, Willie (Brother-in-law of Dick Zindorf)	Machine shop; made metal hoops and welded
Bowman, Carl related to	Pearl room
Bowman, Levi related to	Night janitor
Bowman, Lynn	Accountant; made the move with Rogers to California, 1969
Buckingham, Buck	Punch press operator.

Once lost a finger in a shop accident; the finger was put in a can and tossed down the hill behind the factory!

ROGERS PERSONNEL, COVINGTON ERA

   father of
Buckingham, Jeannie .... Assembly
Burns, Roy .... Endorsee, consultant, clinician
Brush, Gary .... Shipping, packaging
Callison, John .... Machine shop
Campbell, Geraldine .... Beater ball assembly
   (Don Martin's aunt)
Canedy, Don ....Hired as education director; became marketing director with CBS
Cippos, Julius .... Cut & laid pearl in bass drum hoops.
   Often sang Hungarian folk songs as he worked. Julius made delicious cabbage rolls that he sold to co-workers.
Clark, John .... Punch press
Clark, Marie .... Beater assembly
Cline, Gladys .... Slide whistles
Collett, Sam .... Drill press
Collins, Bobby Jr. .... Assembly
Cool, Wilbur
Cross, Ruby .... Screw machine
Curtner, Bob ....Assistant plant manager (Covington,) purchasing agent (Dayton)
Davids, Bill .... J. Thompson understudy
Davis, Dan .... Supervisor 1964–1969, went to California
Davis, Mary Kay .... Assembly
Diltz, Doug .... Machine shop
   Married to
Diltz, Mary .... Assembly
Dunlap, Harvey .... Original employee
   Married to
Dunlap, Audrey .... Original employee
Ellis, Ellen .... Drum head assembly
   Married to
Ellis, John .... Drum head assembly
Ellis, Lorren .... Machine shop
   (Son of John and Ellen)
Engle, Dorothy; see Platt, Dorothy
Ewing, Roger A. .... Painting and pearling
Fricke, Harold .... Shipping agent
   Married to
Fricke, Roberta .... Drum assembly
Geis, Louis .... Engineering draftsman
Griffin, Hazel .... Beater assembly
Hahn, Ralph
Harmon, John .... Assembly, original employee
   (Not related to Marky.)
Harmon, Marky
Marmon, Mike .... General maintenance
Hartley, Billie .... Lug assembly
   Daughter of
Hartley, Eileen .... Beater assembly
   Married to
Hartley, Paul E. .... Maintenance
Hetzler, John .... Machine shop
Hill, Jessie .... Beater assembly
Hittle, Gene .... First plant manager
Holms, Ray .... Truck driver
Horlocker, Humpty
   Made the first Rogers drumsticks when Rogers got their stick machine. Humpty was a timpanist and drummer who participated in jam sessions nearly every day with Joe Thompson and Biddie Etter. These jam sessions were generally carried out with the aid of the plant intercom, with the three in different parts of the plant!
Houck, Edna .... Lug assembly 1963–1969

ROGERS PERSONNEL, COVINGTON ERA

Hughes, Charles..	General manager, 1968 (CBS)
Johnson, Ralph Sr..	Lug assembly
Father of	
Johnson, Ralph Jr...	Machine shop
Kimmel, Forrest...	Machine shop, drum assembly
Kritzer, Betty...	Secretary
Landis, Alice..	Original employee
Leopard, Roberta..	Assembly
Leopold, Ronald..	Research and development
Manning, Diane...	Secretary
Martin, Don...	Covington Production manager, Fullerton plant manager
Nephew of	
Martin, Esther..	Beater assembly
Sister-in-law of	
Martin, George "Wes"...	General foreman.

    Wes used acetone to melt the color off of scrap pieces of pearl to make his own fishing lures
  Married to

Martin, Helen..	Head sewer
Minnich, Luellen...	Assembly; put heads on drums & helped out wherever she was needed
Mullenix, Gorden..	Cut & glue pearl
Nicholas, Bill...	Machine shop
Father-in-law of Don Martin	
Parks, Edith...	Packer & assembled slide whistles
Parks, Ray..	Truck driver, laid pearl, etc.
Platt, Dorothy..	Assembly, secretary

   Dorothy was hired as Dorothy Engle; while in Rogers employ she married Jim Platt. She worked as a secretary and in assembly. Dorothy suffered a broken toe during the cleanup after the big fire when a piece of machinery fell on her foot.

Platt, Jim...	Truck driver.

   Between trips with his truck, Jim would sometimes hang out with Joe in his "lab." He relates that he was once there when Joe was taking the dent out of a horn and was amazed at the patience Joe demonstrated as he sat and slowly rolled a marble back and forth across the brass tubing of the horn. Jim finally asked if that method could really get dents out. Joe assured him that it did, and that he had a collection of six different sized marbles specifically for dent removal. Jim was present when Gene Krupa visited the factory and pulled a set of drums right off the assembly line. They set the drums up in the shipping area and Krupa treated the employees to a drum solo. Jim stood guard after the big fire.

Poor, Wilma...	Beater assembly
Rantz, Darla...	Drum Assembly
Rhodes, Leonard...	Electrician

    Along with Joe Thompson, Leonard did most of the electrical work. He also assembled timpani & bass drums, was a driver, and later was the Dayton warehouse manager. Leonard worked in a separate building referred to as "the chicken house," making timpani and large mahogany bass drums. One day he borrowed Bob Curtner's new GTO and wrecked it. Curtner salvaged some parts from the car, but had to junk most of it. Thirty years later he bought a similar car and installed those rare options he had saved all those years.

Rice, Jim..	Machine shop.

    Came out of retirement to work at Rogers after having served as the Covington chief of police.

Bob Curtner with his restored GTO, 2003

photo courtesy Dave Simms & Bob Curtner

ROGERS PERSONNEL, COVINGTON ERA

Ross, Helen.. Assembly
  Mother of
Ross, Paul... Drill press
Seth, Frank... Third plant manager
Shappe, ?.. Machinist
   Known around the plant simply as "Shappe," he was one of the first Rogers tool and dye makers. He and Joe taught Don Martin most of what he knew. Shappe lived in Dayton and worked all over the country (for clients other than Rogers.)
Shields, Jerry.. Drum tuner, truck driver, warehouse manager in Dayton.
    Jerry stood guard with Jim Platt and Gordon Mullinex after the big fire.
Shields, Ophie... Assembly
Spay, Herb.. Jig and fixture builder
Stahl, Eileen........Sister of Audrey Dunlap................Put drumheads on.
Stein, Harold... Fourth plant manager.
   Harold once passed his pants out through the door to head sewer Helen Martin so she could mend the crotch.
   Knowing Harold would be stuck in his office, Helen kept the pants for several hours.
Stein, Betty (Zimmerman)... Harold Stein's secretary; they later married
Strait, Byron
Strauss, Ben.. Marketing director, sales manager
Studebaker, Richard.. Assembly (late 1950s)
Supinger, Ruby.. First Rogers secretary. Responsible for Don Martin's hiring.
Thompson, Joe.. Chief engineer. (see "Joe Thompson")
Thompson, Helen.. Worked as a substitute for sick workers.
Thompson, Marvin (not related to Helen and Joe)................ Painter
Trostle, Kay... Drum Assembly
Wagner, Othal... Lug assembly
Walters, Frank... Lug assembly
Warner, Mark.. Shipping
   Mark was a teenager who was a bit of a smart-aleck. One day Joe Thompson decided to "take him down a peg" and told Mark there was something Joe could do that Mark could not, even though he was in his late sixties. Mark shot back that he could do anything Joe could do. Joe laid down on the floor, flat on his back. He then crossed his arms. Then, with his arms still crossed and without leaning on or touching anything for support, he stood up. Mark tried and tried and tried, but failed and was humbled. (Don Martin, who witnessed all this, waited until he got home before trying this so he wouldn't publicly humiliate himself. He also failed.)
Way, George... Sales
Welldy, Jack.. Drilling (drums)
Wenrick, Levi.. Painter
Whitenack, Joe.. Second plant manager
Wolford, John.. Scheduling, purchasing.
   John was one of the few Covington staff who transferred to the Cleveland (Grossman) offices
Zimmerman, Betty..........Married to Harold Stein..............see Stein, Betty (Zimmerman)
Zindorf, Dick..........Brother-in-law of Willie Bowers................ Purchasing, foreman

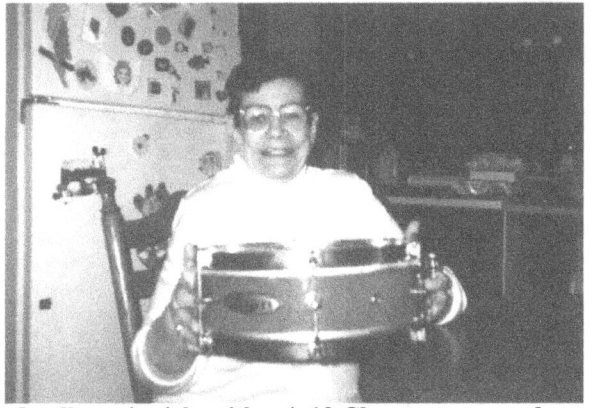

Luellen minnich, with a 4x13 Classmate snare drum   **Sam Collett, with a 5x14 Luxor snare drum**
both photos taken by Dave Simms, 1996

photo courtesy Dave Simms

**Joe Thompson supervises Les Martin's work.
(The two workers at right are unidentified.)**

**Bill Nicholas filing burrs from
Dynasonic snare frame castings.**

**George Martin applying pearl covering
material**

Byron Strait stacking shells

THE ROGERS BOWLING TEAM
left to right: Joyce Bashore, Dorothy Platt, Ray Holmes, Helen Beireis, Kay Trostle

Practical jokes on Joe

One morning someone placed plastic "gag" vomit on the floor and when Joe came along, they told him his dog had done it. Joe quietly fetched a mop to clean up the mess he felt responsible for before discovering it was the latest in a long line of humorous exchanges between he and his "family."

The plant was heated by steam. To clean out the chimney which tended to quickly accumulate soot, they would wedge part of an old tire into it from inside the furnace while it was cold. Then they would light the fire and close the door. After the fire got hot, the door would be opened, and the tire chunk would get sucked up through the chimney, knocking the soot loose on the way. The chimney had not originally been built high enough, so one time Joe went up on the roof to work on extending it. Don Martin and "Shappe" wedged the tire in the chimney and lit the furnace. A few minutes after they opened the furnace door and blew the soot out, Joe came stomping in mad as a hornet and covered head to toe in thick black soot.

Wildlife in the Rogers Factory

Joe's chickens and ducks had free reign of the facility, and often surprised visitors by pecking at them. Joe almost always had a dog. For many years his constant companion was a German Shepherd named Lady. There was an ancient International pickup truck used for plant errands which everybody recognized as Lady's domain. Everyone at the plant shared Joe's sorrow when Lady was struck by a car and killed on the highway near the factory. About a year after losing Lady, Joe got a boxer which he named King.

One of the employees owned a spider monkey named Suzy which lived in the plant all the time except in the dead of winter when it was taken into the house at night.

Probably the most unusual pet was Joe's pet wasp. The wasp stayed near Joe's workbench. Joe would talk to the wasp and it would crawl up and down his fingers. If anyone else came near, the wasp would buzz them and chase them away. Don Martin remembers that both Joe and Helen Thompson would annually catch a wasp and let it sting them as an arthritis treatment.

GEORGE WAY AND ROGERS

There has been no single person who enjoyed as long, varied, and productive a career in the American percussion industry as George Harrison Way. His association with the Rogers Drum Company was in the twilight of his career, and was unfortunately not a happy chapter in his life story.

Way spent his boyhood in Boston, where he took lessons from George B. Stone. He came from a wealthy family, but was practically disowned when he chose a career as a vaudeville drummer. Way traveled extensively with minstrel shows and circuses, finally settling down in Edmonton, Alberta, with a job as house drummer in a vaudeville theater, the Pantages, in about 1918. Together with the house electrician (who specialized in electroplating), Way started the Advance Drum Company. His design, marketing, and sales skills brought him to the attention of U.G. Leedy, who convinced Way to move to Indianapolis to work for the Leedy Drum Company. For over twenty years (which included an era during which Leedy was the world's largest drum company) Way was sales manager at Leedy. During this era he was responsible for numerous historic innovations such as pearl covering on drums, self-aligning lug inserts, and the "floating head" concept.

George Way's job with Leedy was "downsized" by World War II, so he set up shop on his own as a distributor of drum heads and other accessories. After a couple years of that he went to work for Slingerland in Chicago for about a year before borrowing enough money to move to California and open a drum shop in Hollywood with two partners. By this time Way was in his mid fifties and, having already worked in the percussion industry for over thirty years, was regarded as being a little old-fashioned– particularly in the "fast lane" of Hollywood drummers. The war was now over, so Way gave up on trying to keep the shop afloat and moved back to Elkhart to once again work for the Conn company, in their Leedy drum division. In 1955 Conn decided to get out of the drum business, again leaving Way out of work. George solicited investors and formed a corporation named the George Way Drum Company.

Just as this new drum company was beginning to establish a serious market presence, George learned from one of his investors, John Rochon, that there was a movement among the investors to acquire another Elkhart percussion business. Rochon was the owner of Camco, a screw machine company in Chicago which supplied drum hardware to not only the George Way Drum Company but also to Rogers and a number of other drum companies.

To head off the unwanted acquisition, George helped Rochon acquire 51% of the stock of the George Way Drum Company. Much to his shock and bitter disappointment, Rochon's attitude toward Way (and his wife Elsie) changed almost immediately soon as he was "in control." He was rude and condescending, and made it clear he would be taking the company in a fresh direction which would be a relief from the old-fashioned ideas of George Way. Rochon called a board meeting for Saturday August 26th, 1961, and during the meeting began to list the changes he meant to effect. Way was afraid many of his longtime customers and friends would think he had gone crazy when they heard about the changes, and suggested (only half seriously) that if Rochon thought George and Elsie were such hindrances, perhaps they should drop out. Rochon grabbed at the suggestion. It was agreed that George and Elsie would stay for five working days to train a new office girl. The meeting ended, and George and Elsie (in a near state of shock) went home for lunch. While they were at lunch, Rochon called another official meeting during which he accepted their "resignations" effective immediately. He then sent a messenger to their home to inform them they need not report back to work.

Soon after that, Rochon changed the name of the company to the Camco Drum Company, and moved production from Elkhart to Oak Lawn, Illinois, where his screw machine business was located.

George Way, now 71 years old and tired, was once again left searching for a way to make a living in the percussion industry. He wasn't out of work for very long before he was hired by Rogers.

George and Elsie's move from Elkhart to Covington was a fairly major undertaking. They rented the largest truck they could find to move over 18,000 pounds of drum material; catalogs, books, experimental parts, old models of completed items, etc. All of this was in addition to the household goods. It took a full day to load the truck, and of course a full day to unload.

George started work at the Rogers factory on Monday, October 12, 1961. The first order of business was helping to set up an office. According to Way, Rogers had never had "this type of office" before.

One of George's first jobs was to organize an inventory control system for drum heads. It wasn't long before it became evident to him that this was the kind of work he would be doing. He had no doubt anticipated contributing more in the way of product design and marketing ideas– these were the activities he had thrived on for decades. After about a month at Rogers he reported to longtime friend Charles White that things were going ok, though it was somewhat different from the old line drum factories. "It must be alright, though," he wrote, "because they are getting plenty of business." About six weeks later, after the two had exchanged a number of tympani design ideas, George wrote to Charles complaining that "I'm not sure when we'll start work on a tymp model. The personnel here and in Cleveland all have their pet ideas; I may be *consulted.*" He was beginning to feel a little out of the loop. His situation worsened rapidly until he found it intolerable.

On June 1, 1962, after less than eight months on the job, Way wrote to White: "We have been in sort of a dither here inasmuch as Elsie and I are quitting this job. Perhaps we are foolish– time will tell– but everything is so unlike the drum business as I have lived it all this time that we just couldn't get ourselves in a happy state of mind. We have no kick whatever coming on the personal treatment, but the fact that the main office is 200 miles away from here and the people up there are basically "packaged merchandisers" who were formerly in the retail business for many years and are now in the jobbing business, naturally makes quite a difference between their outlook and mine, which is based on the manufacturing end. There are a million details which would be impossible to explain in a letter, but the truth is their manpower and department heads are adequately filled and there really was not much of a place for us. We have been sitting around here for 8 months with hardly anything to do and, while I think they could have made some improvements, they have gotten into the habit of doing things a certain way and.......well, the damn thing just wouldn't work out no matter how we figured it. Their very strong point is a large group of exceptionally good road salesmen: they are the best and the highest paid in the business, and of course nowadays the the public –especially these modern drummers– are very gullible and fast-talking salesmen can sell them. This is practically our last day here. The big boss from Cleveland will be down next Tuesday and that will wind it up. The following weekend we are going to drive to Elkhart and look for a house to live in. We have no connections with any other company as yet and doubt if we can get one because they are too well filled up and the "old school" that we knew does not seem very important to any of them. We might as well get settled for our old age in Elkhart as in this part of the country, which we don't care for one little bit."

ROLAND "PEEWEE" DAVIDSON

Roland "Peewee" Davidson was one of six brothers born in Sidney, Ohio, and raised in Troy; about ten miles from Covington. He graduated from Troy High School in 1936, and shortly thereafter married Evelyn Wilson, the niece of Joe and Helen Thompson.

Peewee worked for the Hobart Cabinet Company until he joined the infantry in March of 1944. On Christmas day, while his Company was combing the Belgian countryside, Peewee was the victim of machine-gun fire from a German tank, suffering severe wounds in both legs. He dragged himself across a nearby road where two buddies found him and pulled him into a heavily wooded area. It was nearly dark, so the three had to spend the night in the woods since they were in unfamiliar territory and still under enemy fire. The next day they were able to rejoin American forces and for the rest of his stay in the Army, Peewee was in and out of various hospitals until his discharge in September of 1945.

When he came home, Peewee went to work for Joe and Helen under the apprenticeship program of the G.I. Bill of Rights, learning how to repair instruments. Peewee worked with Joe and Biddy Etter at the shop on Joe's property all the way through the Rogers Drum Era. Joe and Biddy opened a music store in Covington shortly before Joe died. The repair operation was moved from Thompson's farm to the rear of the store, where Peewee continued to help with the instrument repairs. (This was now a part-time job, as he had begun working for the Post Office as a carrier and clerk in 1952.)

When Biddy died and the store closed, his will included a provision that Peewee should take whatever repair equipment he felt would be helpful to him in keeping the repair business going. He did so, moving equipment to the basement of his house where, at this writing in 1998, he is still repairing instruments. (He retired from the Post Office in 1982.) He once went away for the weekend with his wife and returned to find nearly twenty instruments stacked up by his back door– kids would just drop them off if he was not home!

The nickname Peewee? He got it from his caddying days at the Troy Country Club. When he applied for the job at the age of eight he was small for his age and the club Pro Eddie Hetzle gave him the nickname which he's been stuck with ever since.

ENGLISH ROGERS

by Dave Seville

English Rogers drums were made from 1961 to 1968. They had standard Ajax shells (three-ply) with reinforcement rings made by Boosey & Hawkes in their factory at Edgeware (North London). The drums were fitted with Rogers-style Swivomatic (and later, Knobby) accessories which were made under license in the UK. Because English engineering standards are different from those of the USA, the English Swivomatic fittings are *not* compatible with their USA equivalents.

The first English Rogers catalogue was A5 size blue and black print, and even bore the legend "USA" on the cover! It featured drums with drawn brass "bread and butter" lugs. The sets were shown with Ajax stands and tom-tom legs. There were three 14"x5 1/2" snare drums available, with wood, chrome or brass lacquer shells. These were all Holiday models, with no Dynasonic range at this time. Available finishes were white pearl, black pearl, blue pearl, blue sparkle, red sparkle, and mardi gras. Throughout this catalogue, there is a combination of English products with other illustrations taken directly from USA catalogues. Also, many pages show standard Ajax products. The script logo used was the one mounted on a straight horizontal plane. The endorsees featured were mainly American stars, but Charles Botterill (Mantovani), Kenny Clare (studio star), Jack Parnell (own band) and Bob Turner (Northern Dance Orchestra) are shown.

Note that these are all Big Band players– no beat group drummers were featured!

All English Rogers catalogues bore the addresses of both Jos. Rogers Inc., Bolivar Rd., Cleveland 15, Ohio, USA and Besson & Co. Ltd., Besson House, Burnt Oak, Broadway, Edgeware, Middlesex. Besson was a musical manufacturing company acquired by Boosey and Hawkes in 1930. Perhaps using the Besson name for English Rogers helped to put space between Rogers and Boosey & Hawkes' continuing Ajax line. It seems clear that the marketing strategy was to blur the distinction between the UK and USA products.

The second Rogers catalogue appeared in 1964. The main changes were the fitting of the more reliable die-cast beaver-tail lugs, Knobby-style tom-tom legs had replaced the earlier Ajax type. A UK version of

An early Dave Clark Rogers kit; "Bread and butter" lugs, small Rogers logo on bass drum head.

the metal-shell Dynasonic snare drum was produced at the mind-boggling price of 44 Pounds. The shell featured the two concave beads typical of the American design but did not have the five smaller beads around the middle. Instead were five engraved lines. The UK Dynasonic drums can also be distinguished from their rather superior USA namesakes by the Ajax internal muffler and the oval "Custom Built" badge *without* serial number or grommet. Where fitted, the UK logo was chrome finish. .

The sets were now available with USA style Swivomatic stands and pedals. Previously, the Swivomatic bass drum pedal was offered only as a separate item.

photo courtesy Dave Seville

The same kit as shown on the previous page, with a larger Rogers logo.

was not long before Dave Clark had negotiated a deal direct with Rogers, USA and he appeared in American catalogues, having the characteristic and, at the time, unusual five-piece "Londoner" outfit named obliquely after him. Dave Clark's face finally appeared in the third English Rogers catalogue of 1966 along with another, perhaps rather more technically accomplished, beat-group drummer, Peter York of The Spencer Davis Group. This catalogue was virtually a reprint of the previous one, with amendments to prices.

In the catalogues, Boosey & Hawkes emphasized the production characteristics of their American counterparts and succeeded to some extent in replicating the Rogers USA product. The triple-flanged hoops, if anything, exceeded the deep profile of the Rogers USA product. There can be no underestimating the superiority of the Swivomatic holders

Finishes were now black, red, blue or marine pearl or grey ripple. The success of The Dave Clark Five in the charts led to his being featured as an endorsee. The catalogue cover showed a mysterious silouette with the legend "Who's playing Rogers?" No prizes for guessing that it was the pop hero from North London although his face inexplicably did not appear on the endorsees' page along with UK stars (and former Ajax players) Ronnie Stephenson, Jackie Dougan, Dougie Wright, Jack Parnell, Mike Waldron, Lennie Hastings, Charles Botterill, Lu Ssanet, Roy Burns (!), and Ron McKay. A page featuring Buddy Rich and Louis Bellson was reproduced directly from the USA Rogers catalogue.

If Dave Clark was considered unqualified to take his place alongside such worthies, he appeared prominently in press advertisements in the teen-oriented magazines such as Beat Monthly. However, because of the success of The Dave Clark Five in the USA, it

"Big R" logo, beavertail lugs.

and stands when compared with those of contemporary competitors. The standard set configuration was based around a 14"x20" bass drum with 8"x12" and 16"x16" tom-toms and matching wood shell snare drum. Finishes were black, red, blue or marine pearl, grey ripple, and later mahogany wood. English Rogers could hardly be regarded as an overwhelming success. A cause could have been the apparent reluctance of Boosey & Hawkes (and other UK manufacturers) to market to the buoyant Beat Group market, preferring to continue to emphasise their track record in the Dance Band and Trad Jazz fields of music.

Whatever the causes, the relatively brief shelf-life of English Rogers ended soon after the introduction by Boosey & Hawkes of the up-dated Ajax Nu-Sound range. Although a further catalogue was published for 1967-68, again showing a mixture of American products and UK Ajax accessories, production ceased at a time suspiciously adjacent to the importation of genuine Rogers USA drums by Dallas-Arbiter.

Author's note: I contacted Dave Seville to see if he had any comments, corrections, or additions for the revised edition of this book and he replied that he'll still stand by every word. He did offer a few additional insights and comments:

- English Rogers/Ajax shells were made with the grain of the wood running from bearing edge to bearing edge rather than around the shell. The British Rogers drums did not conceal the grain with an interior paint like the American ones did.
- The color of Dave Clark's kits was most likely red sparkle. This is rather difficult to document, as most photos and video from that era are black and white.
- The light-colored hoops (see Dave Clark kit, page XX) were silver-grey (aluminum) paint that many of the UK drum companies of the era used, including Premier, Ajax, John Grey, and Trixon.
- Queried about the size of the "backwards" tom-toms, Dave expresses the opinion that they are 8x12 and 9x13 because those were the catalogued sizes. (It should be noted that this was the first time a 9x13 tom was offered by any UK drum company.) Certainly his outfits were custom made to order, as there were no outfits offered with twin toms on the bass drum.

Peter York

> **Dave Seville** was the publisher of a newsletter called "The Old Drummer's Club". The newsletter featured reminiscences of drummers who played in bygone eras, articles about drums and drum companies, as well as advertisements for drums and replacement parts.

ARBITER AUTOTUNE DRUMS

Bring up the Arbiter Autotune drums to most anyone who was working for Rogers (America) at the time (1977) and they shake their head. According to one former executive, the only reason it was ever considered in the first place was because Arbiter was selling tremendous quantities of Fender instruments in England which gave them the leverage to force American consideration. A number of prototype snare drums and outfits were put together. There were Rogers strainers on the snare drums, Swiv-o-matic type tom holder assemblies on the tom toms, Rogers style floor tom legs, etc. The snare drum stand (pictured with the outfit above) had to be a new design to keep the snare drum from moving when it was "tuned". The surveys conducted by CBS reported overall disappointing response to the drums. The "easy-tuning" concept was easy to sell but they found stiff resistance to the product's quality, performance, weight, unusual appearance, and lack of choice of colors. CBS decided not to go into full production of the drums.

The gear teeth on the underside of the counterhoop.

The shell-mounted gear mechanism

The basic concept of these English-made drums is an old one that seems to be reinvented every few years; "one-touch tuning". The principle behind the concept was decribed by *International Musician* Magazine (December, 1977) as a "jam jar" principle: "The skin is inserted in the hoop and screwed on with a half twist on nylon blocks which are fixed to the top of the shell." From there you would simply ratchet the whole assembly (the "jam jar lid") with a huge key on the tuning nut.

Because the counterhoops shifted position in relation to the shell, the snare gate was very wide.

Exterior view of the gear-tooth housing with tensioning point

The Arbiter snare drums were fitted with Rogers strainers and butt assemblies

photo courtesy Dave Drew

GROSSMAN SELLS ROGERS TO CBS

Why did Henry Grossman decide to sell his drum company to the Columbia Broadcasting System? The move surprised many in the industry. Here was a company that had grown from a dilapidated tannery/machine shop into the most innovative drum company in the industry. The Rogers name had come to mean quality. The endorsee roster had exploded and was headlined by the world's greatest drummer, Buddy Rich. The manufacturing staff was a dedicated extended family unit. The face of popular music was rapidly changing, and the changes were translating directly into demand for popular instruments such as the guitar and the drum set. The distribution network and dealer base were in place to deal with the new demand for product.

One employee (and friend) of Grossman's is of the opinion that he felt he had taken the Rogers company as far as he was capable of taking it. He could see that the company was positioned to continue on with the growth curve and market share gains, but such expansion was beyond the scope of Grossman's vision in terms of his own involvement.

Another company insider feels that it was nothing more than a case of Grossman getting an offer that was too good to refuse. The company had not really been for sale– the amount of cash being offered was simply too tempting.

It was the beginning of the age of corporate diversification. Within a few years Ludwig would sell to Selmer, and Slingerland would sell to the publishing company Crowell-Collier-McMillan. Pearl drum distribution would become a function of CMI, and later Norlin– a division of a large South American corporation. The point man for CBS acquisitions of musical instrument manufacturers first went to the Ludwig Drum Company– the largest drum company in the industry. He arrived at the Ludwig factory and was given a personal tour of the facilities by Wm. F. Ludwig, Senior. At the end of the tour Mr. Ludwig, knowing that the visitor was a CBS employee but not knowing why he was there, thanked the man for his interest. "But," he added, "We're really not interested in buying any advertising right now." "Oh, but I'm not selling advertising," the man replied. "I'm here to buy your drum company." Mr. Ludwig was reportedly as much angry as surprised and informed the visitor in no uncertain terms that the company was not for sale and he should leave immediately!

When CBS approached Grossman, he was more receptive. The negotiations included considerations which led Grossman to feel comfortable that there would not only be a smooth transition of ownership, but that this move would be better for everyone concerned; the customers, the employees, and for the marque itself.

Since Grossman had a profit-sharing arrangement with employees, the sale meant a cash bonus to employees. Joe Thompson agreed to stay on as a consultant, and before the deal was consummated an agreement was reached in which Ben Strauss would continue to work in much the same capacity as he had, only now as an employee of CBS instead of Grossman. The drums would continue to be manufactured in the same place and the same way, by the same people. They would even be warehoused in the same place, as the agreement called for CBS to lease warehouse space from Grossman in Cleveland.

The warehouse situation was one of the first sources of disagreement and/or change. Grossman had constructed heavy fencing from floor to ceiling around the section of the warehouse which was to be leased to CBS for Rogers. When officials from CBS came to inspect the warehouse, they expressed surprise that the space was inside Grossman's building, even though it was physically separated by fencing. They insisted that their warehouse space should be a separate facility. Grossman's response was that if they wanted separate warehousing facilities, all they had to do was go find them. They did, in Dayton. This is why some Ohio-era Rogers drums have stickers inside which say Cleveland and others Dayton. Most of these drums were in fact made in Covington. None were actually assembled in Cleveland, although CBS did in fact move full production to Dayton for a short time before finally moving to California. (See page 46.)

Ben Strauss had every reason to believe under CBS ownership the growth and development of Rogers would continue; market share would continue to expand, new markets would be developed, and manufacturing processed would be kept updated and innovative. One of his moves which demonstrated this was his hiring of Don Canedy. Canedy had been a Rogers advisor for some time. When Strauss approached him about joining Rogers as an assistant marketing director, he was quite reluctant because he had just been hired by the University of Illinois. Strauss made it clear that the Rogers job would give him an opportunity to develop the educational market; CBS was ready to go ahead with Thompson's tympani design, there would be a new emphasis on marching, percussion, etc. Canedy agreed to come to work for the Rogers division of CBS.

THE COVINGTON FIRE OF 1967

When CBS purchased the Rogers Drum Company from Grossman, they leased the Covington factory building from Joe Thompson. Less than a year after the sale, on Saturday, February 4th, 1967, disaster struck.

The pearl drum covering material was a cellulose nitrate based material which is highly flammable. Footlights have been known to ignite drums covered with this material, and vintage drum buffs have been known to burn the covering off drums because it burns so fast it does not even char the wood underneath if done with care. Evidently there were at least two electric heaters in the pearl storage area, used to keep the temperature in the room high enough to keep the material pliable and easy to apply to the drums.

Foreman Robert Blankenship was the first to note something was wrong, as he worked in the basement with seven other men. He saw smoke coming down the stairway, and yelled out "The place is on fire!" He and Ralph Hahn tried to put the fire out with portable fire extinguishers, but were driven back by intense smoke. Even though the firemen wore masks, the dense black smoke was very dangerous and difficult to work through. In the meantime the Covington fire department had been called, and responded with five pieces of equipment assisted by a pumper and tanker from the Newton Township fire department.

According to Covington Fire Chief Roger O'Donnell, the entire building was engulfed in heavy black smoke when they arrived, and he thought surely the entire facility would be lost. Soon after that, however, the pearl room exploded, blowing out some of the walls and letting the firemen get at the actual blaze. The blast tore out the southwest corner of the concrete block building, but a firewall kept the explosion from ripping through the interior of the factory. Flames, however, did sweep through portions of the assembly area. The intense heat even buckled lugs.

The total dollar amount of the losses was estimated at $75,000.00 to $100,000.00, plus damage to the local economy. It is big news when the largest employer in a town of under 3,000 is out of business. Covington Mayor Herbert Edwards was quoted by local papers: "It's bound to hurt the town– it's very unfortunate."

The Rogers "family" acted quickly to put things back together again, and the company was back in business within two weeks. Some of the equipment was stored in a Covington warehouse until reconstruction at the plant could be completed.

photos courtesy Dave Drew

CBS MOVES ROGERS FROM COVINGTON

Though the point has already been made in a number of ways, the author must again return to the topic of the importance of the Covington community to Rogers.

Rogers was brought to Covington because owner Henry Grossman had recognized the critical role Joe Thompson would play in the company's future. It would be hard to overstate Thompson's bond with the area. The Thompson land, Joe used to tell visitors, could be traced back to around 1798 when his great-great-grandfather Sylvester Thompson settled 360 acres which legally became family property when President James Madison signed it over on a land grant. Joe was very proud of that land grant, and once showed the document to Henry Grossman. Sylvester Thompson was reportedly killed by a renegade Indian's arrow near the cabin he built on the property. Legend had it that his wife and son both witnessed the murder.

Joe Thompson had been born and raised on this same property, and would consider such a major role with Rogers only if it was located where he could work in his own "lab." The first payroll (in August of 1954) listed only five employees. As the manufacturing facility (and the payroll) grew, the whole operation maintained a sense of community– see pages 29–35.

When CBS purchased the firm, it appeared, at least on the surface, that they recognized the importance of Covington to Rogers. Immediately after the purchase of Rogers on April 5th, 1966, CBS named Richard Sievert the new General Manager. Within a few weeks, on May 26th, Sievert addressed Covington area residents at the annual Covington Chamber of Commerce Guest Night Dinner. It is possible that Sievert got carried away by the down-home reception he received– a home-cooked dinner was prepared by the PTA and was served in the multi-purpose room of the Covington Elementary School. Entertainment was provided by a barbershop quartet from Piqua, the Scalemates. After a report from the Fourth of July celebration committee and a sidewalk-sale message, Sievert was introduced as the keynote speaker. Sievert announced that he and his family were from a small town like Covington, near Battle Creek, Michigan. No one, he pointed out, visits Battle Creek without knowing they are in the corn flake capital of the world. The people of Covington, he said, should be even prouder of Rogers than the Battle Creek folks are of Kellogg's, and actively promote the Rogers marque. He assured the group that the factory would be in Covington "for some time to come" (adding that no one could predict exactly how long that may be) and that "we hope to be able to expand in this immediate area." He pointed out that the only significant change that had already taken place in the first few weeks of new ownership was to move the sales and warehousing facilities from Cleveland to Dayton. The company planned, he said, to eventually get all functions under one roof.

Joe Thompson died on March 8, 1968. A few months later CBS moved to combine all operations in their rented Dayton facility. By this time Sievert had been replaced as General Manager by Charles Hughes, who told the media that the move was imperative to reduce material handling costs. 95% of the production staff, he said, would be changing their place of employment from Covington to the Dayton location. Very few of them were actually needed there, however, since sales had dropped alarmingly. In two short years CBS had introduced problems which the Covington workforce was helpless to overcome. Though these folks were still making good drums, they pretty much had their legs cut out from under them by distribution policy changes and order-filling problems. See page 44.

All operations were combined in Dayton, and drums were assembled and shipped from there for a time. Within a year, however, the decision to relocate to California was announced. A few Covington natives made the move along with Rogers, but for the most part the Rogers "family" was left behind.

Author's note: Another special thanks to Covington resident Kathleen O'Roark, who provided local newspaper articles from the time of these events via Dave Simms!

CBS-ERA ROGERS

The date generally accepted for the founding of Rogers is 1848. For better than 100 years the firm remained family-owned with measured growth. There were rarely more than a half-dozen employees, though Rogers became the world's best known supplier of calf heads for the booming banjo market.

In the space of twelve short years (1954-1966) under the guidance of three men, the marque had been transformed from little more than a drum head company to one of the world's largest and most respected manufacturers of high-quality drums. The last 19 years (1966–1985) were filled with paradoxes. The product innovations continued and visibility reached an all time high, but the company was in a tailspin. The causes of the inevitable failure were primarily within– so far within that dealers and field sales staff had no idea there were problems. The author was a Rogers dealer from 1974 until they stopped shipping drums, and did not really understand why that happened until the research for this book was conducted.

It was the best of times....
Drum quality was high
Lighter (yet stronger) hardware was developed, there was more attention to bearing edges and high-quality lacquer finishes, shells were isolated and lugs packed: some of the highest quality American drums ever made were shipped by Rogers as a division of CBS.
Memriloc hardware developed
Rogers for years had dominated the drum hardware market with Swiv-o-Matic. Memriloc again set the standard and left every other manufacturer scrambling to catch up. More pioneering product developments were in the works such as a rack system, new snare drum designs, built-in microphones, and more.
New Markets were targeted
Instruments for the marching and educational marketplaces were developed; marching drums, timp, etc.
Paiste cymbal distribution established
A well-orchestrated introduction of a product line the marketplace was ripe for was a tremendous success. Paiste sales through CBS reached nearly $3 million in a year when Rogers accounted for only $2 million!
Experienced, respected staff
The legendary Ben Strauss was "part of the deal" when CBS bought Rogers. The Covington manufacturing staff remained pretty much intact, and several of the most experienced even made the move to California in 1969. New executives such as John Cermenaro and Dave Gordon sought to carry on the Rogers traditions of excellence and innovation.
Endorsee roster developed without payola
In an era when endorsees started to command five figure annual fees plus clinic and ad guarantees, Rogers artists were content to play the gear and consult. Staff Artist Roy Burns and long-time endorsee Louis Bellson helped maintain a continuity of the Rogers public image while new artists such as Dave Ganduglia and Craig Krampf brought new excitement to the marque.

It was the worst of times....
"Sawdust factory" mentality
Nearly all executive decisions affecting Rogers seemed to reflect the thinking that Fender products were musical instruments while Rogers products were wooden crates with a few metal attachments. It was this mindset which led to nearly all of the following problems:
Drum quality was low
Disruptions in production made it impossible to maintain a skilled production workforce. While the designs were sound, quality was inconsistent.
Product innovations were copied
Patents were not protected through litigation against infringers who sold knock-off product at lower prices.
New markets were not developed
Educational and marching markets were ignored; the products proposed for these arenas were not put into production. Existing instruments were not promoted at a time when imports began an aggressive marketing thrust in these areas.
Paiste cymbal distribution was lost
The Rogers division of CBS/Fender-Rogers-Rhodes took a tremendous hit when Paiste distribution was taken away to be handled by the newly created Paiste America.
Product disasters
More than just embarrassments, some ill-conceived products proved very costly. Millions of dollars were lost when literally thousands of drums were destroyed in a series of engineering and marketing fiascos.
Foreign competition
It was the worst possible time for Rogers to falter as Pearl, Yamaha, and Tama began to take over the American market through quality, attention to educational and marching markets, and lower prices.
Corporate sabotage
Profitability plunged as executives made decisions which seem to have no explanation other than deliberate devaluation of the company. See page 62.

Wildwood was a pet project of a short-tenure president of the Fender/Rogers/Rhodes division of CBS musical instruments. The extremely thin veneer came from trees which had been stained by spikes of food coloring driven into the ground near the roots. (See color photo, p. 90.) Although the matching Wildwood Fender guitars were quite successful according to former Fender DSM (District Sales Manager) salesman Ken Feist, the drums did not sell very well.

An even bigger loss was incurred on wooden shells for snare drums at about the same time. Someone made the mistake of ordering thousands of wooden shells for snare drums at a time when nearly every snare drum being shipped was metal. The original cost, according to a former marketing executive, was about $1.20 per shell. Reluctant to write these shells off as a loss, Rogers execs ordered the shells warehoused. This caused the unit prices to rise. When the move was made to California the shells were moved, adding yet more to the cost. By the time someone finally bit the bullet and ordered the shells destroyed, the unit costs had gone up to over $12.00 per shell. By the time over 7000 shells were destroyed, a $8,400.00 problem had turned into a $84,000.00 problem.

Ben Strauss, marketing director at the time, was not even made aware of the shell situation at the time. "It was a very turbulent time," he explains, "I had my hands full in a number of areas just trying to keep order-filling accurate, etc."

The leadership and direction-setting at Rogers as a CBS division was disjointed and almost immediately set patterns of self-destructiveness. One very major change (not obvious at the time to consumers) was the reorganization of the distribution network. The reader will recall that when Henry Grossman owned Rogers, the Rogers Drum Company sold exclusively to jobbers, including the Grossman Company. CBS decided to pattern Rogers distribution after their Fender distribution, as a manufacturer selling directly to a network of authorized retail dealers. Production foreman Don Martin recalls that when CBS bought Rogers they were shipping about 1800 drums per week. CBS sent a letter to the jobbers explaining the change in distribution, informing them that they would be permitted to purchase Rogers products for one more year before they would be cut off. This angered the jobbers, some of whom responded by returning existing stock. Shipments dwindled in a very short time to 250 drums per week. "When we started getting drums back from angry jobbers," Martin says, "it seemed like we were receiving more than we were shipping!"

See page 90 for color sample.

NEW Wildwood
choose from two outfits

The shift of warehousing to Dayton had brought additional headaches for Rogers. The order-fillers there were not familiar with the stock numbers, or even the nomenclature of the product. A couple of examples cited by Ben Strauss:

– When an order for one pair of hi-hat cymbals was picked, the order picker would pull just one hi-hat cymbal.

– Marching cymbal sets had a catalog number but the order-filler was expected to "build" this product from cymbals, straps, and pads; all of which had separate catalog numbers. There never was actually stock of the complete assembled set. The untrained order-fillers hired by CBS at the Dayton warehouse did not realize this. Although there were plenty of cymbals, straps, and pads in stock the orders for complete marching cymbal sets were back-ordered.

It is not surprising in light of all this that Strauss was not aware of the Wildwood shell disaster described on the previous page.

JOYCE BASHORE

It would be difficult to overstate the importance of Joyce Bashore to the quality and continuity of Rogers drums, particularly during the transition from Grossman to CBS eras. Rogers was much more than just a job to Joyce, who moved to California to continue her work with the company even though it meant leaving her husband behind in Covington. (They did not divorce!) This was a time of extreme confusion and chaos for Rogers; stories abound of problem situations caused by inept order-pickers and untrained production workers. More often than not Joyce Bashore had a hand in straightening out the confusion. John Cermenaro recalls that to anyone who was confused about the function or identification of a Rogers component, she was a virtual lifeline, and encyclopedia of discontinued part numbers and assembly procedures. Whenever the author mentioned her name when interviewing a CBS-era executive they quickly responded with enthusiastic compliments, and a number asked for her phone number so they could call to wish her well in her retirement.

photo courtesy John Cermenaro

Joyce Bashore   April, 1983

MEMRILOC HARDWARE

Just when the industry was getting caught up to Rogers Swiv-O-Matic hardware, Rogers leapt way out front again with the introduction of Memriloc hardware. Their tenure on top was shorter this time, however, as competitors (particularly the imports) quickly came to market with copies. The CBS legal department pretty much shrugged off patent infringement complaints from Rogers. See page 147 for photos.

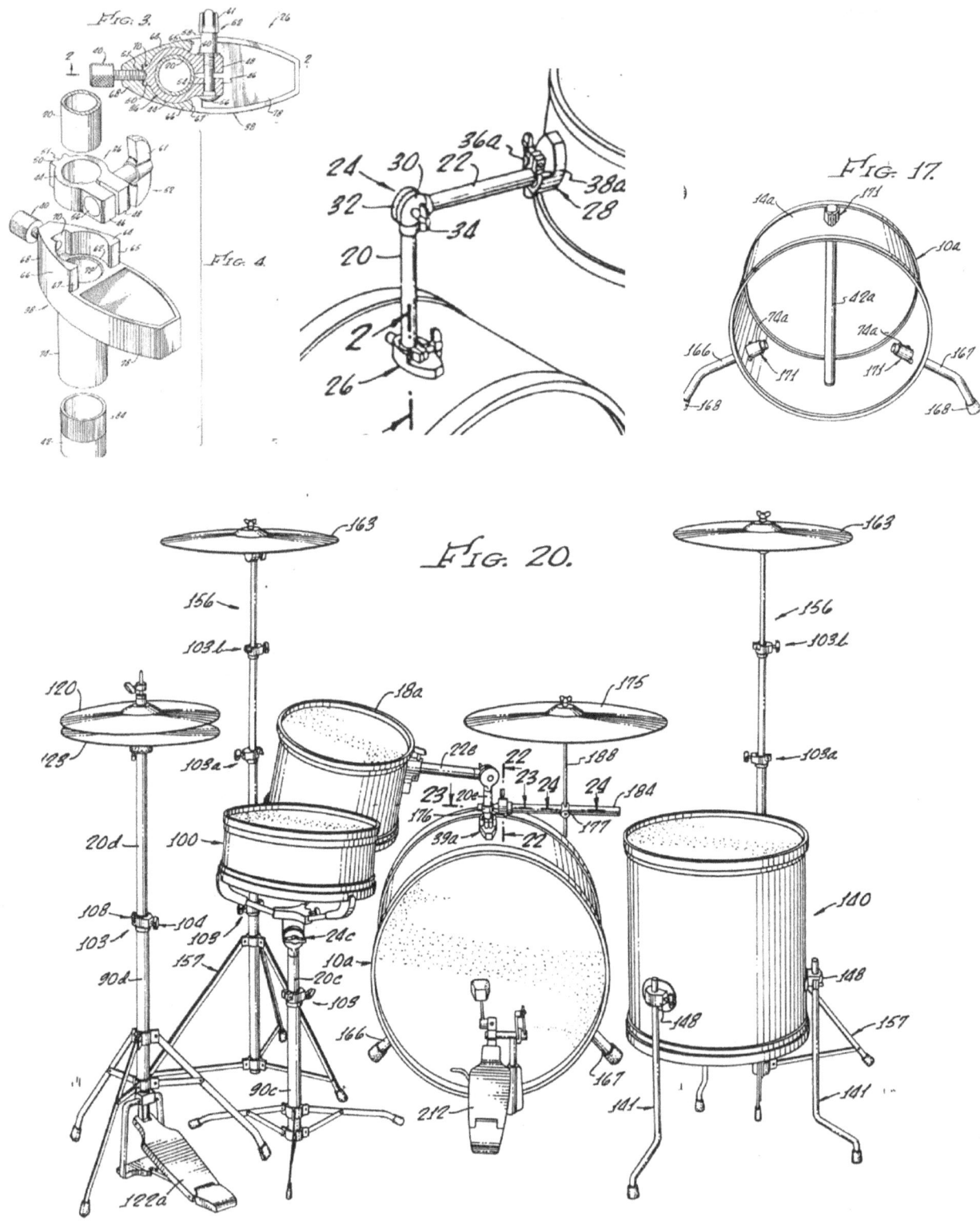

46

THE ROGERS RACK SYSTEM

A classic example of the right product at the wrong time, the Rogers rack system fell victim to the raging executive apathy of the early 1980s. Limited by an R&D budget that let them do little more than come up with new trap cases, John Cermenaro's team came up with a Memrilock rack system. To this day most rack systems which were developed later are comparatively bulky and unsightly. The real beauty of the Rogers rack was its natural coupling with the whole Memriloc hardware series of tom holders, etc.

photo courtesy of John Cermenaro

The Gatlin Brothers' Phil Fajarda's Rogers rack setup, January 1984

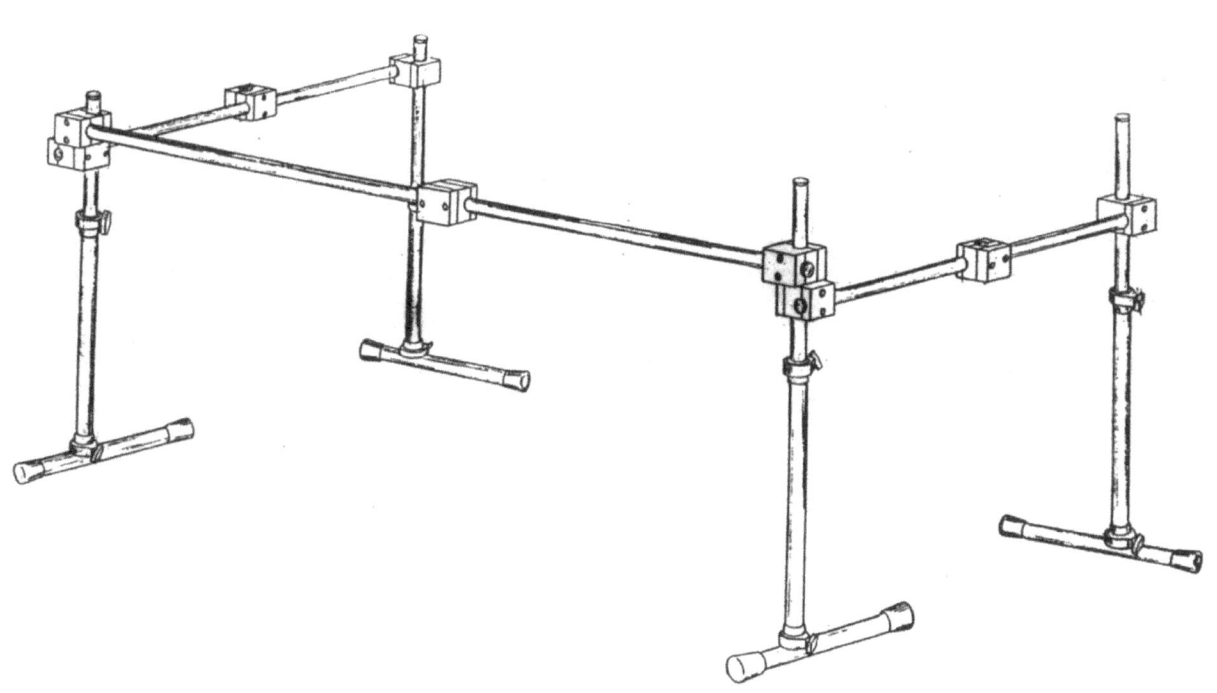

THE ROGERS SNARE MACHINE

The Rogers "Snare Machine" was a snare drum invented by Rogers employee Forrest Clark in the mid 1970s. Each head is attached to and tensioned on a hoop assembly which was independant of the shell.

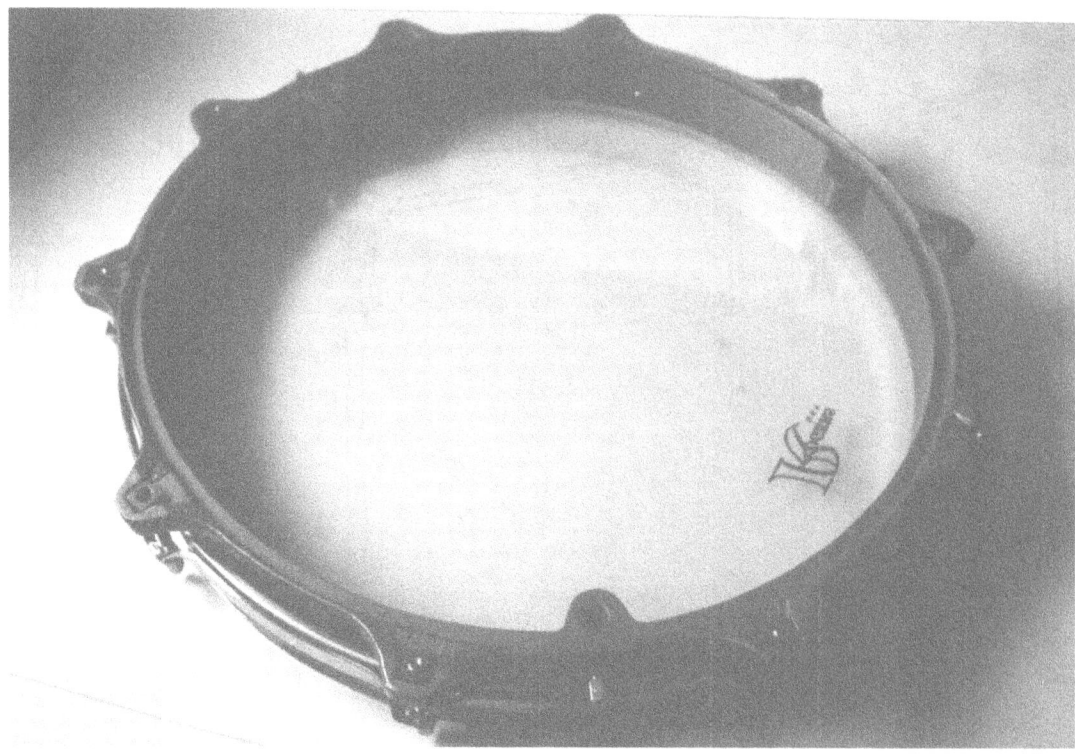

Clark's design allowed for a 360-degree vent in the shell, just below the top head. The top and bottom head assemblies are connected by three support rods.

According to Clark, the Rogers marketing staff was uneasy about sinking enough into the drum to actually put it into production, so only a couple of the prototypes were made. (Clark was not even aware of the plexiglass-shell version in these photos; this drum now belongs to former Rogers R&D engineer John Cermenaro.)

How does it sound? According to both Clark and Roy Burns the drum had a tremendous biting high-end crack from the middle of the room, but the drum's sound was all projection– it was difficult for the drummer himself to hear it. Clark says Harvey Mason used the drum on an album and liked it, but after that the design was quietly forgotten.

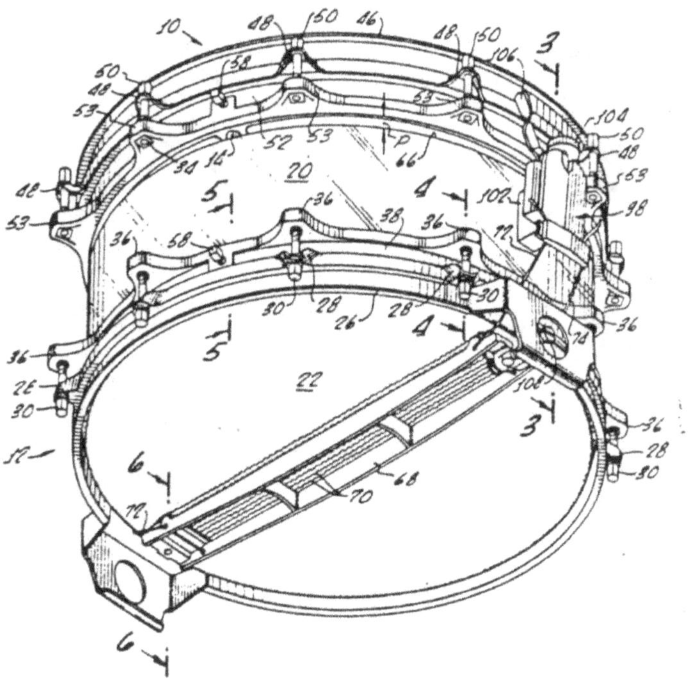

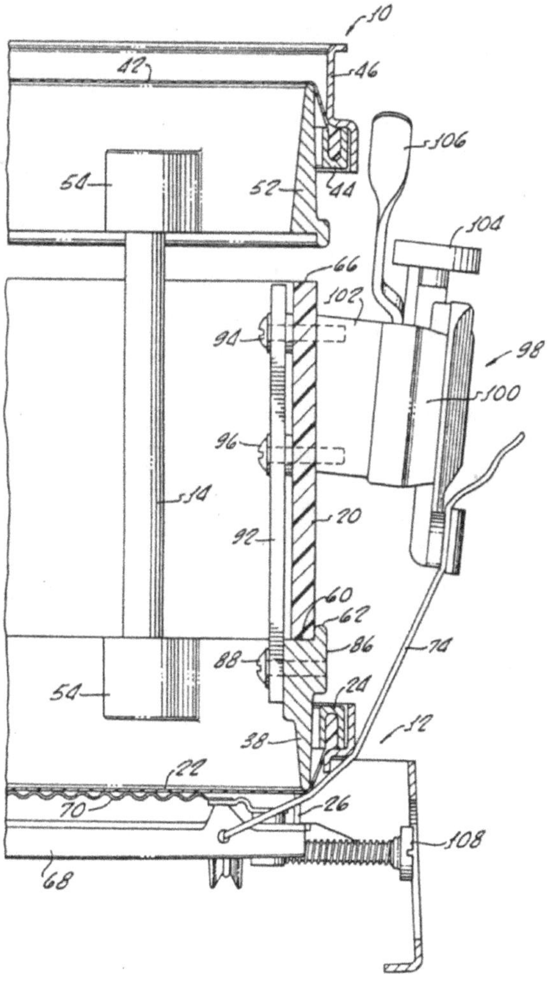

CBS QUALITY

Ben Strauss felt that the best drums Rogers ever made were from the early CBS days. Some of the metal fittings which had earlier been machined from steel were cast, making the drums lighter. The Covington extended family factory staff continued to make drums under the supervision of Joe Thompson until production was moved to Dayton and eventually to Fullerton, California.

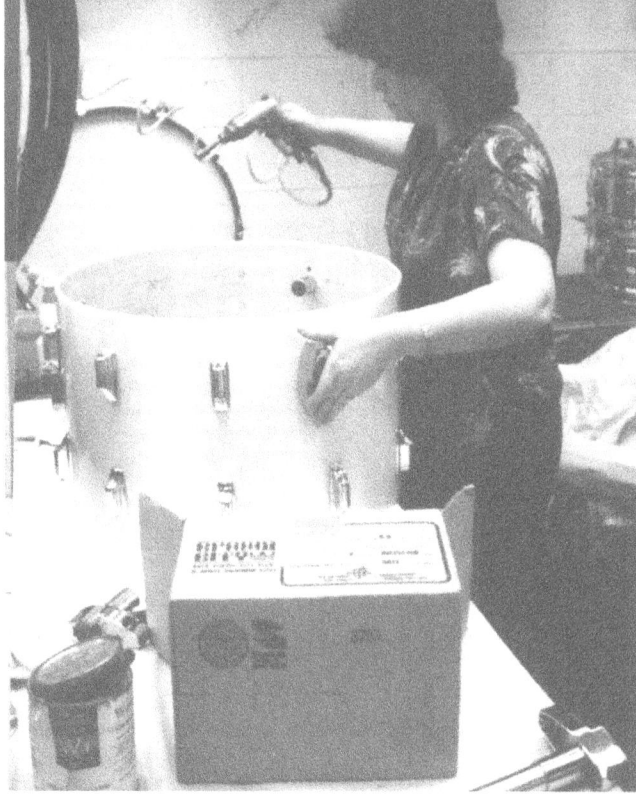

Fullerton, California drum production, clockwise, from upper left: cutting bearing edges, badge application, lug assembly, tables for leveling bearing edges. (Photos courtesy John Cermenaro)

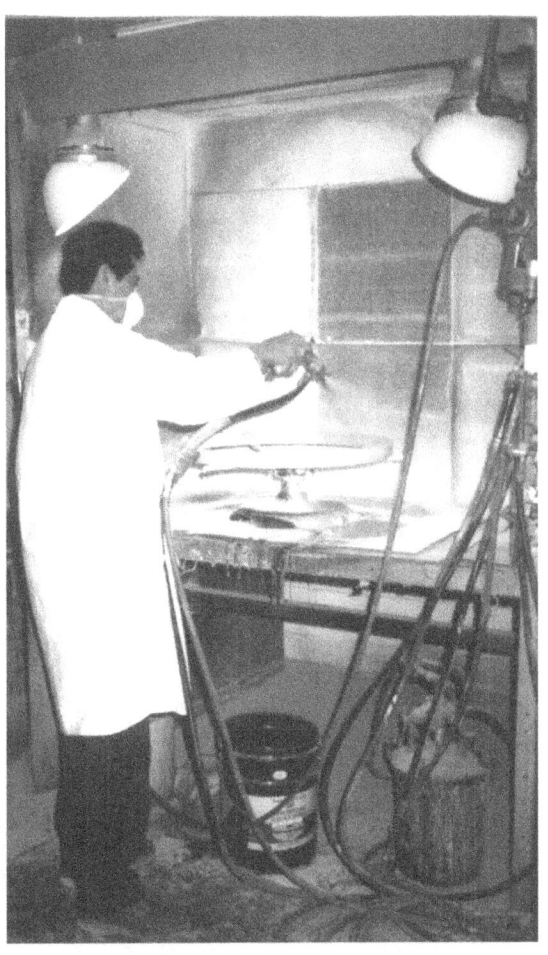

Fullerton, California, production. Clockwise, from upper left: Pearl with contact cement applied drying to tackiness, spraying hoops, stripping misapplied covering, applying pearl to shell. Photos courtesy John Cermenaro

THE SUPER SET 24 OUTFIT

photos courtesy John Cermenaro

The Rogers R&D and Marketing people meant for this to be a satiric comment on the Ludwig Octaplus outfit. Though it was designed strictly as a trade show display, they gave the configuration a part number and price. (It was the "Super Set 24 Outfit" with a retail price of $6,797.50 at a time when the five-piece "Londoner Five" sold for $1710.00.) To their surprise they sold a number of the outfits.

John Cermenaro (right, at his Rogers R&D desk in 1984) remembers that it took all morning to assemble the drums for the photo shoot which produced the shot shown above. When the photographers got their shots they broke for lunch, telling John to turn the set around so they could shoot it from the front after lunch.

52

R&D PROJECTS, 1980s

Borrowing the vent concept of the Rogers Snare Machine, this prototype snare drum was an R&D experiment by John Cermenaro in the early 1980s. The vents near the top head added high-end punch, especially from a distance. (Also note the isolated lugs, tension-rod tightening nuts and custom finish.)

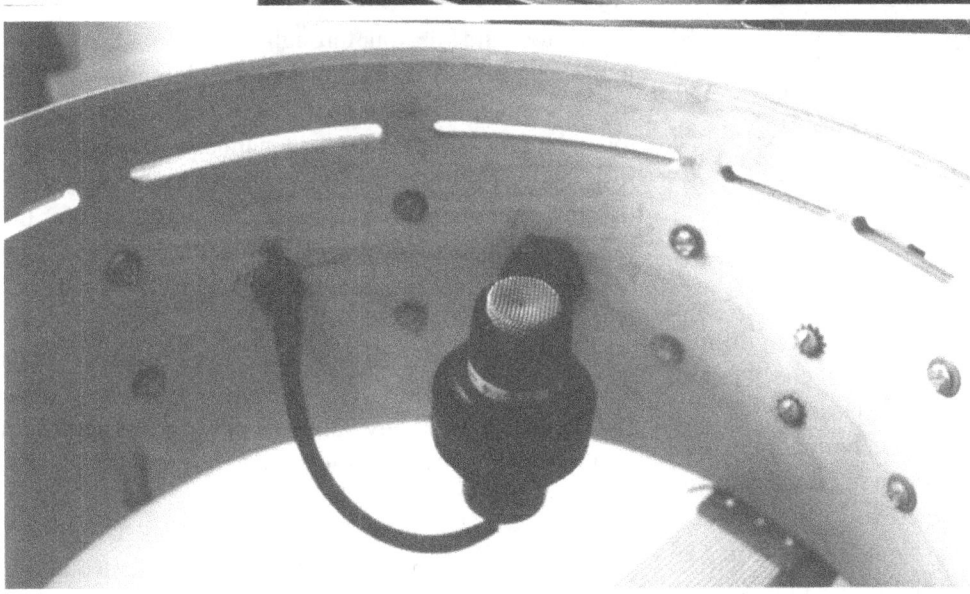

Before Randy May worked out his deal with Slingerland to offer a built-in "May EA" microphone option he worked with Rogers in developing prototypes.

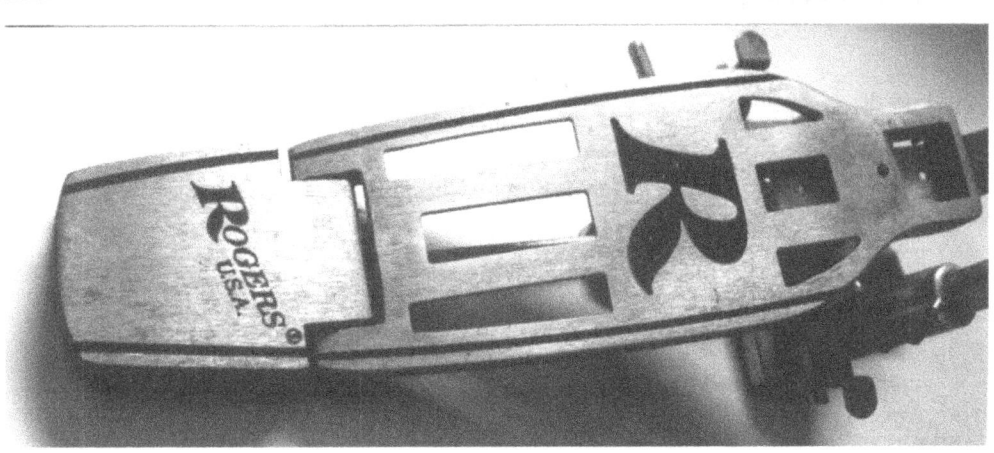

The slots cut in the Supreme pedal footboard significantly reduced the weight of the pedal.

CRAIG KRAMPF

Also see pages 78–83.

Former Rogers executives still speak glowingly of the artist roster from the last days, the early 1980s; particularly Craig Krampf. In an era when the other big drum companies were knuckling under to demands from big name endorsees (annual cash into five figures, clinic guarantees and ad budgets), Rogers had to depend on artists willing to trade gear and design input for endorsements. (CBS did not have to pay anyone to play Fender guitars, and did not feel compelled to do any such thing for the division's smaller companies.) Craig's Rogers story, in his own words:

"My relationship with Rogers started in early 1978. I'd been a Camco endorsee in the mid-seventies. I loved my drums, but throughout the years of heavy touring with Flo & Eddie and the Turtles, my hardware was getting tired. I played a large double-bass set with six toms.

The tom mounts left a lot to be desired, as some of my toms would sink during the course of a show despite how hard the roadie or I would tighten them. I was shocked to learn that Camco was going out of business. Owner Tom Beckman said that he was going to get out of the drum business and become involved with this "new little company out of Japan– Roland". The rest is history! Some Camco endorsees were invited to make a last run through the factory to gather up parts, etc., but I was out on tour and wasn't able to do that. I had joined Nick Gilder and the first single that we recorded "Hot Child In The City" had just begun to climb the charts. (It eventually went to #1 and holds the record for the longest time it took for a song to reach number one!) Tours were being booked and I felt that now was the time for a new set of drums.

Every time I went into a drum shop I'd check out all the different drum makes. After my experience with the fairly weak Camco hardware I was becoming impressed with the companies that were starting to beef things up. Rogers really stood out from the crowd with their large tube hardware and Memriloc system, and I decided I would pay them a visit since Fullerton was fairly close to my home in the San Fernando Valley. My wife Susie typed up a bio for me and off I went.

When I arrived at Rogers, I asked the receptionist if I could speak to the artist representative. She told me to have a seat while she tried to find someone for me. After a short while a man appeared with a curious look on his face and introduced himself as Greg Perry. He asked me whom I was representing and I responded "Myself– who else can talk better about me?" He laughed and said he liked that and that it was a refreshing change from seeing managers and agents. I handed him the bio and explained my interest in playing Rogers drums. He said to have a seat and that he'd be back. He came back shortly

Nashville-based producer& drummer Craig Krampf, 1998

and said "You got it– what do you want?" I was thrilled, to say the least.

Greg took me for a tour through the factory. It was really interesting to see the research and development and then the whole manufacturing process. I was introduced to a lot of people, including Dave Donahoe, who was the man responsible for inventing the Memriloc memory system. It is my opinion that if a list was to be comprised for the top ten innovations in drums during the last fifty years that Dave's name should definitely be on it. "Memriloc" was copied by every single drum manufacturer and truly revolutionized a drummer's set up. Dave was an employee and as such his patent was assigned to CBS. I don't think Dave ever received any compensation for his invention or any royalties from all the copies; he certainly has not received the recognition that is his due.

After my tour of the Fullerton facilities, Greg and I got into specifics about what my new drumset would be. As previously mentioned, I had been playing a large set and Greg helped me put together my order: two 14x24 bass drums, 6 and 8 inch concert toms, an 8x12,9x13,10x-14,12x15,16x16, and 16x18 tom array, several chrome snare drums and all the neccessary hardware, stands, etc. I felt as though Christmas was coming early that year. My new set was going to be manufactured for me and shipped within two weeks. When it arrived, I set it up in my living room and quickly adjusted the positions of everything and set the memory clamps. Wow, everything worked with a standard drum key. I played a show with Nick Gilder that very night in Hollywood and was thrilled with my new set. I still have that drumset and after twenty years all that hardware is just as strong as it was on that very first day– quite unbelievable and quite a testament to their quality.

My relationship with Greg Perry was the best one that I have ever had with an artist rep for a company. I would call up and schedule a visit and I would spend the day in Fullerton. We would always go out to lunch and it was during those culinary adventures that I had a chance to get to know Roy Burns, Don Canedy, John Cermenaro, Jim Ganduglia, Gil Madrid, Dave Garibaldi, Alex Acuna, Alvino Bennett, Sherman Ferguson, and some of the other Rogers endorsees. There was a special vibe about the whole company for a little while back in '78 and '79. Everyone cared, believed in their product and appeared to have fun working on some of the finest and most innovative drums of that era. This vibe carried over to the endorsees and it was special to meet a fellow Rogers player. It was at a percussion show that Rod Morgenstein and I finally met, and felt an instant bond because of our love and endorsement of Rogers drums. It was a great time.

New products were always being developed. Greg called and said that he would like me to come down and try out a new snare drum. We went back to R&D and there was a wood 7x14 snare. Roy Burns played some amazing stuff on it– my jaw dropped watching his technique! After several minutes, Roy handed the sticks to Jim Ganduglia, who wowed me in a similar fashion. The sticks were passed to me. I turned my left stick over (I have played for years with the butt for my left stick and correctly with my right stick). I hit *one* loud rimshot with my left hand and proclaimed, "This drum is incredible!" Everyone fell on the floor. That story was passed around for quite some time. I was able to take that drum home and I immediately used it on an album. The producer was blown away with the sound. It detuned very nicely and it had that "Al Green" snare sound. I had to return it after three weeks so that another Rogers player could try it out. Of course I got a call from that same producer for another session, and he asked me to bring "that unbelievable drum". I couldn't get it back– someone had it on the road. I went down to my local drum stores and tried out virtually every wood drum they had in stock. Finally I found a 6 1/2x14 Sonor. It came really close. I bought it and used it for those next sessions. The producer never knew, but I was certainly sweating it for a while. The next time I went down to Rogers, I inquired about that drum. I was told that the decision was made not to manufacture it. The competition was all coming out with 8x14 drums and Rogers felt there would be no market for a seven inch drum. I fought hard saying that this drum was incredible and it should stand on it's own merits. "Why chase the competition?" I asked. I was told that was the way the business worked and that drum was never produced. Years later when Rogers was folding Roy Burns presented me with that drum. "Craig, you were the only one who truly loved that drum and it's only fitting that you should have it." It's still in my working collection.

I have great memories of my first few years with Rogers. Greg had me bring down my 5x14 Dynasonic (serial number 2651) that I think I bought in 1960 or 1961. He took it to a woman who worked on the line. She beamed. "I probably put that drum together for you; I've been with Rogers since Ohio!" She talked about the family atmosphere of Rogers back then. I felt some of that attitude still existed when I first became an endorsee. Greg and some of the other executive's attitude and spirit was reflected by many of the workers. Visiting the line was always fun for all involved. People were given respect and I believe that helped create a work ethic. Pride was obvious, as the drums were as near perfect as could be. People cared. For a moment in time, Rogers was the epitome of what drums and a company should be.

Author's note: Right up until the last few American-made Rogers drums were assembled in Fullerton in 1984, there were at least a couple people there who had the "Rogers spirit" Craig describes. Their numbers had steadily dwindled since the mid 1970s and, unbeknownst to Craig, most of the other endorsees, and the dealers, the handwriting was on the wall.

ROGERS FACTORY MOVES 1952–1984

Moving a business of any type is disruptive to its operation. The main problem with moving a drum factory is the down time due not only to the movement of physical facilities, but the retraining of personnel at the new location. Beginning with move number four, there was another challenge for Rogers; by this time there was a game of executive musical chairs in progress which left a vacuum when it came to total responsibility. Roy Burns remembers that more than a truckload of cartons sat in an outdoor area in Fullerton for a full year and no one seemed to even know what was in the cartons– everyone assumed soneone else was taking care of it.

MOVE ONE Rogers first began to manufacture drums in Farmingdale in the 1930s; until then Rogers produced only skin heads. The first real move of the Rogers Drum Company was from Farmingdale, New Jersey, to Covington, Ohio in 1952. (It would really be closer to the truth to say a new factory was built rather than one moved.) While H.S. Grossman owned Rogers, the manufacturing was done in Covington and the warehousing and distribution was in Cleveland.

MOVE TWO Soon after CBS purchased Rogers in 1966 the Cleveland functions were moved to Dayton. This was a time of general turbulence for a number of reasons: 1.Most of the employees at the Dayton facility were new not only to Rogers, but new to drums. 2.Although the manufacturing personnel and their immediate supervisors in Covington remained pretty much unchanged, they were under new corporate jurisdiction; there were new procedures to follow, additional paperwork to deal with. 3.Manufacturing in Covington was knocked out of its groove when the distribution network was changed, resulting in reduced demand.

MOVE THREE Drill presses and other manufacturing equipment was moved to Dayton in 1967 and drums were made there for nearly two years. Now Rogers lost the Covington "extended family" sense of community.

MOVE FOUR CBS moved all Rogers operations to Fullerton in 1969. Not all of the heavy equipment was moved; it fell to Bob Curtner to sell it off in Dayton. It finally got down to one drill press and a safe. Curtner contacted CBS and asked what he should do. They asked him to make an offer and he bought the last two items. (The drill press is still in his garage workshop!)

Only a handful of manufacturing personnel and/or supervisors made the move to California. According to Jack Sprouse, the first California line supervisor, they had a terrible time getting parts. "They were losing their butt at first," he says, "the parts were not coming in, and so on. It took two years for drum production to climb to 1000 per week in 1971." (This was little more than half the weekly production of Rogers in it's Grossman/Covington era when they were producing 1800 drums per week.)

Corporate sabotage? From this point on, Rogers "inside executives" such as marketing and R&D people, line supervisors, etc. have a difficult time understanding why the moves were made, or even who ordered the moves. The orders came from "higher up", and often with very little notice. More than one former Rogers employee has suggested to the author that these decisions were so obviously flawed that they represent corporate sabotage– deliberate devaluation of the Rogers division!

MOVE FIVE In June of 1979 Rogers was moved from Fullerton to Monrovia, California, where it was supervised by Jerry Ayles (production engineer) and Gil Madrid. The best explanation for this move seems to be the one from Ayles, who feels that the Lesley division of CBS Musical Instruments was in serious financial trouble and Rogers was moved to the Lesley facility in an attempt to lower Lesley overhead.

MOVE SIX Suddenly in 1981 it was announced that Rogers final assembly was being moved back to Fullerton, while shell and hardware subassembly work would be done in San Luis, Mexico (across the border from Yuma, Arizona). Jerry Ayles remembers being surprised and dismayed by the move. "It was unbelievable. I don't know what they were thinking! It was as if someone just said "Hey! Let's pack up our drum company and go put it out across the desert somewhere!" While someone probably rationalized it as an attempt to save on labor expense, this move was a disaster. There were terrible quality control problems.

MOVE SEVEN Within a few months all operations were moved back to Fullerton again (November, 1981).

MOVE EIGHT Subassembly work was moved to Mexico again in 1983, to Ensenada. This time the quality of the work was better. One former R&D executive explains that this was a logical move since Fender had been building amplifier chassis' down there earlier and it seemed a good way to save some labor expense.

MOVE NINE Everything Rogers was back in Fullerton in 1984. A letter dated August 6, 1984 advised Rogers dealers that XP-8 manufacturing was being "curtailed" while a complete redesign and repackaging was undertaken.

ROY BURNS

photo courtesy of Dave Drew

Roy Burns was born on November 30th, 1935, in Emporia, Kansas. His professional career started with a six-month stint in New Orleans before going to New York in 1955. In 1957 he got the drumming job with Woody Herman's band and six months later he auditioned for Benny Goodman and got that job– a move up since it meant more money and less traveling. Goodman had recently done the movie *The Benny Goodman Story,* so there was a lot of renewed interest in the band. By 1960 Burns had a son and had grown tired of all the traveling so he left Goodman's band to settle down in New York and do studio work. A short time later Roy got a phone call from Ben Strauss, who wanted Roy to check out the Rogers drums. Burns was not particularly interested, but it was the first NAMM (National Association of Music Merchants) convention to be held in New York and prominent drum shop owner Henry Adler encouraged Roy to go and check Rogers out. Adler felt that an association with the rapidly growing Rogers would be good for Burns in terms of publicity.

RC: So you went to the New York NAMM show....

RB: I went over and met the folks from Rogers, and found them to be a very nice group. The drums were pretty good, and they were obviously trying to make them even better. They asked me if I could do clinics because my elementary drum method book had done so well in the schools. That kind of brought me to a crossroads because right at the time they wanted me to go to Europe on a clinic tour I had an opportunity to do another Merv Griffin show. I'd done two or three of the Griffin series' in a row, and it was wonderful work. I talked to Merv about the schedule and he said he just couldn't let me miss six weeks of shooting because he already had too many guys who wanted to start the show late. He said either do the trip or do the show– we'll still be friends either way. So I did the trip which was really terrific and what really got me into the clinic business.

RC: From that time on your endorsement arrangement was more than just loaning your name...

RB: Right– I was an endorsee and a clinician.

RC: And when CBS bought Rogers from Grossman you went to work for Rogers full-time?

RB: Yes, I went to work for Rogers on a full time basis in 1968 as an artist in residence.

RC: What was happening at Rogers then?

RB: Rogers was not the largest in the business, but I

Roy Burns, early 1960s

feel they were the most innovative. They put the tilter screw under the hi-hat cymbal, put spurs on the hihat, developed large spurs and other innovative hardware. If it weren't for Rogers the guys out there today wouldn't know what to make! In that sense it was a great experience.

What happened to the company has come increasingly clear to me as I've gained more business experience in the years since. What really caused the company to collapse was that there were incompetent people running it. I don't mean people like Ben Strauss and Don Canedy who really approached it from the drummer's perspective– I mean corporate types at the top. Bob Bull was an exception; he was a president (of CBS Musical Instruments) who really gave us attention and helped us solve problems. A lot of the other executive types, however, shied away from the Rogers division because they figured it was safer to do a program with guitars and amps. That area was such a fantastic money-maker you could hardly mess it up. Bull understood that the drum business is a low-margin industry; you have to be very careful with your money.

RC: But some of the executives who came after Bull...

RB: Many of them came in with attitudes. It was as if these big businessmen looked at us at Rogers as if to say "we're going to teach you guys how to be in the music business" but they didn't really know anything about the music business. They didn't know anything about drummers. They didn't even know anything about music stores. It was just a spiral case of bungling at the management level. I once was in a meeting where one of them said "you're not here to make musical instruments; you're here to make a profit." Many of those corporate decision-makers were Rogers' worst enemies because they refused to be competitive. Take the franchise system, for example. We sold Rogers drums through authorized, or "franchised" dealers. The number of authorized dealers was drastically reduced in an effort to make it a more valued line. In Denver, Colorado, we had only three dealers, while Ludwig had about 28. The theory was that those three dealers would push our product over all others. Instead the kids bought Ludwig since they saw it everyplace and felt that was the drum to have.

The sales force was quite capable; probably the best I've ever worked with. Their main focus was, however, guitars and amps.

RC: I remember as a dealer at the time being impressed with the cymbal knowledge the field salespeople had when they were selling Paiste....

RB: Paiste ended up being unhappy with what was happening at CBS and ended the distribution arrangement to start up Paiste America. I don't think it was strictly for lack of sales. I remember that at one point Robert Paiste and I went on a six-week dealer tour and in the space of just six weeks we doubled the Paiste sales volume. It was very important to us– at one point the annual sales volume was something like $2.7 million in Paiste while Rogers was only at about $2 million.

RC: What frustrated me as a dealer was ordering merchandise that never came...

RB: When we introduced the XP-8 8-ply shells one September we actually got more orders than Fender guitars did. But by December we had shipped less than half of those orders and people were starting to cancel their orders, or at least try.

RC: Try?

RB: Here's how ridiculous the situation became: Fender

1970s Burns clinic promotional sheet

introduces a new guitar, and a dealer orders heavily. He phones the factory after a few weeks to ask where his order is. The conversation goes something like this;

"About those new guitars I ordered..."

"Sorry; we're behind in manufacturing; it could take as long as six months before we can ship them..."

"Ok.. Well, in the meantime I need to order some current models, to hold me over..."

"Sorry; you're at your credit limit; we can't enter additional orders for you right now."

"How can that be? I don't owe you that much right now..."

"It's that big order for the new guitars. All pending orders are charged against your account's credit limit."

"Ok- So let's cancel that order for now and I'll reorder when the new stuff is ready..."

"Sorry. Those orders were placed on a non-cancellable basis."

"Well, let's talk about getting some Rogers drums on order."

"Sorry. Fender, Rogers, and Rhodes all go through the same credit department."

"Let's see if I have this straight. You're telling me that you can't ship me the guitars I ordered and because I ordered them I'm at my credit limit even though I don't owe you any money right now. I've been a Fender dealer for 15 years and a Rogers dealer for 10 years. I've always paid my bills on time. Now you won't send me any Fender OR Rogers products."

"Sorry; that's the policy."
RB: That's how stupid it got. Anyone with an ounce of business sense knows that is a stupid system.
RC: I didn't get held up by the credit situation, but I did keep ordering drums that never arrived...
RB: You may be referring to the time when they started to have quality control problems. We started to get a lot of complaints, expecially when manufacturing moved to Mexico. Jim Ganduglia and I went to inspect drums and found all kinds of problems. The guys were not sharpening their drill bits or they'd put too much pressure on and splinter the inside of the shell. I think we rejected 260 drums in one day. The people in charge of manufacturing went bananas.
RC: Was that the last straw?
RB: I really felt the heat from dealers when it came to stuff like quality problems, because I was in the field all the time. I'd take what the dealers were saying back with me and eventually it got to the point where some of the executives would actually dodge me in the halls. By that time the people I'd worked with in Ohio were all gone; Ben Strauss, Don Canedy, etc. I just felt that I was fighting a war that couldn't be won. There were still some people trying to carry on the Rogers tradition but we were so constrained that it simply was not worth the frustration. I resigned just before the huge embarassment of the Series II drum line.
RC: That was when you got involved with Aquarian?
RB: Exactly. In fact at the very same NAMM show that I announced Aquarian at, CBS brought out the Series II. I was not happy that they tried to hang that one on me. It was almost funny because at the NAMM shows they have a daily newsmagazine called the *Upbeat Daily*. On one page of the *Upbeat Daily* there was a picture of me with a caption describing me as the developer of this new drum line. I actually had nothing to do with that; they'd asked me to stand by the drums and they snapped my picture! On the very next page of that *Upbeat Daily* was the announcement that Roy Burns has left CBS/Rogers to start Aquarian!

1978 Roy Burns Clinic at Cook's Music, Alma, Michigan

I've got to say that the two biggest lessons I learned in going through all of that were to maintain product quality and to provide customer service. I'll never forget a meeting I had with H.S. Grossman in his Cleveland offices. A manager of his print music department was trying to get me to do some kind of little instructional book that I didn't really see the value of, and I wasn't having any of it. H.S. wasn't saying much of anything. After the guy left the office, H.S. looked at me and said "You're right. Always go with quality." It seems like a simple enough concept, but people do lose sight of it in the business world. And the same goes with customer service. Corporate types can sometimes focus on what they want to sell instead of what people want to buy. You have to listen to your customers!

Rogers sales 1971–1980*

In spite of the problems that frustrated Roy Burns during the 1970s, sales steadily increased. At perhaps the most critical time in the firm's history, just when the American drum companies were beginning to feel the tremendous pressure from foreign lines such as Pearl, the direction and future of the company was pretty much put in the hands of Bill Schultz and several others whom were hired away from Yahama by CBS in 1981.

Year	Sales	Year	Sales
1971	$2,371,000	1977	$4,922,000
1972	$3,738,000	1978	$5,733,000
1973	$4,370,000	1979	$5,617,000
1974	$4,738,000	1980	$6,503,000
1975	$3,623,000		
1976	$4,769,000		

*Source: Dave Gordon

DAVE GORDON AND JOHN CERMENARO

By the time Dave Gordon and John Cermenaro joined Rogers, it was a sinking ship. Neither knew at the time they were hired that the entrenched corporate mindset precluded their success.

RC: Dave; I understand you worked at Gretsch prior to joining Rogers?

DG: Yes; actually John and I both did. I worked as a drummer for several years before opening a drum shop in Kansas City. Though we carried all the major brands, I was always partial to Gretsch and Rogers. I was building customized drums and became interested in manufacturing. I approached Gretsch and was hired in to assume responsibility for the drum division. Duke Kramer had been General Manager for Gretsch drums, guitars, etc. for years and was preparing to retire.

Dave Gordon

John Cermenaro

RC: Duke Kramer was still with the firm, though?

DG: Yes. Although he had stepped back from day to day management, he remained involved for several months helping the new guys with the transition.

RC: And John, you also worked at Gretsch?

JC: Yes. I found out that Baldwin Piano and Organ Company, who owned Gretsch at that time, had a "co-op" internship program. I was working toward my mechanical engineering degree at Worcester Polytechnic Institute in Massachusetts and, as a drummer, I thought the ultimate job would be to do engineering design work for a drum company. Somebody has to design all of the metal parts and assemblies, why not me? I worked for nine months at their headquarters in Cincinnati, which was two back-to-back programs. Dave was pretty much my mentor there.

RC: And you somehow both ended up at Rogers?

DG: I made the move first. There was a marketing director for the Fender/Rogers/Rhodes division of CBS Musical Instruments who had marketing people for each division under him. The Rogers guy was Roy Burns who was obviously not just a marketing executive but also staff artist, dealer liason, etc. He had just left when I was hired to become sort of "Mr. Rogers."

RC: This was around 1980, and you were hired shortly after that, John?

JC: Right. It was pretty much a case of being in the right place at the right time. I had sent in a resume that landed on Mike Fleming's desk right when they needed an R&D engineer. I didn't even know Dave was there until after I started. I still laugh about being "introduced" to the Marketing Manager. It was great to work with him again.

RC: So what was happening when you got there?

DG: Sales were flagging a bit, and Memriloc was starting to get a little dated already. Everybody in the marketplace was copying it. My first priority was to hit the road and see what concerns the dealers had. It became obvious to me that quality was a big concern, and the first thing we had to do was really make Rogers a premium instrument. My goal, then, was to produce the finest instruments we could within the practical limitations of manufacturing economics. Every component of the instrument was thoroughly scrutinized for its contribution to the overall sound quality. All of the tooling was inspected and revised where necessary to bring it within specs. Our requirements for shell quality were tightened. Felt gaskets were incorporated to isolate the shell from the lugs and attached hardware. Bearing edges were inspected on flat granite tables to assure true accuracy. A line of deep toms and bass drums was added. Wood and natural brass Dynasonics were added, including an 8-inch deep wood shell version. The memriloc mounting system was expanded to provide unlimited multi-drum mounting configurations. The improvements were incorporated into production supported with a marketing program. We were determined that through quality control and accurate assembly, we were going to produce drums that were second to none on the market. At this point, we were not coming out with conceptually new equipment, but better versions of existing gear. We did a lot to make that happen in the early 1980s. We installed granite flat tables so we could make sure the bearing edges were perfectly flat. We checked over all the tooling although it meant battling accountants. We isolated the lugs on the snare drums with felt strips. We were determined that through quality control we were going to produce drums that had round shells, excellent bearing edges, accurate hardware, and padded hardware. We wanted to really kick the quality up several notches. The problem we ran into was that for all of that effort and expense, what we really accomplished was to bring Rogers quality up to what it should have been in the first place. We were not coming out with conceptually new equipment; just better versions of the existing gear.

JC: These were things we could do with minimal investment in new tooling. There always seemed to be budget problems that kept us from really taking it the next step to make rogers a real industry leader and innovator. In R&D we were working on things like collapsible Memriloc hardware and some other exciting things, but none of it ever saw the light of day.

DG: Right. What we had accomplished was "Phase 1" of a complete product development program that included a total redesign of the Memriloc hardware and mounting systems, low-end drum outfits, new designs for a reentry into marching percussion, a school percussion program, and so on. They were willing to let us spend modest amounts of money to improve the premium drum line, but the pressure was really on to come up with a lower-priced line to compete with the influx of imports. Series II had failed miserably. I went to Taiwan to and met with a drum export broker named Joe Chen. That was an eye-opening experience. It amazed me that we literally waded through rice paddies to get to seemingly primitive facilities that somehow managed to produce drums that were actually very nice products. When I made it clear to Joe what we wanted he had only two questions; how many and when? It was incredible to me that his work force could produce under those conditions.

RC: Not exactly a union workplace?

DG: The union was one of our problems in California. At one point we were told by the union that we had to rotate the workers to different jobs every thirty days. This made it impossible to maintain a skilled workforce. We were trying to produce high-quality musical instruments but had to constantly retrain workers who had just transferred in from the guitar line or the guitar string division.

JC: Personnel-shifting happened at the management level also. Mike Fleming, the man who hired me, moved to a new postition shortly after I got here. His replacement only stayed a short time before Roger Cox, who had been in charge of Fender/Rogers/Rhodes marketing, took over. This was all being driven by changes at the very top. CBS hired a top manager from one of our up-and-coming Japanese competitors to run the place, and in a relatively short period of time several of his former co-workers were also hired. A lot of changes came down fairly quickly , really before they had won the confidence of the "troops." We really didn't know what was going on.

DG: Really it began to seem as if the mold had been cast. We made our presentations for the new product and marketing programs and were told that there was no room in the budget.

JC: Here's how bad it got. We literally were down to so little R&D budget that for the better part of a year we couldn't do anything except design some new cases, mainly because we wouldn't have to pay for any tooling to do it. When Dave had the pre-NAMM sales meeting and showed the sales force the new cases, they couldn't believe it. They were incredulous. "Cases?" they asked. "We have to go out and battle the competition's gear with the same old stuff because all you came up with was *cases*?"

RC: You guys were there in 1981 when production was moved from Monrovia back to Fullerton, with the subassembly work being done in San Luis, Mexico. Whose idea was that?

DG: We didn't know anything about it until it was suddenly announced that the decision had been made.

JC: We don't know to this day exactly who made that call and why.

RC: But I understand it was a mistake?

DG: It was a bad decision for a couple of reasons. It made quality control practically impossible and we were just launching a "Proudly Made In America" advertising program!

JC: I'm sure the labor rate was virtually nonexistent compared to what they had to pay factory people in Fullerton. In reality, there couldn't have been any real savings because just about everything that came out of that plant was rejected. There was no supervision of the manufacturing by our people. Wehn I went down there for inspections with Jerry Ayles, the manufacturing engineer, there were times when we had to cobble together tooling with duct tape and vise grips! Ultimately, it was brought back to Fullerton.The second time production was moved to Mexico, it went to Ensenada. I think that was in 1983. It was more productive and modern facility, but the move was still a surprise and quality was not very consistent.

DG: Finally the R-360 and R-380 lines pretty well took over. With those lines it was pretty much an accounting situation instead of a manufacturing situation; it was just box-in and box-out. That was hard because this was a 100-year-old company. I felt a responsibility to the people who went before me.

JC: You feel like you're the caretaker!

DG: Well, you *are*! It was my responsibility; I'd been given the baton and I darn sure didn't want to drop it. But the budget cuts continued– three or four a year. Significant layoffs were made, and not just at Rogers. One Friday 700 people got the ax company-wide.

JC: Purchasing was done very selectively toward the end. Market demand was ignored and we built only what could be assembled using up what we had in stock.

RC: Were both of you finally laid off?

DG: I was. I was called into an office where a complete executive restructuring was explained to me. There was a big chart with names and responsibilities.... When he was all done I nodded and asked "Well where do I fit into this?" and the response was simply "You don't."

JC: It was ruthless and in some ways nearly inhumane. I remember the Friday that one manager was given a list of people to terminate, and a schedule. All day long people went to his office at fifteen-minute intervals, all to be fired. At the end of what had to be an already terribly depressing day, he himself was fired. It had all been planned out!

JC: I was there for another year after Dave left. The mindset continued– all we heard was "cut it back, cut it back." Joyce Bashore was told to split her time between Rogers and Squire strings. Gil Madrid, the Rogers operations manager, got laid off. Jerry Ayles was moved to Fender. Rogers marketing responsibilities were given to Ed Rizuto. He was also responsible for acoustic guitar marketing and he had no experience with drums whatsoever. I was called in and told that I was going to be in charge of the Rogers assembly line because they had laid off the production foreman. "What about the R&D?" I asked. "Oh you can still do that– you can keep that office and do that when you have time, but this is now your main responsibility." Later I was called in again. "We can see from your personnel file," I was told, "that you're an engineer. We need engineering talent over at Squire. We want you to spend part of your time over there, and part here at Rogers." I simply said no. I was not willing to do that. They made it quite clear that by refusing I was cutting myself off from growth in the corporate structure– this was going to have a very negative impact on my ability to move upward through the organization. I said "OK! That's not a problem!"

It was the general perception that things had been winding down for a long time, and now that process was accelerating. By 1983 it was clear on the production line that this was not a career opportunity. My own mission ultimately became to sit at a desk with huge printouts, figuring out how the production line could convert existing stock into sellable finished goods. The goal was to deplete the inventory of raw materials so when they pulled the plug, they'd have a minimum scrap rate.

Eventually I was the last full time staff employee of Rogers. There were a few hourly employees doing some assembly, but I received the only salaried paycheck that was paid solely on Rogers as a cost center.

I finally quit in 1984 because I was just too stressed. Here I was in my early 20s feeling like I was pounding nails into the coffin of a 100-year-old American drum company in the face of Tama taking off like a rocket, Yamaha taking off, and Pearl doing real well. The foreign stuff's doing great and I've got one of the last American drum companies slipping through my fingers. The icing on the cake was that we were also selling an offshore product– I resented that product line terribly. To this day, those little gold "Made In Taiwan" stickers give me the willies.

Author's note: After speaking with these two men for several hours, the real cause of Rogers' demise was starting to come into focus, but was still rather fuzzy. I was a Rogers dealer from the late 1970s through the end and had always found it a little perplexing; the quality had been excellent, the prices reasonable, but deliveries simply stopped. The talk with Dave and John certainly gave me some insights, but even they still had questions about some of the decisions that had been made. To research this a little further, the three of us made some conference calls to some of the people wo had also worked at Fender/Rogers/Rhodes/Squire. The people we spoke to asked that their observations remain anonymous. The intent was to gain some additional insight as to what factors led up to the eventual closure of Rogers drums. There is nothing to be gained by attempting to attach "blame" to specific individuals. Everyone can claim to have 20-20 hindsight. Decisions made at any given time are based on the information and circumstances of the moement. These comments may help us to understand what forces may have been at work in the final two years that Rogers produced drums in North America.

Anon 1: I really think that they (company management) simply did not want to be in the drum business. They understood that it was a much lower-margin business than the making of guitars and saw no need for it.

Anon 2: I was in a corporate meeting once when

someone made the point that our (Rogers) division was not profitable enough. I started to point out that our market share had been steadily growing and was cut off in what I considered a very rude fashion. His words were something to the effect of "We're not in business to increase market share. We're in business to make a profit!"

Anon 3: At the time I was under the impression that we were the third largest American drum company, behind Ludwig and Slingerland. I later learned that we had actually passed Slingerland and were the second-largest. It was not like we were losing money. I know for a fact that while I was there we were making an 11% pre-tax profit on gross sales of nearly $5 million. That, however, was not much compared to the profit on guitars.

Anon 4: You were a Fender dealer then?

RC: Yes.

Anon 4: And how much were you paying for a Fender Stratocaster in the late 1970s?"

RC: As I recall it was somewhere around three or four hundred dollars.

Anon 4: Well, the manufacturing cost of those guitars was about $75.00. Multiply that by the 300 guitars we were making every day. That's where the money was. I think they saw the opportunity to just sell prepackaged drums as a way to solve a lot of problems with manufacturing– it's much easier to just buy and sell boxes. Box in, box out!

Anon 5: At one point the Fender/Rogers/Rhodes division was quite profitable. It represented only 1/10th of the gross sales of CBS yet accounted for nearly 50% of the profit. For some reason, however, in a relatively short period of time the profit of around $1 million a month shifted to losses of almost $600 thousand a month.

Anon 2: (A manager) said we have to do some major restructuring of the dealer network. It was decided to cut the number of dealers in half with the logic that we would be left with the most loyal dealers. Instead we ended up with the most profitable dealers because they had less competition. Though the *dealers* were making more profit, the *company* was not. Once you get below the breakeven point, losses pile up in a hurry.

Anon 1: The designer of the Series II knew that it wouldn't work and he didn't want to do it. He was pressured into it. When he had the engineering work completed on it he brought the designs to me. He handed me the stack of papers and announced that he was quitting. You know, man– it seemed to me like everything that _____ & _____ did seemed to negate the value of the company. In my humble opinion I think they came to the decision that here was a chance to run this thing into the ground so they could buy it cheap.

Anon 3: Some of the decisions that were made, quite frankly, made no sense unless you consider them to be deliberate actions to devalue the division.

Anon 6: We made profit until certain people came in, they did some things, and eventually there was an ownership change.

POST-CBS ROGERS

From January of 1984 through March of 1985 the Fender/Rogers/Rhodes division of CBS Musical Instruments was for sale. It had become evident to CBS executives that the real estate could yield more than they could ever realistically hope to make in profit if they could stop the losses at all. In the summer of 1984 there literally was a "For Sale" sign out in front.

A consortium put together by William Schultz purchased the division from CBS in March of 1985. By this time little to no effort was put into maintaining the Rogers marque. When contacted for comment about the last days of Rogers as a division of CBS and what he did with the division, the response from William Schultz through his Public Relations liason was "I politely and respectfully decline to comment."

Parts and equipment were sold off in bulk, much of it in three lots. John Cermenaro acquired a small portion, some was sold to a Chicago-area distributor (now-defunct *Music-Dealer-Service*), and much of the remaining stock of parts was sold to Dave Drew of *Al Drew's Music* in Woonsocket, Rhode Island.

In the late 1980s the Rogers name was licensed to an importer-distributor (also now-defunct), *Island Music*. Island planned to import inexpensive copies of the Rogers drums which had been produced in the last CBS days as well as restarting production of some high-quality American-made drums. They approached Dave Drew with a proposal which in Dave's opinion called upon him to do most of the work while they collected most of the profit. He respectfully declined the offer. The imported Rogers that Island distributed was of decidedly inferior quality and was only on the market for about a year.

By the time Fender arranged to sell Rogers, there was not really very much left to sell; there was the Rogers name, the rights to all Rogers patents, and a few pieces of equipment. This was all sold to Matthew Spitzer. Spitzer owned retail music stores in California (Spitzer Music) as well as a distributing company (jobber), Sahlein Music. Sahlein distributed Fender acoustic guitars, so Spitzer had a working relationship with Fender owner William Schultz.

Spitzer purchased Rogers as an investment and to protect the name from further damage. He turned down an offer from one of the "superstore" chains to license the name for use on inexpensive imported outfits.

William Schultz (left), President of Fender, at the closing of the sale of Rogers to Matt Spitzer (right) on December 1, 1993.
Spitzer sold Rogers to Bill Everitt of Brook Mays Music in June of 1999.

It seemed to the author at the time he conducted the interviews on the preceding pages (particularly the conference call to former Rogers employees) that fingers were pointing at William Schultz with rather serious allegations. They were basically claiming corporate sabotage for the failure of Rogers. They claimed, in no uncertain terms, that under the leadership of Schultz, Fender/Rogers/Rhodes/Squire slid from making $1 million profit per month to showing losses of $600,000.00 per month. This served to devalue the Fender division also, prompting CBS to sell the whole Fender/Rogers/Rhodes/Squire division. Who stepped up to buy it? An investor group headed by Bill Schultz. Rhodes was sold off to Roland in 1987, but there were no ready buyers for the thoroughly trashed Rogers division.

Seeking comment from Schultz, the author tried to set up an interview in 1998. An assistant to Schultz explained that before an interview would even be considered, it would be neccessary to supply some biographical information, an explanation of the work-in-progress, and a list of the questions to be asked. The author complied, only to be told, "Mr. Schultz respectfully declines to comment."

The questions which the author was trying to ask Mr. Schultz:
1. When did you first come to work for CBS, and in what capacity?
2. What was the financial situation for Rogers when you first joined CBS/Rogers/Rhodes?
3. How did that change between when you joined the company and when you purchased Fender from CBS?
4. Who was responsible for the business end of Rogers during that time period?
5. From when you joined CBS through to the date you sold Rogers to Spitzer, did management ever perceive of Rogers Drums as a vital part of the company's product mix, or was it perceived early on as something that would eventually need to be "spun off?"
6. Did management believe that the Fender division was the company's core and that so long as Rogers did not cost the company any money or resources, it should be kept?
7. Did the Rogers division accumulate debt? If so, why was it not sold sooner?
8. Who made the decision to move drum manufacturing to Mexico, and why? In retrospect was this a good decision?
9. Why was the Rogers name licensed to Island Music? Were there other bidders?
10. What was the final disposition of the Rogers parts inventory and production equipment?
11. Is Fender considering getting back into the drum business?
12. Who decided to restructure the dealer network? (the restructuring referred to by Roy Burns, page 58)

In preparing this revised and updated edition of *The Rogers Book* in 2004, the author tried once again to get some kind of comment from Mr. Schultz. Still no comment.

ROGERS ENDORSEES

No endorsees were listed in the Rogers catalogs prior to 1958. Most endorsee agreements were set up by Ben Strauss. (He shared this job with Don Canedy beginning in 1966.) It was a simple agreement that contained a cancellation clause that could be exercised by either party after the first year. The 1962 and 1964 catalogs featured full-page spreads of small endorsee photos (see pages 68–70;) a number of these endorsees Strauss never actually met. They were players who were prominent in their locales, and set up on the strength of the local dealer's recommendation. The standard deal was that the endorsee got a Rogers outfit at a reduced price plus a trade allowance. The dealer got to keep the trade-in outfit, and Rogers took care of getting photos of the artist. Artists who were more visable and influential were supplied with an initial equipment package.

Louis Bellson and Buddy Rich agreements called for two outfits per year though they did not always take that amount. Many times all that was required were new heads because the drums were in good condition.

Strauss says that endorsees occasionally demanded more, such as full page ads like the ones they saw featuring Bellson and Rich. He politely but firmly explained that while he respected their abilities as a player, they simply did not have the same influence as the two big names in the Rogers stable. If they persisted with an ultimatum, they were reminded of their option to terminate the agreement, which they sometimes exercised.

(The years listed here are based on artist listing in catalogs, so they do not represent exact dates that artist agreements were consummated and terminated.)

Name	Years	Pages
Abel, Alan	1964	
Adamson, Freddy	1967	
Alpert, Dave	1962–1964	68
Anderson, Rags	1958–1960	
Anton, Art	1962–1964	68,72
Appleyard, Peter	1964	
Barnett, Dick	1962–1964	68
Beck, John	1964–1973	
Bellson, Louis	1959–1973	67,71,76,77
Bellson, Tony	1964	68,70
Bennett, Alvino	1983	
Bethancourt, Jose	1964	
Black, Dave	1962–1964	68,74
Blaine, Hal	1958–1964	70,74
Bonita, Freddy	1960	
Bookspan, Michael	1964	
Botterill, Charles	1959–1967	67
Bourg, Ned	1964	
Bourne, Eddie "Mole"	1960–1964	70,73
Bowden, Mark	1962–1964	
Breines, Gil	1964	73
Bridge, Danny	1962–1964	70
Britton, Mervin	1964–1964	
Brokensha, Jack	1960–1964	70
Brooks, Roy	1962–1964	68,73
Brush, Howard	1958–1964	68
Buckley, Damon	1958–1964	68
Burns, Roy	1959–1983	67,68,77
Caimi, Frank	1958–1960	
Cameron, Charles	1962	70
Capp, Frank	1960–1964	68
Carto, Lou	1964	
Cattini, Clem	1966–1967	
Chapin, Jim	1959–1968	67,70,75
Chavez, Frankie	1962–1964	69
Clare, Kenny	1959–1964	67
Clark, Mona	1960–1964	69
Clark, Dave	1965–1967	
Coldren, Dave	1960–1962	69
Cole, Cozy	1958–1967	67
Collins, Rudy	1962–1964	69
Cooper, Jackie	1958–1960	
Cooper, Ray	1967	
Cottler, Irv	1959–1964	67,69
Cusatis, Joe	1962	70
Dahlgren, Marvin	1964	
DeSoto, John	1962–1964	68
Devens, George	1964	
Devito, Frank	1958–1964	68,74
Dougan, Jackie	1963–1967	
Edwards, Paul	1962–1964	68,73
Elliot, Don	1964	
English, Paul	1983	
Ettleson, Steve	1973	77
Falls, Skip	1960	
Feld, Morey	1960–1964	68
Feldman, Victor	1964	
Ferguson, Sherman	1983	
Fine, Elliot	1964	
Floyd, Ray "Red"	1962–1964	
Flynn, Frank	1962–1964	68
Friedman, Jerry	1962–1964	70
Frost, Ritchie	1958–1960	
Gadzos, Ernie	1958–1964	69
Gagliardi, Frank	1958–1964	69
Gall, Jim	1964	
Ganduglia, Jim	1973–1976	77
Garibaldi, Dave	1983	
Gibbs, Terry	1964	
Gilgor, Jerry	1962	69

Name	Years	Notes
Girone, James	1962–1964	69
Goldenburg, Morris	1964	
Greb, Ronnie	1958–1964	69
Gubin, Sol	1962–1964	69
Guerrero, Chico	1964–1964	
Gustofson, Gus	1962–1964	70
Hampton, Lionel	1958–1960	67,68
Hardy, Hagood	1964	
Harmon, Murray	1958–1960	68
Hastings, Lennie	1963–1967	
Hayes, Louis	1958–1967	68,72
Heard, J.C.	1958–1964	68
Heath, Albert	1958–1964	68
Hinger, Fred	1964	
Holland, Milt	1958–1964	70
Hunton, Eddie	1960	
Ippolitto, Frank	1958–1964	69,70
Irwin, Russ	1964	74
Jansa, William	1964	
Johnson, Jimmy	1958–1964	69
Krampf, Craig	1983	78,80,83,83
Kraus, Phil	1964	
Krell, Stan	1958–1964	67,69,73
Lackey, Jim	1964	
Lampkin, Chuck	1958–1964	69
LaPron, Dennis	1958–1964	70
Lawrence, Stan	1958–1964	68,72
Leavitt, Joseph	1964	
Lewis, Sabby	1958–1964	68
Leyland, Ken	1967	
Lillo, Don	1958–1964	68
Lordan, Bill	1983	
Ludwick, Rex	1983	
Luty, Chet	1958–1964	68
Maineri, Mike	1964	
Malin, Lou	1958–1964	68,74
Manton, Freddie	1958–1964	70
Mason, Harvey	1976	
Matson, Robert	1964	
McCartney, Jack	1958–1964	69
McKay, Ron	1963–1967	
McKenzie, Jack	1964	
Meaney, Gerry	1958–1964	69
Miles, Barry	1958–1964	
Miles, Buddy	1976	
Monte, Al	1958–1964	69
Montgomery, Buddy	1964	
Morales, Lloyd	1958–1964	69,74
Morales, Humberto	1967	
Morgenstein, Rod	1983	88
Morris, Weedy	1958–1964	70
Neel, Bob	1958–1964	68,72
Norvo, Red	1964	
Oliphant, Grasella	1958–1960	68
Oliver, Howie	1958–1964	68
Owen, Charles	1964	
Palmer, Earl	1958–1964	68
Palmer, Mike	1965–1967	
Pangborn, Robert	1964	
Parnell, Jack	1959–1967	67
Patton, Pat	1958–1964	68
Perry, Bey	1958	70
Perry, Charley	1958	67,69,70
Pettica, Carl	1958–1964	69
Phillips, Rich	1964	74
Press, Arthur	1964	
Price, Ray	1958–1964	69
Puente, Tito	1964	
Raynor, Joe	1958–1964	73
Reilly, Ray	1962	
Rich, Buddy	1960–1967	67,71,76
Ricord, Chet	1958	
Rosen, Gerry	1958–1964	70,74
Rosengarden, Bobby	1964	74
Rully, Ron	1962	
Sage, Walt	1958–1964	70
Sheen, Mickey	1958–1964	70,73
Shiraki, H.	1964	
Siconolfi, Angelo	1950–1964	70
Silva, Mike	1964–1967	
Smith, Ethel	1960–1962	
Solvick, Gina	1983	
Sperling, Jack	1964–1967	75
Ssanet, Lu	1963	
Stalcup, Josie	1958	70,73
Stephenson, Ronnie	1963–1967	
Testa, Joe	1958–1964	70
Thaler, Gene	1958–1964	70
Thompson, Porter	1958–1964	
Tjader, Cal	1964	
Tucker, Ray	1958–1964	
Turner, Bob	1959	67
Tutt, Ron	1983	
Volk, Jack	1958–1964	
Walden, Narada Michael	1983	
Waldron, Mike	1963–1965	
Wallace, Harold	1958–1964	69
Walsh, Dave	1967	
Wilson, Harold	1958	
Wilson, Dennis	1958–1964	69
Worth, Bobby	1967	
Wright, Dougie	1963–1966	
York, Peter	1965–1967	
Young, Lee	1958–1964	70

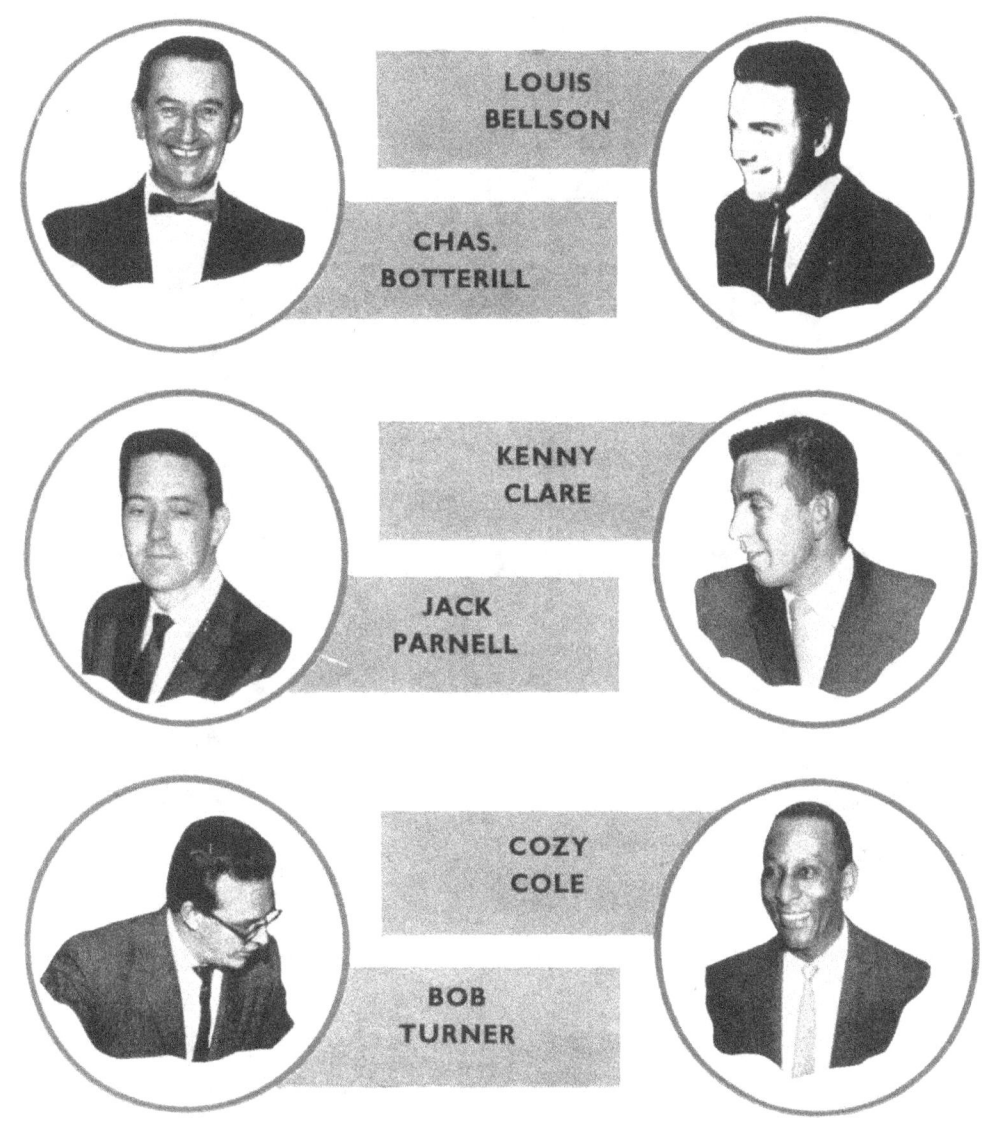

1962

1962

 FRANKIE CHAVEZ
 MONA CLARK
 DAVE COLDREN
 RUDY COLLINS
 IRV COTTLER

 ERNIE GADZOS
 JERRY GILGOR
 JAMES GIRONE
RONNIE GREB
SOL GUBIN

 FRANK IPPOLITTO
 JIMMY JOHNSON
 FRANK GAGLIARDI
 STAN KRELL
 CHUCK LAMPKIN

 JACK McCARTNEY
 GERRY MEANEY
 BARRY MILES
 AL MONTE
 LLOYD MORALES

 CHAS. PERRY
 CARL PETTICA
 RAY PRICE
 JOE RAYNOR
 CHET RICORD

 PORTER THOMPSON
 RAY TUCKER
 JACK VOLK
 HAROLD WALLACE
 DENNIS WILSON

The artists on this page and the two preceding pages were pictured in 1962's catalog 62R. A very similar spread was in catalog 64R of 1964, with some exceptions: Lionel Hampton, Murray Harmon, Grasella Oliphant, Josie Stalcup, Charles Cameron, Jay Collins, Ned Bourg and Lou Carto, were replaced with Jim Lackey, William Jansa, Jim Gall, Chico Guerrero, Jay Collins, Ned Bourg, and Lou Carto.

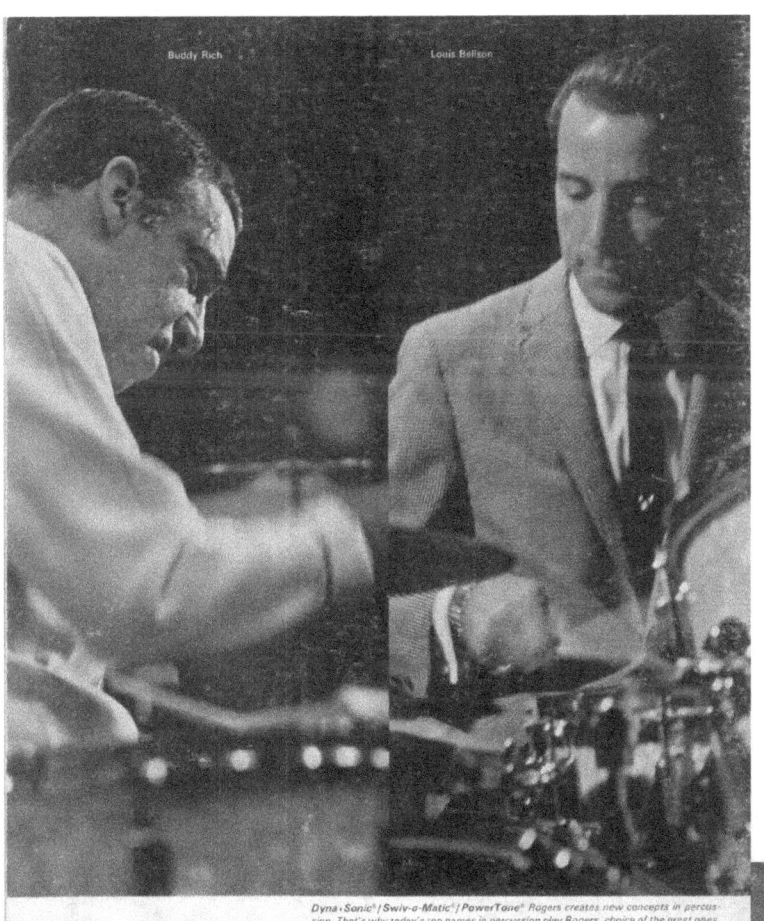

Now you see him...
(Buddy Rich (far left) with Louis Bellson on the back cover of the first edition catalog 67-68)

Now you don't.....
(back cover, second edition catalog 67-68)

Buddy Rich endorsed Rogers drums for nearly ten years, and may well have continued had Grossman not sold Rogers to CBS. Rich felt that not only should he receive a cash payment for his endorsement (he reportedly was demanding $55,000.00 annually) but also expected his band to be supported by the CBS recording label. CBS declined the ultimatum, and published a second edition of catalog 67-68 which removed his photo from the back cover (above) as well as all mention of him with the two signature outfits and drum sticks.

Stan Lawrence   **Louis Hayes**   **Charles Perry**

Tony Bellson   **Frank Ippolito**   **Bob Neel**

Art Anton   **J.C. Heard**   **Gene Thaler**

| Josie Stalcup | Paul Edwards | Gil Breines |

| Roy Brooks | Barry Miles | Eddie Mole Bourne |

| Stan Krell | Joe Raynor | Mickey Sheen |

Russ Irwin

Lloyd Morales

Lew Malin

Rich Phillips

Gerry Rosen

Dave Black

Hal Blaine

Bobby Rosengarden

Frank De Vito

Chapin was a Rogers endorser from August of 1959 to November, 1968.

Louis Bellson with an experimental outfit; bass drums down to 16 inches. Ben Strauss once told Joe Thompson that Rogers could not afford to have him spend so much time making prototypes for Bellson which were based on concepts unlikely to lead to mass market sales. Thompson responded that he enjoyed working with Bellson so much that he would do it on his own time.

Catalog 73/74, 1973. Clockwise from upper left: Steve Ettleson, Roy Burns, Jim Ganduglia, Louis Bellson

CRAIG KRAMPF

Although Craig Krampf's association with Rogers was during a relatively brief slice of his career (see pages 54,55), his story is such a remarkable one that the author felt compelled to include it here. Craig's love of music, his love of drumming, and his willingness to make the most of his opportunities have seen him through the lean days: by any standards today he is enjoying success as a seasoned session drummer and top producer, based in Nashville.

RC: Let's start all the way back a the beginning; how'd you get started playing drums?

CK: Every German Polish boy in Milwaukee had to play accordian (laughs). My older brother, at ten years old took accordian lessions. He was playing polkas and waltzes. I don't know why, but there were drumsticks around the house and I picked 'em up. My dad was a railroad man and he loved music. Every paycheck he brought home records, so there was always music being played in the house. I think that because of the records I just kind of knew what to do with the sticks. Carl would play the accordian and I'd play pots and pans and wooden chairs. At Christmas when I was eight years old I got a forty dollar Sears drum set. That was fairly expensive for them back then.

We gradually built up a real drum set a piece at a time, and I played my first job when I was 9. It was a Polish wedding or communion party and Carl played the accordian and we played waltzes, polkas, and standards. I just kept at it and we played more and more jobs. I didn't really plan on a music career. I went to Marquette University planning to become a social worker. The family band finally broke up when my brother went to graduate school, and I was asked to join some brothers from Milwaukee who had a band that was scheduled to open up for the Beach Boys at the Milwaukee auditorium. I went and rehearsed and it really worked well– the band clicked. That next summer (1965) we did a tour for RCA and DuPont fasshions. Kids would come to the show, we'd play some rock and roll, then there'd be a fashion show. We did that the whole summer, and got an RCA recording contract. They took us to New York, we recorded– but never had a release. The band was "The Robbs". So we went back to school– I started my junior year and we continued to play quite a bit. By that time, I was going to class every day from 9:00 A.M. until about 2:00 or 3:00 P.M., teaching drums from 3:30 P.M. to about 8:30 every night, then playing from 9:30 'til two in the morning. Then we heard about a Battle-of-the-bands and we entered. We won every round, and the

playoff was in Chicago. That really was not our "turf"; nobody down there had heard of us, but we won that too. Grand Prize was an appearance at Dick Clark Teen World's Fair. This was in March or April of 1966. So now we're on the big stage show as part of a nine-day festival. *Everybody* was coming through; Paul Revere and the Raiders, Johnny Rivers, Sam The Sham, Mitch Ryder, The Angels, The Turtles– it was just an amazing rock and roll festival. Dick Clark was upset when he saw an unfamiliar name on the schedule. He was losing it. The promoter explained that there'd been a battle-of-the-bands and the winner was playing this slot. Clark was not at all happy about that. We went on stage, and the crowd went wild. They mobbed the stage. It was unbelievable. Dick Clark met us backstage and said "I want to put you guys on again tomorrow." By the third day we couldn't go back to the hotel. It was like Beatlemania. It was like the movies. Girls screaming, tearing at our clothes, tearing our hair- it was absolutely amazing. Then Clark came to us and said his TV show *Where The Action Is* was coming to town and he wanted us to be on. We said we didn't have anything on tape and he just said go make a recording. So we went in with Lou Reisner who produced Rod Stewart's first album– we went to Universal in Chicago and recorded two songs. Mercury Records was aware of what was going on at the amphitheater; Mercury signed us on the spot and two days later our songs were getting airplay on WLS in Chicago. Nowadays we record something and we don't hear it on the air for six or nine months, but in those days it happened fast. So *Where The Action Is* came to town and Clark announced us as a band he discovered in the Chicago area who was going to be the next huge hit.

So the fair ended, and we went back to Milwaukee with a song playing on the radio. It was amazing. And to this day hearing myself on the radio is a thrill.

Dick Clark then called the promoter of the Teen World's Fair and told them "I've got to find the Robbs! I want them to be regulars on *Where The Action Is!*" The promoter told him "Well, I manage them!". Then he called us and told us if we'd sign with him he thought me might be able to get us a regular spot on *Action*. . Well, of course we signed– our first experience with a crooked manager.

So we left for California in May of 1966 We replaced the Knickerbockers; they had their hair pulled back and wore sharkskin suits. Clark thought they didn't have the image there that fit as well as ours, with the long hair, denim jackets, etc. Every day when Dick Clark introduced us he'd give a big buildup about the new band he'd discovered that was going to be the next big thing.

It was an amazing experience to be 20 years old, involved in music and to be getting to California in 1966. Dylan, The Byrds on the Sunset Strip, Buffalo Springfield– I remember seeing the Doors at the Whiskey as an opening act. There were just countless acts we saw before they were signed or got big.

We went out and did the Dick Clark tours; 80 one-nighters in a row, traveling in buses that didn't have bunks. We'd drive 400 to 500 miles, get our 20 minutes on stage, pile on the bus, and travel to the next town.

Something developed out of that time without my realizing it until a producer pointed it out. There was a producer I worked with quite a bit, who loved my playing, and loved it especially because I did all snare drum fills. I'd occasionally hit a tom-tom, but I was not really a tom-tom guy. When I thought about it, I realized that came from those days of touring when the toms were not miked and you just could not hear them.

As far as record success, we came really close. Billboard magazine had their "Hot 100" chart, and under that they had a list called "Bubbling Under". We were the kings of "Bubbling Under". We'd constantly be at 103, 102, and every time a record came out I'd call my mom and say "Ma! This one! This is the one!" We had one record, our third record, that was top 3 in every market that it came out in but it was over a nine or ten month span. It's be number 3 in Atlanta, but nowhere else in the country. Later it was #1 in Las Vegas... I think during the course of that band we had something like 15 or 17 singles... We went with Atlantic records for two releases, then we went with ABC Dunhill.

I met my wife during that period- around 1969 or 1970. By this time we'd changed our name from the Robbs to Cherokee. (People were beginning to think that if the disc jockeys got one more Robbs record they'd just say "Oh not THESE guys again!")

Suzie and I decided we were going to get married. I was 25, she was 19. She's still my best friend and during the rough times, I think she had more faith in me than I did in myself.

We had never really captured on record what we were live so we thought "Let's buy a 4-track and record demos so we can show the producers what we're really all about". We started with a four-track in the garage and a year later the studio had grown to 24-track doing like Steely Dan's *Pretzel Logic*. At the studio everybody was engineering and assisting... The studio was getting booked; ELO was out there, Ricky Nelson, Del Shannon (who was a close friend), there were just a lot of people recording there. I went through a lot of soul searching because six months had gone by and I hadn't been playing my drums much. It was like "What is the premise of my life?" I knew it was to be a drummer and a musician, not to be an engineer. I'm grateful, though, for what I learned by being on the "other side" of the glass.It was really a hard decision after being with those guys for so long. We'd been through so much together and now this studio was a group effort but I thought about it a lot, talked to Suzie, then I went to the three brothers (Dee, Joe, and Bruce) and said "Guys, I can't do this. I'm a drummer- I've got to find out about that." It was hard– it was a breakup. They understood, and then like a year later they're all driving Cadillacs and Corvettes and my wife and I were barely getting by. Did I make the right decision? Yes. They bought the old MGM studios on Fairfax Avenue in Hollywood and they opened up a great studio which is still a world-class facility today (Cherokee Studios), so they're doing good. We still stay in touch.

So I went off and did stuff with the Hudson Brothers who had a television show that summer– it was a replacement for the Sonny & Cher show. Right afterward, I did a soundtrack for a cartoon with Mark and Howard (Flo & Eddie) from The Turtles. It clicked really well so I joined up with them, touring through 1974, 1975, 1976, in that era.

Our first child was born, Carrie, in 1973. Suzie worked up until the 9th month of her pregnancy. I was working in a convalescent hospital; it was like, "What can I do? I have to help pay for this baby, but I'm a musician." Then Suzie's dad got me a job at the stationery company where he worked. Suzie was also working there. I started as a truck driver, then went to shipping clerk, then promoted to purchasing agent. I could

see Suzie's mom and dad breathe a little easier. We saved money, paid for the baby, and Carrie was born in January.

Then in April, Little Richard called. He was familiar with my work because there was a movie called *Let The Good Times Roll* and something happened to the soundtrack where they lost the drums and the tenor sax solo. So I overdubbed all the drums to a live performance for Little Richard for this movie. He calls me on a Wednesday and says "Craig, I need you!" I ask "When?" He says "Friday! We open up at Madison Square Garden." So I talked to Suzie, and of course we decide I have to go. Thursday I went in to the office and I talked to all the bosses and to Suzie's dad and I said I got this call from Little Richard and that I was really sorry and I knew that the only fair thing to do was give two weeks notice, but.... we leave tomorrow. My father-in-law just stood there in disbelief. So off I go. All I knew was that I was going to get paid $400 a week and it was a four week tour. I was going to come home with $1600. What was going to happen after that? I didn't have a clue. Thank God for Suzie understanding– "Of course– you're a musician, you've got to go."

That was quite an experience. Madison Square Garden, no rehearsals. 18,000 people. Before the show Richard's bodyguard came up to me, "Richard wants to see you." So I go, and Richard for some reason was sitting on a chair in a shower stall. "You're gonna be fine! You grew up with all this stuff! It's all in here! Watch my shoulder for tempo, you're gonna be fine!" And he was right. He just had to let me know that even though we hadn't played this stuff together before, it was gonna be ok. Richard had to have the bass drum touch the end of his piano bench– it almost had to be that close. He wanted to be able to feel the bass drum. So we go on, there's 18,000 people and I'm this far from Richard and there it was– *Lucile, Keep a Knockin'*, etc. The show was unbelievable. So I spent roughly a year with Richard.

I had been playing Slingerland from the start and had a Capri Pearl set early on, then when I went with the Robbs it was arranged for me to pick up a Silver Sparkle set at Franks Drum Shop– two 20" bass drums, two 8x12s, two 16x16s. Then when I went with Flo and Eddie I went in to see Tom Beckman and that's when I got the Camcos. They had an interesting way of using serial numbers. Inside every drum of the set there was a number 181; that meant this was the 181st set they made. I still have that set.

In 1977 Steve Perry and I put a band together. We're on food stamps again, starving. Steve Perry's on food stamps, starving. We found a bass player, Richard Michaels, and a great guitar player, Stevie DeLacey. Chrysalis and Columbia both wanted to sign us. The band was magical. I'd borrow thirty or forty dollars from friends and I'd put like ten dollars toward the phone bill, the rest we'd get a rehearsal hall.

RC: What was the name of the band?

CK: We never had one. Some of Steve's fans and CBS Records have referred to us as *The Alien Project*. This story is a strange one. The record people were blown away. They said "We want to see the whole package.

We'll sign you tomorow if we can see like managment, lawyers, all of that in place." So we said ok– I got some spec time, from the Robbs at Cherokee, we went in and we did some demos. Steve and I would go around to various lawyers and we're trying to get a vibe to get the right lawyer. We finally thought we'd found the right one– he puts the tape on and says, "This is big! This is really big! We're talking a million dollar deal here." And in 1977 they were giving million dollar deals. Then we started playing for management– we played for Leber and Krebs who managed Aerosmith, Aucoin who had Kiss. Every single managment company wanted to manage us. The band was batting 1000. We hadn't made a decision yet on management. There was a CBS record convention in Hawaii and when the CBS people got back from the convention we were going to sign the contracts. Our bass player, Richard, was from Detroit. Although he was white he played with Detroit soul; everything had this "thing" to it. The kid sang high– he sang a third above Steve Perry. It was an amazing band. Richard and his girlfriend were on their way to our house and he was killed in a car wreck. It's even stranger– I was taking out Carrie to her Grandma's house to spend the night, and I passed the wreck on the highway. I said to Carrie "Don't look. This is a bad one." I didn't recognize the wreck– they were in her car. I dropped Carrie off at Grandma's, came back to our house, no Richard, no Richard, and finally I get a telephone call. So I called Steve– we were just devastated. I had been through a rock and roll death the year before with Flo and Eddie- we lost Phil, our guitar player, on the road- he was found nine stories down the first day we began a Doobie Brothers tour. (Nobody to this day knows what occurred.) I kind of knew what was going to happen– for a while you can't play, but are you going to give up music? No, eventually you go on with life. You go back to it when it feels right. With Flo and Eddie we came off the road and we didn't do anything for months, then finally said ok, let's get back to it. The same thing was going to happen with this band– let's let some time go by, and if it feels right, let's get a bass player and carry on. I called CBS in Hawaii and told them the news, and the wheels started turning by all the brass at Columbia and Journey's manager. Here we have Journey, a 4-piece band with two releases that doesn't really have a lead singer; and here we've got a great singer who doesn't have a band anymore– so that was put together.

So finally a couple months went by and it was like "Steve- let's get going." But every bass player I bring in Steve would be going "no, no–" After about the third day of this he said "I've got to talk to you. I've been given an offer to be in this band Journey and I've gotta do it." I completely understood because every person should follow his heart in life, but I was crushed. Our band just wasn't meant to be... the hand of fate has other ideas. Steve and I remain good friends.

So our second daughter was born a month following Richard's death. Back when I'd been working in the hospital an old lady told me "Don't worry– when a baby is born they always bring their own bread." The day Katie was born I landed this album project, so all of a sudden there was a month or so of work.

Throughout the mid 1970s I was playing on tons of demos. If people called up and said they had no money, it didn't matter. I was learning about my craft. Better to be doing that than watching television. Sometimes it was ten bucks a song, maybe twenty bucks a song. I just wanted to keep on learning about recording. Then Chrysalis Records needed a drummer for Nick Gilder. They were aware of me because they wanted to sign the band I had with Steve, so I got together with Nick Gilder and started rehearsing and there was a regular paycheck and all that. We went in and did *Hot Child In The City* with Mike Chapman. That song went to number one and was only the 12th single to ever go platinum. We did a lot of touring in 1978 and 1979; this was the era of Rogers affiliation; some of those photos were taken at Nick Gilder concerts.

I've always maintained that you do need a lucky break, but that you have to be ready for it when it does happen. Well, in '79 this producer called me because Jeff Porcaro was supposed to do this album but was sick. "I hear you're a great rock & roll drummer." I said, "Yeah." He said Jeff was sick, and how soon can I get to the studio? I said probably about an hour and a half, he said be there in an hour and you've got the whole album. So I went to do that album and I think that was the start of jumping in to a different level. So the studio thing started happening in about 79.

RC: What was that album?
CK: It wasn't a success, but shortly after that the same producer, George Tobin did Kim Carnes *More Love* and I played on that. Kim wasn't happy with the mixes, so Kim was going to have Val Garay (because of the Linda Ronstadt/James Taylor thing) mix the album. So the tapes come over to Val and he brings up the drum faders and asks, "*Who* the heck is *this*?" So Kim tells him, "Craig Krampf." That's how Val found out about me and I became his drummer for about seven years. We did all of Kim's albums, *Betty Davis Eyes*, The Motels' *Only The Lonely*, Joan Armatrading, etc That really began a really good run. I was still playing the Rogers.
RC: The same sizes?

CK: As soon as I got into the studio I dropped the other bass drum. Sometimes I'd set up two little concert toms. I wound up just taking the larger two of the mounted toms. It was 10x14, 12x15, 16x16, and to this day that's what I play when I'm in the studio. When I went with Tama they made me an 11x14, but it's still 14,15, and 16 toms. I get in there and sometimes the engineers say "Gosh– those drums are... large!" I always say they're not power drums– I never did like the power sizes; I just couldn't relate to the sound.

RC: Coated ambassadors?

CK: Yeah, coated ambassadors on top, clear ambassadors on the bottom, clear ambassador on the kick.

RC: Snare drum?

CK: Back then, it was either my Dyna-sonic or my Powerten. I've also got a Camco snare drum at home that played on both *Hot Child In The City* and *Betty Davis Eyes*– two number one records.

So then I went out and toured with Kim, and that was sort of the end of my touring. I think it was three weeks or a month. After that it was all in the studio. The 80s in LA was fantastic. Finally there was financial security; our third daughter was born in '82.

I don't change drums often, but finally in 1987 I went with Tama. I'm still playing a Tama set that's ten years old now, an Artstar II outfit.

RC: What's the snare drum with the Tama set? Is it a Tama?

CK: It's probably the greatest snare drum I've ever played in my life. It's a Tama bell-brass drum- it weighs 23 lbs and I think in ten years that thing has only missed 8 or 10 songs out of all the thousands of songs I've recorded. It loves a clear CS. Maybe it's a little fanatical, but I've always maintained that a drum sort of dictates where it likes to be tuned– it sort of lets you know. And I've tried different heads on that drum and there's something about the black dot. I break an occasional lug because of the way I play, and Tama no longer has any spare ones, so I've stashed a few away; last year I found four in a drum store in New Orleans, three out in LA.

So I was probably in the top three to five guys in LA, working nonstop doing album after album... Then in 1983 a producer brought me to Nashville, telling me there was noone here like me, blah blah blah... They even flew Suzie in and were showing her houses while I was in the studio– they were serious about us moving there. It just didn't feel right to do at that time.

The last album I did in LA was Melissa Etheridge's first album– I co-produced that and played on it. We had pretty much made the decision by then that it was time to go. The earthquake of October '87 was the final kick in the butt. One of our daughters was at school and as a parent you don't know if that school is standing– it was an eery, horrible feeling to have the family separated when that hit. Our youngest daughter, who was a very stable child, not emotional at all, she gave up sleeping. She'd hear garbage trucks, or a helicopter... even I was weirded out. That one got to me for some reason. The aftershock comes two days later and we're all under the dining room table, the pool water is sloshing, the kids are looking at you like "make this stop" so Suzy and I said "What the hell are we doing here?" I finished Melissa's album, I delivered all the tapes to the record company, and I told Melissa we were moving. "Where?" "Nashville." "When?" "On Monday." It was that quick. Today is our tenth anniversary of when we landed in Nashville.

I went from working two or three albums at a time, working nonstop, back to nothing. I sent 70 resumes out and I think in 87 it almost had an adverse effect. People saw nothing but Rock and Roll on there– 200 albums, a Grammy, blah blah blah and all they thought was, "He's a rock n roller." So the first two years there was practically nothing. We lived off our savings, we got over the hump, and every year has been better than the year before. Susie and I have three wonderful daughters, Carrie, Kaie and Courtney. I still love drumming. Life is good. I love making records– it kills me. Production has been the natural progression because of that. I haven't been too active with songwriting lately, I kind of put that on the back burner. I co-wrote *Oh Sherry* with Steve and I had a song in *Flashdance* with Kim; we won a Grammy for that which was an honor. Actually I think it's an honor and an unbelievable thing to be a musician and it's something I'm really thankful for. I've been blessed. I've never had a day when I woke up and thought, "Oh no, I've got to go to work." Every day I wake up and say, "Thanks for another day and great, I get to play today!"

"I was honored and thrilled when Greg Perry informed me that Rogers would like me to be on the cover for the new drum catalog and ad campaign for the new XP-8 series of drums. It was a most interesting photo shoot. The photographer was quite famous. I was set up in a pure white alcove where the floor actually blended and curved up and around the wall and ceiling. It was an eerie feeling being in this environment for a whole day– I actually lost the true understanding of perspective and where I really was. The photographer said that it was sometimes impossible to get animals to enter this space; they would freak. The drums were positioned mainly by Greg and the photographer for the best camera effectiveness. Polaroids were constantly shot and the two of them would confer and then change heights and angles of various drums and stands. They explained the concept of time exposure and two poses molded into one. Finally after many hours and many test shots we were ready. I had to hold the pose looking right for a given amount of time and then immediately swing to my left and grasp a mirror-like pose on the left side. It was really an experience. That shot was used throughout the whole campaign for the XP-8s and it was an incredible honor to be on the cover of the catalog. When I was a kid I would look at Gene Krupa on the covers of all those Slingerland catalogs, never thinking that someday I would also be on the cover of the catalog– quite a thrill. Dreams *can* come true." Craig Krampf

Rogers drum dating– an interview with Bobby Chiasson, proprietor of Jollity Drum Farm

There always seems to be an exception or contradiction to the most carefully considered dating guidelines. The people best qualified to render expert opinions on identifying Rogers drums are therefore the people who have handled the largest number of them while examining each one in minute detail. Probably the leading expert is Bobby Chiasson of Argyle, New York.

RC: How long have you been at this?

BC: I'm 50, & I've played Rogers drums all my life. I hung around them from 1964 to 1969 along with all the other American brands that were stocked at the Freddy Blood Drum Studio in Glen Falls, New York. I became one of his 3 or 4 teachers– one of the other teachers, Willy Wilcox, became Todd Rundgren's drummer (His brother Jimmy wound up with Blue Oyster Cult). Freddy Blood knew Krupa, Roach, Morello, Arsenault, etc. and had them all in for clinics. The stories about his shop go on and on, but Rogers was his number one brand. They were the most expensive, but by far the best. I got my first set from him in December, 1963, when I was in tenth grade. I've found it helps to date drums when you can get the original purchaser to reference the purchase to some landmark in their life– Christmas, birthday, etc.

One thing that concerns collectors is whether a set is all original. To illustrate what may have happened, I'll tell you about what happened in Freddy's shop. If a customer came in and wanted a spring for a Rogers pedal, Freddy would walk over and take one off a new pedal, then re-order a new pedal spring. Was the pedal still all original? The drums got the same treatment. I bought my Buddy Rich Celebrity kit, as I say, in 1963. The serial numbers are 13- 26325, 16- 27784, 22- 29555. You can see a 3000-number spread in serial numbers there. Now sometimes an outfit will have drums in almost sequential numbers but if they do not, it does not mean they were not an original factory kit. In 1968 I ordered another 20 and 12 to go double-bass. Though the factory shipped them both at the same time, the 12 has a serial number (92574) that's 12000 numbers back from the 20, which indicates to me that the drum had been sitting around for a while– maybe half a year to a year. All the manufacturing clues are identical; we've now got hex-driven scews, we've got the same Fender flat washers which are one big, one small... The tension rods on the tom-tom now have the little "blips" on the side like all Ludwig's do, unlike the square-headed early Leedy, Slingerland, Gretsch, Rogers etc. My 1968 bass drum also has the new T's and claws... all bread and butter lug bass drums have the old bow-tie t-handles and horseshoe claws. This switch was gradual; I've had 3 or more bass drums with the old t-handles and new claws. That's the case with most manufacturing clues– everything was transitional since they didn't just throw away old parts- they used them up.

I decided after a while that double-bass wasn't really for me, so I made a separate small kit out of that 12 and 20 I had added. I went in and asked Freddy to order me a 14" floor tom. He sold me one from a kit he had in stock. That 14 had probably already been in the shop for nearly three years. And that tom (11593) has one of those labels I call the "blank" labels- the model is typed in like the earliest Dyna-Sonic labels. (Some of those labels have serial numbers as low as three digits.) Freddy was not the only dealer that realigned drums within outfits– let me tell you a Henry Adler Drum Shop story. Paul Buhler from up around the Troy area went to Adler's with the idea of getting a kind of a "Captain America" outfit. Henry sold him a 20" blue sparkle Rogers bass drum from one set, 12" and 16" red sparkle toms from a Rogers Dayton kit with flat grey inside paint, and a 13" red sparkle tom from a speckled Dayton kit. So by the time Henry re-ordered drums to put all those sets back together, there were three Rogers outfits he had for sale that were not factory-original outfits.

Manufacturing clues are going to be the definitive answer. I've seen a Cleveland tag on what I know are Fullerton drums; it has Fullerton star washers, speckled grey paint on the inside, it's double-tagged which they only did during Fullerton, it's got the little blip-headed tension rods, the chrome rims begin to take a slightly different flange in the Fullerton era and actually look a little better made– the chrome is better.... I see all those clues on a drum that has a Cleveland label tag which has the model typed in and another model crossed out with magic marker- it was probably Newport, Banner, Luxor, Tower, or Classmate. My theory is that CBS simply did not want to spend the money to have new labels printed. Don't believe everything you see- if it says Cleveland it may be a sheep in wolf's clothing. That's why I believe my sale lists are more complete than the other lists I've seen; I abbreviate all the manufacturing clues and list them for every drum on my list!

Bobby Chiasson
420 Coach Road, Argyle, NY 12809
(518) 638-8559
www.drumfarm.com, drumfarm@global2000.net

ROGERS CATALOGS

c. 1925
3.5"x6.25"   16 pages
Farmingdale, N.J.
This leaflet describes the different grades of Rogers heads and how they are processed. Makes it clear that Rogers is a *tannery, not an instrument manufacturer*.

1937
6"x9" 80 pages
Farmingdale, N.J.
Bass drums & most parade drums either single-tension or tube lug; rest of drums have Gretsch lugs. Also includes Deagan instruments, Walburg & Auge hardware.

1940
5.5"x8"   16 pages
Farmingdale, N.J.
First catalog with tunable toms and Rogers' own lugs.

1946 (poster) 18.75"x24.25"
Farmingdale, N.J.
Five outfits with tunable toms (tacked bottom heads).

1955
8.5"x11.5"   4 pages
Three outfits, seven snares, bass & parade drums.

Catalog #56 1956
8.5"x11"   20 pages
The first real Ohio Rogers catalog; preceded only by several fliers listing accessories and a few drums.

1957 8.5"x11"   20 pages
Nearly identical to #56, plus color swatch cover.
(Same form number on back.)

Catalog E, Spring 1957
9"x11 1/2"   8 pages
Parade drums and snare drums, all b&w.

Catalog #59R 1958
9"x12"   60 pages
First catalog with Swiv-O-Matic and Knobby hardware, endorsees.

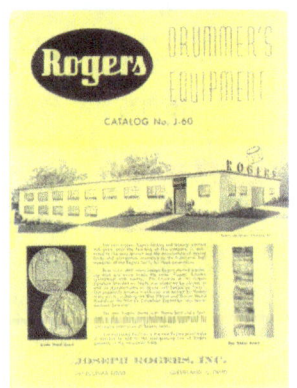
Catalog J-60 1960
9"x12" 20 pages
No drums; this is a "Jobber's catalog" for distributors featuring hardware, parts, rhythm band equipment, and marching accessories. An updated version (J-63) was printed in 1963.

Catalog 60R 1960 (c.)
8.5"x11" 84 pages
Very similar to catalog 59R.

Catalog 62R 1962
9"x12" 100 pages
First catalog with Dyna-Sonic, Buddy Rich, ripple and onyx colors and mardi-gras finish.

Catalog 64R 1964
8.5"x11" 100 pages
First catalog with beavertail lugs.

Catalog 67-68 1967
8.5"x11" 64 pages
(First CBS-era catalog.) Best looking Rogers catalog so far, with nice full color photos on nearly every page. There are two versions of this catalog; one with Buddy, another with he and all his signature models deleted.

1968
8 1/2" x 11" 4 Pages
Leaflet on first R-360 series

1968
8.5"x4" 20 pages
Pocket catalog; popular outfits, snares, hardware

1969
8.5"x11" 22 pages
First parts catalog; parts were previously included in drum catalogs..

1971
8.5"x11" 22 pages
Second parts catalog (shown here in b&w)

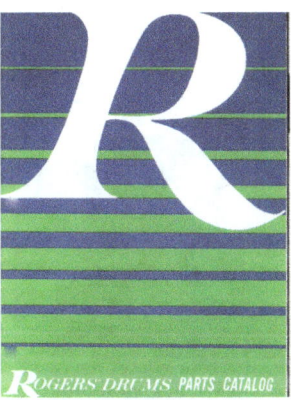
1973
8.5"x11" 12 pages
Third parts catalog

late 1970s
8.5"x11" 12 pages
Several versions from 1975–1979
(shown here in b&w)

1970 8.5"x11"
The 1970 catalog was split into three sections. Pages 1-20 comprised the drums and outfits section.

Reproduced here in black and white; original was in color.

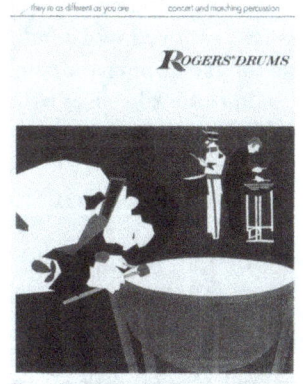
1970 8.5"x11"
The pages of the concert and marching section were numbered 21-40.

1970 8.5"x11"
The pages of the accessories section were numbered 41-64. Two updated price lists were published for this catalog "trilogy" in 1972; January 1 and June 1. Each price list covered all three catalogs, with catalog page reference numbers next to each price.

Catalog #73/4 1973
8.5"x11" 36 pages
Last catalog with Swiv-o-matic hardware.
Published in 1973, with copyright notices for 1973 and 1970, demonstrating CBS concern for legal protection.

Catalog '76/'77 1976
8.5"x11" 32 pages
First Memriloc hardware catalog.

Series II leaflet; 1979
8.5"x11" 4 pages

1980
8.5"x11" 8 pages
Introduces XP-8 series;
8-ply all-maple shells.

1980
8.5"x11" 4 pages
"Second generation" R-360-R-380 leaflet. These drums were entirely different than the earlier R-360 and R-380 drums. There was also a 1980 8-page leaflet (basically a Remo PTS catalog) on the R-340 (Pre-Tuned) series.

1983
8.5"x11" 8 pages
Last CBS-era Rogers "catalog"

1987
8.5"x11" 6 pages
Leaflet produced by Island Music for the imported drums they sold (under license) with the Rogers name.

Other Rogers literature not pictured: First Ohio circular (accessories only, 4 pages) 1954, Second Ohio circular (a few inexpensive outfits, 8 pages) 1954, Third Ohio circular (slightly expanded line, 12 pages) 1954, Catalog J-63 (30 page jobber's accessory catalog) 1963, First generation R-380 circular (2 pages) 1968, Accessory catalog (8 pages, with Paul Whaley of Blue Cheer on cover) 1969, Wildwood drum flier (single sheet double-sided) c.1975, Memriloc setup book (8 pages) 1977.

1959 5.75"x8" 24 pages
First English Rogers catalog

FOREIGN CATALOGS

ENGLAND
There were at least four English Rogers catalogs produced, as well as two English Rogers newsletters. These were printed between 1959 and 1967 and were quite similar to U.S. catalogs, but with a much more limited selection of outfits, colors, etc.

CANADA
At least one catalog was produced specifically for Canada, in about 1963. Rogers was at the time distributed in Canada by the Selmer Co.

JAPAN
Japanese Rogers literature was first printed in about 1975, featuring drums and hardware only.

ROGERS COLORS

The years listed below represent the years these finishes were listed in Rogers catalogs. These dates should not be construed as the *only* dates these finishes were available; there was often a gap of two to five years between catalog printings.

Scotch Plaid appeared only in a couple of 1950s catalogs and was a finish developed specifically for Bob Reynolds, director of bands at Carnegie Tech. Former marketing director Ben Strauss recalled that the school's band had a Scottish theme (see page 92), with tartans and bagpipes, etc., so at a Rogers salesman's request a plaid finish was made. Strauss remembered this as a contact-paper type of finish as opposed to a pyralin.

Finish	Years
Black Onyx Pearl	1962–1964
Black Oyster (R-360 series)	1968–1972
Black Strata Pearl	1967
Block	1973–1976
Blue Diamond (R-380 series)	1968–1972
Blue Mist	1980–1984
Blue Onyx Pearl	1962–1967
Blue Oyster (R-360 series)	1968–1972
Blue Ripple (R-360 series)	1968–1972
Blue Strata Pearl	1967
California Wine	1980–1984
Combination Pearl	1964–1973
Duco Combination	1958–1964
Duco Ebony	1938
Duco White	1938
Emerald Pearl	1938
KOA	1973–1976
Mahogany	1938
Metallic Gold	1976–1984
Metallic Silver	1976
Mardi Gras Pearl	1958–1962
Midnight Mist	1980–1984
Mojave Red	1973–1976
Natural Maple	1980–1984
New Blonde	1973
New England White	1973–1976
New Mahogany	1972–1976
Pacific Blue	1973–1976
Pearl White	1938–1976
(name changed to white marine pearl in 1958)	
Pearl Black	1938–1973
(name changed to black diamond pearl in 1958)	
Pink Champagne Pearl	1964–1967
Pink Strata Pearl	1967
Platinum	1980–1984
Red Onyx Pearl	1964–1967
Red Oyster (R-380 series)	1968–1972
Red Ripple (R-360 series)	1968–1972
Red Umber (R-360 series)	1968–1972
Scotch Plaid	1958
Sky-blue Ripple Pearl	1960–1962
Solid jet Black Pearl	1958–1976
(name changed to Ebony in 1973)	
Spanish Gold	1976–1984
Sparkling Blue	1958–1967
Sparkling Gold	1938–1967
Sparkling Green	1938–1967
Sparkling Red	1958–1967
Sparkling Silver	1938–1967
Steel-Gray Ripple Pearl	1960–1967
Tobacco Sunburst Lacquer	1979–1984
Wildwood	1967
Wine Red Ripple Pearl	1960–1967

Purple Diamond Pearl: See page 93.

Sunburst: The tobacco sunburst drums were originally produced with dark brown edges, fading to a yellow midsection. When John Cermenaro was working as R&D engineer in the early 1980s, he saw a drum in the paint shop which was unfinished, and faded from the dark brown to a natural midsection. He thought this was an appealing color, and had the paint shop switch. He later realized that this would create problems matching drums to older sets, and had production switch back to yellow in the midsection.

Sparkle note: See page 105 for examples and explanation of Glass vs. non-Glass glitter.

Variations: Patterns such as Ripple, Strata, and Onyx finishes fluctuate quite a bit in both tightness of pattern and contrast. This is primarily due to the pyralin manufacturing process. A few shells were painted black before these translucent coverings were applied, resulting in darker hues.

Wildwood was a which never appeared in a regular Rogers catalog. The color shown here is orange; it was also offered in Green and Blue. This (very thin) veneer was dyed while the tree was still living; fertilizer spikes with tint were driven into the ground, and the tree sucked the color up! See page 44.

SKY-BLUE	BLACK AND GOLD	BLUE AND SILVER	SPARKLING SILVER PEARL
*COMBINATION	STEEL-GRAY RIPPLE PEARL	WINE-RED RIPPLE PEARL	MARDI GRAS PEARL
RED ONYX PEARL	BLUE ONYX PEARL	BLACK ONYX PEARL	PINK CHAMPAGNE PEARL
BLACK STRATA PEARL	PINK STRATA PEARL	BLUE STRATA PEARL	GREEN SPARKLE PEARL
BLUE SPARKLE PEARL	RED SPARKLE PEARL	GOLD SPARKLE PEARL	BLACK DIAMOND PEARL

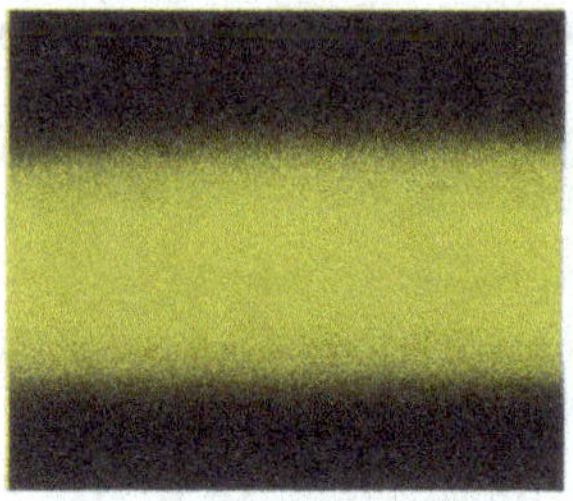

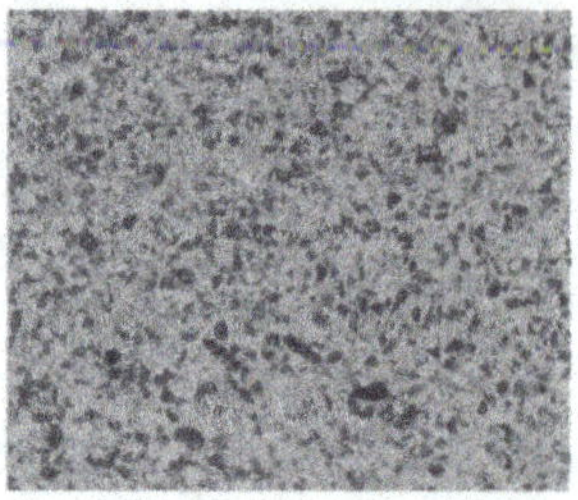

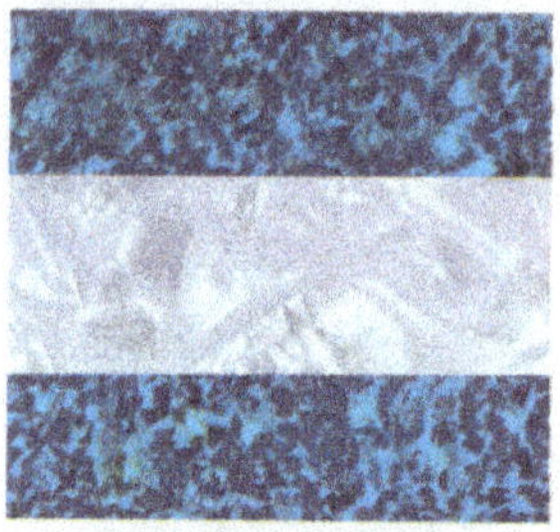

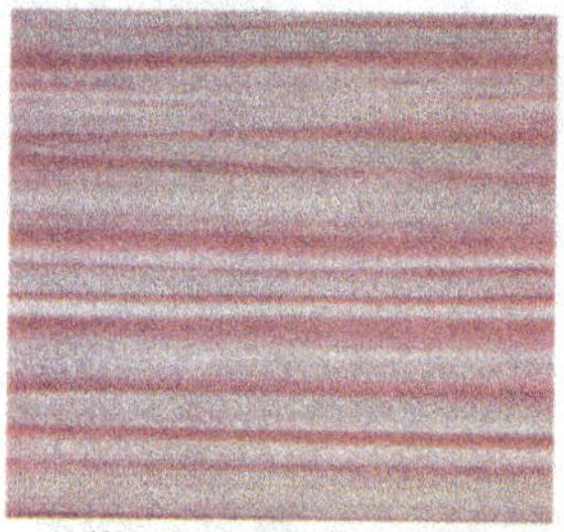

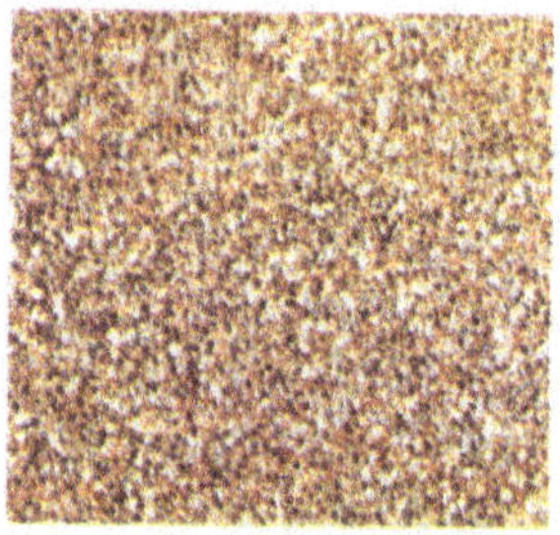

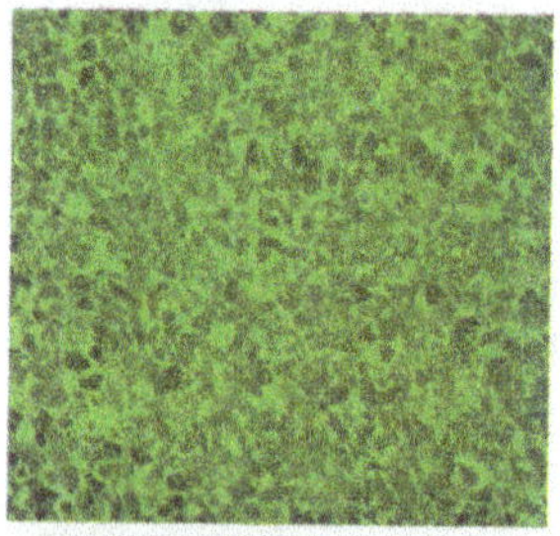

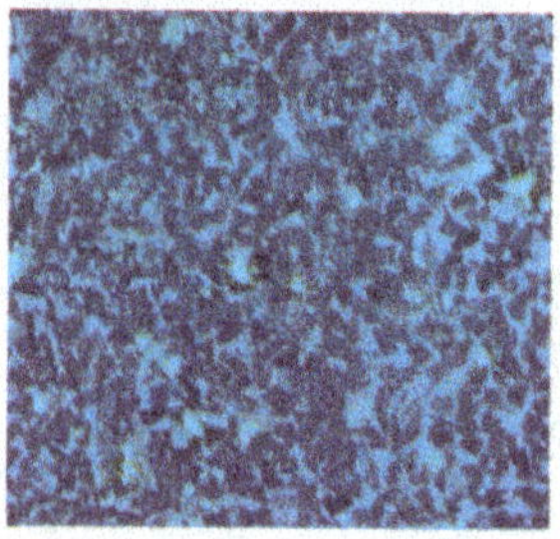

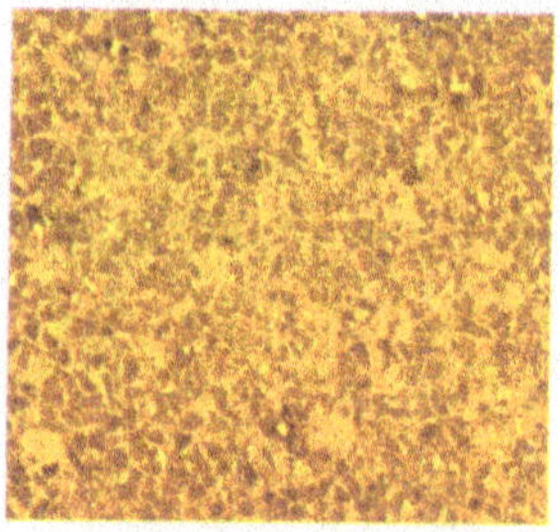

EBONY—089	BLOCK—081	KOA—063	NEW ENGLAND WHITE—082
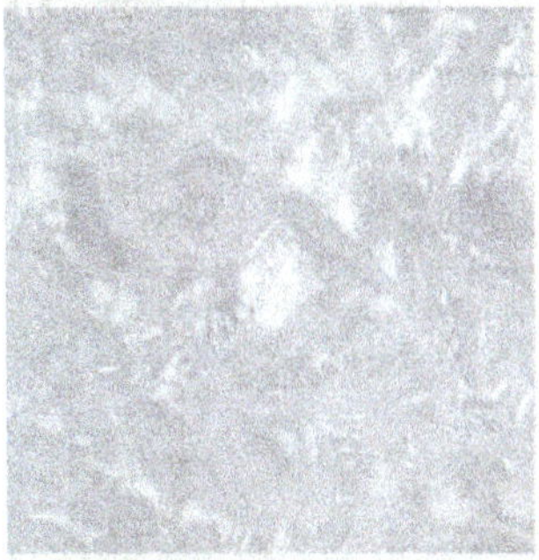 MARINE—010	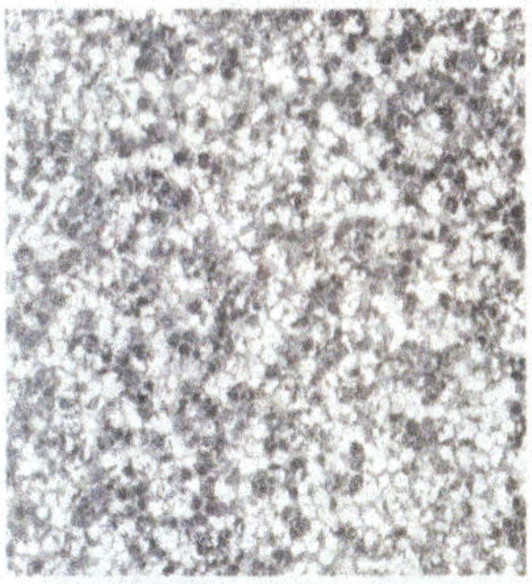 SILVER SPARKLE—011	NEW MAHOGANY—086	 BLUE ONYX—012
 BLACK STRATA—032	PACIFIC BLUE—088	NEW BLOND—080	MOJAVE RED—084
METALLIC GOLD-090	SPANISH GOLD - 085		

R-360   1968–1972

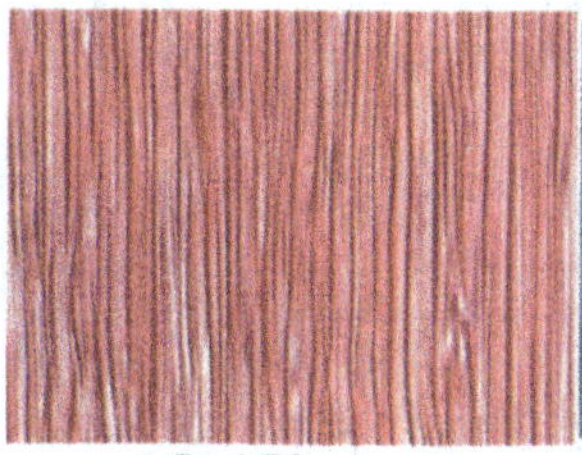

Red Ripple    Blue Ripple

Twister outfit available in the above colors only.

Double Soul and Rock Solid outfits available in the above colors only.

The Scotch Plaid finish was catalogued only in 1958. The finish was developed specifically for the Carnegie Tech Kiltie Band (below,) but added to the catalog. Sales were slow, and the finish was soon discontinued.

drum photos courtesy Gary Nelson

photo courtesy NotSoModernDrummer magazine

Purple Diamond Pearl

This color was never catalogued and when the author questioned him before his death Ben Strauss did not remember this finish. Still, there evidently were a fair number of drums produced in this finish over the space of at least several years. Collector Gary Nelson of New Jersey has accumulated a number of drums with this finish, with distinctively different vintages of hardware features, badges, etc.

Nelson heard about the finish before he ever saw one, and began searching for one to determine whether it was simply a faded Black Diamond Pearl. Removing a lug proved that the original color was a vibrant purple.

All drums on this page are from the collection of Gary Nelson.

photo by Gary Nelson

photo by Gary Nelson

ROGERS COLORS

  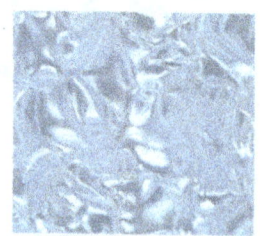 

RED OYSTER **JET BLACK** **MARINE PEARL** **BLUE DIAMOND**

R-380 Series, 1968–1972

R-360 Series c.1980

1980s, left to right, top to bottom:
Mojave Red, Midnight Mist
Tobacco Sunburst, Metallic Silver, California Wine
Blue Mist, Ebony, Natural Maple, Metallic Gold
New England White, Platinum, KOA

Steve Maxwell Collection

Steve Maxwell has been an avid Rogers fan and wood Dynasonic collector for many years and has accumulated some of the rarest and most unique Rogers snare drums in existence. Maxwell can be contacted at his vintage and custom drum shop in Chicago; www.maxwelldrums.com.

Very rare 6.5x14 Wildwood Dynasonic, Serial #12237. "When I was authenticating this drum, I learned from sources employed at Rogers at the time that during this era no wood dynasoncs in this finish were built for stock. They were done on a special order basis only. That fact plus the unique 6.5 size indicates that this drum may in fact be unique."

Wine Red Ripple Dynasonic, Serial #1808
"This is one of the early Bread & Butter lug drums made soon after the introduction of the external badges, which started with serial number 1001. This color is rare and the finish on this particular drum (which came from the collection of noted historian and author Harry Cangany) is extremely vivid."

White Marine Pearl Pre-Badge Dynasonic
"A New Old Stock drum purchased from the music store that bought it new from the factory and never sold it. This is a superb example of the earliest wood dynasonics. These drums predate the use of an external badge. Instead, there is a paper tage attached to the inside of the shell with the word "dynasonic" typed on it. Although it is nearly impossible to verify with total accuracy, it is believed that fewer than 3000 wood dynasonics were built, and of this number, probably less than 50 were pre-badge drums, most of which did not survive."

White Marine Pearl Transition Dynasonic
"This Cleveland-era drum bears serial #3132 and was made at the time that Rogers switched from the crack-prone "bread and butter" lugs to the sturdy, attractive "beavertail" design. During this transition period, the rounded "clockface" strainer and the high hoops used on the earlier B&B drums were carried over until the stock was used up. Rogers then moved to a "straight-sided" version of the strainer and lowered the height of the hoops. Very few drums are seen in the configuration shown here."

Steve Maxwell Collection

Dayton-Era WMP Dynasonic- No internal muffler.
"This drum has not been drilled for an internal muffler. According to the late Ellis Tollin, this drum was built for an endorser, most likely Buddy Rich or Louis Bellson, both of whom ordered their snare drums without mufflers. All special orders of this type were processed through Tollin's Philadelphia shop. Buddy Rich usually also requested additional lacquering of the interior of the shell. The interior of this drum is lacquered beyond what is normally seen on these drums."

6.5x14 Red Onyx Dynasonic, Serial #17961
"6.5 Wood dynasonics are exceedingly rare. Very few were made. I've handled only a few, and have never seen another one with this finish."

Mardi Gras Dynasonic, Serial #1034
"Although WMP is a rare finish that is highly sought after, Mardi Gras is even more scarce. This is apparently the 33rd wood dynasonic built after the introduction of the external badge, which started at #1001."

Blue Strata Dynasonic, Serial #20337
"Blue Strata was a color listed in the Rogers catalog only in 1967. Rogers drums in this finish are rare, and this is the only dyna I have ever seen in this finish. The drum is extraordinarily clean and looks like a brand new drum."

Ellis Tollin's White Marine Pearl Dynasonic
"This Dayton-era drum bears serial #15220. Ellis Tollin was one of the founding fathers of the dynasonic snare drum. Ellis's first WMP dynasonic had been stolen many years ago. The drum shown here was left to me by Ellis, who played it until he passed on in 2001. Ellis signed the inside of the shell, and it is complete with documentation between Ellis and myself, as well as Ellis's widow."

Gary Nelson Collection

Gary Nelson (New Jersey,) shown below with a portion of his remarkable Rogers collection. Gary can be contacted at fltgrycleav@yahoo.com

Gary Nelson Collection

Bruce Felter Collection

The late Bruce Felter was a San Francisco native and jazz drummer who lived in the San Francisco Bay Area. His first set, purchased in 1964, was a Holiday Black Onyx 20,13,16 with matching Dynasonic.

Gold Plated Dynasonic

The late Brian Allman brought this drum to the Chicago show in 1997 where the author took the photo below. The other three photos were taken by Richard Egan and provided courtesy of Brian's sister Christine Allman.

Joe Thompson Prototype Dynasonic

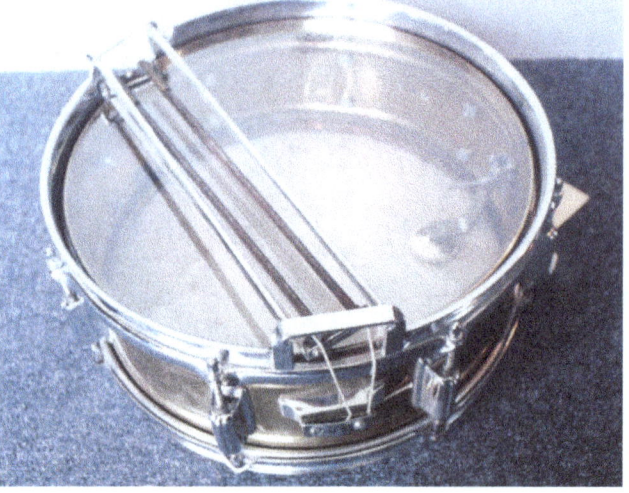

Ray Bungay Collection

All three of the drums on this page are the prized possessions of Rogers expert Ray Bungay. The photos were taken by Dan "Skitch" Williams of Metro Studios.

Pink Strata Dyna-Sonic
Serial Number 26983 Fullerton c.1971
All wood-shell Dyna-Sonics are becoming collectors items, but what makes this particular drum very rare is that as a Fullerton drum, this could not have been made earlier than 1969 yet is covered with rare pink strata, a color which was catalogued only in 1967.

"Bread & Butter" lug Power-tone
Serial Number 1541,
c. 1963
When the Powertone was introduced, it was with cast lugs. It's predecessor, the Holiday, had "B&B" lugs.

10-lug Powertone
c. 1965
Serial number 6194
The Powertone as catalogued was an 8-lug drum. This particular drum was made for Ellis Tollin of Music City in Philadelphia, a Rogers consultant. He gave it to one of the drum instructors at his store. (The color is a yellowed silver sparkle.)

Bobby Chiasson's Jollity Drum Farm

The author has encountered a great many people who are passionate about their drums, but finds it neccessary to put Bobby Chiasson in a class of his own. When Bobby takes a set of photos of a drum, they not only show the drum inside and out and from every angle, but often as a work of art, as demonstrated below with this 1963 Luxor. Contact information for the Drum Farm can be found in the resources section, page 227.

Steel Gray Ripple Swingtime Bop
12x20,8x12,14x14
(not shown; the wide reinforcement hoops found on earlier bread & butter kits such as this one.)

1965/1967 "Comet" kit;
Tower 14x20 and 8x12, Luxor 5x14

1962 "Cozy Cole Constellation"
14x22,9x13,16x16

c. 1965 "Swingtime" Red Onyx;
14x20,8x12,16x16

c. 1972 Gloss Black 14x22,8x12,9x-13,16x16

Patriotic Sparkle bands

Dyna-sonic with collet for cocktail setup

Steel Gray Ripple Dyna

Tobacco Sunburst

Wine Red Ripple

Silver Sparkle- faded

1964 5x14 Luxor Blue Sparkle

1965 Luxor 5x14 Blue/Silver/Blue

1958 Holiday 5x14, BDP (faded) with Swivomatic arm holder

1959 Holiday 5x14 Silver Sparkle (faded)

1960 Luxor 5x14 White Marine Pearl

1964 Luxor 5x14 Black Diamond Pearl

1962 5x14 Holiday Sky Blue Ripple

1960 5x14 Holiday, Mardi Gras finish

c. 1968 Silver sparkle 8x12,9x13,16x-16,14x20

c. 1965 Delta 8x12,14x14,14x20 (Tower series drums)

This drum set was used for the Johnny Cash movie which at this writing is still pending release. It is not a real set that did come together, but the movie required a Rogers drum set in these sizes and color for the Folsom Prison scene, so a set was assembled odd Jollity drums.

c. 1979 New England White 14x22,8x12,9x13,16x16

c. 1968 Blue Onyx Louis Bellson twin bass 9x13,9x13,16x16,14x22,14x22

c. 1970 New Mahogany "Celebrity" 9x13,16x16,14x22

All that glitters is not glass...

Glass   **Non-Glass (aluminum foil)**

All early Rogers pearl finishes had a smooth glossy finish. Around 1964, there was a change in the sparkle material; the surface was slightly textured; what Bobby Chiasson refers to as "puddled" or "orange peel" finish. (The non-sparkle finishes remained glossy.) The textured finishes tend to be less prone to fading, while the early glossy reds fade to tangerine and the blues fade to darker colors. Silver and gold finishes fade markedly regardless of gloss or textured finish. In the early 1970s all sparkles were discontinued except for silver, which became the none-glass type (aluminum foil bits were used in production instead of actual glass shards.) Note: Ludwig used non-glass sparkles throughout the 1960s and 1970s.

c. 1967 Wildwood 8x12, 16x16, 14x20

Red Onyx Rarities

1964 Chrome Powertone

Brook Mays Music Company

In June of 1999, Rogers was sold to Brook Mays Music, headquartered in Dallas. The transaction seemed to slip by under the music industry radar, primarily because the intentions of Brook Mays chief Bill Everitt were not to re-establish Rogers as a drum company selling to drum shops and music stores, but rather to supply his own stores with Rogers product.

Bill Everitt

Bill Everitt is CEO of Brook Mays Music Company. The company operates 63 stores in multiple states but has its roots in Texas. Bill has grown up in the music business in Texas and began full time employment with Brook Mays in 1972 after graduating from Southern Methodist University. Bill has seen the company grow under his leadership from 3 stores to 63 stores. Bill has been an active participant in support for music education throughout his career. He is currently the President of the American Music Conference . AMC's goal is to promote the importance of music making and music education on a national level. Bill has also served on multiple boards throughout the music products business including a term as President of NAMM (the International Music Products Association.) Bill's committment to support for music education is evident in his sustaining membership role within the Texas Music Educators Association, Texas Bandmaster's Association, Texas Orchestra Director's Association, Texas Choir Director's Association and other organizations focused on the importance of a musical education.

Brook Mays Music Company

Brook Mays, the man who founded the company that bears his name and ran it for nearly 40 years, was a transplanted Tennessean. Mays was no musician himself, but as a shrewd businessman, he saw a need for a first-class piano dealership in Dallas, and that was exactly what he established when he opened his original store in a building at Elm & Poydras.

Originally, the firm dealt exclusively in pianos and became the largest dealership of its kind in the entire region. It was the only major music company to survive the Great Depression of the 1930s.

In the 1940s, Brook Mays Music Company began to expand its merchandise lines to include organs, sheet music, and a band instrument division. Soon after World War II, the downtown store was extensively remodeled. This growth spurt which extended through the early 1950s included the development of a band instrument division which was destined to become the largest supplier of band instruments to school groups in the Southwest. Much of that growth was attributable to the phenomenal expansion of the high school band and orchestra programs at that time. Brook Mays is proud to be an active part in what has become the most impressive music education state in the country.

Dallas was in the era of the player piano and Sunday afternoon concerts when Brook Mays Music Company first opened its doors for business in August of 1901. Ever since then, through more than 100 years of changing sounds from the patriotic fervor of George M. Cohan and John Philip Sousa, to Irving Berlin, flappers, and the Charleston, to the big bands of the Dorseys, Glenn Miller, and Harry James, and right on down to today's amplified guitars and digitized rock, Brook Mays has been helping to create music throughout the USA.

The 1960s, with the arrival of the Beatles and rock 'n' roll, brought about an entirely new demand for musical instruments. Electric guitars, amplifiers, and drums were added to the extensive Brook Mays inventory. The musical trends of the 1970s and 1980s introduced high-end electronic instruments including keyboards, synthesizers, and drum machines.

Today, Brook Mays Music provides the latest state-of-the-art musical electronics to students, performing professionls, and to the recording and broadcast communities.

The last decade has seen an overall committment to excellence and community service. Now with sixty-three retail locations and mail-order and e-commercee divisions that serve both national and international customers. The company offers a broad range of educational services (for both students and music educators,) complete repair facilities, and the Southwest's largest instrument rental program.

Bill Crowden

It's not often that a CEO can with one hire demonstrate a profound understanding of an entire industry. Brook Mays Music head Bill Everitt did just that when he named Bill Crowden managing director of Rogers Drums & Percussion. Crowden (whose wife Brooke is the daughter of William F. Ludwig II) has for decades worked near the epicenter of the percussion industry. His career path has wound around a bit, from drum shop manager to owner, to consultant and Director. Along the way he has always found time to hold trade association positions, volunteering his time in a clear demonstration of his love and respect for the percussion business. When he announced the appointment of Bill Crowden, Bill Everitt made a statement about his plan for the Rogers name.

RC: Did you get started with drums as a kid in school, Bill?

BC: Well, I played, but badly. My strength, the thing that really appealed to me, was fixing them. That's why I did all the repairs for the Chicago Symphony and the Lyric Opera. I really loved working with the mechanics of it rather than the playing. People like the timpanist at the Chicago Symphony were very fine musicians, but they spent all their time at their craft rather than the mechanics of it. He had 40 timpani over there of various sizes. I had them all numbered so he could call and just say, "Bill, #22 and #23 don't sound right, I don't know what's up..." You'd have stagehands moving them and knocking them out of alignment and so forth. I'd go over and make sure that mechanically he could tune them. Once they were at that stage, then he could apply his talent.

RC: That was really the start of your music industry career?

BC: Yes. I really honed my skills working at Franks Drum Shop. I started there in May of 1957, about a month after Maurie Lishon bought it from Frank Gault.. I honed my skills working with a repair guy named Stewart– it was like going to Harvard. I was with him for six years.

Bill Crowden

RC: I'm not familiar with him. Was he before Clarence?

BC: Yes. He was there with Frank Gault and stayed on when Frank sold the shop to Maurie. Stu had been there for 15 or 20 years already when I started. He was simply incredible. If he couldn't fix it, you threw it out.

I learned a lot about business in general while at Franks, of course. It wasn't strictly repairs. I learned sales, and general operations. When Maurie bought the shop, he had an agreement with Frank to pay on an installment basis. He worked at CBS to pay for his household expenses, so the money he made at Franks could be used to make the shop payments. I was in the shop every day; he'd come in about 2:30 or 3 in the afternoon.

RC: There was some kind of an agreement for you to become a partner after a certain period of time, wasn't there?

WC: Yes, we had an understanding that after 5 years I could buy up to 25%. We got to that point and he didn't say anything, so I let another year go by. Still no decisions were made, so I went to Maurie. I reminded him of the understanding and pointed out that in six years I'd never been absent or sick. He said he wasn't sure how we were going to work it out, because he had sons who were going to be coming into the business. We talked a little more and it became clear to me that I needed to wish him luck and make my own way in my own shop.

RC: Your shop was pretty close to Franks.

WC: Anywhere else would have been suicide. At one time, Rob, on both sides of Wabash Avenue for about a five block strip, there were something like 35 or 40 stores.

RC: Was it rough getting started so close to an established operation? Were vendors reluctant to disrupt their relations with Franks Drum Shop?

WC: Very much so. I had to start with the fringe suppliers like Camco and Leedy.

Buddy Rich with Bill Crowden in Crowden's Chicago shop, Drums Ltd, March 19th, 1967. Rich did a clinic in the shop that day.

WC: Gretsch was in the same building as I was. Do you remember that?
RC: No. I wasn't aware of that.
WC: Anything that was shipped to points west of Chicago was shipped out of the same building that I was in. They had a huge warehouse there. That was part of the reason I went into that building. Basically their warehouse was my warehouse. If you came in and wanted a Gretsch outfit, you'd pick out what you wanted, then you and I would go downstairs. You'd get your set, I'd pay Gretsch, and off you'd go. I was very strong with Gretsch. Maurie for some reason was not a Gretsch guy. At that time the top 8 or 10 drummers in the Downbeat poll were all Gretsch players. Max Roach, Don Lamond, Philly Jo Jones, Charlie Persip,...
RC: What about Rogers?
WC: At Franks we started with just the Rogers hardware, and worked into it from there. After I started out on my own, they wouldn't sell to me for three or four years. Finally they sold me hardware, but it was quite a while before I could get the drums.
RC: Your shop was very close to Franks, wasn't it?
WC: Right. I was at 218, he was at 226 South Wabash.
RC: You eventually purchased the name Franks Drum Shop. Were there any other assets? I understand that by that point it was no longer a going concern...
WC: There really was not much that was worth anything at that point. There were some old timpani trunks that I donated to the Salvation Army, some chime tubes, flesh hoops, and so forth. I bought it mainly for the name; not so I could do business as Franks Drum Shop. I didn't want anybody else to have the name and have it come back to haunt me. It was a very powerful name. To this day I still have people calling me and asking about Franks Drum Shop. Most of them are just nostalgia calls; folks wanting to know what happened to so-and-so, people doing articles about "Tin Pan Alley Chicago" and so forth.
RC: So then when you sold your business, was it a matter of simply being ready to retire, or shift gears in the music industry?
WC: Well, it just got to a point where I'd had enough retail. I'd been at it from 1957 to 1991. As I'm sure you know, Rob, from your retail experiences, there can come a point where you have so many things going on that you can just cease being creative. The hot credit cards, the stolen checks... it just stopped being fun. I'd been in it nearly my whole life and had loved it, so I knew when it was not fun any more that it was time to do something else. Another factor was that I had the opportunity to sell the business. The buyers were able to pay the entire purchase price so I didn't have to wait for my money.
RC: Did you stay on for the changeover?
WC: You know, Rob, that's something that always baffled me. There was a clause in the purchase contract that I was to work for two months at no charge on an "on call" basis. What baffled me was that I never in that time frame got even one call. I just couldn't believe the new owners could take over that kind of operation and not have any questions for me! Two and a half years later they were out of business. I don't mean to say that they went out of business because they didn't ask for my help– the big box stores were moving into Chicagoland, and the mail-order discounters were putting more pressure on. It gets tough to keep your niche in the face of all that.
RC: You certainly didn't leave the industry altogether. I understand you worked with Paiste next?
WC: Yes. At that time I saw that Paiste was very thin on their hand cymbals. I approached them with a proposal to do a survey at a PAS convention, and they approved it. I quizzed a lot of people who I knew would be honest with me about cymbals. It was just a quick "recognition" kind of checklist. I presented the results to Toomas and Eric Paiste and they were very interested in doing something more to develop their hand cymbals. We started working on a few things. Prototypes would be sent in from Switzerland and we'd get an off-site room at the Midwest Band Director's conference every year. Michael Paiste would come over from the factory and he would work closely with some of the elite cymbal players I'd send up. There were guys from the Indianapolis Symphony, guys from Oberlin... I'd work with Sam Denov from the Chicago Symphony and various other guys who had the credentials. They'd give us input on the cymbals and Michael would go back and either add to the high end or take away from the low end and so forth. We'd take prototypes over to the Chicago Symphony Hall; the cymbal players would play while Michael went out into the seating area to listen. We went to the Lyric Opera where, as you know, the orchestra is under the stage. like a lot of the opera houses in Europe. The bottom line really was that I helped him gain access to a lot of venues and personnel that otherwise would have been very hard for him to get to on his own. After five years we pretty much had everything started. They now have five lines of cymbals and it pretty much took all of that to really seriously break into the whole cymbal market.
RC: How did that project wind down?
WC: Well, it was a five-year project that saw all the hand cymbals developed. They're all in the catalogs now and they really didn't need any more developmen-

tal help. I took a little time off, then then went to work for Brook Mays.

RC: How did you get hooked up with them?

WC: Bill Everitt, the owner of Brook Mays, and I were on the NAMM board together. We became friends and I offered to help out by looking over the percussion departments at his stores. I have to admit that part of my motivation was to get away from the Chicago winters. I'd go to each store every week and look over the product mix; point out if they had too many bongos but not enough congas, that sort of thing. Three years after I started with Brook Mays we bought the Rogers name. Bill said he wanted me to develop it. I was based in Houston at the time. Bill said it would be possible to do it from there, but he really preferred that I move to Dallas where the corporate offices are, so I did.

We not only have drums, but we have a line of educational kits; bells and so forth that are absolutely the best in the business. We are very actively involved with the Texas music educators in particular. We exhibit at their conferences and so forth. I'm very impressed with the level of support for the arts in Texas. A music education is still a high school graduation requirement in the Texas school system.

RC: What was your thinking when you first heard that Bill had bought Rogers or was thinking about it?

WC: Well, my reaction was largely shaped by the fact that I knew Bill very well. He's really a first-rate guy and I know that he respects my opinion on drums and such. I knew from the start that if I gave him an honest opinion along with some of the reasoning behind it that he'd back me up. He knows that I would not ask him to do anything that I wouldn't do if it were my business. Right now I'm happy with the progress we've made. We have the beavertail lugs; I looked at five prototypes of that before I ok'd one. The lacquer shell-packs are now out and are doing very well.

RC: Do you anticipate a Dyna-sonic revival?

WC: Well, of course that's something that a lot of people ask about. I've looked into it, but the mold costs are going to be at least $60,000.00 and frankly I just don't know if we're at a point where that would be a prudent business decision. I'm certainly not saying it will not happen, but at this moment in time I can't say it's going to happen.

RC: We should probably clarify the current and anticipated distribution situation. Do you think that Rogers drums will ever be available through retail outlets other than Brook Mays stores?

WC: Well, it's certainly possible. We have 63 stores to supply right now, and these stores are doing very well with this Rogers line. We've got an RD2000 that we sell for under four hundred dollars; it's got suspension toms and it's just great. It took me a year and a half to get the hardware line where I wanted it. We have a great snare drum stand that we can sell for just sixty bucks. Now I'm kind of tweaking the line by adding things like holders and so forth. I recently brought out a "stick brick;" a cellophane-wrapped assortment of various-sized sticks.

It's no secret that these days you have to work very closely with off-shore vendors to make it clear that your parameters are very narrow. We have found some folks who realize that if they listen closely, they can learn something. I've been at this for over 40 years and I'm not saying I've never made mistakes– we've all made them. I've learned from my mistakes, however. You just don't make too many mistakes in this business and stay around this long.

Bill Crowden's career milestones

May, 1957 Manager, *Franks Drum Shop*, Chicago
November, 1963 (Until January, 1991) Owned and operated *Drums, Ltd.*, Chicago
1970 Produced two award-winning instructional films; *Timpani Techniques* with Chicago Symphony timpanist Don Koss, and *Cymbal Techniques* with Chicago Symphony cymbalist Sam Denov.
1973 Awarded patent for seamless acrylic drum shells
1974 Awarded patent for internal drum baffling system.
1980–1982 President, Percussive Arts Society, Illinois Chapter; active membership doubled!
1984–1986 Secretary, NAMM Board of Directors
1984 Purchased assets of *Franks Drum Shop*
1990 Recipient of *Music & Sound Retailer Magazine*'s "Drum Shop Of The Year" award
January, 1991 Sold *Drums, Ltd.*
1992–1997 Educational Director of Sales, Paiste America
1999– 2005 Managing Director, Rogers Drums & Percussion, Brook Mayes Music Group, Dallas, Texas

November, 2002 Recipient, PAS President's Industry Award for outstanding service and dedication.

Bill Crowden passed away Feb 15, 2013

"By the time I was doing the page layout for this section, I was burning with curiosity. Could these drums possibly be as nice as they looked in the literature and still be sold this cheaply? I ordered a set for myself, shown here. This RD-3000SP Shell Pack (16x20,14x14,8x10,9x12) is, in my opinion, a remarkable value."

Rob Cook

Brook Mays Music era

"I had five prototypes made before I approved the new beavertail lugs. They had to be right."
—Bill Crowden

Product innovations and improvements such as the beavertail lugs and recently introduced Silver Sparkle lacquered shell-pack have been made possible by the success of the entry-level Rogers products such as the student percussion kits (bells, snare drums, stands,) wide range of hardware, cymbal packages, thrones, congas and bongos, and accessories such as practice pads, sticks, etc.

Brook Mays Music era

RD2000 (wrapped) 16x22,10x12,11x13,16x16,6.5x14,stands

RD500(wrapped) 14x22,8x12,9x13,16x16,5.5x14,stands

RD4000SP 16x22,8x12,9x13,16x16, lacquered finishes

RD3000SP 16x20,8x10,9x12,14x14, lacquered finishes

RCS5514 5.5x14 Steel Shell

RCS 3.5x13 steel shell (also made in 3.5x14)

RBS6514 6.5x14 brass shell

RCS6514 6.5x14 Steel Shell

RMS6514 6.5x14 9-ply maple

RMS3514 3.5x14 9-ply maple

Brook Mays Music era

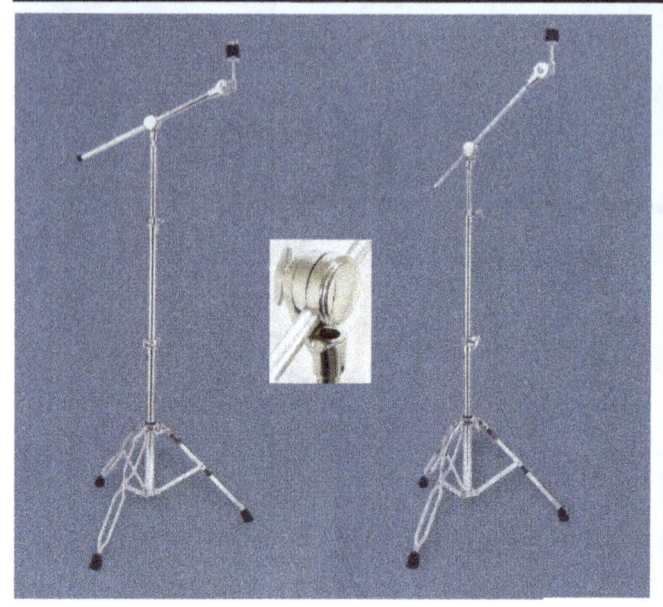
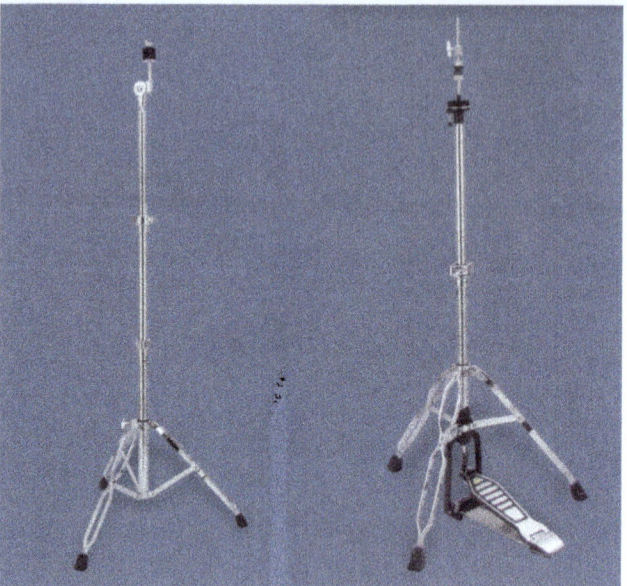
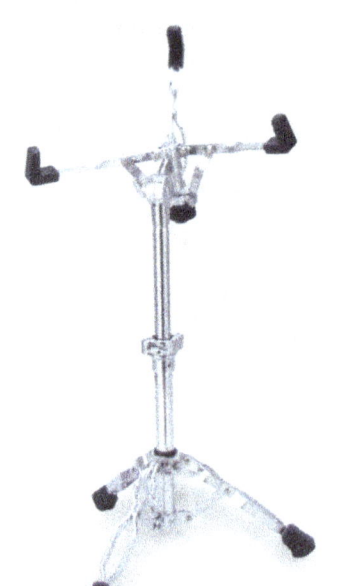
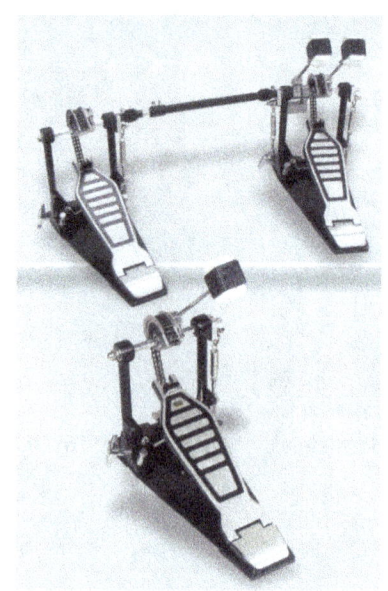

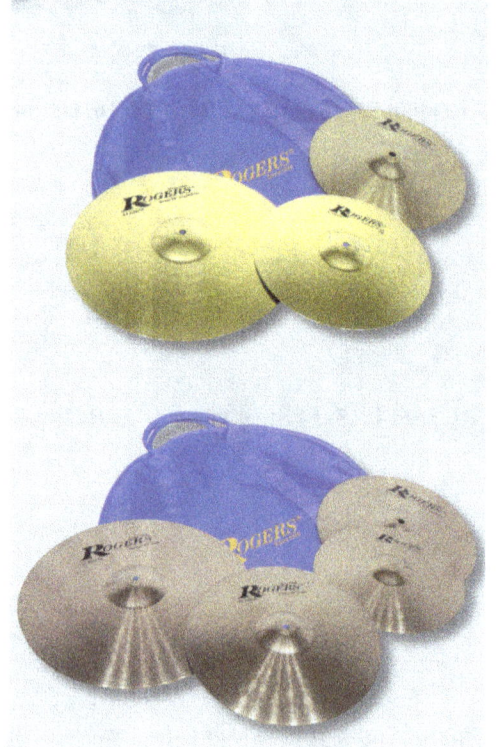
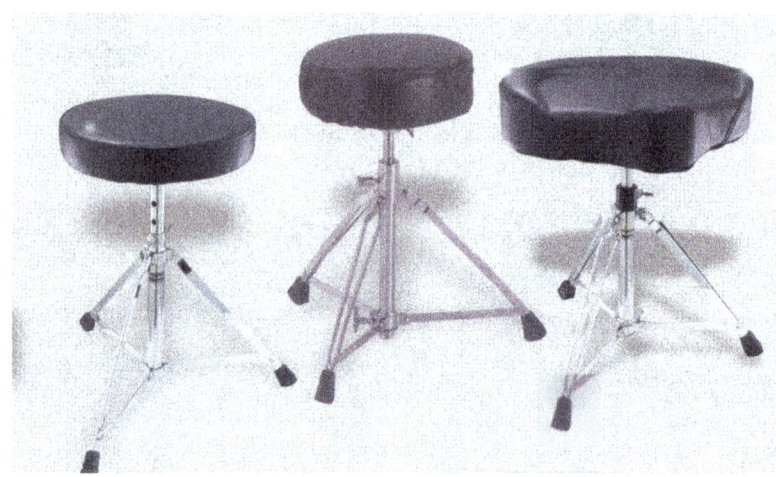

ROGERS SHELLS

The Rogers drums made in Farmingdale, New Jersey, were steam-bent solid mahogany. Shell-making did not continue in Ohio; the raw shells were purchased from other vendors (usually Jasper or Keller) and finished at Rogers.

Many long-time Rogers fans are surprised to learn that the shells used throughout the Ohio and California eras were not made by Rogers and were made of the same woods as several of their competitors.

"The type of wood you use when you're making drums is important, but not *that* important," the late Ben Strauss told the author. "The *most* important factors were the level and the bearing edges."

Jasper Wood Products (Jasper, Indiana), supplied the shells for all of the earliest Ohio-era Rogers drums as well as Gretsch shells until as recently as 2002. (The only exceptions were special-orders for bass drums which required shells larger than Jasper made for Rogers; Rogers purchased these shells from Slingerland.) Keller (New Hampshire) also supplied some shells in the 1960s, and became the exclusive supplier of Rogers shells by the time of the XP-8 8-ply all-maple shells.

Slingerland and Ludwig both made their own shells from plywood that was dry-heated; the seams had tapered overlap points that resulted in shells which could not be perfectly round. In 1963 Slingerland switched to "Unimold" construction similar to the way the Jasper shells were made. Plies of wood were placed into molds one at a time so that the seams of the plies were staggered. This made it possible to use seams that butted together instead of a tapered overlap, and resulted in rounder shells. Gretsch was the first company to use this type of shell, in the 1920s. A basic difference between these brands throughout the 1950s, 1960s, and into the early 1970s was that the outer ply of Gretsch and Rogers drums was always maple. Slingerland used an outer ply of mahogany on drums which were earmarked for pearl covering, while drums to be lacquered or stained were the only only ones with an outer ply of maple.

Over the years Rogers used a number of different bearing-edge designs and reinforcement-hoop designs. Early Ohio-era drums were three-ply (maple/poplar or mahogany/maple) while later Ohio-era and early California drums were five-ply (maple/poplar/maple/poplar/maple).

Ben Strauss, on shell diameter, thickness and bearing edges: "Joe was a firm believer in how thick a shell could be. We put a five-ply liner (reinforcement hoop) top and bottom, but we never thought the body of the shell itself should be any thicker than five plies. The biggest part of the sound is from the edges, not the shell. We had a tool that took a little off the outside and the rest off the inside, leaving a bearing edge of just 1/16". If you look around at some of the other drums you'll see bearing edges that are more rounded off than that. We felt that the least amount of shell in contact with the head, the better the sound. Look at the bass viol bridge or violin, or a good guitar– there's hardly anything touching the strings. Lay your finger on a batter head. It muffles it. Obviously the same thing works when you lay the head on the drum. Leedy developed the floating head principle. We took the floating head principle and made smaller shells because heads forced onto shells kill the sound. Rogers drums were always 1/8" smaller than the head size for that reason."

From left: Henry Grossman, Joe Thompson, Gene Hittle, Harvey Dunlap, Don Martin. Gene, Harvey, & Don had a combined weight of 420 pounds. This photo was used to demonstrate the strength of the Rogers mahogany parade drum shell. (A laminated Jasper shell.)

TESTING PERMA-BUILT SHELLS

The 1956 catalog featured this photo of five employees (with a combined weight of 824 pounds) standing on a 10"x14" parade drum shell.

Catalog descriptions of shells:

Prior to 1970, catalogs made no mention of the type of wood used in Rogers shells, referring to them simply as laminated (or perma-built) shells, although whenever reinforcement rings are mentioned, they are identified as maple. The premium drums were usually three-ply, with inner and outer plies of maple, middle ply of poplar. Entry-level drums were often made of mahogany rather than maple.

Catalog nomenclature:

1962 through 1967: Cross-laminated wood shells with rock maple reinforcing rings.
1970: Cross-laminated maple shells with maple reinforcing rings. (3 ply)
1973: All Rogers hardwood power shells are three-ply, cross-laminated with rock maple reinforcing rings.
1976: Rogers exclusive 5-ply hardwood power shells
1979: XP-8 power shells... created from 8 individual layers of prime New England rock maple

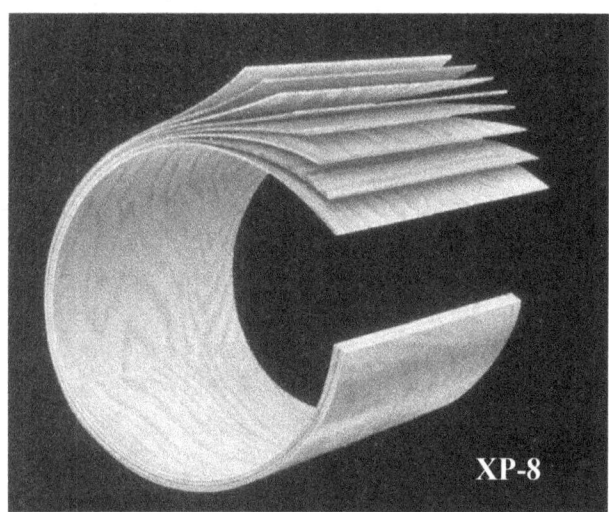

The XP-8 shells were introduced in mid-1979 after the move to California. XP-8 shells were 8 plies of maple, probably the best quality shells ever used for Rogers drums. Inner and outer plies were matched finish layers. The seams were staggered, and the bearing edges were cut to a perfect 45-degree angle.

Inside the shells

Ben Strauss recalled that Rogers was the first company to begin finishing the inside of their shells.

The first 9000 or so Grossman-era Holiday model shells were painted flat black on the inside. Somewhere between Serial Numbers 9,000 and 10,000 there was a switch to flat grey. Dyna-sonic snare drums received three coats of clear varnish instead. Buddy Rich insisted that all of his drums receive the clear varnish instead of grey paint, and asked for extra coats of the clear varnish. A few (very few) kits have surfaced which have what Bobby Chiasson describes as a "murky clear lacquer with grey mixed in."

CBS-era Rogers shells from 1966 until the XP-8 series was introduced in 1979 were painted with "trunk paint;" greyish colored with speckles. There are variations of that according to Rogers expert Bobby Chiasson; the earlier drums have a finer-grained speckle. The XP-8 shells were sealed with a clear varnish unless they were made to match older drums; a supply of trunk paint was kept for that purpose.

Shell, badge, and serial number notes, from an interview with Bobby Chiasson:
-The earliest serial-numbered drums were the Eagle-badge Rogers drums from 1956 forward, which had the interiors painted black up until near serial number 9000.
-From 9000 up (1959 or 1960,) the interiors were painted grey.
-At around serial number 13000, the Eagle badge was replaced with the earliest script badge. (See page 128.)

Other Rogers shell materials:

R-360, R-380 first generation "Select Asian Hardwoods"
Series II Made from chemically-treated cardboard tubes used by local (Southern California) garlic growers.
R-360, R-380 second generation 9-ply mahogany
R-340 Remo "Acousticon" shells.

ROGERS LUGS

GRETSCH "ROCKET" LUG
Rogers drums of the 1930s

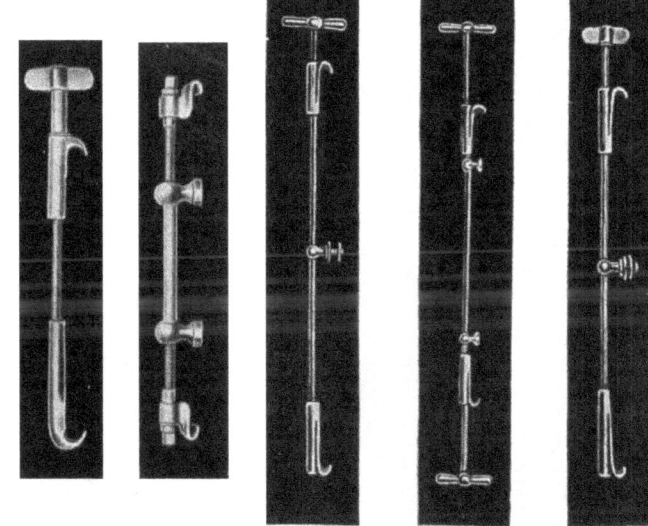

TUBE LUGS, SINGLE TENSION LUGS
Rogers drums of the 1930s; mainly used on field drums, though both types were used on orchestra drums as shallow as 4".

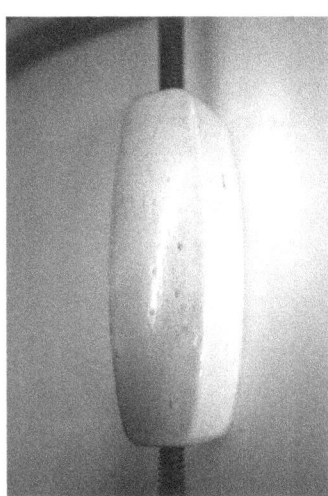

ROGERS WARTIME LUG
The War Production Board decreed that no more than 10% of the weight of a drum could be metal. Like Ludwig, Leedy, Slingerland and others, Rogers lugs were wooden during this period.

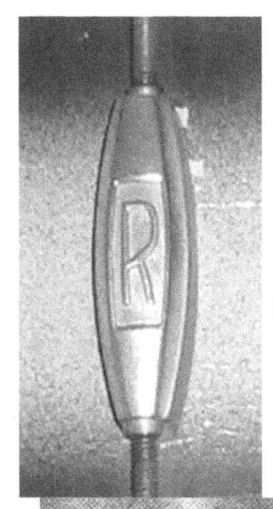

1940s "BREAD AND BUTTER" LUG
The only "bread and butter" lug made by Rogers prior to the move to Ohio, these lugs feature a large letter R.

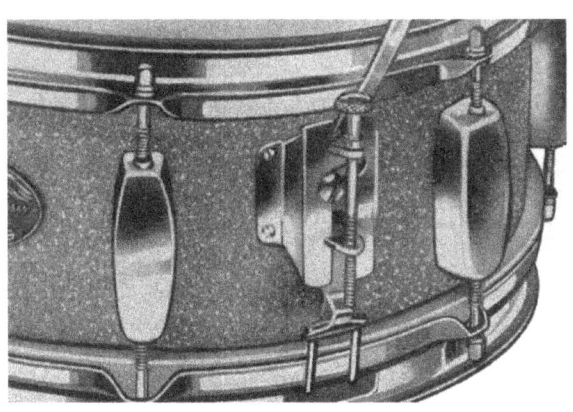

PLAIN DRAWN BRASS LUG
("Bread and Butter" lug)
1950-1959

COCKTAIL DRUM BEAVERTAILS
These lugs were never listed in parts sections of catalogs or shown on any drums other than the "Champion" (mid '50s) cocktail drums

RIDGED "BREAD & BUTTER" LUGS

According to Rogers authority Bobby Chiasson, there were at least three generations of drawn brass ridged "Bread & Butter" lugs from 1959 to 1963. They differed in both size (overall length and hole spacing) and shape (slightly rounded vs. squarish corners). Earliest mounted tom-toms have the smallest of the three lugs with newer drums getting slightly larger lugs. Earliest floor toms and snare drums have the largest lugs while newer models got slightly smaller lugs. If you need a replacement "Bread & Butter" lug, be prepared to supply the exact measurments to insure you get the right one.

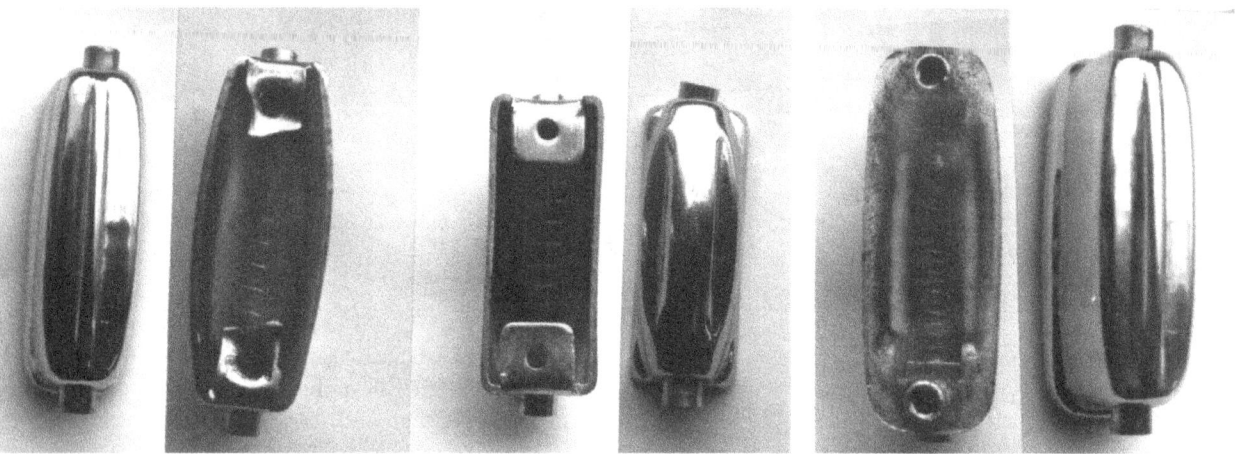

This is the lug found on most Rogers drums made between 1959 and 1964. Rogers referred to it as the "Drawn Brass Lug" (see page 198).

Collectors usually call it the "bread and butter" lug or "tab lug"– a reference to the two threaded tabs which serve to secure the lug to the shell. These tabs are prone to breakage, as are the tops and bottoms of the lug.

Collector Dave Simms found this lug style on his "Cleveland" Luxor, Serial number 1951. It is similar in appearance to the 1955 Slingerland lug, though that lug was cast while this is drawn brass. Screw spacing is 1 1/2".

A rather rare "bread & butter" lug, again supplied by Dave Simms: this one is die-cast. It is from a "Cleveland" Luxor snare drum Serial number 3840. Hole spacing is 2".

Note: "Bread and Butter" lugs could be special-ordered even after they were replaced by the beavertails shown on the next page. The lug style does not, therefore, definitively date the drum.

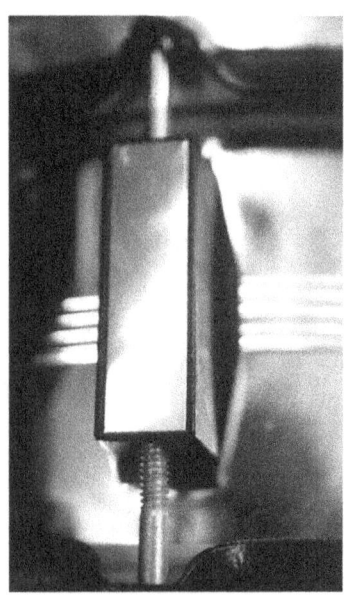

SERIES II Lug;
plastic & metallic tape

This lug was designed by Joe Thompson, with the patent being taken out in his name (and assigned to CBS) after he died. This lug design showed up on two different series' of drums; the Yamaha-produced R-360 and R380 series as well as the Grossman-produced Duplex drums they made after selling Rogers to CBS.

The catalog excerpt below is from Rogers catalog 64R of 1964, the first catalog to feature the new cast lugs. Dealers and collectors usually refer to this series simply as "cast center lugs" and "beavertails". These lugs were manufactured in Dayton, Ohio, until about 1972 when CBS switched to foreign vendors. Although the screw spacing of the new imported lugs was the same, there were various other changes:

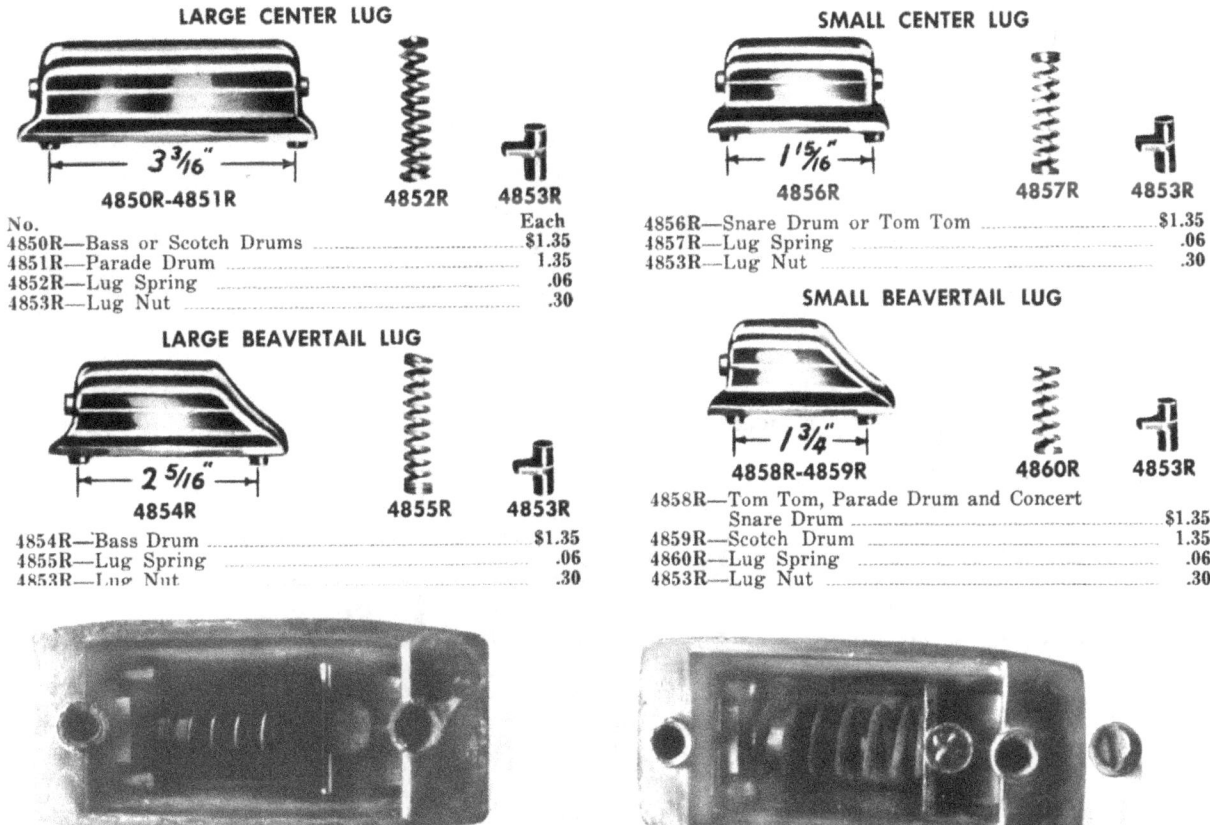

The first beavertail lugs were much more rugged than the drawn brass lugs they replaced, but there were problems with the screw posts breaking off. The screws used on this lug were the same #8 24 tpi slotted machine screws used on the drawn brass lugs which preceded the beavertails. It's difficult to see in this photo, but there is a felt pad between the spring and the lug.

Beginning with the second generation beavertail lug the screw post breakage problems were eliminated by a reduction in the the size of the screws to #7 28 tpi slotted hex-head screws. This photo is of the third-generation beavertail which differed very slightly from the second; a little lighter (though still much more substantial than it's successors) and elimination of the felt pad.

CBS-era beavertail lugs were much lighter-weight than Grossman-era castings. (The earlier lugs were cast Dayton, CBS lugs were imported.) The first of these lugs were shorter (by 1 mm) than their predecessors. (Note also the scallopped top edge.) The hex-head screws were no longer slotted.

The last CBS beavertail had no internal spring; the threaded insert was held in place by a ring on the threaded insert outside of the casting (above). This change was made in about 1975. These lugs (and sometimes the immediate predecessors) sometimes damage the pearl covering material because of the sharp edges, causing a crack that tends to spread like a windshield crack.

ROGERS STRAINERS

 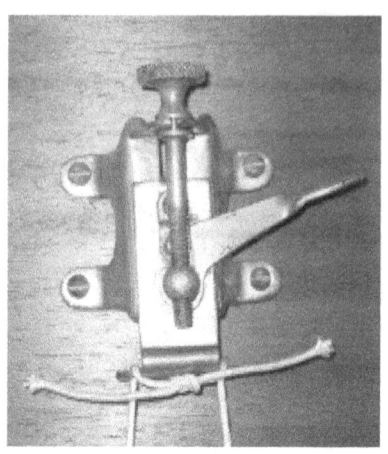

The Leedy Presto Strainer (dubbed simply the "Throw-off Snare Strainer") was standard equipment on lower-priced drums from the late 30s to the early 40s.

From 1938 through the late 40s Rogers used the Slingerland "three-point" strainer on top-of-the-line drums.

The "Improved Snare Strainer" was one of the first strainers designed and built by Rogers, in 1938. It was standard equipment on mid-range snare drums for a couple years, discontinued by 1940.

Another Leedy strainer, their "Utility Combination Snare Strainer and Muffler" was used by Rogers on entry-level snare drums in 1938. They simply called it the "Throw-off Strainer".

 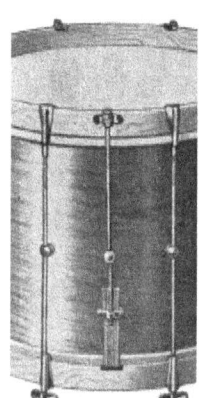 

No. 4474

Several different types of strainers were used on early Rogers marching drums. The 4474 (above) remained in use through the late 1950s.

This strainer was brought to the attention of the author by Rogers collector Kirk Higgins of Prescott, Arizona. This stamped metal strainer does not appear in any Rogers catalogs and may be an experimental or prototype model of the early 1950s. The snares are released when the lever is either straight up or straight down, and tightened when the lever is raised either to the left or the right. The tension of the snares is adjustable via the screw on the top of the boxlike butt assembly (above right). The drum this strainer is on also is an uncatalogued model. It most closely represents the *Monitor* model; 8 plain drawn brass lugs, single-flanged hoops with double-claw collar hooks. The only differences are the finish and the badge. The Monitor was offered only in a natural mahogany finish while this drum is lacquered white. The badge text under the air vent of the Monitor reads "The Quality Drum" while the badge text under the air vent of *this* drum reads "Union Brand" under which also appears "The Quality Drum."

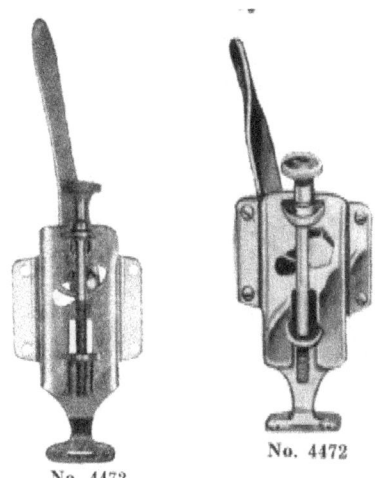 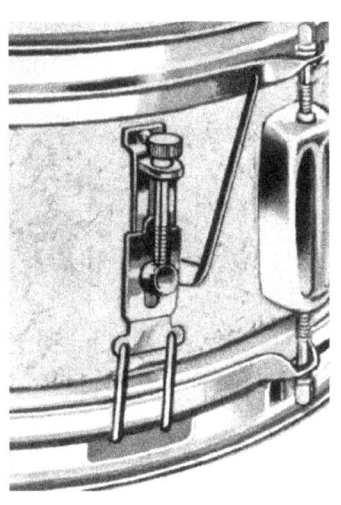 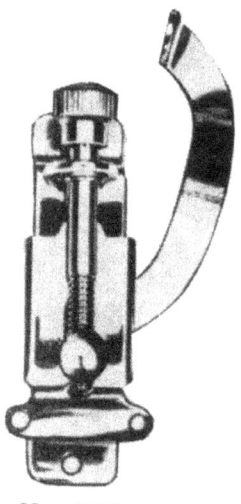

The first 4472 "Orchestra" strainers (1954) had a straight lever. By 1960 they had the twisted lever pictured above right. The name also changed, to the Universal Throw-off Strainer.

The 4476 "Orchestra" strainer was introduced in 1958 and was discontinued by the time of the 1960 catalog.

The Utility Throw-off Strainer was in use from 1960 through 1964.

1964   **1967–1969**

The Sta-Tite Strainer was on mid-level snare drums (Tower, Luxor) from 1964 through the late 1960s. When introduced in the 1964 catalog, this strainer had the v-shape on the face pointing down (above left). All subsequent catalogs and parts lists have the v-shape pointing up (above right.) Rogers expert Bobby Chiasson theorizes that this strainer was put on a few Dyna-sonics between the clockface and the strainer that replaced it.

The 393 Bantam Strainer was a slightly less expensive version of the Sta-Tite. Introduced in 1967 on the Luxor, it was used as late as 1970 (on the R-360 snare drum).

Both versions of the Sta-Tite, the Bantam, and the clockface all used the same core mechanism.

Front and back of the Sta-Tite strainer front plate

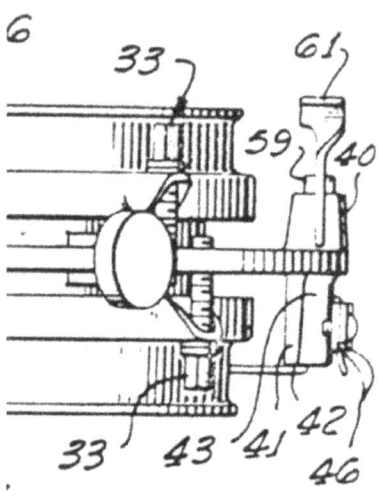 

The Skinny Drum strainer (C. 1970) was little more than a simple lever attached to the cast shell.

  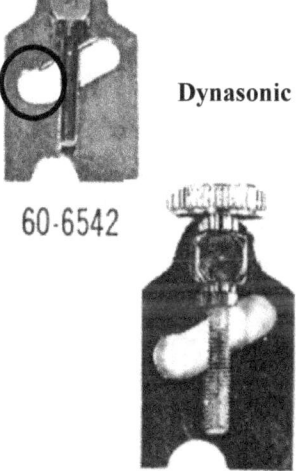

Dynasonic

60-6542

Powertone

60-6540

Commonly called the "clockface" by collectors, the catalog name for this strainer when it was first catalogued in 1959 was the Swiv-o-matic Perma-Tension Snare Strainer. The area around the logo was black on earlier versions, then (about 1964) was left unpainted. Early ads for this strainer show it with a rubber handle (above left).

Around 1967 the "clockface" was elongated. Note the letter D stamped just below the knob at the top. This identifies this as a Dyna-sonic strainer. The Cam and Tension screw assembly for the Dyna-sonic (part #60-6542, above right) differed from the powertone version in that the lower left portion of the cutout had a more pronounced hook to keep the snares locked in place.

photo courtesy Dan Coluccio

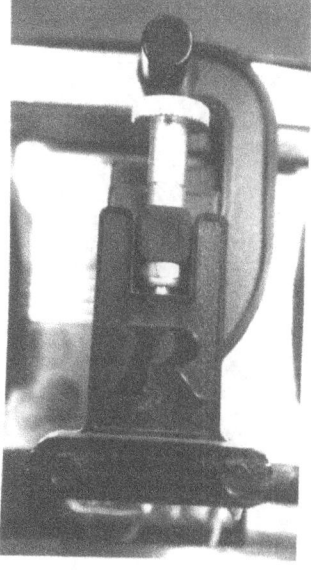

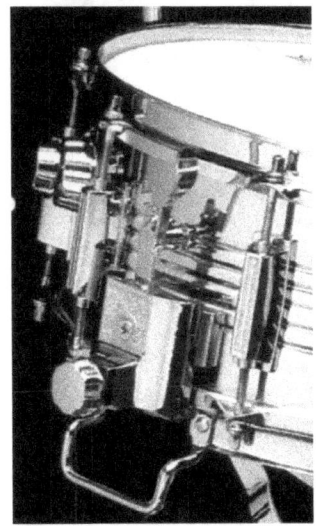 

R-360 (right) and R-380 (left) drums of the early 1980s were fitted with imported strainers.

SERIES II, c. 1986 The strainer, like many of the parts for these drums, was largely plastic and aluminum.

ROGERS SPURS

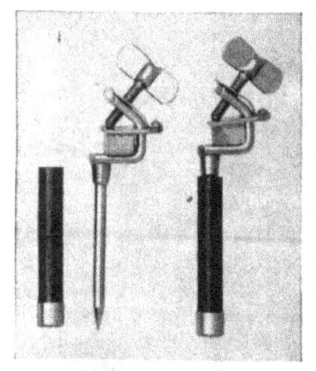

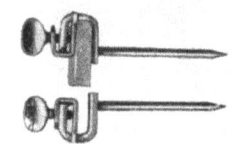

1930s
top #982W middle #122W bottom #206E

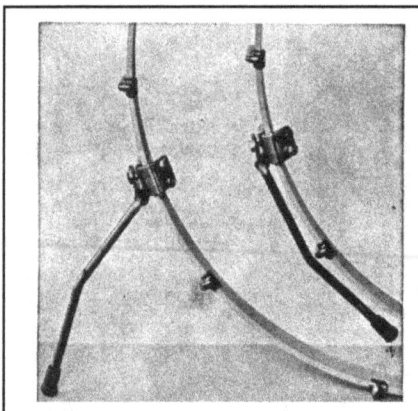

1940s – 1962
#1469

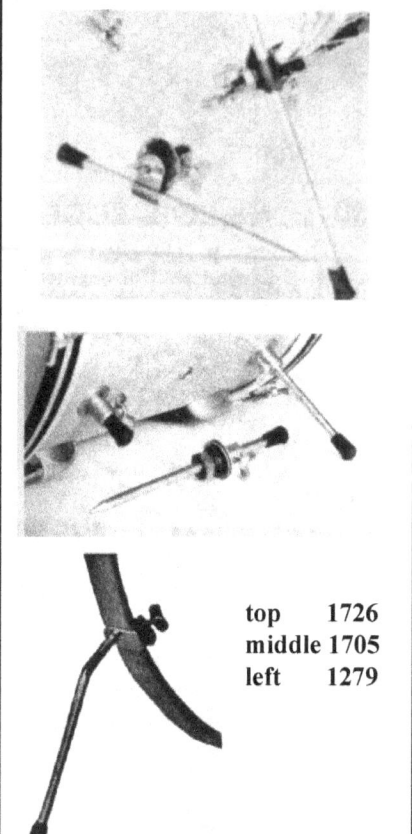

top   1726
middle 1705
left   1279

1950s – 1962

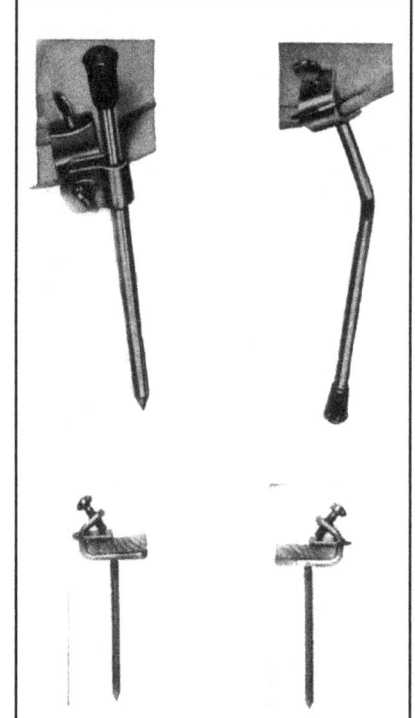

1950s – 1964
top left #4410, top right #4412,
bottom #1542

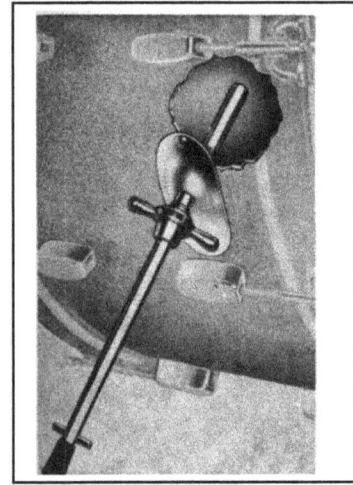

1964 – 1970
335R for 20" bass wide spread
340R for 22" bass
338R for 20" bass shorter angle

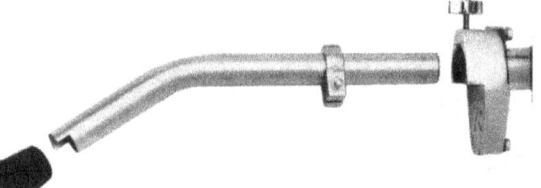

1976 – 1980s
1960 – 1962
240R -shell mount
241R hoop mount

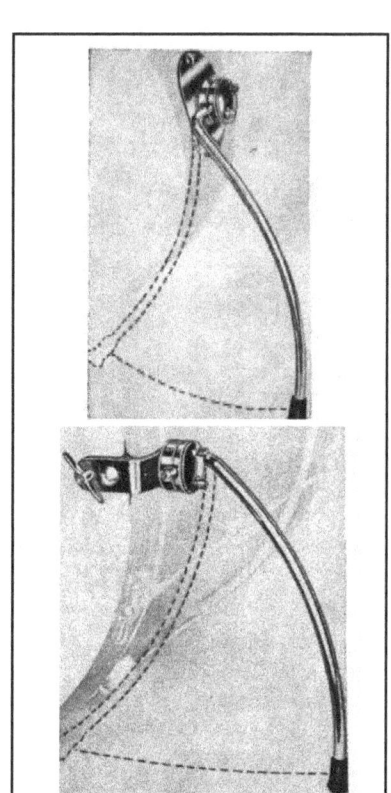

BADGES

Badges from the Farmingdale, New Jersey, era; late 1930s–1952

The small rectangular badge on the parade drum at the upper left was used on Daisy, Soo, and Union Brand parade drums. The small oval (upper right) appeared on tom-toms. The scalloped rectangles were embossed with the model; Soo Brand (entry level), Daisy Brand (better), Union Brand (better yet), and Three Star Brand (best).

The "Eagle Badge" was apparently the earliest Grossman-era Rogers badge, used from the mid to late 1950s.

Corrugated aluminum oval badge; Classmate and Banner entry-level snare drums of the 1950s. (These drums were also made with Eagle badges.)

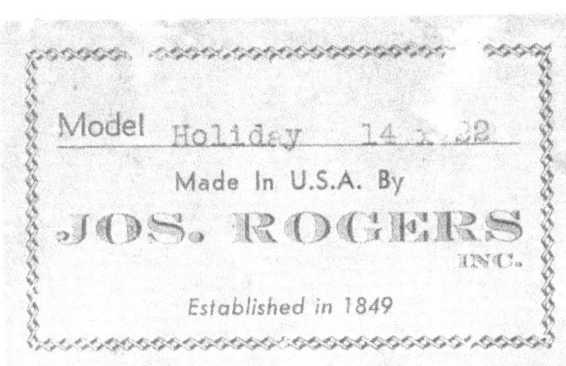

The internal shell stickers on the earliest Grossman-era Rogers drums; 1956

There was some overlap between the first sticker (above left) and this one; collector Kirk Higgins found both of these stickers in drums from the same outfit, evidently made in 1957. This serves as an indication of when Rogers began using serial numbeers.

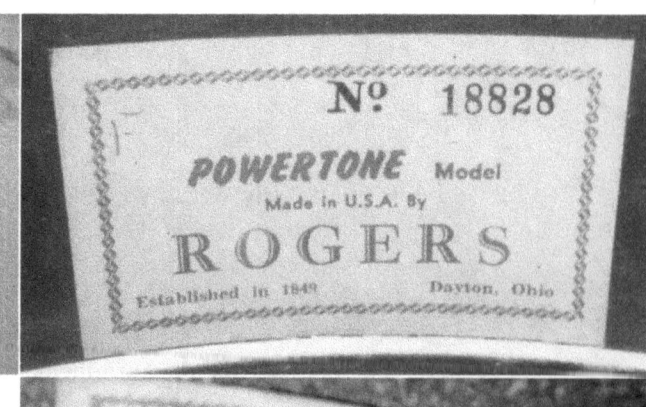

Above: Cleveland, Ohio. Assembled in Covington, warehoused and distributed through Grossman in Cleveland 1956–1965

Above Right: Dayton, Ohio. Assembled in either Covington or Dayton, warehoused and distributed through CBS in Dayton 1966–1969

Right: Fullerton, Calif. Assembled in Fullerton, warehoused and distributed there 1969–

The riveted script badges appeared in the late 1950s. There were a couple very short-run versions such as the oversized one shown at the left. The three most common versions are shown above. Of these, the first (and shortest-lived) version was the one above-left. The 1960 catalog pictures both the above-left and above-center versions. The version at the above-right was used from 1964 until 1976 with the only change being a difference in thickness; the older badges were slightly thicker. This is the style in use at this writing on the Brook-Mayes Rogers drums.

The Champion badge; used on entry-level drums and cocktail outfits in 1954.

Duplex badge and internal shell sticker; used by Grossman in the 1960s on drums they manufactured after they sold Rogers to CBS.

First-generation R-360 and R-380 series drums. Made for Rogers by Yamaha c. 1968

photos coutesy Bobby Chiasson

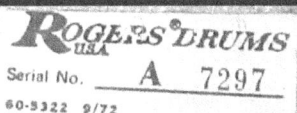

FULLERTON, CA stickers: In 1969 production and warehousing moved to California. Some drums made in and shipped from California actually have Cleveland labels- see the Bobby Chiasson interview on page 94. The earliest "Fullerton" drum labels had a border similar to the Ohio labels. Later badges were nearly identical except for the deletion of the border. The next generation of serial number labels (above) were tiny (about 1/2"x1 1/2") white labels with a 9-72 in the lower corner. These internal shell stickers spanned the years 1972–1975 in the order shown above from left to right; number underlined with no letter prefix, letter prefixes, then number only with no underline. (Special thanks to Dan Colluccio and Bobby Chiasson for sorting this out.)

Arbiter Autotune; made in England in the late 1970s on little more than a prototype basis.

Series II; The CBS debacle of the late 1970s.

The R-340 appeared with the second-generation 360 and 380 drums in the early 1980s. The R-340 drums were made by Remo; phenolic shells with "pretuned" heads.

In addition to the Dyna-sonic (see page 186,) two other snare drum models had their own badge; the SuperTen and Powertone.

The "Big-R" Badge

Introduced by CBS in 1976, there are a number of versions of this badge. The most common is the version pictured. Some were applied to floor toms without a vent, some do not have the "U.S.A." under the Rogers name, and some do not have serial numbers.

These badges are made of a metallic tape which was supplied to CBS in roll form. There was a fairly high rate of waste plus in the 1980s each time badges were ordered they started back at the same starting number, so serial numbers do not reflect actual drum production numbers.

The offshore drums imported by Island Music in the late 1980s did not have serial numbers or "U.S.A.".

Bass Drum Logos

Probably the best-known bass drum logo is the one shown here; the "Big-R logo", used from about 1965 through the 1980s. Through this era a few variations were used:
– Budget lines all had their own logos; R-340, R-360, R-380, and Series II.
– When the XP-8 shell was introduced (about 1980) a small "XP-8" was added below the big R.
– When Island Music licensed the Rogers name in the early 1990s, the logo was slightly smaller and the "U.S.A." was deleted.

The logos on this page are arranged from oldest (top of page) to newest (bottom of page), pretty much in order. All of these head logos were produced between 1956 and 1962. Bass drum t-rods are pictured to give a size reference to the logo.

ROGERS CYMBAL STANDS

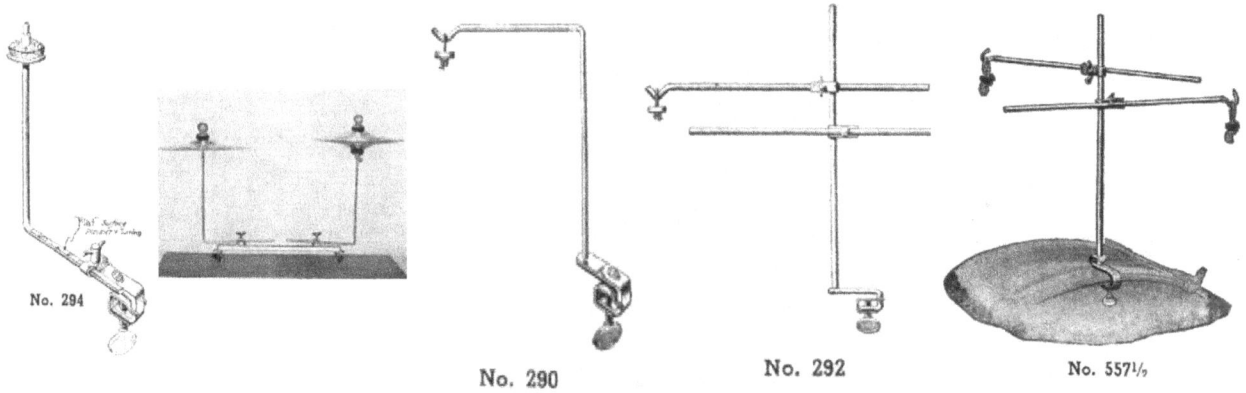

No. 294　　No. 290　　No. 292　　No. 557½

1930s – 1940s   hoop-mount cymbal holders

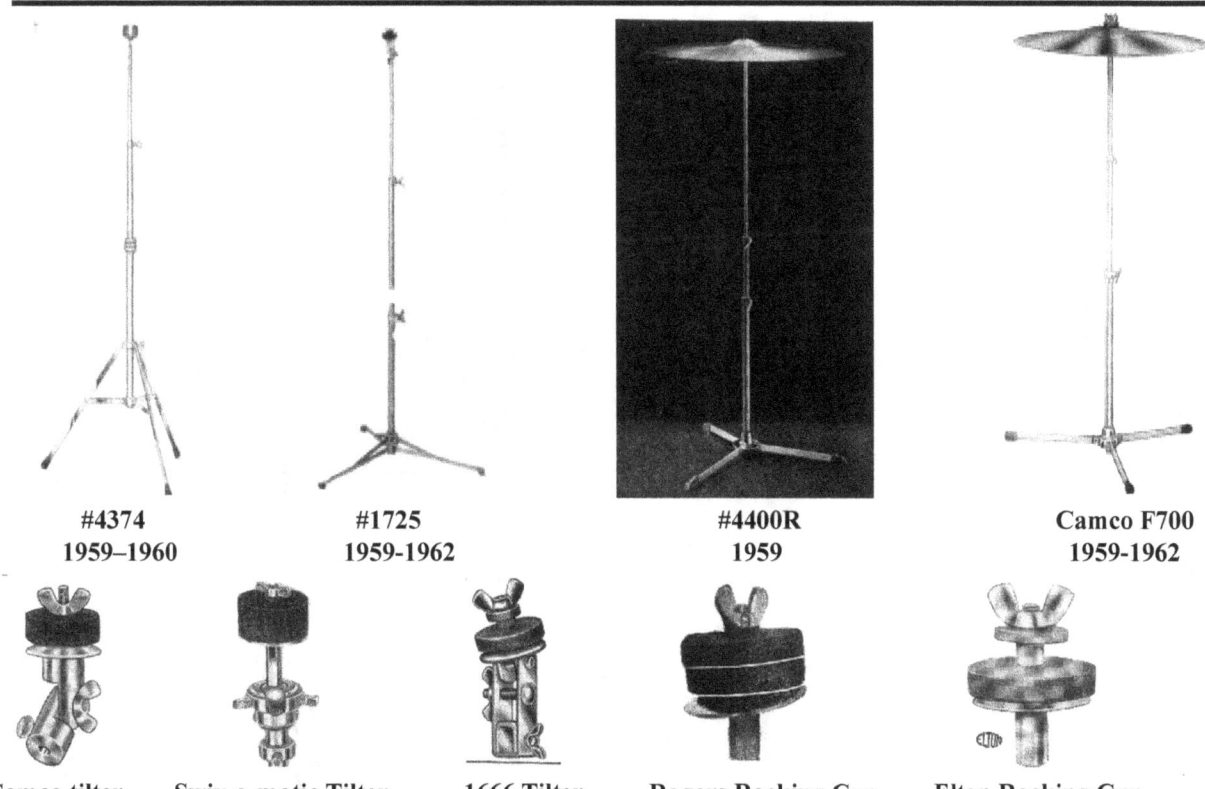

#4374　　#1725　　#4400R　　Camco F700
1959–1960　1959-1962　1959　　1959-1962

Camco tilter　Swiv-o-matic Tilter　1666 Tilter　Rogers Rocking Cup　Elton Rocking Cup

From the late fifties through the mid sixties, the actual cymbal holder was a separate (interchangable) part of the stand.

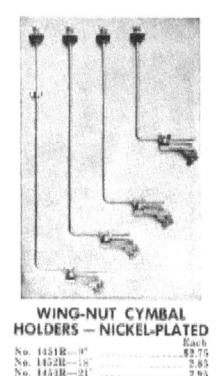

1946 – 1962

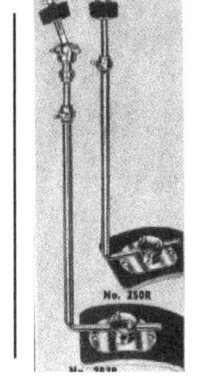

The "Knobby" system was introduced in 1958. The "Wonder Bar" (see tom holder section) was only in the line for a year or two, but the Knobby cymbal arms were catalogued until the early 1970s. (9", 12", 15" & 18" lengths).

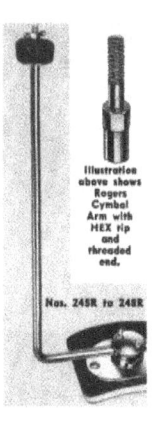

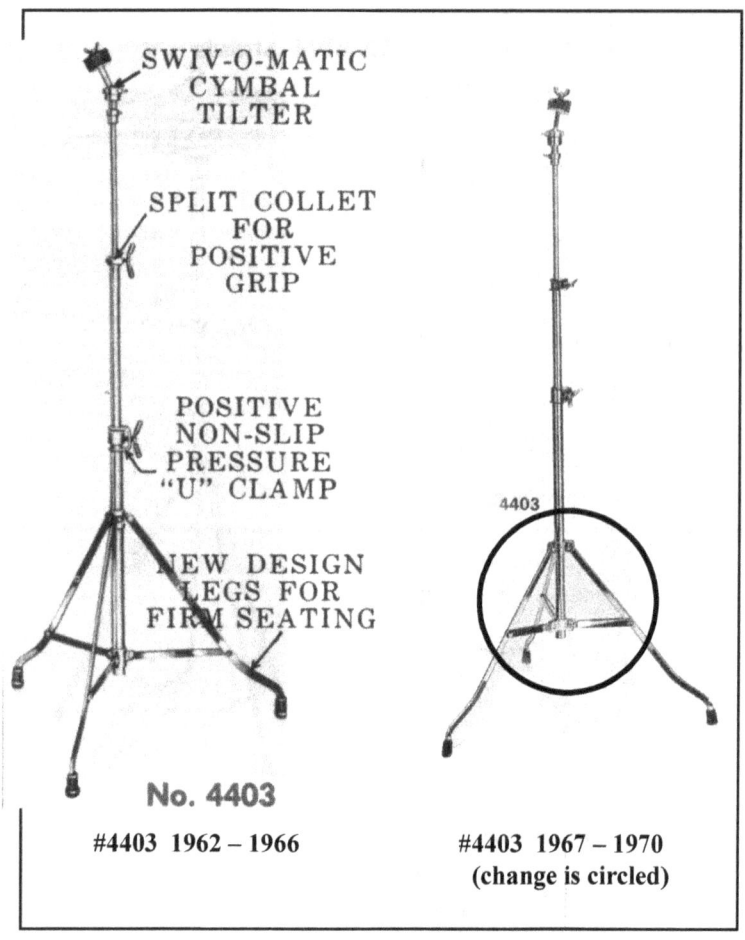

#4403 1962 – 1966

#4403 1967 – 1970
(change is circled)

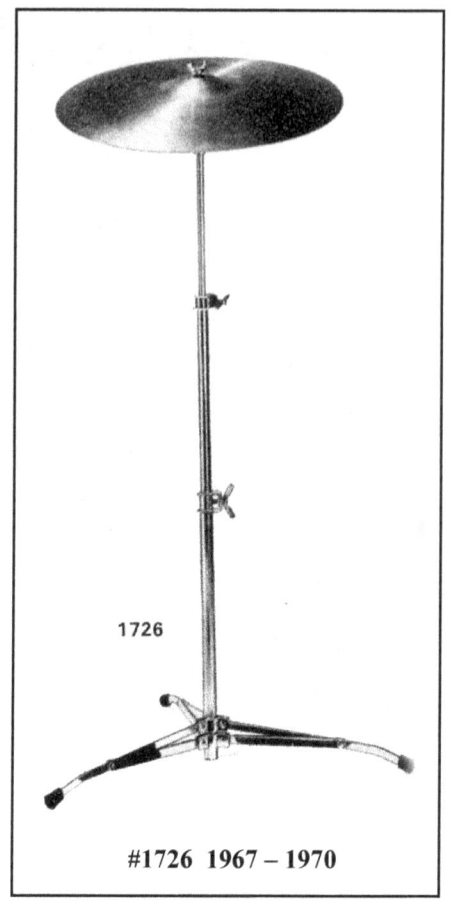

#1726 1967 – 1970

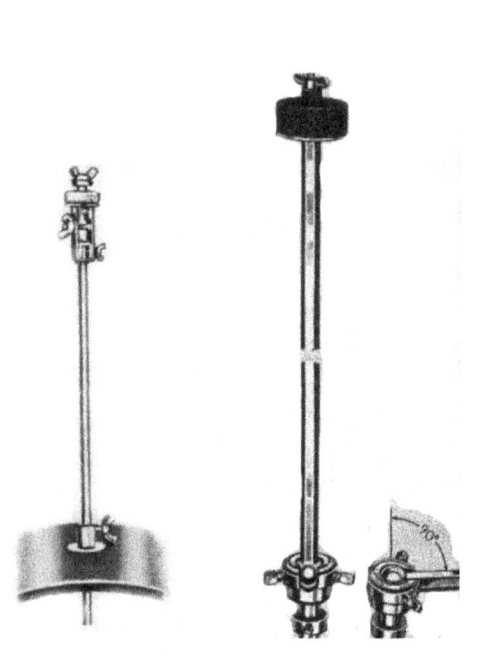

1704A
1962 – 1964

Swiv-o-matic extension arm
1964 – 1973

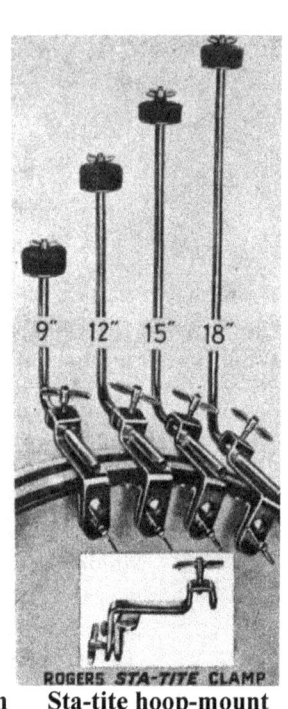

Sta-tite hoop-mount
1964

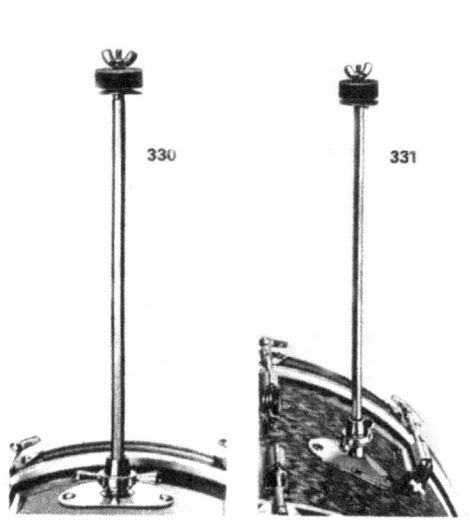

Swiv-o-matic disappearing
1964 – 1970

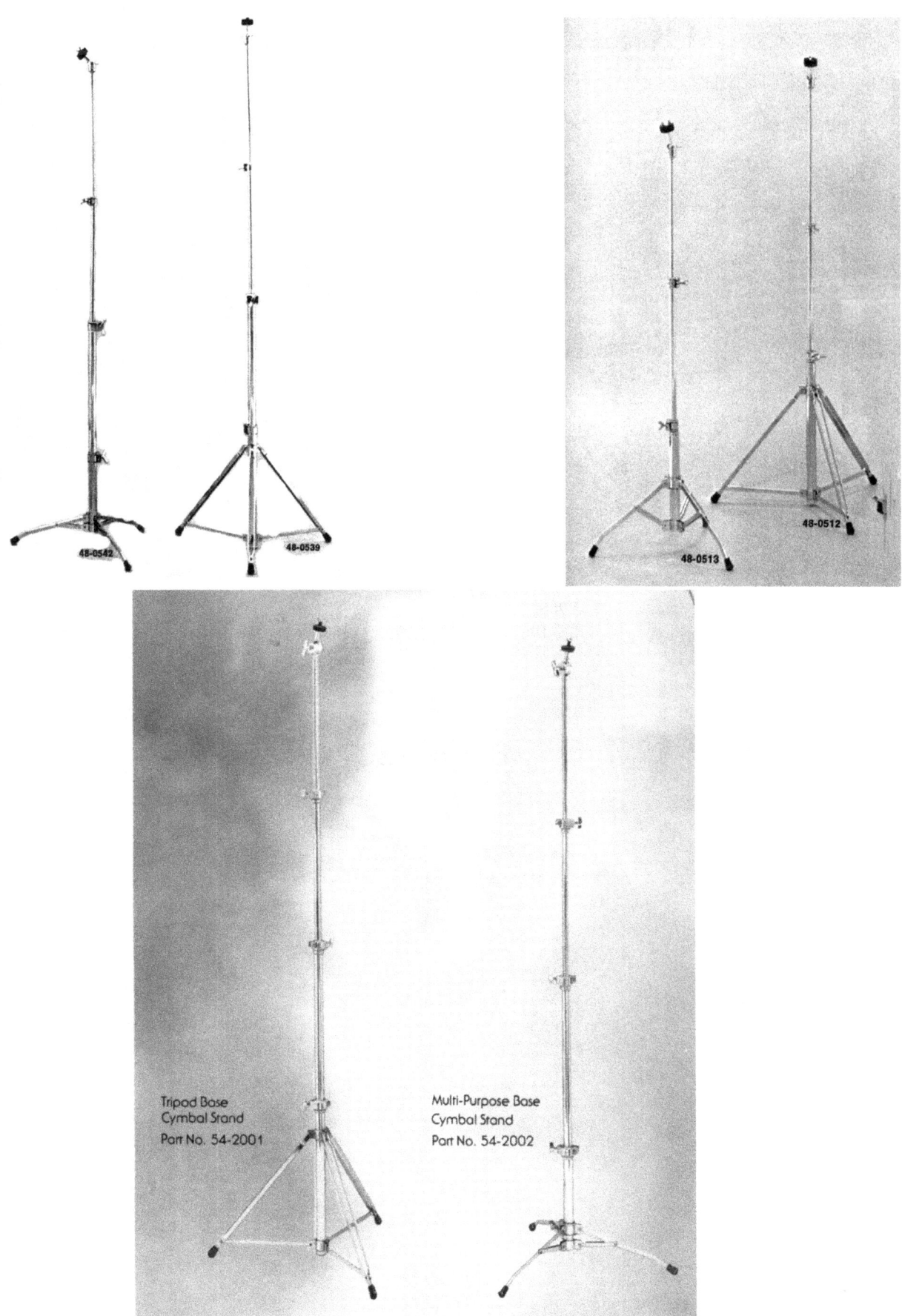

The four top stands were introduced in 1973. This series was replaced by the lower two stands in 1976; they were the same as the taller two upper stands except for the Memriloc height adjustment and ratchet tilter.

ROGERS HIGH HAT STANDS

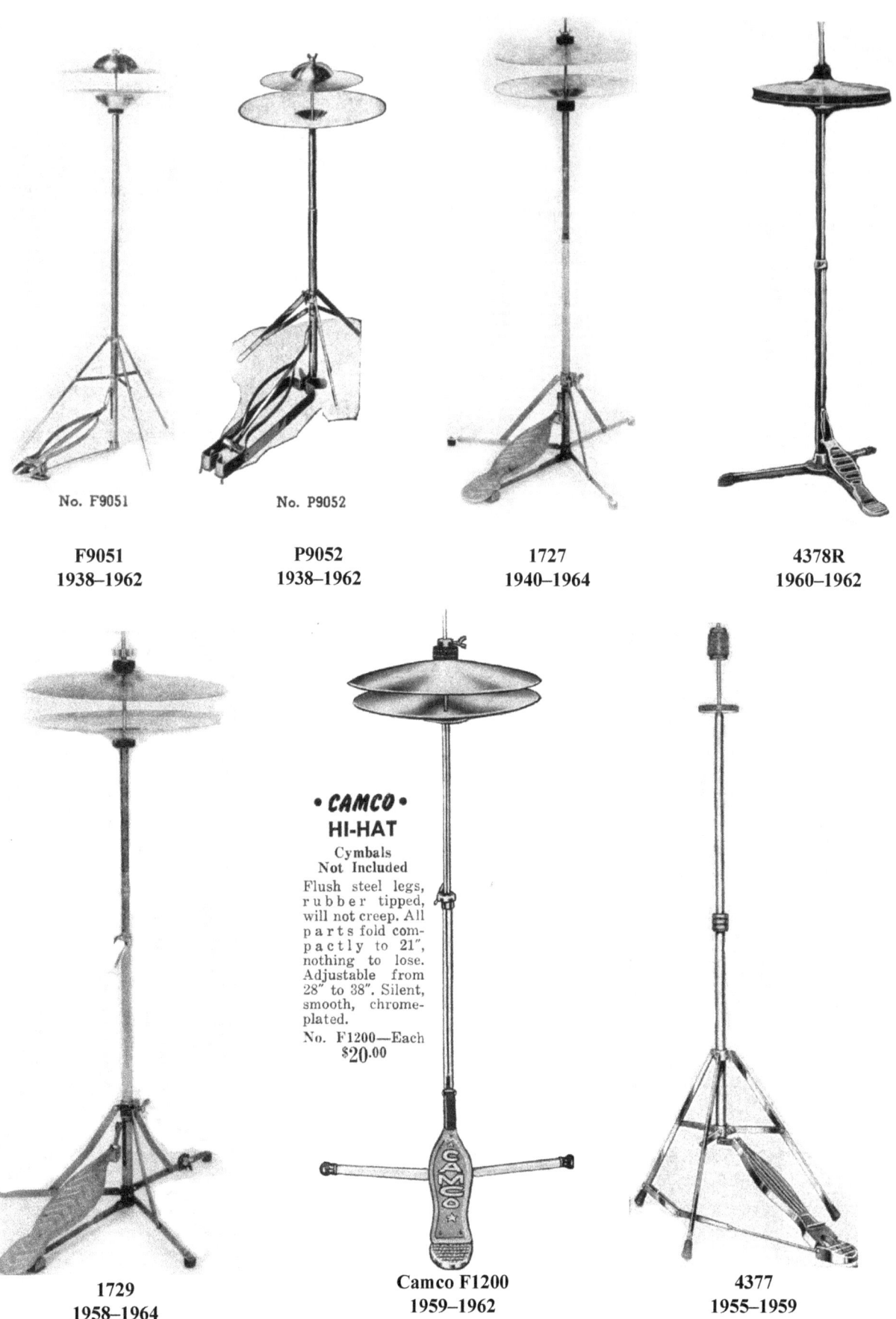

4399 JET
1967

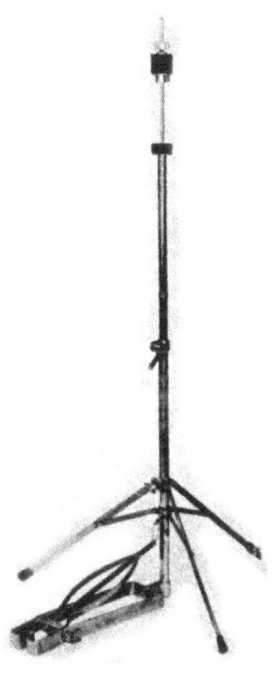
502 Hollywood
1962

1680 Rhythm King
1962

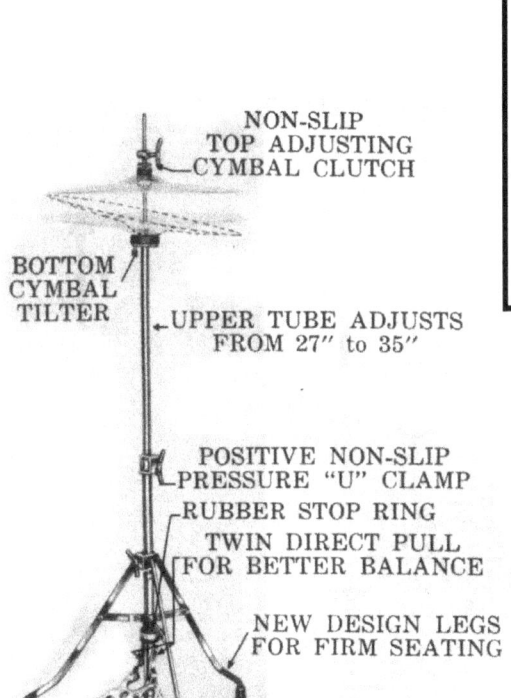
Swiv-o-matic 4401
1962–1973

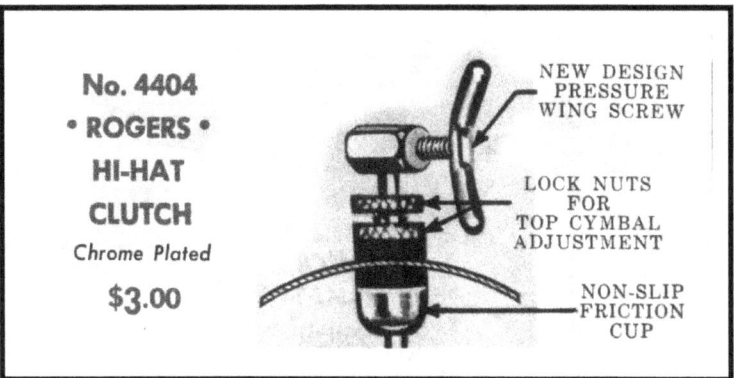

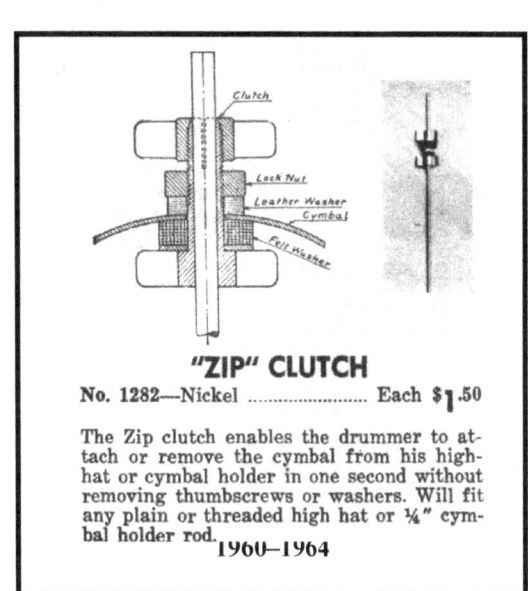

Supreme
1973–1975

Dualmatic clutch
1976–1980s
Releases top cymbal
when bar is struck,
reconnects when
pedal is pushed
down.

Supreme
1976–1980s

ROGERS SNARE STANDS

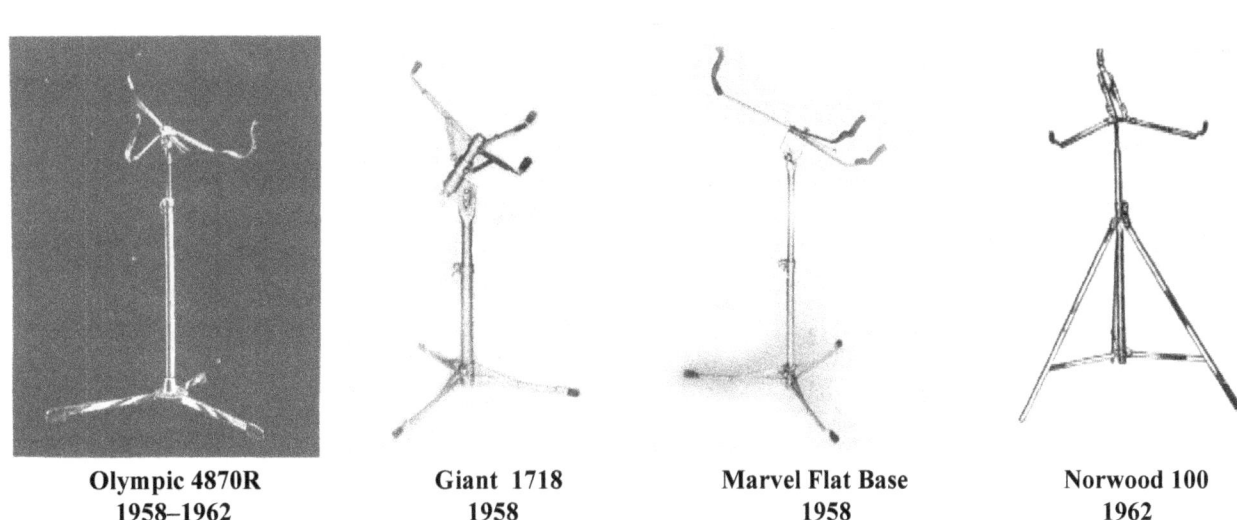

| Hamilton #7 1938 | Hamilton #8 1938 | Lone Star #9 1938 | #36 1938–1964 | Super Marvel #918 1938–1964 |

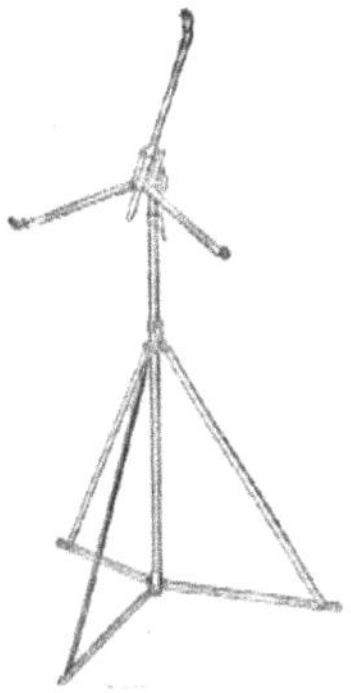

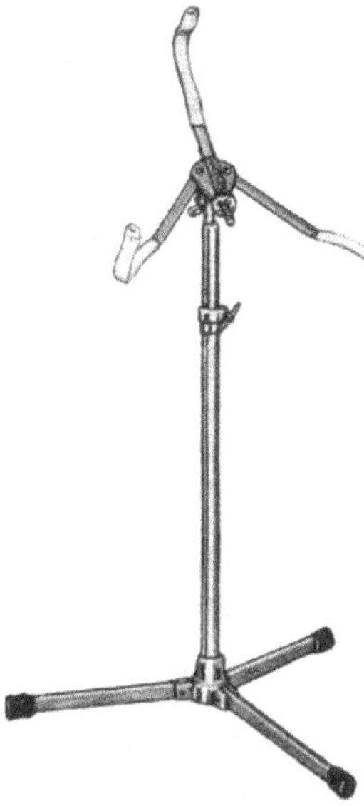

Camco F800 1958–1962 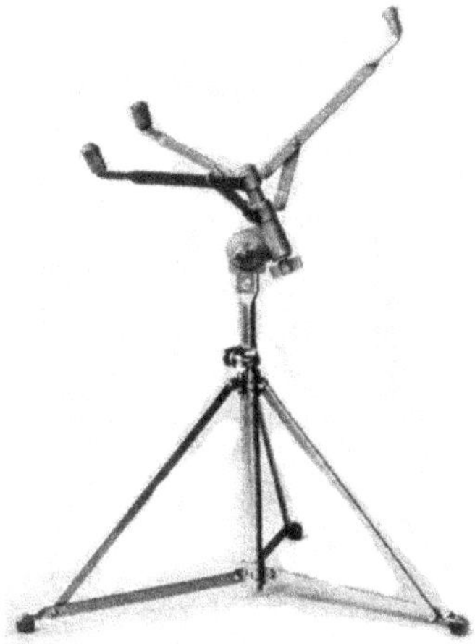   Super-Grip 1946    Super-Grip Junior 1946–1962

Olympic 4870R 1958–1962   Giant 1718 1958   Marvel Flat Base 1958   Norwood 100 1962

Perfection 525 1962–1964   **Norwood Empire 1962**   **Hamilton 275 1962–1964**   **Super Marvel 1962**

**Buck Rogers
1962–1964**

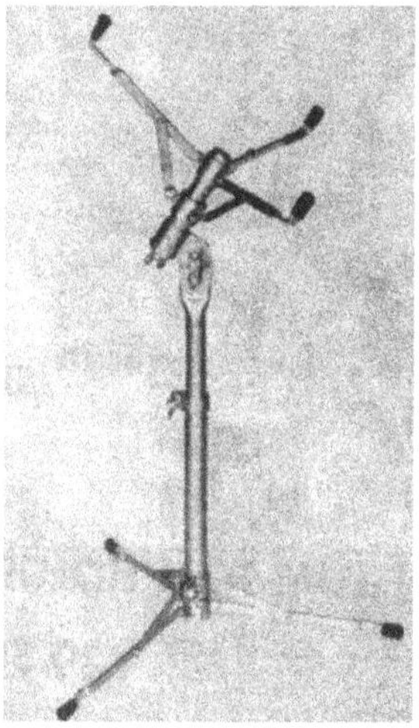

**Buck Rogers Junior
1962**

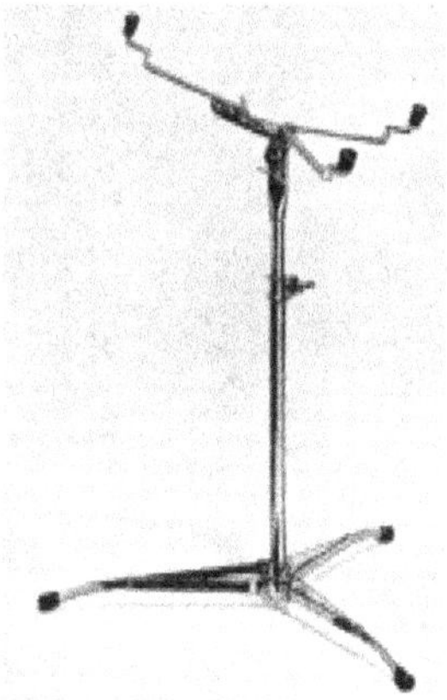

4040 Banner 1967    **4011 Pro 1962–1967** 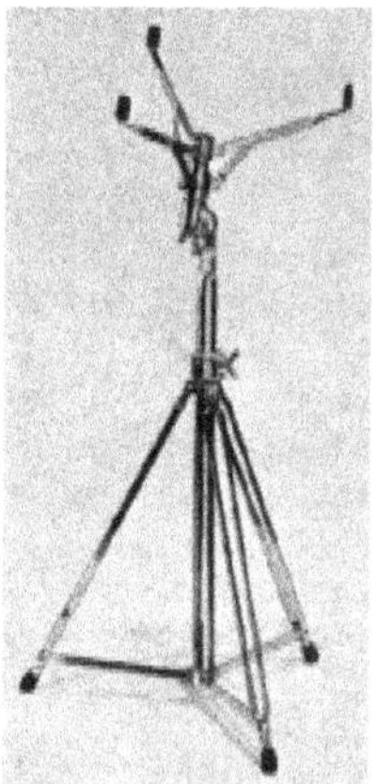   **4019 Sampson 1967–1970**

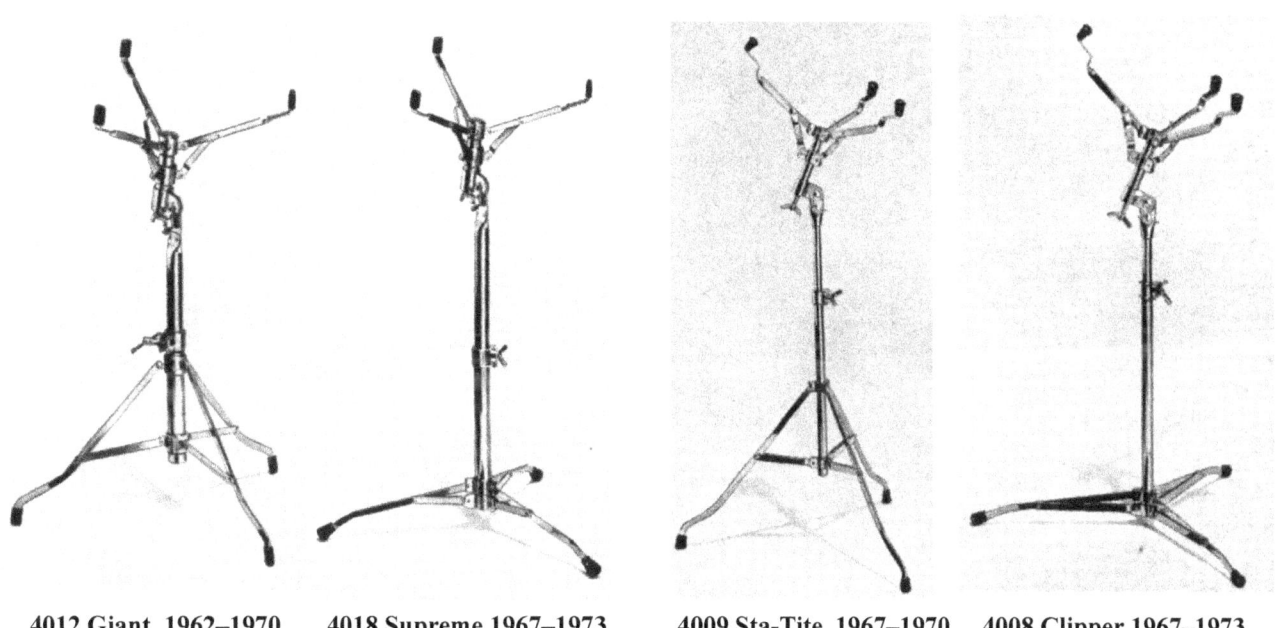

4012 Giant 1962–1970 **4018 Supreme 1967–1973** **4009 Sta-Tite 1967–1970** **4008 Clipper 1967–1973**

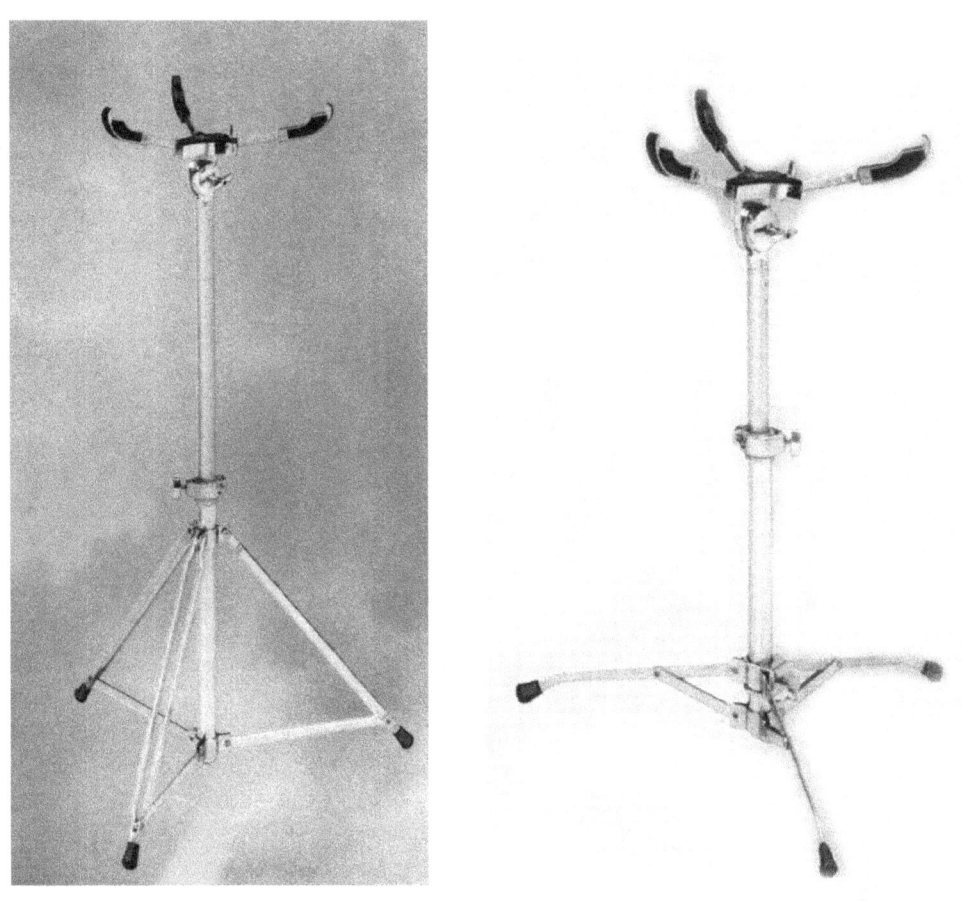

Memriloc Snare Stands 1976–1980s

ROGERS PEDALS

9056 Universal 1938 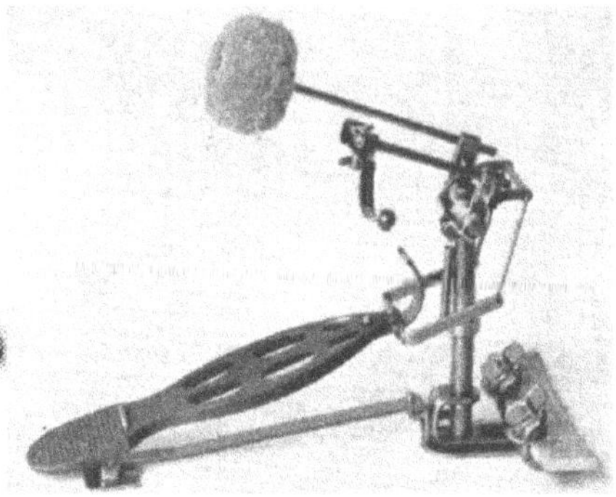   **9054 Whirlwind 1938** 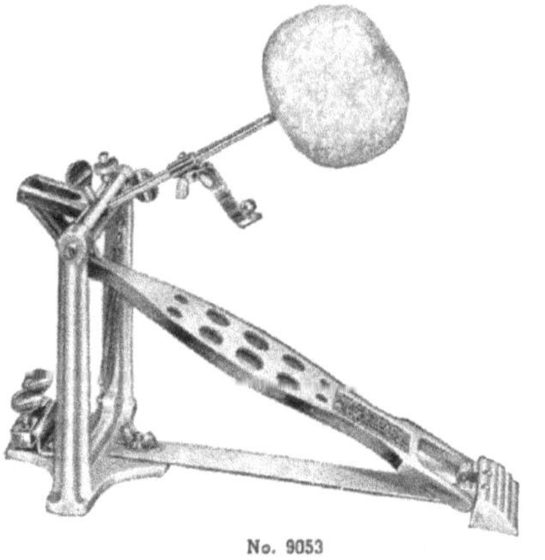   **9053 Heyn 1938**

9055 Eclipse 1938–1958 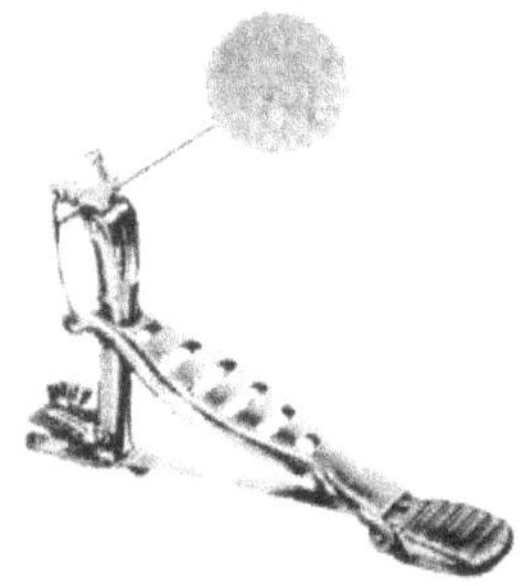   **4438R Utility 1958–1962**    **4441 Champ 1962**    **Acme 1946**

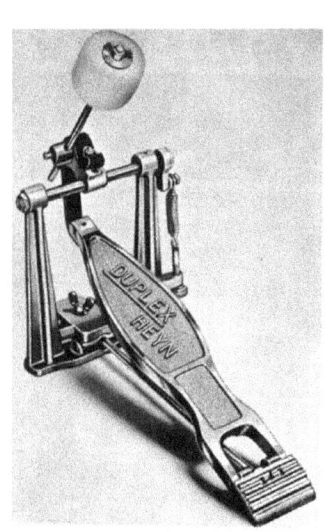

Duplex-Heyn 1964

399 Jet 1960–1966

4425   1954–1958

• CAMCO •
De Luxe Model
FOOT PEDALS

Deluxe model. Highly polished aluminum, no painted parts. Folds without taking anything apart. Features fast, quiet operation with complete tone control; tension control; power action; vertical stroke adjustment; footboard adjustment.

No. F4462
Each $22.50

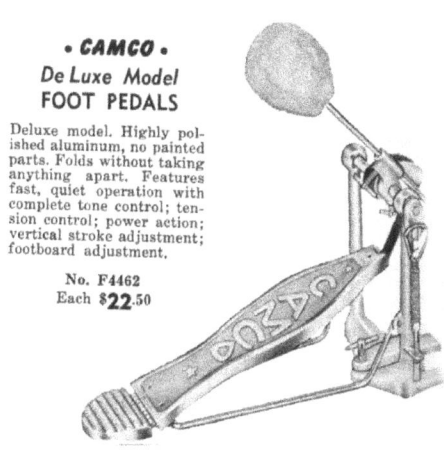

Camco (Deluxe or Standard) 1958–1962

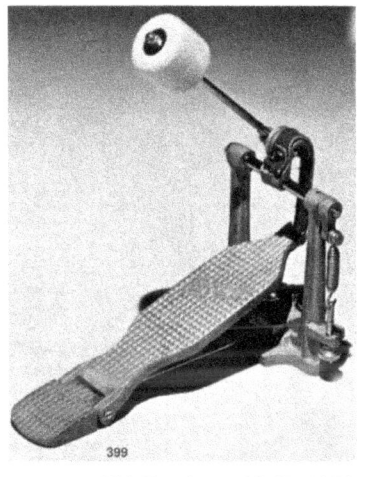

399 Rocket 1967–1970

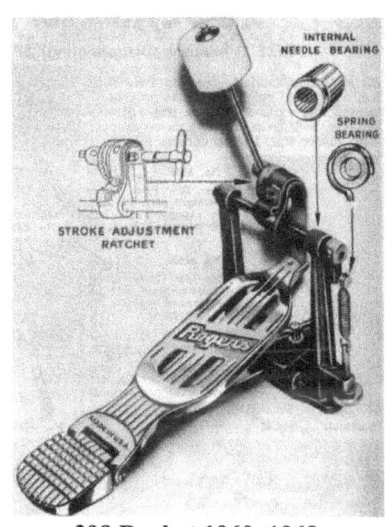

398 Rocket 1960–1968

ROGERS "UP BEAT" OR "COCKTAIL" FOOT PEDAL

Designed for use with any type tom-tom leg. Eliminates special brackets, plates or bars. Attaches quickly and easily. Footboard design permits positioning to any comfortable angle, for playing in either sitting or standing position. A smooth, fast action pedal—complete, with directions.

No. 205R $22.50

ADJUSTS FOR
- HEIGHT
- STROKE ACTION
- FOOTBOARD ANGLE
- BEATING POSITION
- STRAP LENGTH
- SPRING TENSION

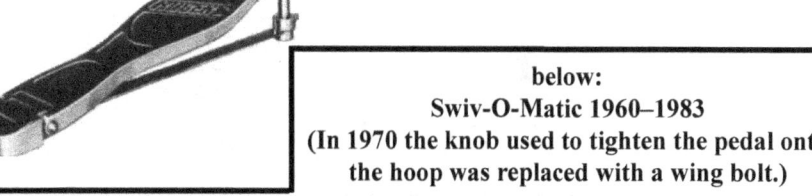

Cocktail Pedal 1962–1964

below:
Swiv-O-Matic 1960–1983
(In 1970 the knob used to tighten the pedal onto the hoop was replaced with a wing bolt.)

•ROGERS• FOOT PEDALS

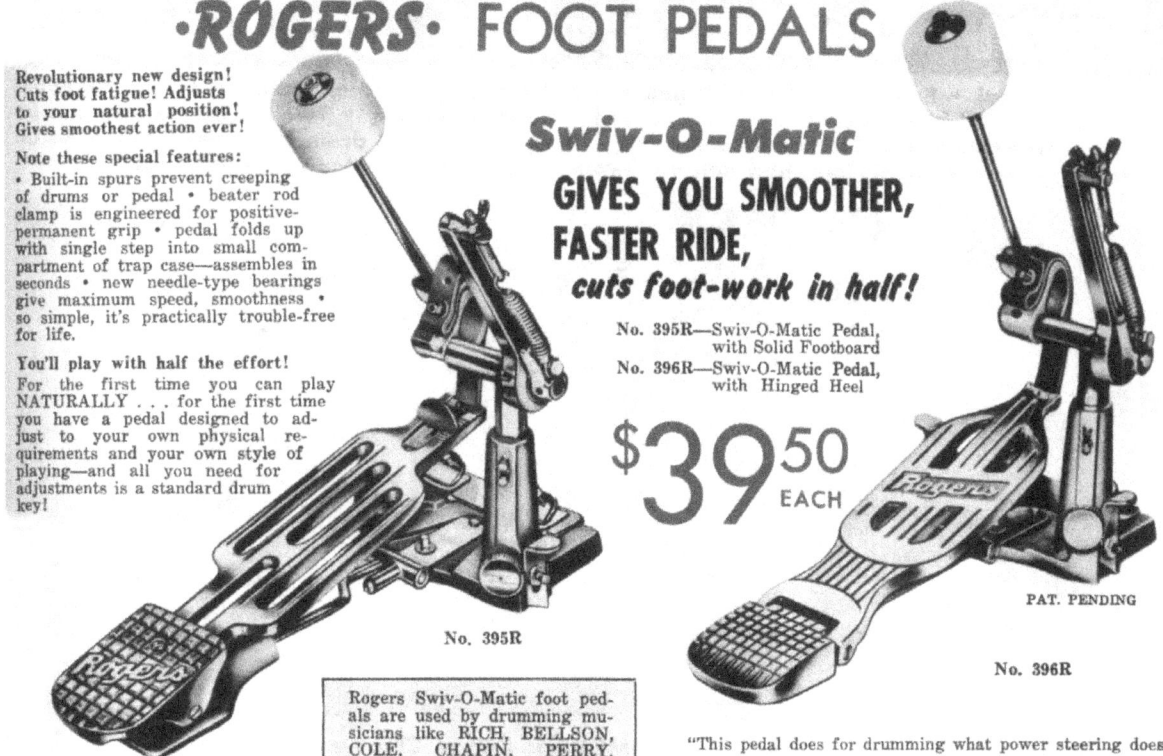

Revolutionary new design! Cuts foot fatigue! Adjusts to your natural position! Gives smoothest action ever!

Note these special features:
• Built-in spurs prevent creeping of drums or pedal • beater rod clamp is engineered for positive-permanent grip • pedal folds up with single step into small compartment of trap case—assembles in seconds • new needle-type bearings give maximum speed, smoothness • so simple, it's practically trouble-free for life.

You'll play with half the effort!
For the first time you can play NATURALLY . . . for the first time you have a pedal designed to adjust to your own physical requirements and your own style of playing—and all you need for adjustments is a standard drum key!

Swiv-O-Matic
GIVES YOU SMOOTHER, FASTER RIDE,
cuts foot-work in half!

No. 395R—Swiv-O-Matic Pedal, with Solid Footboard
No. 396R—Swiv-O-Matic Pedal, with Hinged Heel

$39.50 EACH

No. 395R

No. 396R PAT. PENDING

Rogers Swiv-O-Matic foot pedals are used by drumming musicians like RICH, BELLSON, COLE, CHAPIN, PERRY, COTTLER, BURNES, KRELL, and many others.

"This pedal does for drumming what power steering does for driving." That's how one top drummer put it! This is a dream pedal. It adjusts exactly, completely to you.

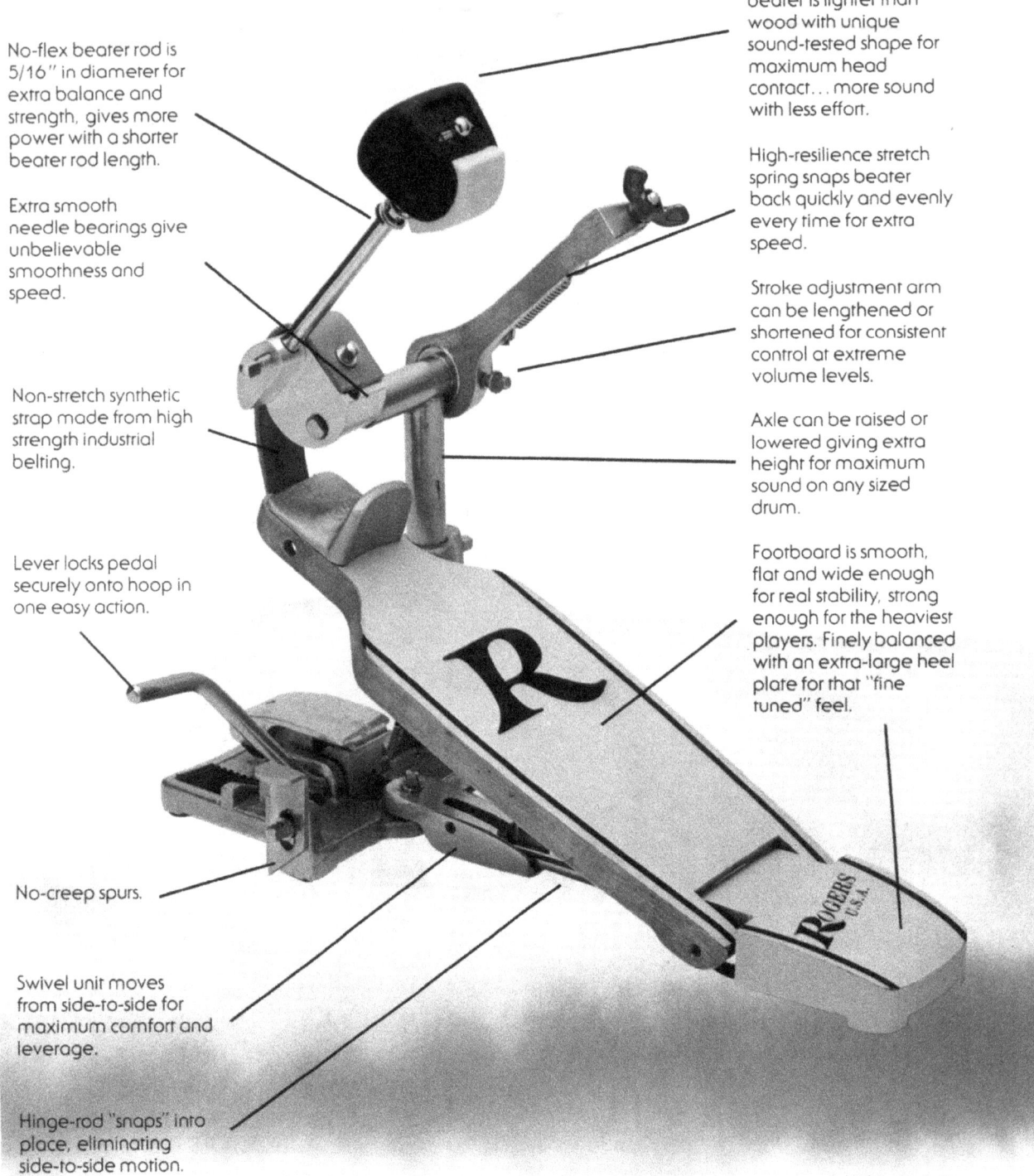

We call this the "Ultimate Foot Pedal". Take a minute or two to study its features and you'll soon see why. There is no pedal on the market that can match the amazing Rogers Supreme! It will help add a new dimension of creativity to all the music you play! Part No. 54-7000

No-flex beater rod is 5/16" in diameter for extra balance and strength, gives more power with a shorter beater rod length.

Extra smooth needle bearings give unbelievable smoothness and speed.

Non-stretch synthetic strap made from high strength industrial belting.

Lever locks pedal securely onto hoop in one easy action.

No-creep spurs.

Swivel unit moves from side-to-side for maximum comfort and leverage.

Hinge-rod "snaps" into place, eliminating side-to-side motion.

"Black Jack" two way beater is lighter than wood with unique sound-tested shape for maximum head contact... more sound with less effort.

High-resilience stretch spring snaps beater back quickly and evenly every time for extra speed.

Stroke adjustment arm can be lengthened or shortened for consistent control at extreme volume levels.

Axle can be raised or lowered giving extra height for maximum sound on any sized drum.

Footboard is smooth, flat and wide enough for real stability, strong enough for the heaviest players. Finely balanced with an extra-large heel plate for that "fine tuned" feel.

Supreme 1976–1980s

ROGERS TOM HOLDERS

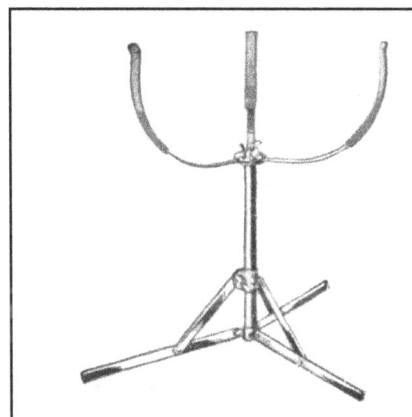

GIANT TOM TOM STAND

No. 815

Holds any 12, 13 or 14" giant tom tom in perfect playing position. Adjustable for height. Arms are rubber covered.
No. 815 .... $ 4.00

No. 815½

Extra large heavy arms to hold giant 16" tom toms.
No. 815½ .... $ 4.00

The first tom toms sold as part of the drum kit were the tacked-head "Chinese toms". The small toms were attached to the bass drum in much the same way as other novelty instruments and cymbals. The larger Chinese tom toms were often referred to as Giant tom toms and were placed in "cradles" which resembled short snare drum stands.

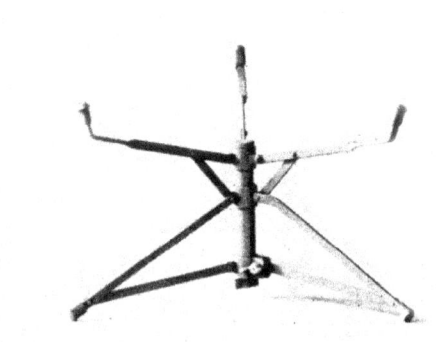

THE "SUPER-GRIP" TOM TOM STAND
(HEAVY DUTY)
(Patent applied for)
For 15" and 16" tom toms. Tom tom locks to stand. Adjustable to height.
No. 1526 .... $6.00

THE "SUPER-GRIP" TOM TOM STAND
(ALL-PURPOSE)
(Patent applied for)
For any size tom tom. Tom tom locks to stand. Adjustable to height.
No. 1527 .... $6.00

THE 'HOLDWELL" TOM TOM STAND
(LIGHTWEIGHT)
For 15" and 16" tom toms.
No. 1529 .... $3.00

THE "HOLDWELL" TOM TOM STAND
(HEAVY DUTY)
For 16" tom tom.
No. 1528 .... $4.00

#1501 All-Angle Holder
1946 – 1956

264R
1958 - 1964

1946 Console; available in models that either clamped onto tension rods or bolted to shell

Shell Mount Consolette
1958 – 1964
(Rod mount version)
1958 – 1960

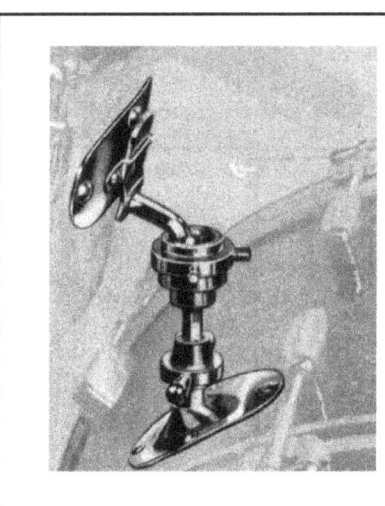
Swiv-o-matic utility holder (left) and demountable holder (right)
1958 – 1962   1958 – 1964

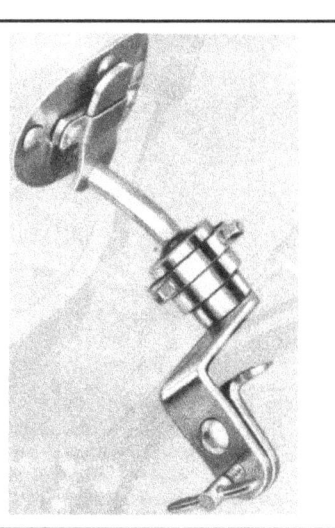

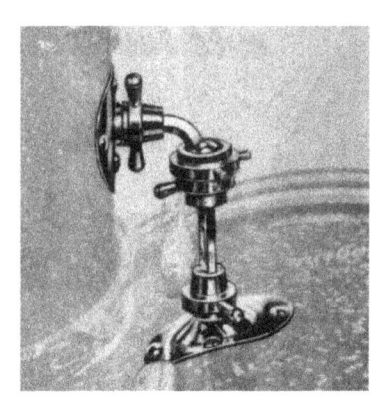   

Swiv-o-matic tom holders
1958 – 1973

144

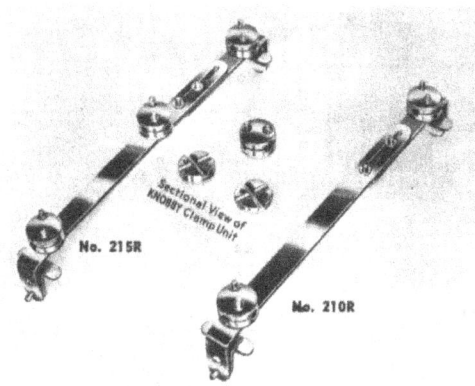

ROGERS • WONDER BARS •

The WONDER BAR consists of 2 steel bands having STA-TITE hoop clamps for firm mounting on both hoops. Slotted top band permits adjustment for head tensioning. Adjusted with any standard drum keys. Compact and flexible. Provided a means of mounting equipment without the need of individual holders. DeLuxe chrome plated.

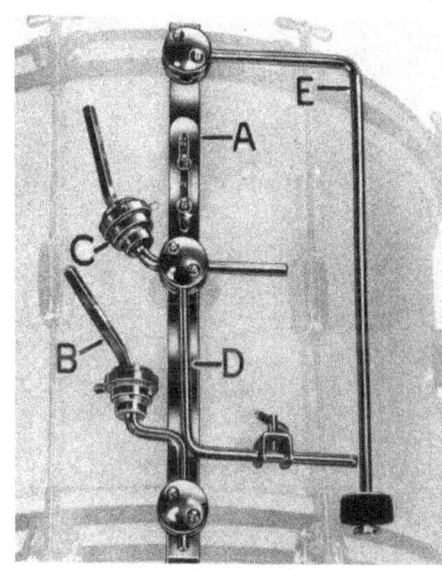

• WONDER BAR •
With Folded Attachments

3-unit WONDER BAR on top of bass drum, showing attachments folded for packing into fiber case, or bag.

A—Wonder Bar (#215R)
B—Snare Drum Holder (#270R)
C—Tom-Tom Holder (#265R)
D—Cowbell Holder Assembly (#239R)
E—Cymbal Arm

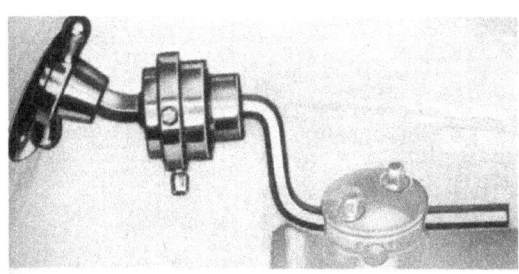

• KNOBBY • SNARE DRUM HOLDER
Wonder Bar To Snare Drum

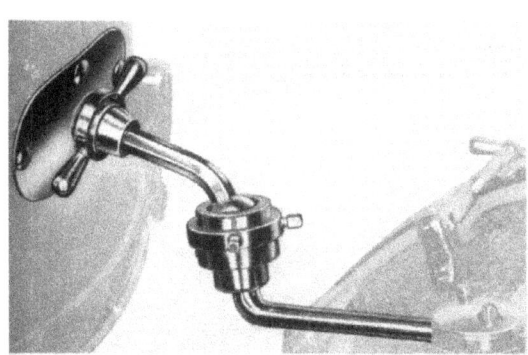

• KNOBBY • TOM TOM HOLDER

• WONDER BAR • IN USE
3-unit WONDER BAR on top of bass drum, showing Snare Drum Holder, Tom-Tom Holder, and Cymbal Holder in use.

KNOBBY BAR SYSTEM 1958

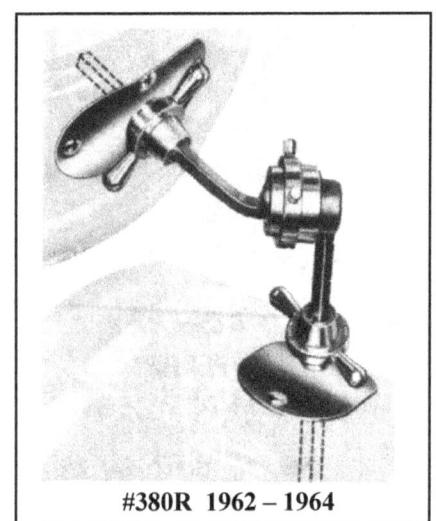

#380R 1962 – 1964

2 Tom Toms Spread Apart

ROGERS • SWIV-O-MATIC® • TWIN TOM-TOM HOLDER

No. 365R—Chrome-Plated _____Each $39.50

Here's a twin holder for double tom-tom, engineered for maximum adjustments. Exclusive Swiv-O-Matic features permit any playable height and angle adjustment, inter-changeable locations — left, right, rear, or front, close together, spread apart, or any desireable position in-between. Individual height adjustments keep top heads level, even when using two different size tom-toms. Unlimited variations to keep pace with the needs of the modern drummer.

1962 – 1964

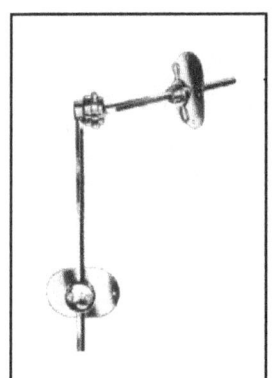

382R For mounting snare drum or tom to floor tom or cocktail drum.   1962 – 1964

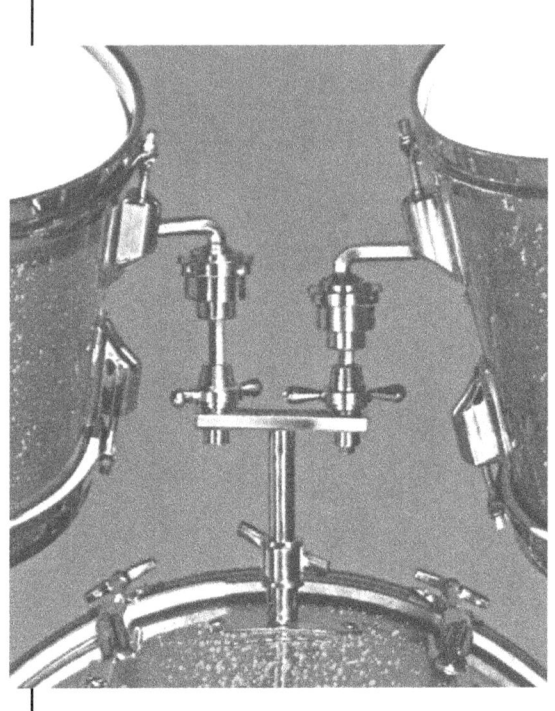

1967 – 1973

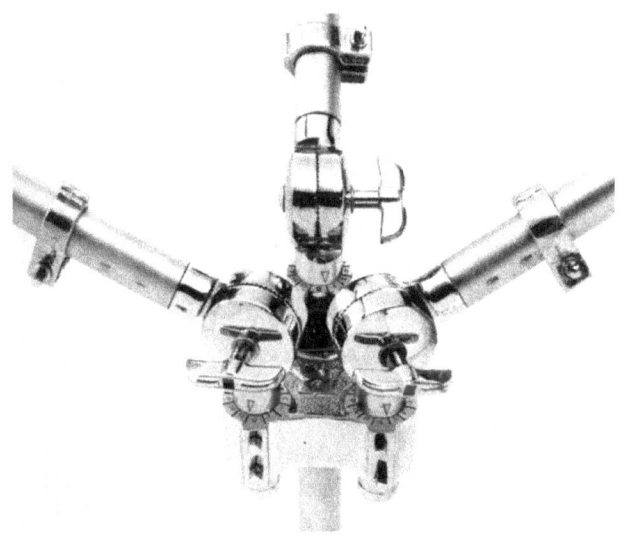

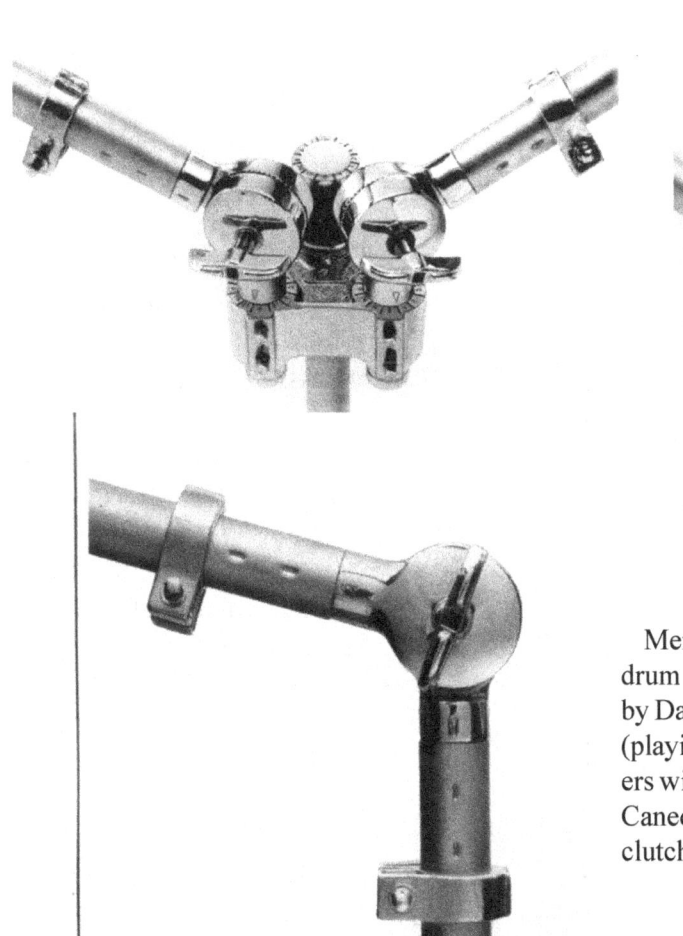

Memriloc hardware was as significant a development in drum hardware as Swivomatic had been. It was developed by Dave Donahoe in the mid 1970s. Donahoe was musician (playing 5-6 nights a week) and machinist who went to Rogers with his prototype Dualmatic hi-hat clutch in 1975. Don Canedy and Roy Burns were impressed not only with the clutch but with Dave, and hired him as a product designer.

MemriLoc System 1976 through 1980s

ROGERS HOOPS

Until the Covington era, Rogers hoops were pretty much the same as everyone else's. In fact they often *were* someone else's– often Gretsch's. Aside from some die-cast hoops in the late 1930s the pre-Covington hoops were single or double flanged hoops used with clips, or wooden hoops with claws.

"**TALL HOOPS**" The triple-flanged hoops Rogers began making in Covington in the early 1960s were what today's collectors refer to as "tall hoops". While the overall height of a Ludwig hoop from the same era is about 1 1/16" and the distance from the mounted head to the top of the hoop is 3/8", the measurements for the tall hoops are 1 1/4" and 5/8" respectively. (Rogers hoops were steel, not brass like Ludwig's.) There was a very practical reason for the extra height: when calfskin heads begin to pull out, the top of the hoop is drawn closer to the surface of the head. While this leaves a Ludwig hoop nearly flush with the head, the Rogers hoop still leaves the drummer some hoop for rim shots. By the time beavertail lugs were introduced in the early 1960s, practically all heads in use were plastic, so the height of their Rogers hoops was reduced to match industry standards. Most (but not all) beavertail drums were shipped with standard-height hoops.

DATING GUIDE – SNARE DRUMS

Three Star   1938
5" or 6 1/2" x 14", 8 lug, 3-ply
Gretsch lugs & rims, Slingerland strainer

Brighton (Daisy Brand)   1938
5" or 6 1/2" x 14", 8 lug, 3-ply
Gretsch lugs & rims, Leedy strainer

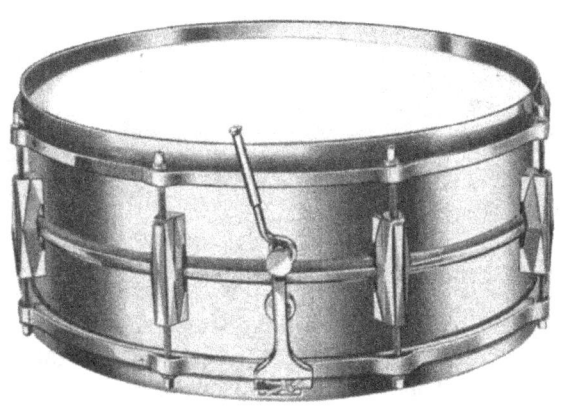

Mercedes (Union Brand)   1938
5" x 14", 8 lug, 3-ply or metal shell
Gretsch lugs & rims, Rogers strainer

Newton (Daisy Brand)   1938
5" x 14", 6 lug, brass or 3-ply shell
Gretsch lugs & rims, Leedy strainer

Manville (Daisy Brand)   1938
4" or 5" x 14", 5"x15", 3-ply mahogany
16 Leedy thumb screw rods, Leedy strainer

Madison (Daisy Brand)   1938
3"x13" or 5" x 14", 3-ply mahogany
8 Leedy thumb screw rods

Princeton (Soo Brand) 1938
5"x14", 6 lug, wood or metal shell

Hawthorne (Soo Brand) 1938
4" or 5"x14", brass or 3-ply shell

Sultan (Daisy Brand) 1940
6 1/2 or 7"x14", 8 lug, 3-ply
R-imprint lug, Leedy strainer

Goodwill (Daisy Brand) 1940
5", 6 1/2", 7", or 8"x14", Duco or Mahogany 8
R-imprint lug, Slingerland strainer

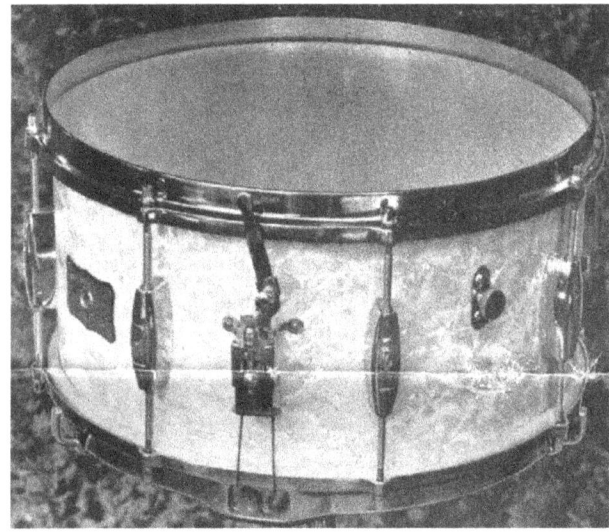

Superior 1940–1946
Union Brand (Nickel), Three Star (Chrome)
6 1/2", 7", or 8"x14", 3-ply shell
8 R-imprint lugs, Slingerland strainer

Utility (Daisy Brand) 1940
5" or 6 1/2" x14", brass shell
6 R-imprint lugs, Leedy strainer

Classmate   1954–1962
4"x13"   Black or white lacquer

Banner   1954–1962
5"x14" Black or white lacquer, mahogany
(pearl finishes added in 1962)

Broadway   1954–1960
5"x14", black or white lacquer   (Ridged lugs at right first catalogued in 1958)

Spotlight   1954–1960
5"x14"   White or black pearl, gold, red, green, or blue sparkle
(ridged lugs at right first catalogued in 1958)

Mercury 1955–1956
5"x14"
1955: Blue & Silver, White Pearl, Black Pearl
1955 & 1956: Black & Gold, Red & White

Luxor 1958–1962 (replaced Mercury)
5"x14"
1958–1960: Blue & Silver, Black & Gold,
White or Black Pearl
1962: Choice of mahogany, lacquer, any pearl
1958–1960: Eagle badge   1962: Script logo

Monitor 1955–1960
5" or 6 1/2" x 14", Mahogany   (change to ridged lugs in 1958)
Catalog photos show Eagle badge except 1956 which shows rectangular badge

Mayfair 1955–1960
5" or 6 1/2" x 14", Black & Gold or Blue & Silver (change to ridge lugs in 1958)

Scottie 1955
5"x14"
Offered in single tension, double tension, and double tension with self-aligning lugs and triple-flange hoops.

Century 8"x15"
Available in mahogany, lacquers, or pearl coverings.
Introduced in 1958 (left), the change to a Swiv-o-matic strainer and script badge was in 1962.

Century 1964
(Change to beavertail lugs)

Luxor   1964–1968
5" or 6 1/2"x14", Mahogany, lacquer, or pearl
Strainer note: Luxor was equipped with the StaTite strainer unless about serial number 10000 in 1967, when it was replaced with the Bantam strainer.

Student 1964
5"x14"
Mahogany, lacquer, or pearl
Replaced discontinued Classmate model

Strainer Note: The Sta-Tite strainer (Luxor and Tower models) shown in the 1964 catalog have the v-shape on the face pointing down like on the drum shown below. The next catalog published was in 1967 and from that pint on all Sta-Tite strainers illustrated have the v-shape pointing up like the one at right.

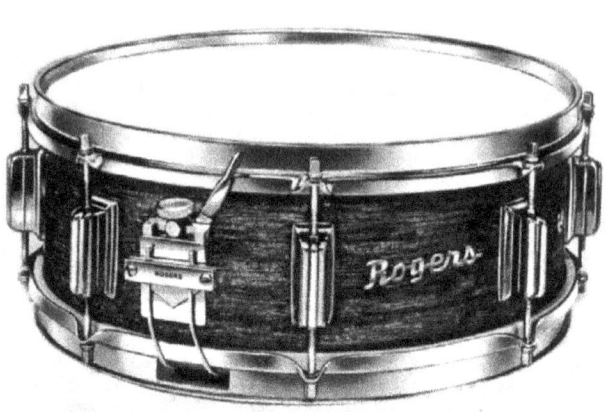

Tower 1962 (left) – 1964 (right)
5" or 6 1/2"x14", 6 1/2"x15" Mahogany, lacquer, or pearl
This 8-lug drum replaced the Monitor, Broadway, and Mayfair models.

Holiday 1955–1962
5" or 6 1/2"x14"
Pearl finishes or Scottie Plaid in 1955 & 1956 when it was the top-of-the-line Rogers snare drum (above left).
Lug and strainer change in 1958 (left).

Changes in 1962 (above):
Swiv-o-matic strainer, Script logo, Metal shell version.
No longer top-of-the-line in 1962, with introduction of the Dyna-sonic.

Powertone 1964–1970

The Powertone snare drums replaced the Holiday models in 1964, and were offered in the same sizes and finishes. The main differences between the Powertone and the Holiday was the updated lug design on the Powertone and the elimination of the snare bed. Early metal-shell Powertones were steel, while the 1967–1970 models were brass.

Superten 1973–1983
5" or 6 1/2" x 14"
1973: Oval badge, metal shell only
1976: "Big R" badge, metal shell only
1983: 10-ply maple shell added in 5",
6 1/2", & 8" depths

The Dyna-sonic (left) introduced in 1962, and the "skinny drum" (right), in the line from 1972 to mid-1974, both are featured in their own chapters; see pages 179 through 196.

1980s Rogers snare drums made for and distributed by Island Music,
under license from Fender Musical Instruments

Although the quality of the plating and general craftsmanship was rather marginal on these drums imported from the orient in the late 1980s, there were some interesting drums nevertheless. The bottom-of-the-line 5"x14" had a rather generic shell with two rows of ridges around the shell. It was nearly identical to a dozen other cheap imports except for the Rogers badge and lug. The Dyna-sonic (pictured here) was offered not only in the steel shell but also in a plexiglass shell, a maple finish wood shell and a gold plated metal shell, all in 6 1/2"x14". There was also an 8"x14" maplewood model.

photos courtesy Bob Andrews

Apparently only a couple dozen of the RSD-146G gold-plated Dyna-sonics were made for Island Music in the late 1980s. The retail price was a quite reasonable $495.00, but the poor quality of the plating impeded sales.

DATING GUIDE- OUTFITS

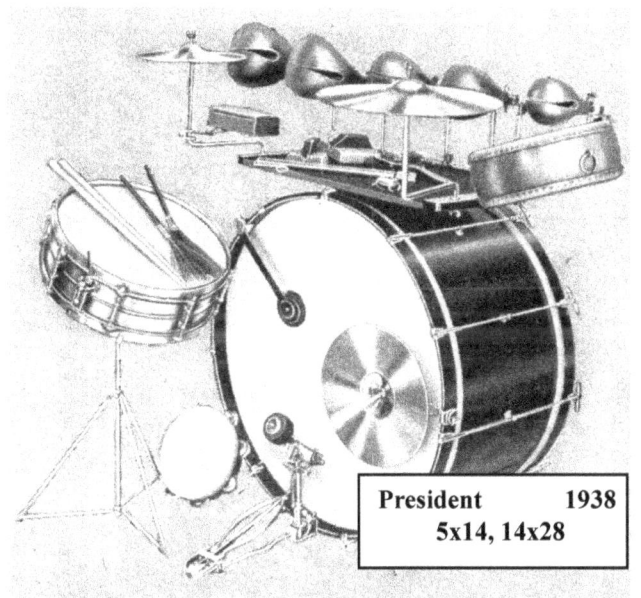

President 1938
5x14, 14x28

Classic 1938
5x14, 14x28

Challenger 1938
4x14, 12x24

Mercury 1938
3 1/2x13, 8x24

DeLuxe 1938
5x14 12x26

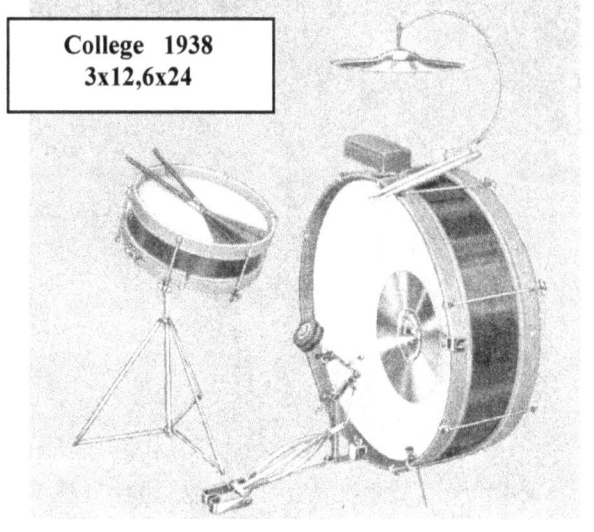

College 1938
3x12, 6x24

Acme 1940 6 1/2 x14, 9x13, 16x16, 14x28

Imperial 1940 6 1/2 x14, 9x13, 12x14, 16x16, 14x28

Outfit #1 1946 6 1/2 (or 7)x14, 8x12, 9x13, 14x28

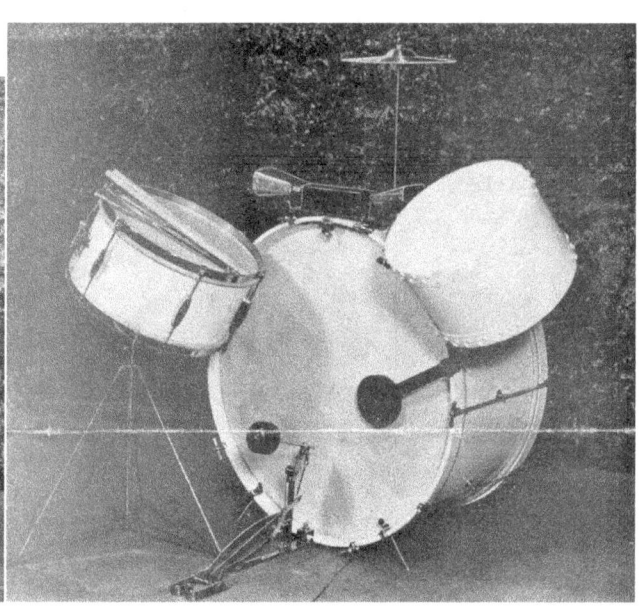
Outfit #5 1946 6 1/2 (or 7)x14, 4x10, 12x24

Outfit #3 1946 6 1/2 (or 7)x14, 7x11, 8x12, 12x26

Superior Economy 1940 5x14, 12x26

Spotlight   1954
Spotlight 5x14, 9x13, 14x20

Scottie   1954–1955
Scottie 5x14, 9x13, 14x22

Holiday   1955–1956
Holiday 5x14, 9x13, 14x22 optional 16x16

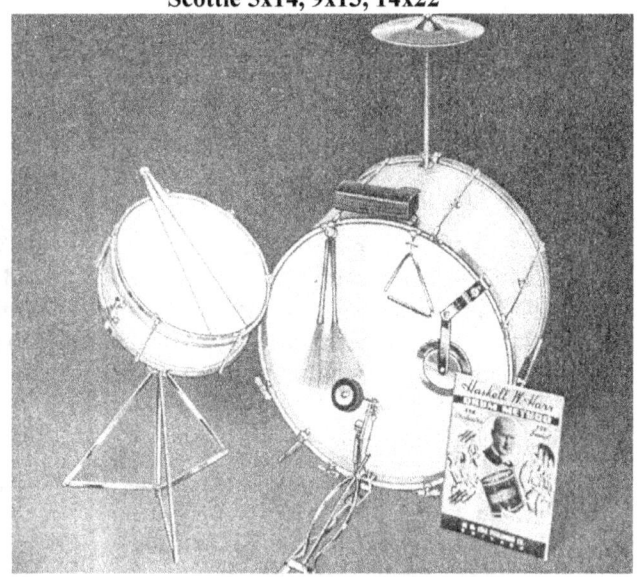
Classmate   1954–1956
Classmate 4x13, 12x22

Mercury   1954–1956
Mercury 5x14, Mayfair 9x13, Mercury 14x20

Mayfair   1956
Mayfair 6 1/2 x 14, 9x13, 14x22

IN RADIANT PEARL and DeLUXE CHROME

DeLuxe "KNOBBY" LEGS

(Also offered with an 8x12 in 1958 as "The Super Constellation")

The earliest Constellation outfits (as pictured here) featured Camco pedals, Eagle badges, and Holiday snare drum. In 1960 the badges were changed to the script logo and the Holiday snare drum was fitted with a Swiv-o-matic strainer. In 1962 the set was shipped with Rogers pedals. Beginning in 1964 the Holiday snare drum was replaced with the Power-tone snare drum and the outfit was renamed "The Cozy Cole Constellation" (pictured below).

160

Meteor 1958–1960 Holiday model drums: 5x14, 9x13, 14x22

Skyline   1958–1962   Holiday 5x14, 8x12, 14x20
1958: Eagle badge, 4476 strainer, Camco pedals
1960: Script logo badge, Swiv-o-matic strainer
1962: Rogers pedals

Rocket   1958–1960
Spotlight 5x14, 8x12, 14x20

Starlite   1958–1962
Holiday 5x14, 8x12, 16x16, 14x20   (Camco pedals until 1962)

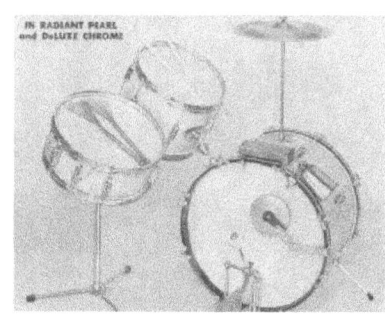

Jet   1958–1960
Spotlight 5x14, 8x12, 14x20

Comet   1958–1967
Spotlight 5x14, 8x12, 14x20
until 1962,
then Luxor 5x14 with
Tower 8x12 & 14x20

Top Hat   1958–1964
Holiday 5x14, 8x12, 16x16, 14x20
until 1964, then Powertone 5x14.
Swiv-o-matic snare holder until
1960, then Camco snare stand.
Camco stands until 1962, then
Rogers.

162

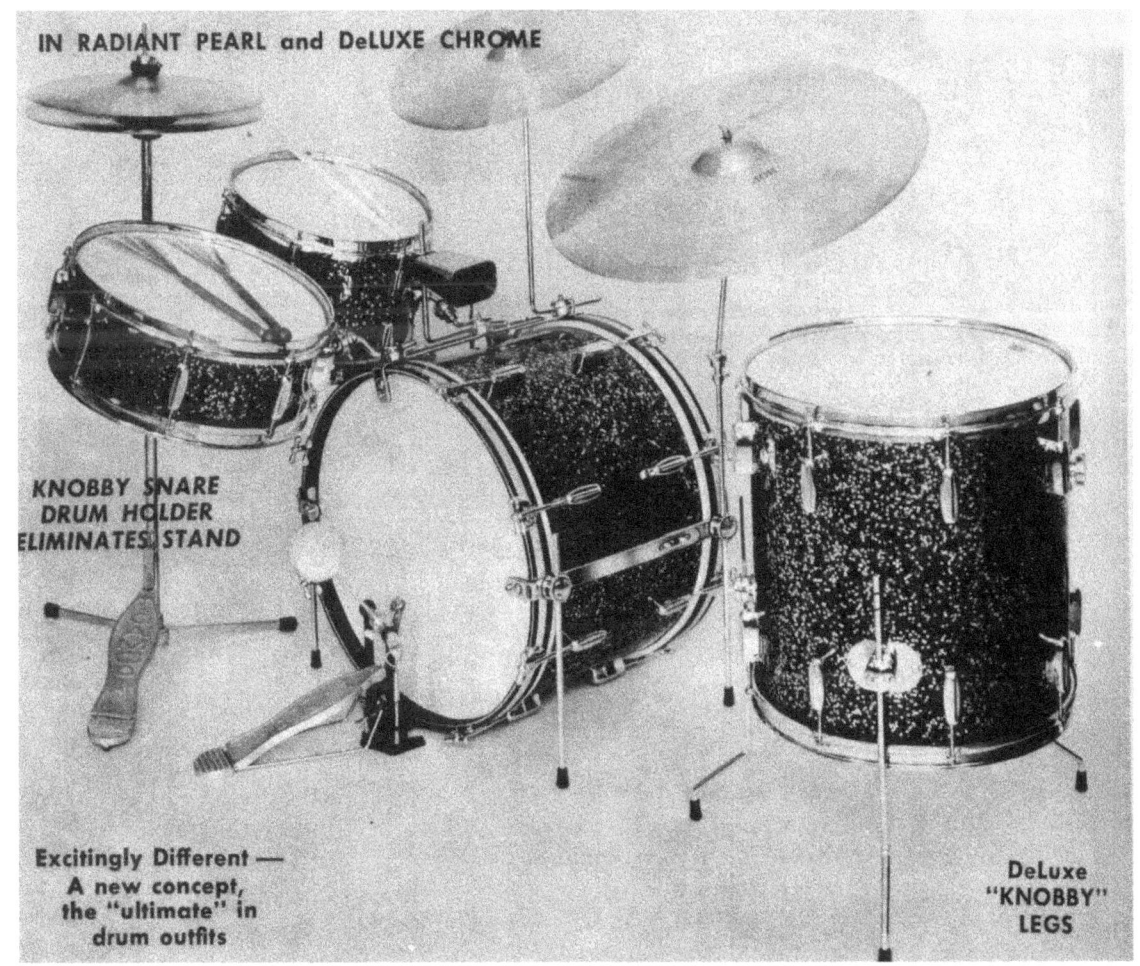

Stagetime 1958 (Also sold without the floor tom as the "Encore" outfit from 1958–1960)
Holiday 5x14, 9x13, 16x16, 14x22

Knobby Spur Rods

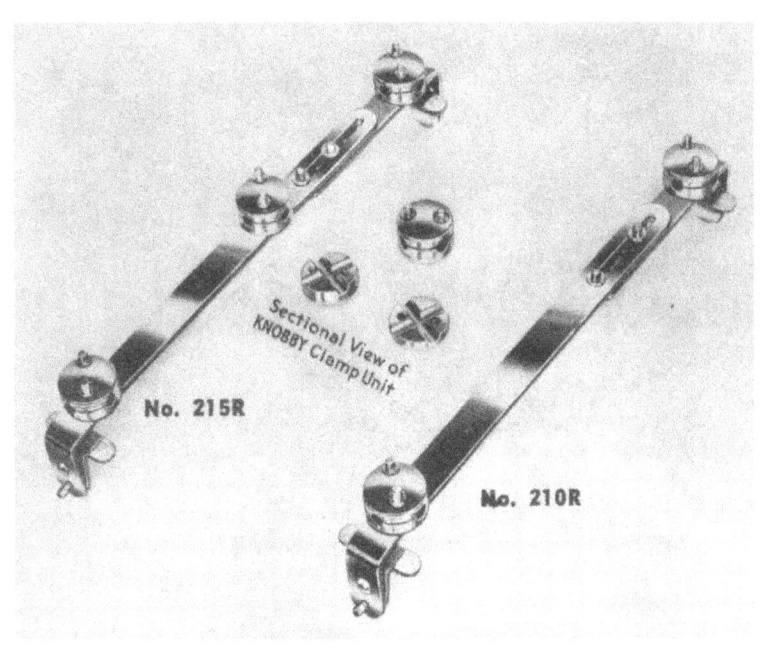

Rogers Wonder Bars

SHOWCASE OUTFIT

The most exciting line in the drum world . . . growing in popularity because of sets like this. Superb Rogers sound, smart and sparkling Rogers styling . . . a terrific set-up at a terrific price. You have to see and try Rogers to appreciate it. Here's why . . . Note how easily this 'Showcase' set converts to a combo outfit. Transfer the snare drum and cymbals to the floor tom-tom and you're ready. Versatility possible only with Rogers and Swiv-o-matic.

← From this to this ↓

"SHOWCASE" OUTFITS

Showcase 1960–1962
Holiday 5x14, 8x12, 9x13, 16x16, 14x20
Camco stands in 1960, Rogers stands in 1962

Cozy Cole 1960–1962 Holiday 5x14, 8x12, 9x13, (2) 16x16, 14x20
Camco pedals in 1960, Rogers pedals in 1962

Festival   1960–1962
Holiday 5x14, 8x12, 14x14, 14x20
Holiday 5x14, 8x12, 16x16, 14x20
(The 5x14 and 14x20 were catalogued as "The Planet")

Orbit   1960–1962
Holiday 5x14, 8x12, 14x14, 12x20
Holiday 5x14, 9x13, 16x16, 12x22

Video   1960–1962
Luxor 5x14, Tower 8x12, 14x20
Luxor 5x14, Tower 9x13, 14x22

Parklane Cocktail Outfit 1960–1962
Holiday 5x14, 8x12 or 9x13, 16x16

Astoria Cocktail Outfit 1962–1964
Holiday 5x14, 16x16

Bandstand   1960–1962
Tower 5x14, 9x13, 12x15, 14x22

Classmate   1960–1962
Classmate 4x13, 14x20

Clipper   1960–1964
Luxor 5x14, Mercury 14x20

Luxor   1960–1964
Luxor 5x14, 8x12, Mercury 14x20

Playboy   1962
Holiday 5x14, 8x12, 14x14, 14x20
Holiday 5x14, 9x13, 16x16, 14x22

Buddy Rich Three-Star   1964
Powertone 5x14, Holiday 8x12, 14x20

Buddy Rich "Celebrity" 1962–1970 (Catalogued 1968–1970 without the Buddy Rich name)
1962: Holiday 5x14, 9x13, 16x16, 14x22 or Dyna-sonic 5x14 with Holiday 8x12, 14x14 or 16x16, 14x20
1964–1967: Beavertail lugs, Dyna-sonic 5x14 metal or wood, Holiday 9x13, 16x16, 14x22
1970: Powertone, not Holiday

Buddy Rich "Headliner"   1962–1970 (catalogued from 1968–1970 without the Buddy Rich name)
1962: Holiday 5x14, 8x12 or 9x13, 14x14 or 16x16, 14x20 or 14x22
1964: beavertail lugs 1970: Holiday drums replaced by Powertone models

Louis Bellson Twin Bass   1962 (above) – 1964 (below) – 1970
1962: Holiday 5x14, (2) 8x12 or 9x13, 14x14 or 16x16, (2) 14x20 or 14x22
1964: Dyna-sonic 5x14, Holiday 9x13, 16x16, (2) 14x22
1970: Clamp for hi-hat added

Delta   1967
Luxor 5x14, Tower 8x12, 14x14

Citadel   1967–1970
Dyna-sonic 5x14, Holiday 8x12, 14x14, 14x20
1970; Powertones instead of Holidays

Swingtime   1964
Powertone 5x14, Holiday 8x12, 16x16, 14x20

Louis Bellson Citation   1964
Holiday 5x14, 8x12, 14x14, 14x20

Viking   1964
Powertone 5x14, Holiday 8x12, 14x20

Timbale Twin   1967–1970
Powertone 5x14, timbales, Holiday 16x16, (2) 14x20

Dave Clark Londoner
Introduced in 1967, this set did not appear in the 1968 catalog but was brought back in 1970 without the Dave Clark name. Powertone 5x14, 8x12, 9x13, 16x16, 14x20

Roy Burns Starlighter   1967–1970
Dyna-sonic 5x14, Holiday 9x13, 16x16, 14x22
Offered in 1970 as "Constellation" with Powertone snare, 2 cymbal holders on bass drum, lightweight snare stand

Starlighter IV 1973–1977
1973 Swiv-o-matic hardware, 1976 Memriloc hardware
5x14, 9x13, 16x16, 14x22

Londoner V 1972–1977
1973 Swiv-o-matic hardware, 1976 Memriloc;
5x14, 8x12, 9x13, 16x16, 14x22

Ultra-Power 1970–1977
(named Ultra-Power VII 1973–1977)
Dyna 5x14, Powertone 9x13, 10x14, 16x16, 16x18, (2) 14x24
Toms were mounted on a Swiv-o-matic dual tom stand until 1976, then bass drum mounted with Memriloc hardware.

Studio X
1974–1974 with Swiv-o-matic hardware
1976-1977 with Memriloc hardware
Dyna-sonic 5x14, 6x8, 7x10, 8x12, 9x13, 10x14, 16x16, 16x18, (2) 14x22

Ultrapower IX   1973
Dyna-sonic 5x14, 8x12, 9x13, 10x14,
12x15, 16x16, 16x18, 14x24

Studio VII   1973
Superten 5x14, 6x8, 7x10, 8x12,
9x13 (all concert toms) 16x16, 14x22

Londoner VI   1973–1977
Superten 5x14, 8x12, 9x13,
10x14, 16x16, 14x22

Compact X   1973
Supterten 5x14, 6 & 8 bongos, 7x10, 8x12,
9x13, 10x14, 12x15, (all concert toms),
(2) 14x20

Ultra-Power VIII   1976–1980
Dyna-sonic 5x14, 8x12, 9x13, 10x14,
12x15, 16x16, (2) 14x24

Londoner VII   1976–1977
Dyna-sonic 5x14, 8x12, 9x13, 10x14,
12x15, 16x16, 14x22

Headline IV 1976–1977
Dyna-sonic 5x14, 8x12, 16x16, 14x20

Heritage   1983
Dyna-sonic 5x14, 10x10, 12x12,
14x14, 16x18

Super Londoner V   1983
Dyna-sonic 5x14, 9x13, 10x14,
16x18, 14x24

The Beat   1983
Superten 5x14, 12x12, 14x14, 16x18,
18x22

THE ROGERS MALLETRON

The Rogers Malletron was an electronic marimba. The brainchild of mallet instrument genius Clair Musser, this instrument unfortunately does not mark a shining moment in his career. Both Don Canedy and Ben Strauss recalled that although the concept seemed viable, the instrument as it was brought to market simply did not work. The problem was that there were no dynamics; the player had a very narrow range to play in. If the player exceeded that range and played too loudly, the instrument choked. Mallet percussionists found this to be unacceptable and the Malletron (introduced in 1970) was discontinued by June of 1972. Remo Belli then took an interest in the development of the Malletron. Canedy explained to him exactly that the problems were, and Belli thought he could solve them. Belli reportedly spent a significant amount of money on the Malletron before he also gave up.

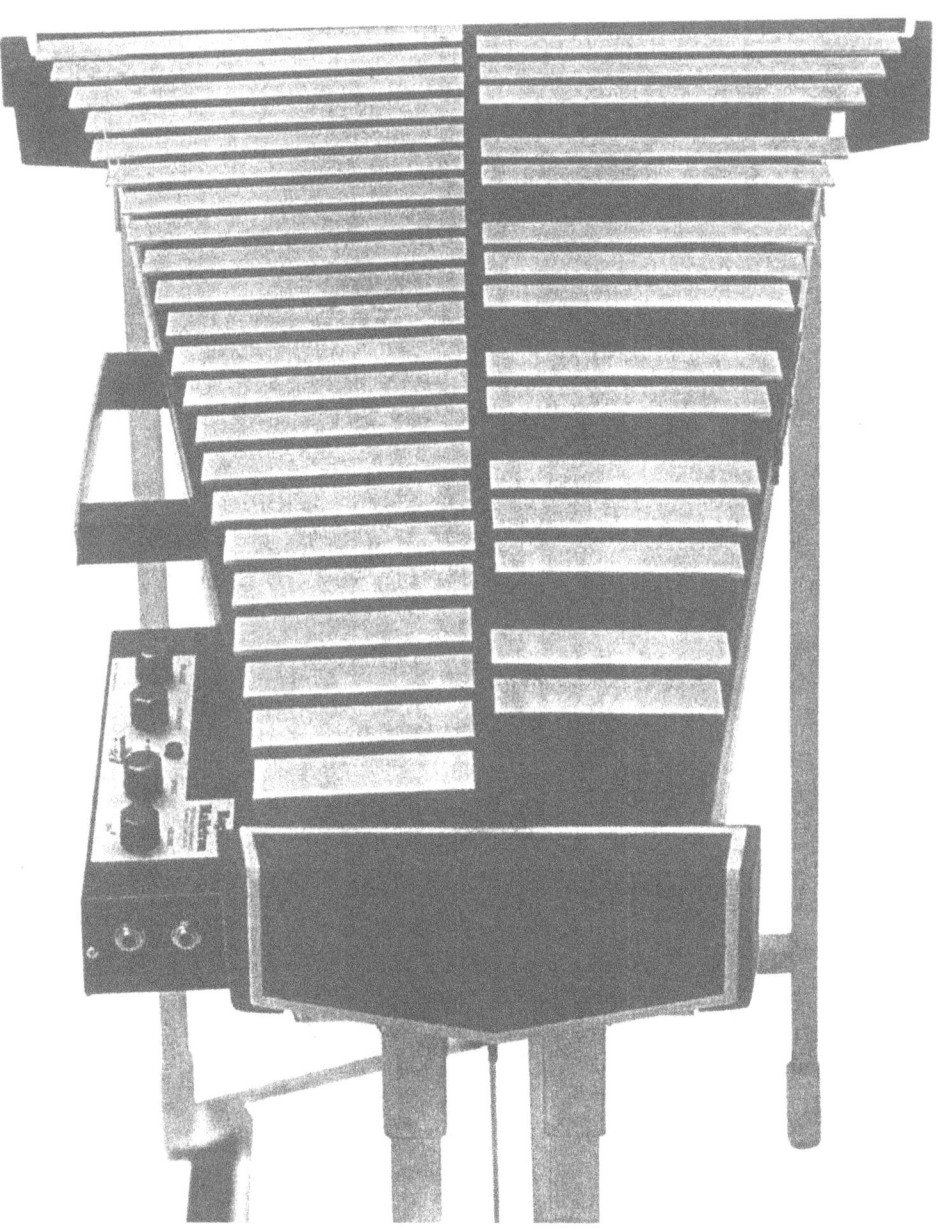

Had it not been for the problem with the dynamics, this instrument may have been a huge success. Rogers had a well-balanced marketing strategy for the Malletron, presenting it as an instrument equally suited to beginners playing with headphones or amplified soloists fronting orchestras. The Malletron was compatible with the Rhodes KBS System which featured a console for the instructor which could single out one connected instrument, a group, or the whole class.

ROGERS TIMPANI

Rogers distributed Jenco tympani for several years in the early 1960s in the interest of becoming a full-line percussion supplier. (They also distributed chimes and piston bugles.) A number of timpani designs were considered through the 1960s, including an all-wooden timpany. It was not until the 1970s that Rogers finally developed an all-new timp design, shown on the next two pages.

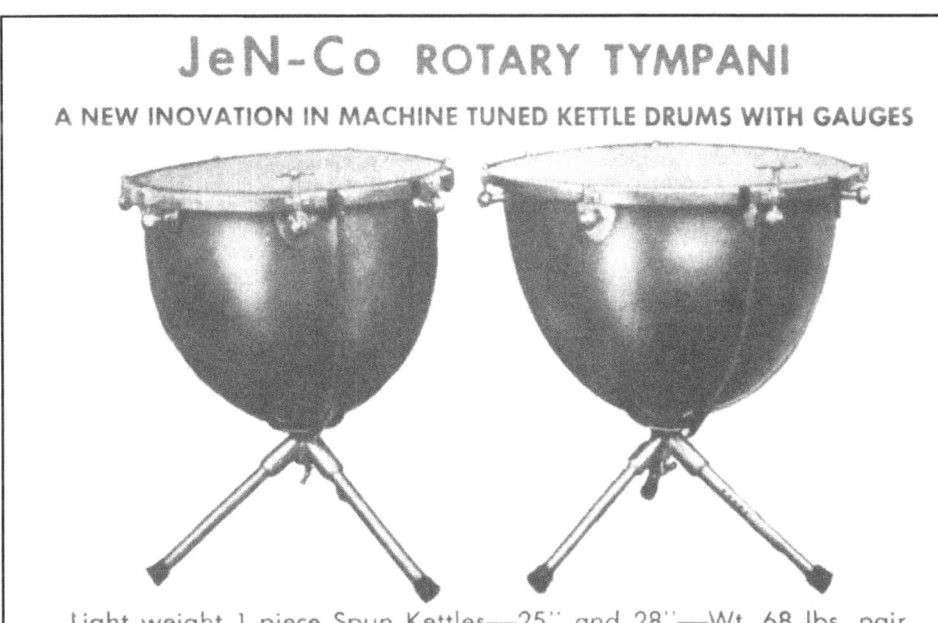

JeN-Co tympani as featured in Rogers catalogs from 1960 to 1962

Prototype of wooden timpany, built by Leonard Rhoades and Joe Thompson in the late 1960s.

ROGERS TIMPANI

Ben Strauss: "Don Canedy helped Joe Thompson design timpani that reduced the problem of tuning. We used the key tension rods; you would tighten them all the way down, which was the opposite approach from the conventional. When you found a spot that was a little sharp, then you'd back off a little.

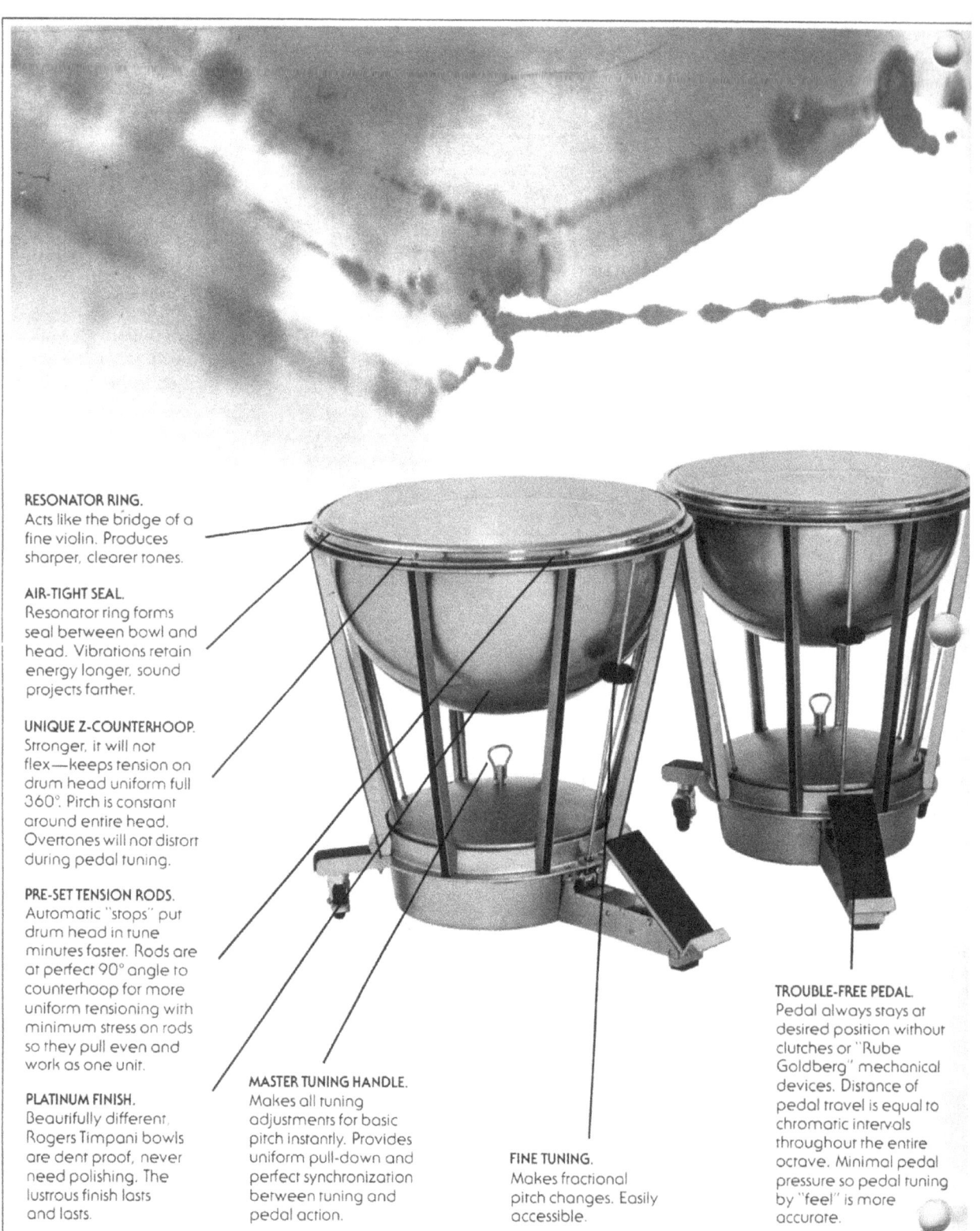

RESONATOR RING. Acts like the bridge of a fine violin. Produces sharper, clearer tones.

AIR-TIGHT SEAL. Resonator ring forms seal between bowl and head. Vibrations retain energy longer, sound projects farther.

UNIQUE Z-COUNTERHOOP. Stronger, it will not flex—keeps tension on drum head uniform full 360°. Pitch is constant around entire head. Overtones will not distort during pedal tuning.

PRE-SET TENSION RODS. Automatic "stops" put drum head in tune minutes faster. Rods are at perfect 90° angle to counterhoop for more uniform tensioning with minimum stress on rods so they pull even and work as one unit.

PLATINUM FINISH. Beautifully different. Rogers Timpani bowls are dent proof, never need polishing. The lustrous finish lasts and lasts.

MASTER TUNING HANDLE. Makes all tuning adjustments for basic pitch instantly. Provides uniform pull-down and perfect synchronization between tuning and pedal action.

FINE TUNING. Makes fractional pitch changes. Easily accessible.

TROUBLE-FREE PEDAL. Pedal always stays at desired position without clutches or "Rube Goldberg" mechanical devices. Distance of pedal travel is equal to chromatic intervals throughout the entire octave. Minimal pedal pressure so pedal tuning by "feel" is more accurate.

ROGERS TIMPANI

It was a very simplified method. The goal for Joe and Don was to provide timpani that schools did not have to spend hours tuning. Each drum had a range of an octave. I don't know if any timpani out there today have that, but at that time no other timpani on the market had that range."

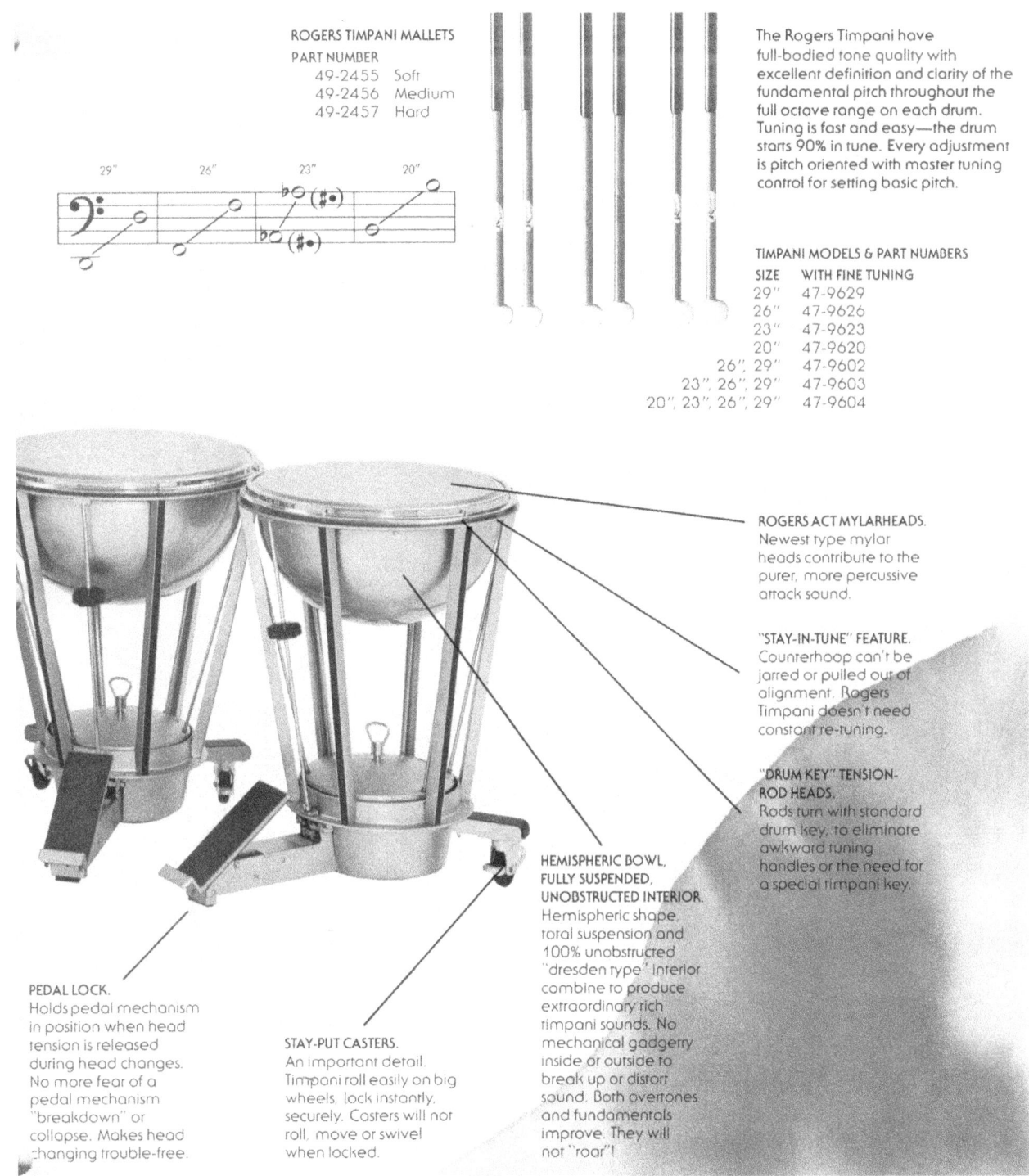

ROGERS TIMPANI MALLETS
PART NUMBER
49-2455 Soft
49-2456 Medium
49-2457 Hard

The Rogers Timpani have full-bodied tone quality with excellent definition and clarity of the fundamental pitch throughout the full octave range on each drum. Tuning is fast and easy—the drum starts 90% in tune. Every adjustment is pitch oriented with master tuning control for setting basic pitch.

TIMPANI MODELS & PART NUMBERS

SIZE	WITH FINE TUNING
29"	47-9629
26"	47-9626
23"	47-9623
20"	47-9620
26", 29"	47-9602
23", 26", 29"	47-9603
20", 23", 26", 29"	47-9604

ROGERS ACT MYLAR HEADS. Newest type mylar heads contribute to the purer, more percussive attack sound.

"STAY-IN-TUNE" FEATURE. Counterhoop can't be jarred or pulled out of alignment. Rogers Timpani doesn't need constant re-tuning.

"DRUM KEY" TENSION-ROD HEADS. Rods turn with standard drum key, to eliminate awkward tuning handles or the need for a special timpani key.

HEMISPHERIC BOWL, FULLY SUSPENDED, UNOBSTRUCTED INTERIOR. Hemispheric shape, total suspension and 100% unobstructed "dresden type" interior combine to produce extraordinary rich timpani sounds. No mechanical gadgetry inside or outside to break up or distort sound. Both overtones and fundamentals improve. They will not "roar"!

PEDAL LOCK. Holds pedal mechanism in position when head tension is released during head changes. No more fear of a pedal mechanism "breakdown" or collapse. Makes head changing trouble-free.

STAY-PUT CASTERS. An important detail. Timpani roll easily on big wheels, lock instantly, securely. Casters will not roll, move or swivel when locked.

ROGERS BUDGET/IMPORT OUTFITS

In an attempt to deal with competitive pressure from the Orient, Rogers began to import drums (and hardware) in the late 1960s. The first 360 and 380 series drums (pictured below) were manufactured by Yamaha for Rogers and were introduced in 1968. In addition to the outfits shown there were two other R-360 kits; a five-piece (Double Soul) as well as a four piece with flat-base hardware (The Twister).

"ROCK SOLID" outfit

ROGERS BUDGET/IMPORT OUTFITS

At the same time the "second generation" R-360 and R-380 drums were introduced, Rogers also introduced the R-340 series (right). These were PTS (Pre-tensioned-system) drums made by Remo; "Acousticon" (synthetic) shells with lightweight paperclip-type attachments holding "pre-tuned" heads in place.

SERIES II

The Series II line was designed by Dave Donahoe, the brilliant engineer who also came up with the much-emulated Memriloc series. His directive was to develop an American answer to the imports; low-cost but impressively bulky, lightweight but durable. Donahoe left Rogers immediately after completing the design stage of the Series II. He now reflects that Series II *could* have been successful had it been done correctly. "Even then," he says, "there really wasn't any point! The Japanese were really producing good stuff, cheaply. The Series II (properly made) would have been just marginally better and/or cheaper. Why bother?"

After Donahoe left, Series II grew into a monster that perhaps can be credited with destroying Rogers. Specs were changed to lower costs. Another way to lower costs was to produce larger quantities, so CBS execs gladly accepted boldly optimistic sales projections. By the time Series II was ready for introduction to the sales force and dealers, it was already clear this was a debacle. District Sales Managers, gathered for a presentation of the new line, witnessed a pedal fall apart as it was passed around the room. At the first NAMM show for Series II, the drums were set up in a corner of the booth with no fanfare. Embarassed salespeople reluctantly took a few orders and within weeks their apprehensions were validated as angry dealers began to call about broken hardware.

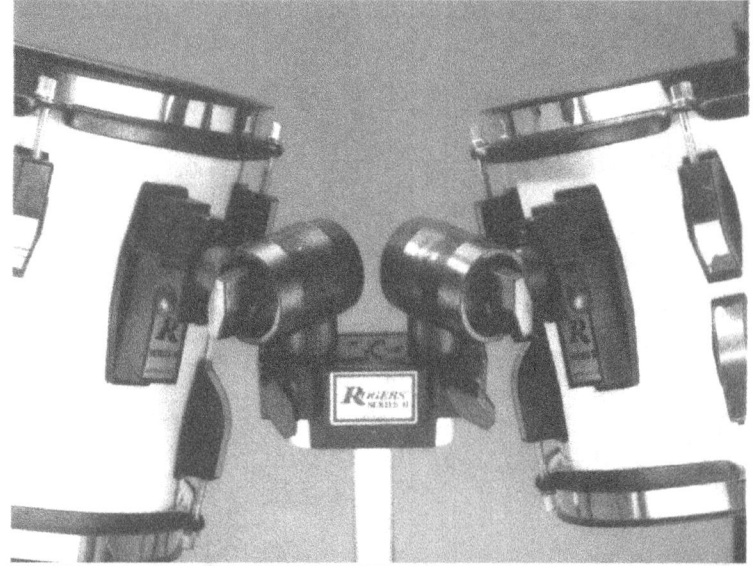

At executive conferences there was an effort to fix blame. Who had come up with the sales projections that resulted in the stockpiling of enough parts to build *thousands* of the outfits? The author learned that these projections came not from a market analyst, but from a *clinician*. He remembers being pressed for comment on the sales potential so he reluctantly threw one out. "The guy who insisted on a number from me," he recalls, "would not later own up to responsibility for the projections, so I kept my mouth shut too."

Division head Ed Lewelleyn (known to show occasional flare) stalked into an executive meeting with a piece of paper stuck to his forehead. On the paper was a large 1 with six zeros. He pounded his fist on the table and pointed to the paper. "I've got a problem!! I've got a *million dollar* problem here, people!!" He was referring to the Series II tooling costs. There was nothing this group or anyone else could do to solve Ed's problem.

THE DYNA-SONIC SNARE DRUM

From the early days of the Grossman Music Rogers era (early 1960s) all the way to the end, the flagship snare drum of the Rogers line was the Dyna-Sonic snare drum. Few drums have a history so filled with contradictions... Most drummers who have had experience with the drum seem to have strong feelings about it, whether positive or negative– some feel it is the most responsive, flexible, and best-sounding drum ever made, others feel it is next to impossible to tune and not worth the effort.

There are even conflicting stories about the genesis of the Dyna-sonic. One story has Henry Grossman quizzing Ellis Tollin (owner of a Philadelphia shop, and sometimes drum consultant to Grossman) for ideas on how to jumpstart Rogers. Tollin responded that they needed a breakthrough product significant enough to attract a big name endorsee. The product and the endorsee would comprise the one-two punch needed to really get Rogers off the ground. In response to the suggestion, Grossman arranged for Ben Strauss, Joe Thompson, and Ellis Tollin to get together. They were snowbound for four days, emerging with the plans for this first Dyna-sonic.

According to Ben Strauss, Buddy was already playing Rogers drums before the Dyna-sonic was developed. Rich was, in fact, the one who suggested the need for such a drum.

Buddy Rich told Ben Strauss he would like a drum that if he touched it, it would respond, and if he played FFF it would not fall apart. He said he did not know of anyone other than Rogers who could make such a drum. Ben considered, and thought that perhaps after so many years it would indeed be possible to change the basic design of the snare drum. So they got busy. Joe Thompson did a lot of research, and the drum was in the making for nearly three years. Joe did most of the design work, though input was sought from many people. Ellis Tollin was very involved; Rogers flew him in several times to offer his perspectives on what was happening with the design. The basic theory was that most snare drums other than the Dyna-sonic were choked.

"When you lay into a snare drum," explained Strauss, "your snares are literally holding the snare head from vibrating. So Joe figured that what was required was a drum with heads that could vibrate freely all the time. Let's say you take a drum and tune it up like a tenor drum. You tune the heads up the way you want them. Now what happens when you engage the snares? You're putting pressure on the bottom head! So the way we described it, in non-engineering terms, was that instead of the snares biting into the head, (forcing themselves into the head), the snare head comes down to just "kiss" the snares. We liked to use the word kiss because it makes it sound light. So– starting from the beginning; you tune up the batter head to the tension you like. Then, our philosophy was, after you get the batter head the way you want it, then the snare head should be a little higher pitch. There are, of course, differences of opinion on that"

As will be seen on the following pages, a great deal of thought and design effort went into the development of the Dyna-sonic snare drum. The fundamental concept the developers were dealing with was the fact that with tradional drums of the day, the snares were pulled into the head. Most snare drums had rather deep "snare beds", the portion of the drum shell which was cut away to the snares could maintain uniform contact with the head when they bowed in the middle as they were pulled upward more tightly from both ends.

As Ben Strauss explains; "My question always was "What happens to the snare head when you do that?" Everyone knows what happens to the top head when you put an internal tone control in- you deaden it. When you pull the snares into the snare head you do the same thing. We tried to change that, and we did. That's really the story behind the Dyna-sonic. The snare bed is barely perceptible. In the days of calfskin heads, customers often took great care to select matching heads for the top and bottom of their drums. Some even brought in micrometers. I used to point out to these guys that when the matching pair of heads is put on a snare drum with deep snare beds, they will no longer match when the drum is tuned up. When plastic heads came out, those drums with the deep snare beds always had wrinkles in the snare head near the beds unless you tightened those rods a little more, meaning now you did not have even tension. If you want to tune a drum properly, you must have even tension. The vibrations you set in motion when you strike the head must expand out evenly, like ripples in a pond when you drop in a pebble. We actually watched this by using a black light with the white drum head. We reasoned that you did in fact need *some* degree of snare bed to allow the head to vibrate down and touch the snares. We used such a shallow, and graduallly tapered, snare bed that you couldn't even really see it. When Joe Thompson was done with his design work on this he ended up with a snare bed that was only .004" deep. If you've ever worked with feeler gauges you know that .002" is like a very thin piece of tissue paper. You can't see it. The Powertone had a snare bed of .008" which is much less than the average drum of the day. It was built on the same principle.

We used a big perfectly flat surface table with a rotary tool. After we determined that the drum was perfectly level (we had a light shining inside of it in a dark room) we used the rotary tool to cut the snare bed, starting at nothing and going down to .004. Every single drum and component was checked. Every snare frame assembly that was put on a Dyna-sonic was checked against a bead of light; when we put it on a shelf against the light we could see if there was any variation in the distance between the top of the snares and that light. The frame assembly was always kept under tension. We had instant response because we had nothing impeding the head motion. The proof of that is when you simply drop a tick on the batter head. The head will kick the stick back if it's free. If the head is choked it won't kick it back quite as much. We used to check that. We used to get a much quicker stick rebound off the Dyna-sonic than we did off any other conventional drum.

The strainer used on the Dyna-sonic was not designed specifically for that drum, but did have to be modified for it. The strainer was designed in response to what we perceived as a need for a strainer that worked more comfortably than the others on the market. This strainer was built on a roller mechanism; there was a little sleeve that just rolled along the slot, and you could flip it off with just a little finger motion. This strainer was first used on the powertone; the version used on the Dyna-sonic had one difference; since there was no pull on the snares, we added a little notch so the strainer would lock in place. (see page 125)

We put a lot of care into making drums– much more than most people realized. It was very difficult to communicate that to enough people."

Joyce Bashore, longtime Rogers employee: "Every Dyna-sonic snare drum was shipped out so that it was ready to be played as soon as it was pulled out of the box. In Covington one of my jobs was to check over and tune up those drums. After the set-up and inspection every one of them went to Joe Thompson for another inspection. If he found anything a little bit off he would show us what problem he found to be sure we understood."

Was the Dyna-sonic a success? The answer can only be yes. Even drummers who hate the drum must admit that it was an unqualified business success. One source estimates that during the 20 year life span of the drum Rogers sold over 50,000 units.

Did everybody love the drum? As has already been stated, the answer is no. Not even all Rogers endorsees liked the drum. Dave Clark reportedly did not play the Dyna-sonic. Some other Rogers endorsers played it in public but recorded on other models. (It should be noted that the reverse was also true. Jimmy Fox of The James Gang says he played the Dyna-sonic for 99% of his career, even when he was a paid Slingerland endorsee.)

Did Buddy love the drum? Stories about Buddy and the Dyna-sonic abound, with varying degrees of accuracy. A vintage drum magazine carried a quote by someone who claimed Buddy hated the thing. Buddy may even have told someone that at some point; he was, after all, known to have strong opinions which were occasionally subject to change. He did, however, play the Dyna-sonic from it's early developmental stages through the end of his relationship with Rogers. Another story the author has heard was that the whole reason for the Dyna-sonic concept was that Rogers (before their affiliation with Buddy) felt compelled to develop a drum good enough to bring him "into the fold". This was not the case according to Ben Strauss, who remembers that Buddy was an endorsee well before the introduction of the Dyna-sonic, playing the Powertone snare drum.

At one point Buddy excitedly phoned Ben Strauss from Las Vegas. He asked Ben if he remembered the white marine pearl 5" Dyna-sonic Ben had just sent him. Ben cautiously responded that yes, he remembered the drum. (Cautiously because he knew Buddy well and was half-afraid that there was something wrong with the drum.) Buddy proceeded to explain to Ben that it was the best snare drum he had ever played. He was simply calling to let Ben know that they had finally really nailed the essence of what Buddy expected from a snare drum. Furthermore, he was so excited about this drum that he was going to actively promote it. He was going to call every drummer he knew who was in Vegas, and have them come and listen to the drum. Ben thanked him and asked if he could borrow the drum back for a few days after the current gig so Rogers could study it and see if they could spot what it was that made the drum special. Buddy was playing at the Flamingo at the time, and did spread the word about the snare drum. A couple days later he again phoned Ben to tell him he had bad news. He had come to work and found the drum gone. Ben always kept three snare drums ready to go to Buddy, so he offered to bring another one out on his next trip to California in just a few days. Ben stopped off in Vegas, and went to the Flamingo. He was not surprised the drum had been stolen when he found how loose the security was. He was able to walk right through the bar and back to the area where the band was set up with no questions asked. The police eventually found the drum– it had been hocked for $50.00. The guy who hocked it had banged it up and screwed around with it; in the estimation of Buddy and Ben it was not even worth getting the drum out of hock. Buddy told Ben that as good as most of the other Dyna-sonics he'd played had been, *everything* was right on that drum.

Dyna-sonic snare frames

As can be seen below, a great deal of thought and work went into the development of the Dyna-sonic snare frames. The prototype frames below were hand-built, presumably by Joe Thompson. Some of these prototypes had "jacking screws" as shown in the diagram below, drawn by Dyna-sonic researcher Charlie Costello. In the final production model Dyna-sonics, a small bar was cast at the spot where the tip of the "jacking screw" comes through on the prototype. The protruding bar bent the entire snare wire end-plate, causing the snares to bow upward in the middle of the drum. This bowing matched the curvature of the drum head to maintain snare contact across the head.

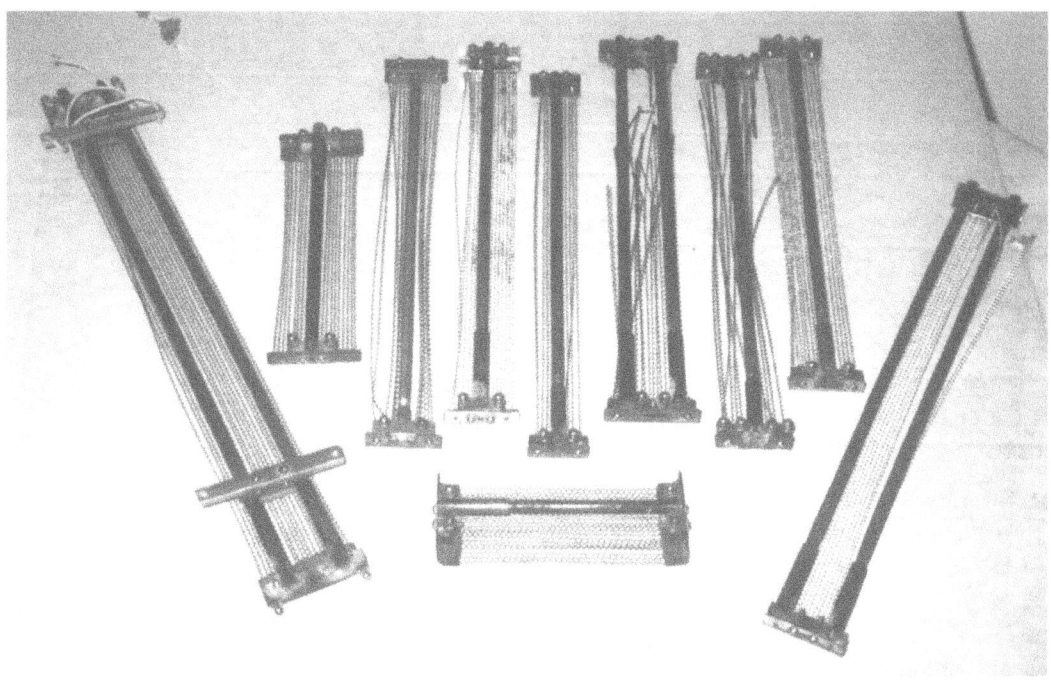

photo by Charlie Costello

More early Dyna-sonic snare frame assemblies, from the collection of Charlie Costello. Note that the top two feature individually-adjustable snares. A few parade drums (with gut snares) were made with this feature.

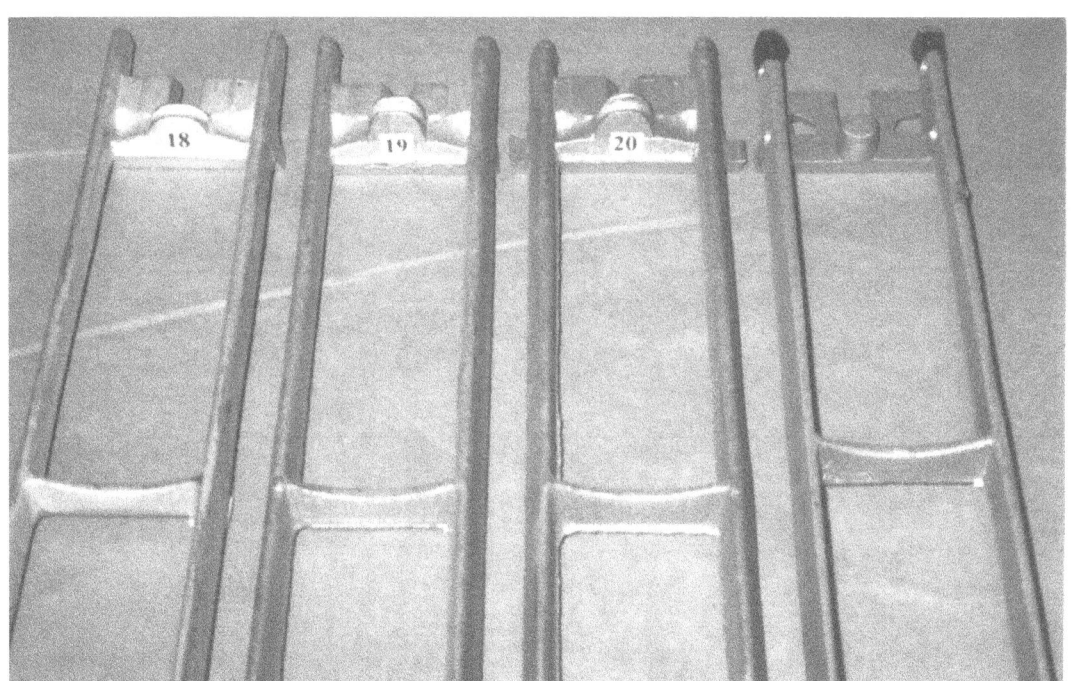

There were numerous versions of the cast aluminum Dyna-sonic snare frame; note the differences in the snare-rope guides. The frame on the right is an actual first-generation production model as used on Dyna-sonics numbered from #1001 to #1999. The other three represent the style that was used on Dyna-sonics from about #2000 to #5000.

Evolution of the wire tensioning device
by Charlie Costello

From left:
A: Prototype

B: As used on the first 1000 Dyna-sonics

C,D,E: The next three generations.

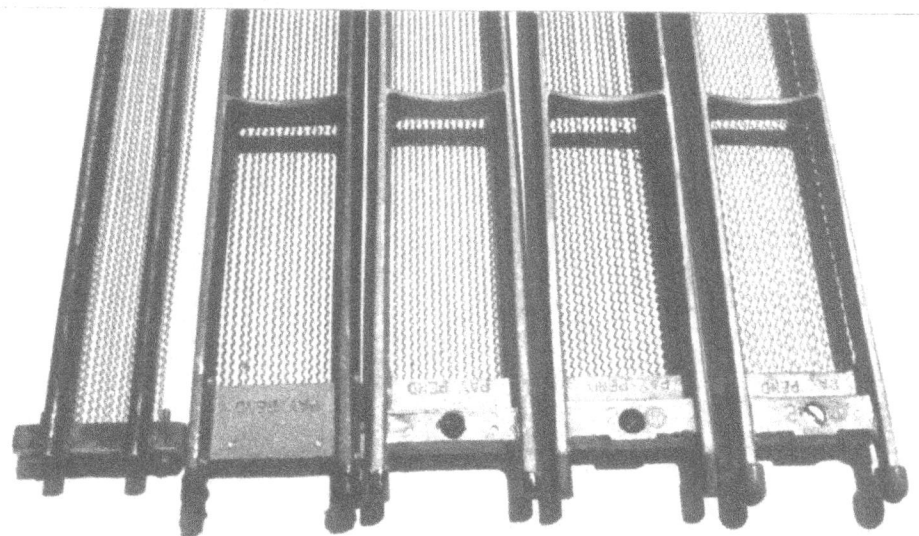

(l to r)
A: Two screws
B: Screw with 2 posts
C: Screw only
D: Height-adjusting center screw

DYNA-SONIC

Joe Thompson made the following points in the text section of his Jan. 16, 1962 patent application:
- A drum is a cylindrical shell having both of its ends covered by heads which together define a "closure containing a confined column of air."
 "Only when both heads have equal areas, and each is under the same tension, is the truest tone quality and maximum volume produced."
- Snare drums to date have always utilized snare beds (the cutting away of a portion of the bearing edge under the head area where the snares pass) in order to insure uniform contact of the snares with the drum head.
- The physical characteristics of the snare and batter heads on a drum with snare beds can never be equal. This results in less than optimum volume and tone, and creates distortion, dead spots, and choking.
- The goal of this invention is to provide a drum with "floating snares" which can be tensioned without putting pressure on the head, on a drum with no snare beds.

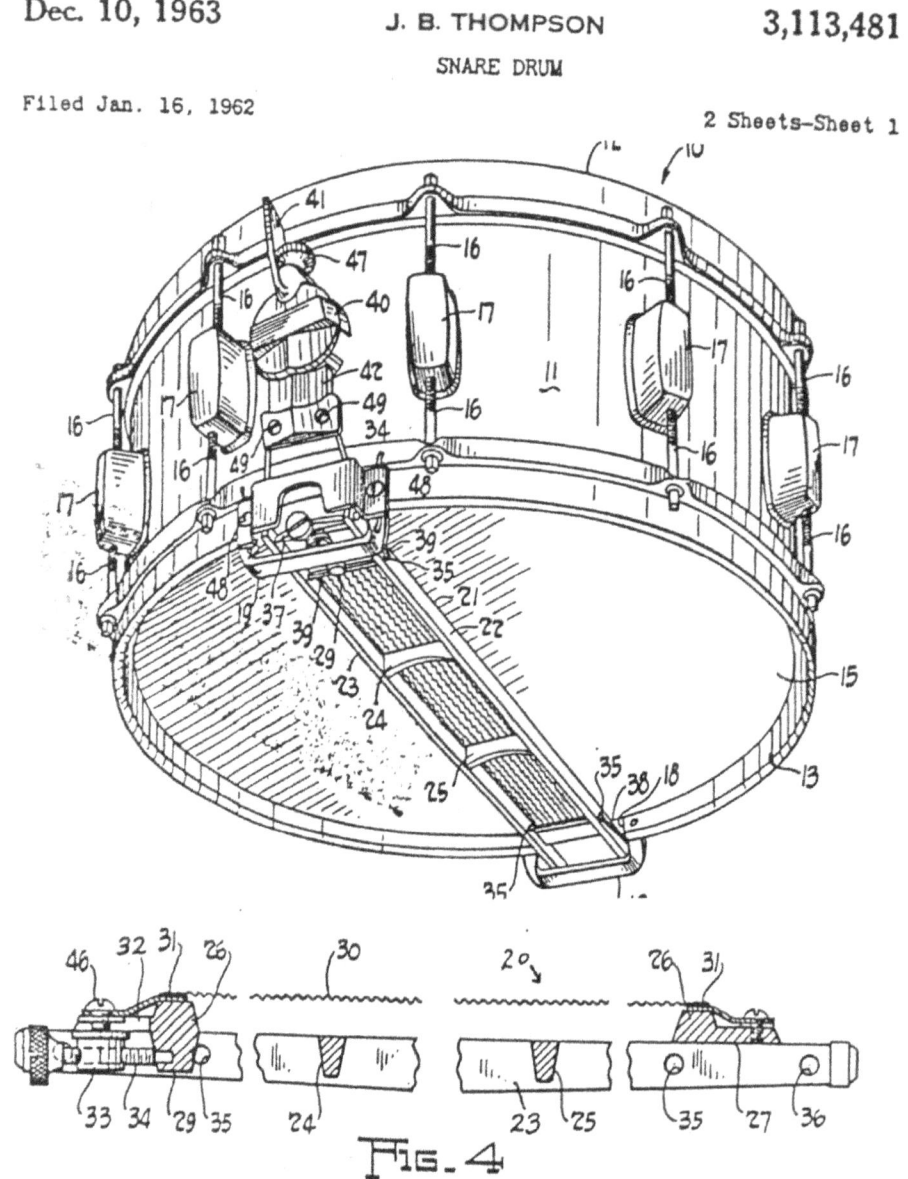

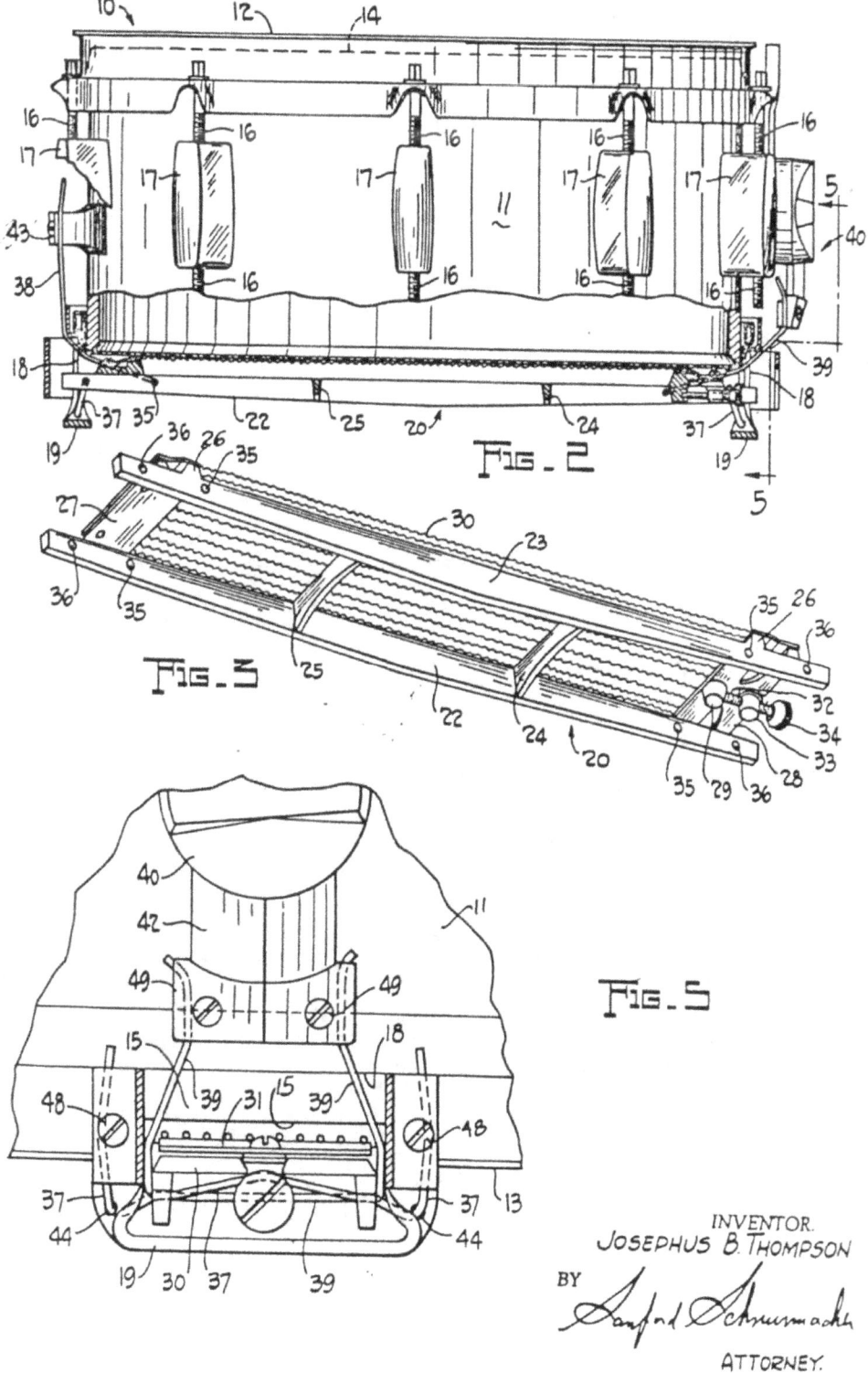

Endorsee Ed Thigpen found that when he was hand-drumming on the Dyna-sonic the snare frame rattled against the snare guards. Ben Strauss relates that when Thigpen pointed out his problem, it became a design challenge which was solved with a system of black elastic bands which kept the snare frame centered between the edges of the snare guards (#37 in the patent drawings, page 202). It solved the problem, but really was unneccessary for nearly everybody else, so the bands were soon discontinued.

Dyna-Sonic badges, serial numbers

The first Dyna-sonic "badge" was the paper tag applied to the inside of the shell, with "Dyna-sonic" typed in. This was used only until the oval "custom-built" badges were screwed to the shell. As can be seen on this tag, the serial numbers of the paper tags are out of sequence with the rest of the Dyna-sonics.

The first metal-shell Dyna-sonics were brought to market in 1961, about three months after the wood shell model. They were the first to bear the exterior metal badge. (Labels inside the shell were discontinued.) The first badge serial number was 1001. This badge was used until about #3000.

Wood and metal-shell Dyna-sonics from very early days up to the "Big R" below all had a script logo in addition to the oval badge.

The majority of Dyna-sonics have one of these two badges. The badge above started around serial #3001. It is unknown when the switch to the badge below was made, but it was probably between 1966 and 1969, under CBS. As can be seen by the number on the badge below (#53639), these badges were used well into the 50000s.

CBS began using the "Big R" badge in about 1976. Later on when Island Music licensed the Rogers name to use on cheap imports, they used the same style badge made of vinyl without the serial number or inscription "Made In U.S.A."

Dating Dyna-Sonics by serial number

Author note: As this edition went to press, I decided that the information I was about to present was simply not good enough. I had updated the serial number chart from the first edition and added a serial number chart for all Rogers drums in the shell section. Before printing this information, I wanted the approval and comments of Rogers expert Kirk Higgins. Kirk responded that the information was simply not reliable. In his opinion a great many more drums must be sampled and in a more formal and scholarly method before such a chart can be useful.

English Dyna-Sonic

There are a few British-made Dyna-sonic snare drums in circulation. (See "English Rogers" chapter.) The drum pictured below is one of ten prototypes made by London's Eddie Ryan for Boosey and Hawkes, the distributors of English Rogers drums just before they discontinued their distribution. This drum has an Ajax shell made of three thin plies of birch and beech, with a very thick reinforcement hoop. The bearing edge is much sharper than the American Dyna-sonics. The inside is stained much darker than the American drums, the lugs are cast, and there is no serial number on the badge.

Dyna-Sonic Wood Shells

The earliest Dyna-sonics were wooden shells only, built on the "Holiday" model shells. (The Dyna-sonic versions were 10-lug drums, the Holidays were 8-lug drums.) These were three-ply shells (maple-poplar-maple) with three-ply reinforcement hoops. These shells were quite thin, and are known to vary in thickness somewhat from drum to drum. Unlike the Powertone drums which were painted grey inside, early ("Cleveland" era) Dyna-sonics were stained with a dark stain that Ben Strauss refers to as a fruitwood stain, and then clear-coat lacquered. (Right) The first few of these drums (reportedly less than 200) had stickers inside identifying them as Dyna-sonics.

Later Dyna-sonics (after serial #7500) were 5-ply (maple and poplar) with 5-ply reinforcement hoops. These drums received a clear lacquer over the natural maple inner ply. (Below, below right.) Charlie Costello speculates that the change from three-ply to five-ply was probably around the time of the change from bread & butter lugs to beavertails, around #3000. The five-ply drums also seem to have individual thickness variances. (The thickness variation observation is from Gretsch expert Lee Ruff who has observed the same characteristics in Gretsch drums of this era.)

In the early 1970s wood shell Dyna-sonics were discontinued, and all Dyna-Sonics were metal shelled until the XP-8 series of all-maple drums of the early 1980s. The last wood-shell Dyna-sonics of the CBS era were ten-ply all maple shells with no reinforcement hoops.

Dyna-Sonic Metal Shells

The Gretsch shell was bent over about 1/2" to form the bearing edge.

The first metal Dyna-sonics were made with thin Gretsch metal shells. It is estimated that only about 200 of these drums were made. There was no bead pressed into the shell, and there were seven lines (cosmetic only) etched into the shell. (The lines were lightly pressed into the brass before the chroming, then enhanced with little "tick marks" after chrome plating.) The first metal-shell Dyna-sonic was serial number 1001. This series numbered from 1001 to 1200.

The next generation of metal shells for the Dyna-sonic were the heavier brass shells with two beads. Ben Strauss points out that the reason for a bead on a drum is for added structural integrity. Rogers felt that their competitors' drums with one bead in the middle rather missed this point because the bead did not add the rigidity where it was needed most– near the point where the shell was subjected to the most torque and stress from the head and lugs.

The first shells produced with this double-bead also had seven etched "mini-beads" at the middle of the drum.

Serial numbers for this series (with the bread and butter lugs); 1201 to 2700.

From #2701 to #14000, cast lugs were used instead of the old brass "bread and butter" lugs, on the "seven-line dual bead" brass shell. The CBS-era drum at right was assembled in Fullerton, California; note that now there are only five lines in the middle. #14001 and up.

Note (photo below) that the bearing edge for the dual-bead drums was formed by bending the shell down and back to the shell making this a much heavier drum than the first generation of the previous page.

bearing edge

shell

Dyna-Sonic Strainers

The "clock-face" throw-off, a 1950s design, was used on early Dyna-sonics. This is seen both with the black and chrome backgrounds (see page 118) on Dyna-sonics up through #5000.

The Swiv-o-matic throw-off replaced the clock-face at about serial #5001 (1965). The Dyna-sonic Swiv-o-matic differed from the standard Swivomatic; see page 118.

1962

 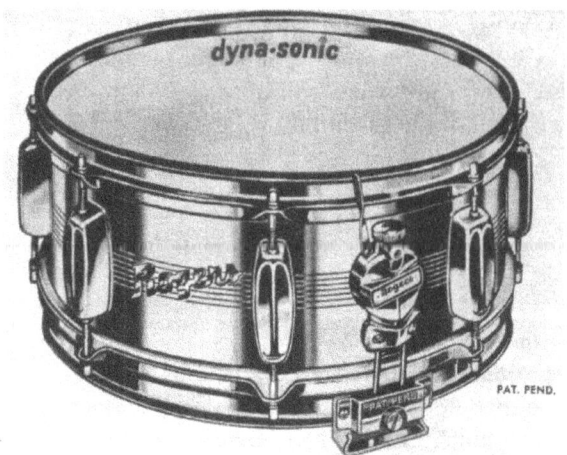

WOOD SHELL MODELS: 5"x14", 6 1/2"x14", 8"x15", 10"x14", 12"x15"
METAL SHELL MODELS: 5"x14", 6 1/2"x14"

1964

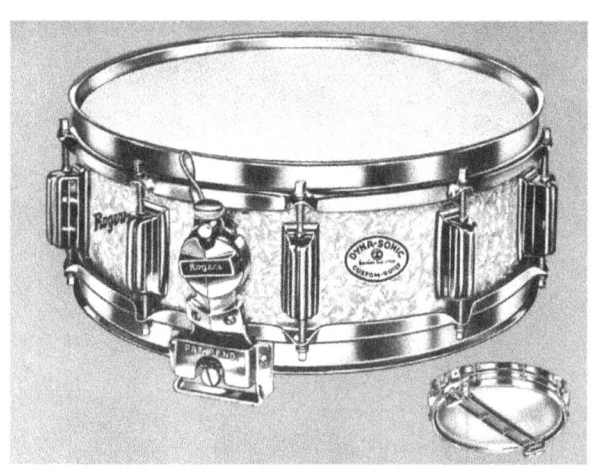 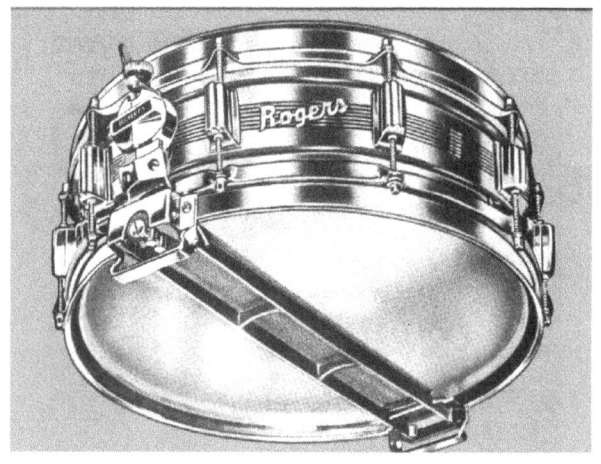

WOOD SHELL MODELS: 5"x14", 6 1/2"x14", 8"x15", 10"x14", 12"x15"
METAL SHELL MODELS: 5"x14", 6 1/2"x14"
CHANGES: Lug design, nylon snare option

The "tall hoops" were replaced by hoops of regular height by 1964– probably around serial #4000.

1967

WOOD SHELL MODELS: 5"x14", 6 1/2"x14", 10"x14", 12"x15"
METAL SHELL MODELS: 5"x14", 6 1/2"x14"
CHANGES: Brass shell, new strainer casting, slotted snare guard (circled, right) gut snare option, screws on badge

 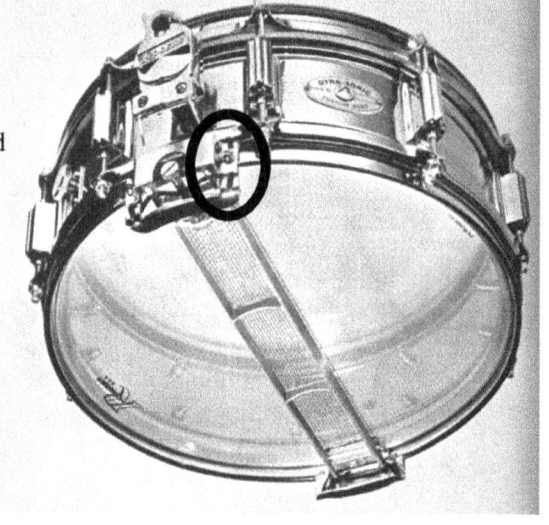

1970 DYNA-SONIC

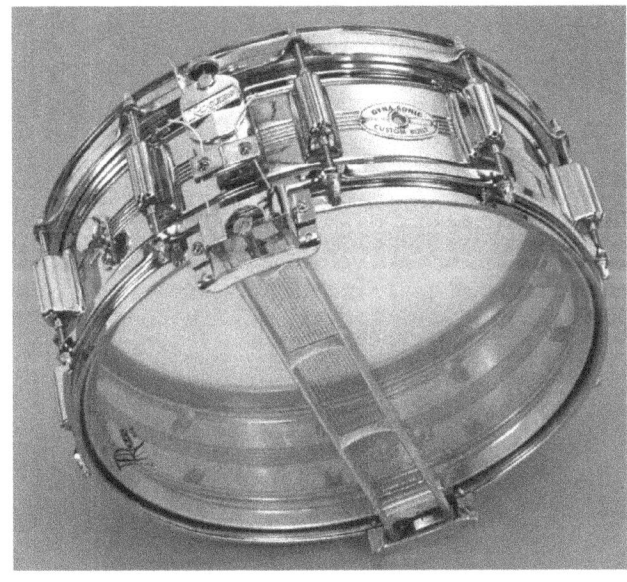

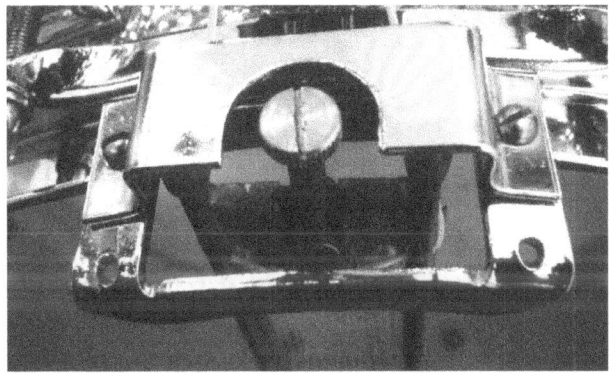

WOOD SHELL MODELS:
5"x14", 6 1/2"x14", 10"x14", 12"x15"
METAL SHELL MODELS:
5"x14", 6 1/2"x14"
CHANGES: All maple shell, redesigned snare guard.
(Wood shell models discontinued by 1973 except for marching drums.)

1976

- Metal shell only, except for marching drums.
- "Big R" badge
- Redesigned snare guard, to allow complete rotation of drum key on tension rods closest to the guard.

1983

Lacquered brass (or chrome-plated) shell, 10-ply maple shell. Isolation gasket/washers between each lug and the shell.

ROGERS PERCUSSION FACTSHEET
HOW TO TUNE YOUR DYNA-SONIC SNARE DRUM

FACTSHEET 01-5

1. Loosen all tension screws (½ turn at a time) in "sequence" (Fig. 1) until all tension on the head is relieved. Then re-tighten all tension screws (again

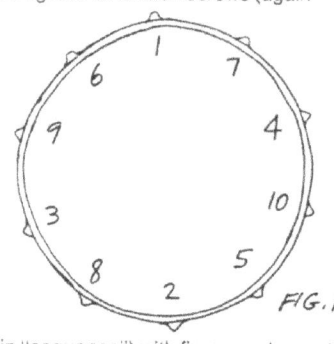

FIG. 1

in "sequence") with fingers or key until the collar on the tension screw seats itself or contacts the counterhoop ear. Having done this, you will have leveled the counterhoop and head onto the bearing edge of the shell. This starts the head 90% in tune.

2. For the top head (Batter head), turn each tension screw with the drum key one half turn in "sequence". Then repeat this sequence with additional one-half turns until you have completed four half turns.

3. For the bottom head (Snare head), turn each tension screw with the drum key five equal half turns in the same manner as described above.

4. Tighten the screw (Fig. 2) at the end of the snare frame (A) all the way with the fingers (without forcing) before adjusting the snare strainer knob (B).

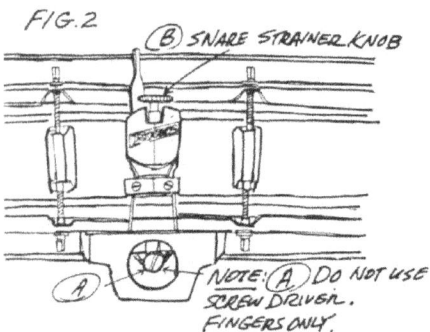

Tighten this screw (A) before adjusting snare strainer knob (B).

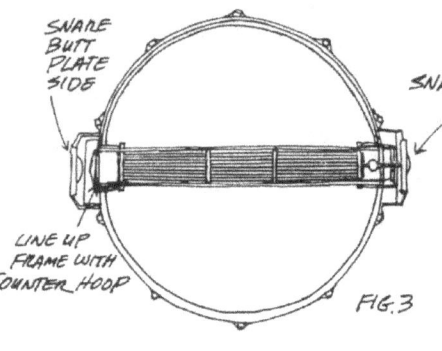

FIG. 3

5. Check to make sure that the snare frame is centered (Fig. 3). Place snare throw lever to the "on" position. Line up the end of the snare frame with the cutaway section of the counterhoop on the snare butt plate side of the drum.

6. Turn snare strainer knob counterclockwise (Fig. 4) until snares are quite loose (tap lightly with drumstick). If snares rattle and are indistinct, they are loose enough.
Now turn snare strainer knob clockwise until rattle disappears and drum sounds crisp when tapped lightly with drumstick.

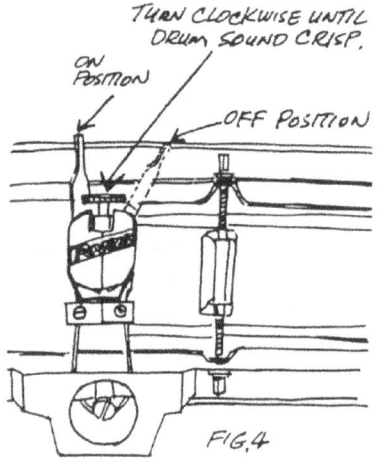

FIG. 4

7. As a final check, tap lightly with a drumstick one inch in from the edge to check for the approximate pitch at each tension screw (Fig. 5).
If any one tension screw sounds higher than the others, loosen it ¼ turn. If any one tension screw sounds lower, tighten it ¼ turn.

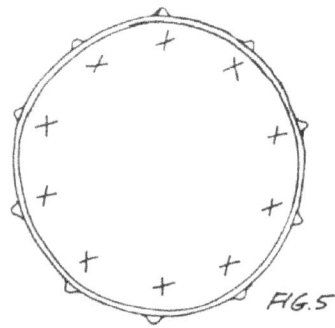

FIG. 5

SUPER TEN SNARE DRUM

To tune the Super Ten Snare Drum, follow Dyna-Sonic steps #1, #2, #3, #6 and #7. Omit steps #4 and #5.

Rogers Drums, CBS Musical Instruments
1300 E. Valencia Dr., Fullerton, California 92631

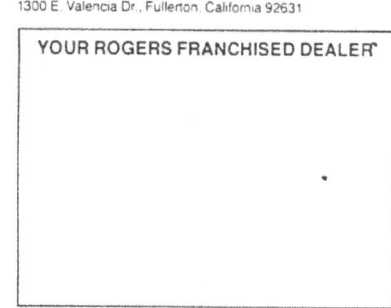

YOUR ROGERS FRANCHISED DEALER

FORM NO. 42-9401 PRINTED IN USA

THE ROGERS SKINNY DRUM

The Rogers "Skinny Drum" patent was granted posthumously to Joe Thompson in 1972, assigned to CBS Musical Instruments. As can be seen from the prototypes and patent drawings, a great deal of work went into the design of the drum. Joe cited the concepts of a cast shell and a tuning flange in patents as far back as 1887 (Boulanger). The points Thompson made in his patent application:

1. The tapered shell and short depth of the shell afforded his drum lighter weight yet higher rigidity than any previous cast drums.
2. The predecessors were too close in size to the size of the flesh hoops used. (His was more of a "floating head" design.)
3. His strainer mechanism was a cast part of the shell.
4. His damper made use of the flange depth for stabilization.
5. The shallow depth of this drum resulted in a very high pitch and a high ratio of "snare sound to drum sound".
6. Instead of using lugs, the tension rods threaded directly into the flanged shell. This afforded the user a visual tuning check.

The final production models were cast at Ross Pattern in Sidney, Ohio, and were introduced in the Rogers catalog of 1970 with a full page spread. The copy touted the versatility of the drum, ideal for recording and concerts.

The most basic problem with the drum (as can be seen in nearly every one that surfaces in the vintage drum marketplace today) was that steel (the tension rods) is capable of cutting aluminum (the shell). When a rod stripped out its shell threads, the damage was permanent.

Sales of the drum were disappointing; it is estimated that only a few hundred of the drums were shipped. By the time of the next Rogers catalog (73-74), the drum was given only a corner of a page. Don Canedy attempted an educational slant on the marketing, trying to sell the drum as a beginner instrument packaged as a kit with a stand, etc., but by March of 1974 the drum was discontinued.

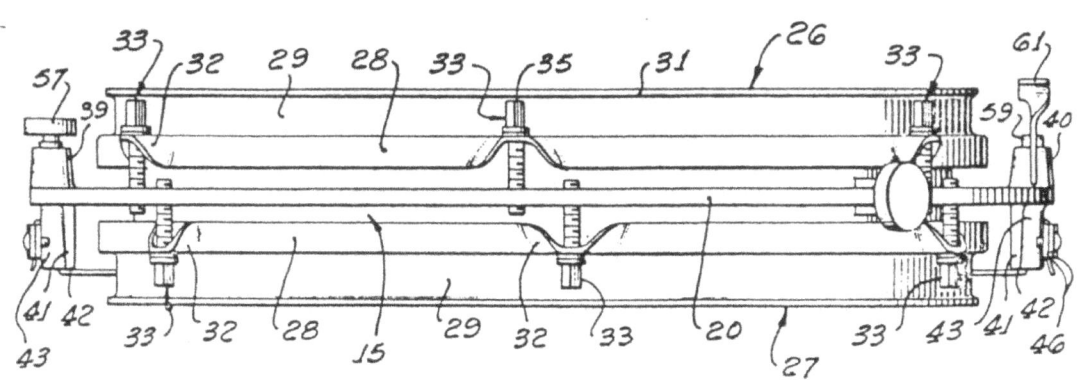

Wooden engineering model, skinny drum

(courtesy Hauer Music, Dayton, Ohio)

Early skinny drum prototype cast shell
photo by Dave Simms

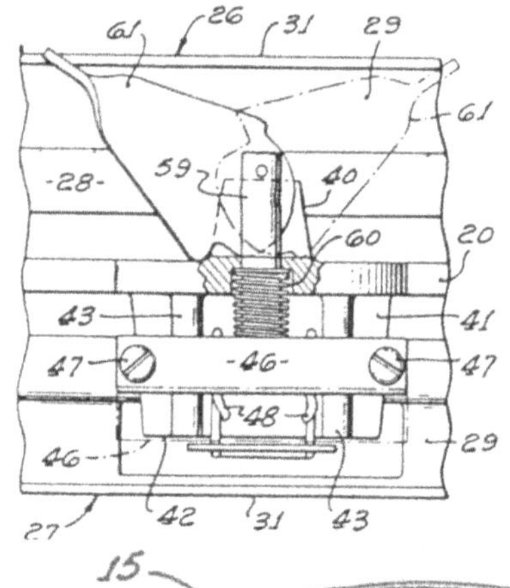

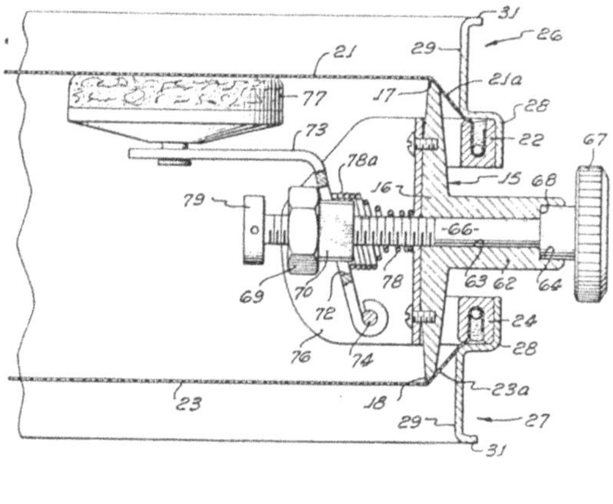

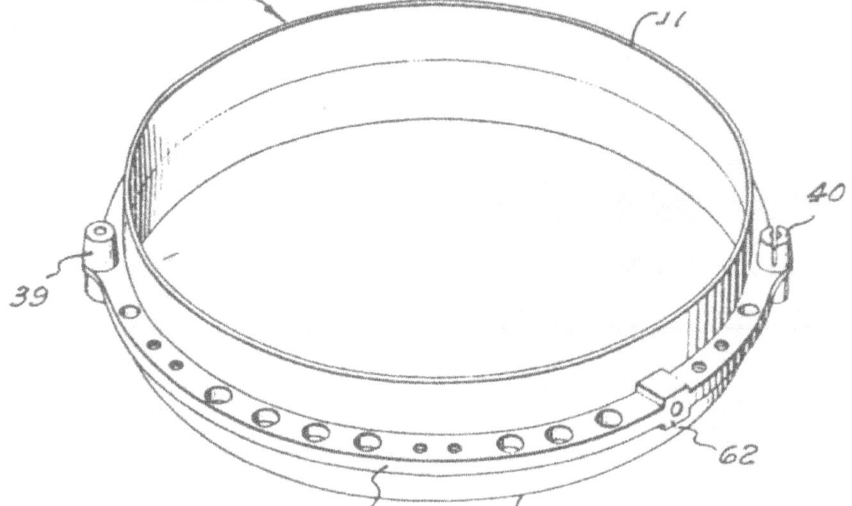

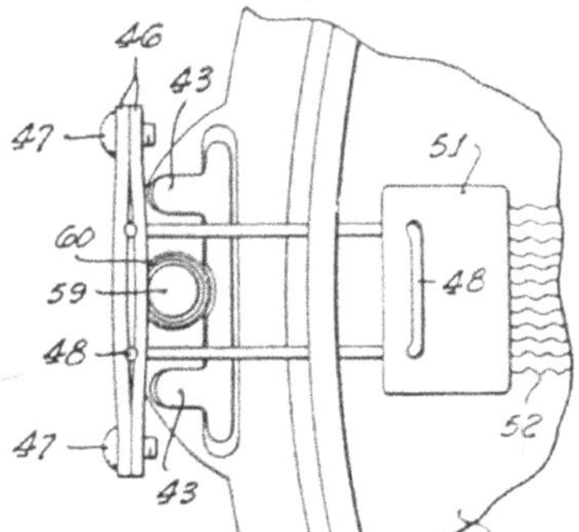

SWIVOMATIC HARDWARE

Swivomatic hardware was so far ahead of it's time that it had no real competition. So many top drummers who endorsed other makes of drums in the late 1960s insisted on having them fitted with Rogers Swivomatic hardware that larger drum shops such as Franks Drum Shop of Chicago ordered all drum sets from all companies with no hardware attached. (Ringo Starr of The Beatles used Swivomatic hardware on his Ludwig drums, and Charlie Watts of The Rolling Stones used Swivomatic hardware on his Gretsch drums.) These shops soon realized that it enhanced their image as full service professional shops to provide the service of mounting hardware, and even ordered Rogers drums with no hardware attached. Though this would seem to be a cost savings for the manufacturers, it actually was the opposite since it meant that the regular production flow had to be disrupted for specific drums.

After the Cambridge Recorder and the Flutophone, Swivomatic hardware was probably Joe Thompson's most significant contribution to the music industry. It was one of the ideas he came up with as he worked late in his laboratory– Ben Strauss recalls that Joe like to work late when there were no interruptions, and they would sit and talk until two or three in the morning.

The ball and socket in itself was not a new concept; what made Thompson's version unique is seen on the patent drawings here– the "ball" here was not a perfect circle which would have eventually slipped when enough torque was applied. There was instead an "equatorial recess" into which the set screws tightened.

> "Originally all the parts were silver-soldered steel. That's a very expensive process. Eventually these parts were cast."
> –Ben Strauss

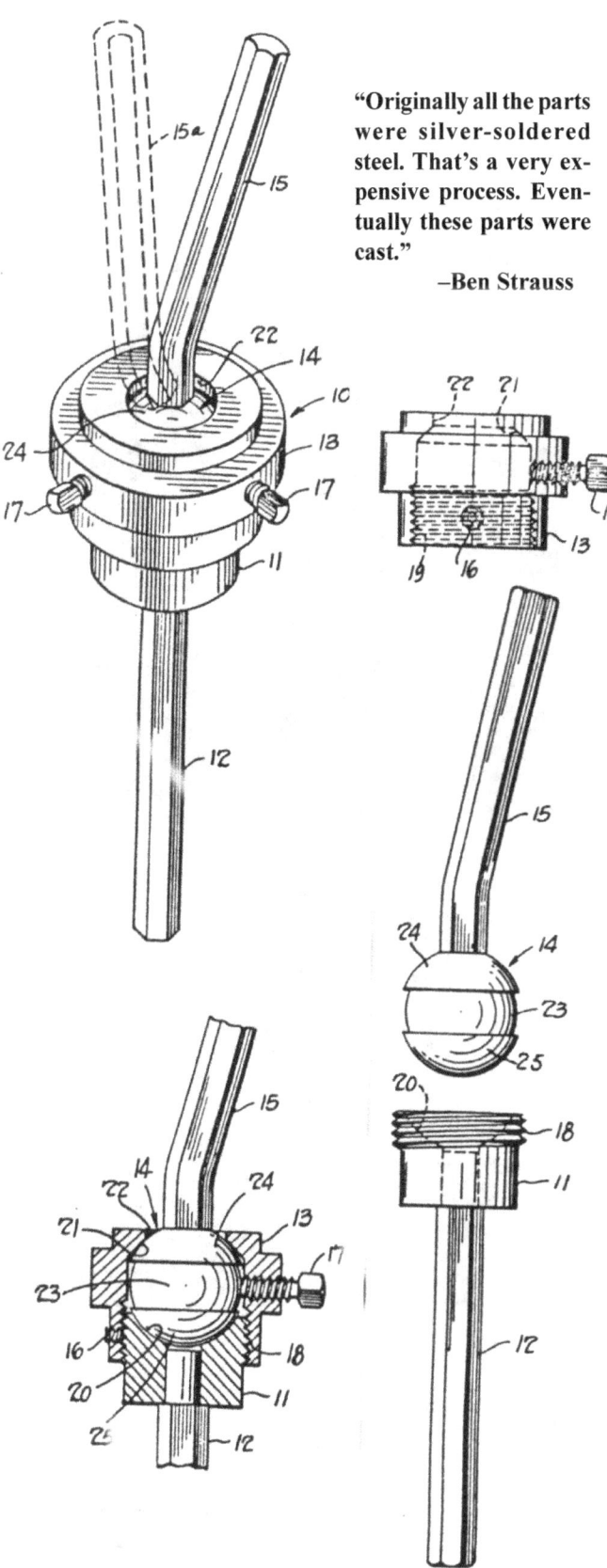

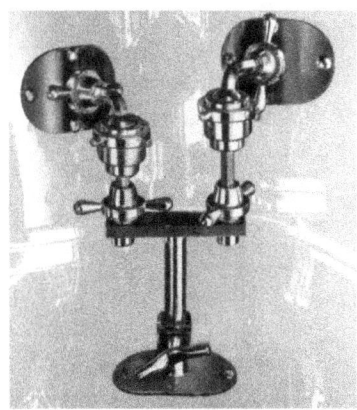

(note: Also see dating guide hardware section and parts section.)

ROGERS PARTS

The parts listings from all Rogers catalogs are included in this section except where there were duplications. The parts listings on this page represent the parts section of the Rogers 1938 catalog.

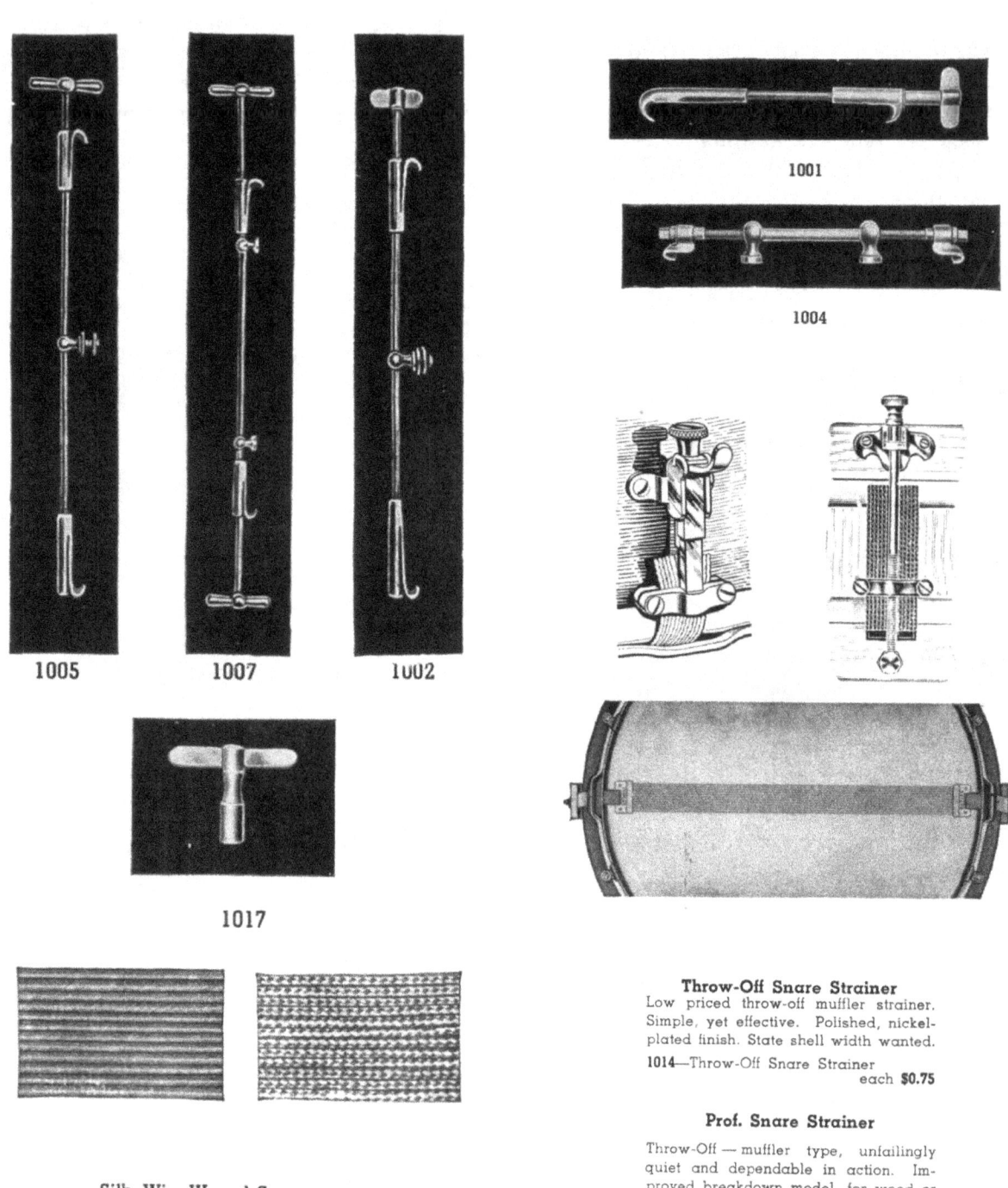

1005 1007 1002

1017

1001

1004

Throw-Off Snare Strainer
Low priced throw-off muffler strainer. Simple, yet effective. Polished, nickel-plated finish. State shell width wanted.
1014—Throw-Off Snare Strainer
each $0.75

Prof. Snare Strainer
Throw-Off — muffler type, unfailingly quiet and dependable in action. Improved breakdown model, for wood or metal drums. Nickel-plated finish.
1013—Drum Strainer..........each $1.50

E-Z Play Snares
(Patent Pending). An improved 12-strand all-metal snare that lies very flat to the head and gives maximum vibration. The snares do not pass the edge of the head. A special feature is the opposite twist of the wire which prevents them from meshing.
1012—E-Z PLAY Snares..........set $1.80

Silk, Wire-Wound Snares
Silvered wire wound over selected silk. Very snappy and responsive. Put up 12 strands to a set, with snare butt.
1008—For Orchestra Drums..per set $1.00
1009—For Street Drums........per set 1.00

Gut Drum Snares
Selected hard finished, natural color gut. Put up 12 strands to a set, with butt.
1010—For Orchestra Drums..per set $1.80
1011—For Street Drums........per set 2.00

ROGERS PARTS

Catalog 59R, 1958

DRUM RODS — HOOKS — LUGS — HOOPS

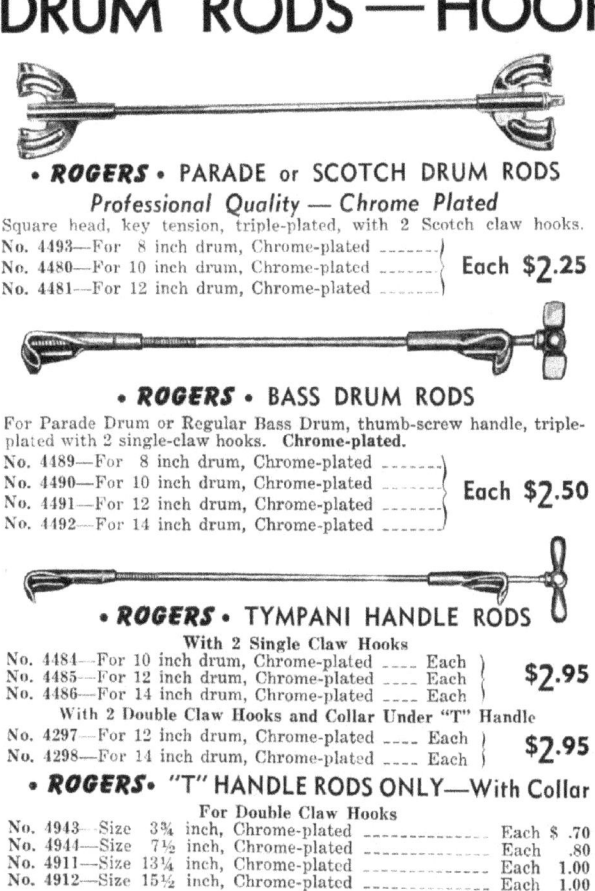

• ROGERS • PARADE or SCOTCH DRUM RODS
Professional Quality — Chrome Plated

Square head, key tension, triple-plated, with 2 Scotch claw hooks.
No. 4493—For 8 inch drum, Chrome-plated
No. 4480—For 10 inch drum, Chrome-plated } Each $2.25
No. 4481—For 12 inch drum, Chrome-plated

• ROGERS • BASS DRUM RODS
For Parade Drum or Regular Bass Drum, thumb-screw handle, triple-plated with 2 single-claw hooks. **Chrome-plated.**
No. 4189—For 8 inch drum, Chrome-plated
No. 4490—For 10 inch drum, Chrome-plated
No. 4491—For 12 inch drum, Chrome-plated } Each $2.50
No. 4492—For 14 inch drum, Chrome-plated

• ROGERS • TYMPANI HANDLE RODS
With 2 Single Claw Hooks
No. 4484—For 10 inch drum, Chrome-plated ____ Each
No. 4485—For 12 inch drum, Chrome-plated ____ Each } $2.95
No. 4486—For 14 inch drum, Chrome-plated ____ Each
With 2 Double Claw Hooks and Collar Under "T" Handle
No. 4297—For 12 inch drum, Chrome-plated ____ Each } $2.95
No. 4298—For 14 inch drum, Chrome-plated ____ Each

• ROGERS • "T" HANDLE RODS ONLY—With Collar
For Double Claw Hooks
No. 4943—Size 3¾ inch, Chrome-plated _____ Each $ .70
No. 4944—Size 7½ inch, Chrome-plated _____ Each   .80
No. 4911—Size 13¼ inch, Chrome-plated _____ Each 1.00
No. 4912—Size 15½ inch, Chrome-plated _____ Each 1.00

HOW TO ORDER DRUM RODS
Give Shell Measurements Only, Without Counter Hoops.

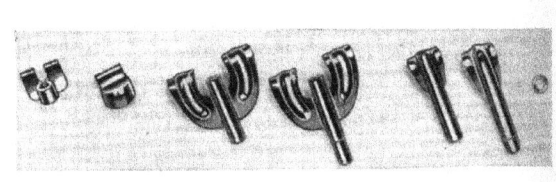

4406 4407 4478 4479 4487 4488 4483

• ROGERS • DRUM HOOKS — CHROME PLATED
No. 4106 —Collar hooks, double claw _____ Each $ .30
No. 4406P—Collar hooks, double claw, threaded insert _ Each .50
No. 4407 —Collar hooks, single claw _____ Each .30
No. 4478 —Scotch type, double claw, plain _____ Dozen 8.40
No. 4479 —Scotch type, double claw, threaded _____ Dozen 9.60
No. 4487 —Single claw, plain, _____ Dozen 8.40
No. 4488 —Single claw, threaded _____ Dozen 9.60
No. 4483 —Washers for drum rods _____ Dozen .35

• ROGERS • DRUM CENTER SUPPORTS
No. 4477—For use with drum rods, complete with screws, washer, etc. Chrome-plated. For snare drum. Each $ .40
No. 4470—Same as above. For bass drum _____ Each .40

• ROGERS • LUGS—LUG SPRINGS—LUG NUTS
No. 4945—Drum Lug, drawn brass, mirror finish, chrome-plated, 2 holes, for single tension, for "L" hoops } Each $1.00
No. 4946—Drum Lug, same as above, but with 1 self-aligning, threaded lug nut and spring, for "L" hoops } 1.25
No. 4974—Same as above, for triple flange hoops
No. 4947—Drum Lug, same as above, but with 2 self-aligning, threaded lug nuts and spring, for "L" hoops } 1.50
No. 4998—Same as above, for triple flange hoops
No. 4948—Lug Spring _____ .06
No. 4949—Lug Nut _____ .20

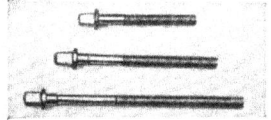

• ROGERS • KEY TENSION RODS
Key Tension Rods, square head, triple-plated. Specify size. (Length from under collar to threaded end)

No.	Size	Doz.	No.	Size	Doz.
4930	1¾"	$1.80	4937	5 "	$3.00
4931	2 "	1.80	4929	5½"	3.00
4932	2½"	1.80	4938	6 "	3.60
4933	3 "	2.40	4939	8 "	4.00
4934	3½"	2.40	4910	10 "	6.00
4935	4 "	3.00	4942	13 "	7.20
					8.40

• ROGERS • THUMB-SCREWS
No. 4232—Thumb-screw for all Rogers clamps. Threaded ½", standard 12-24 thread. Chrome Plated. Each $ .30
No. 4233—Same as above, threaded ¾" __Each .30

• ROGERS • FLESH HOOPS
SNARE and PARADE FLESH HOOPS

No.		Each
4572—For 13" snare		
4573—For 13" batter		
4574—For 14" snare	}	$ .75
4575—For 14" batter		
4576—For 15" snare		
4577—For 15" batter		

BASS DRUM FLESH HOOPS

No.		Each
4878—For 20" Drum		
4879—For 22" drum		
4580—For 24" drum	}	$1.80
4581—For 26" drum		
4582—For 28" drum		

• ROGERS • COUNTER HOOPS
Maple, Lacquered

SNARE and PARADE COUNTER HOOPS

No.		Each
4584—For 13" snare		
4585—For 13" batter		
4586—For 14" snare	}	$2.85
4587—For 14" batter		
4588—For 15" snare		
4589—For 15" batter		

BASS DRUM COUNTER HOOPS

No.		Each
4877—For 20" drum		
4880—For 22" drum	}	
4592—For 24" drum		$5.40
4593—For 26" drum		
4594—For 28" drum		

• ROGERS • WHEEL TUCKER
No. 4599—"ROGERS" Tucker, novel and practical, with wheel _ Each $3.00

• ROGERS • METAL COUNTERHOOPS
Specify Size and Type of Drum
No. 4230—Batter side, "L" shaped. For parade drums, or tom-toms. Chrome-plated Each $5.50
No. 4231—Snare side, "L" shaped. For snare drums, or tom-toms. Chrome-plated Each 6.00
No. 4295 — Batter side, Triple Flange. For parade drums, or tom-toms. DeLuxe Chrome. Each 9.50
No. 4296 — Snare side, Triple Flange. For parade drums, or tom-toms. DeLuxe Chrome. Each 10.00

ROGERS PARTS

Catalog 59R, 1958

SNARES — STRAINERS — TRAPS

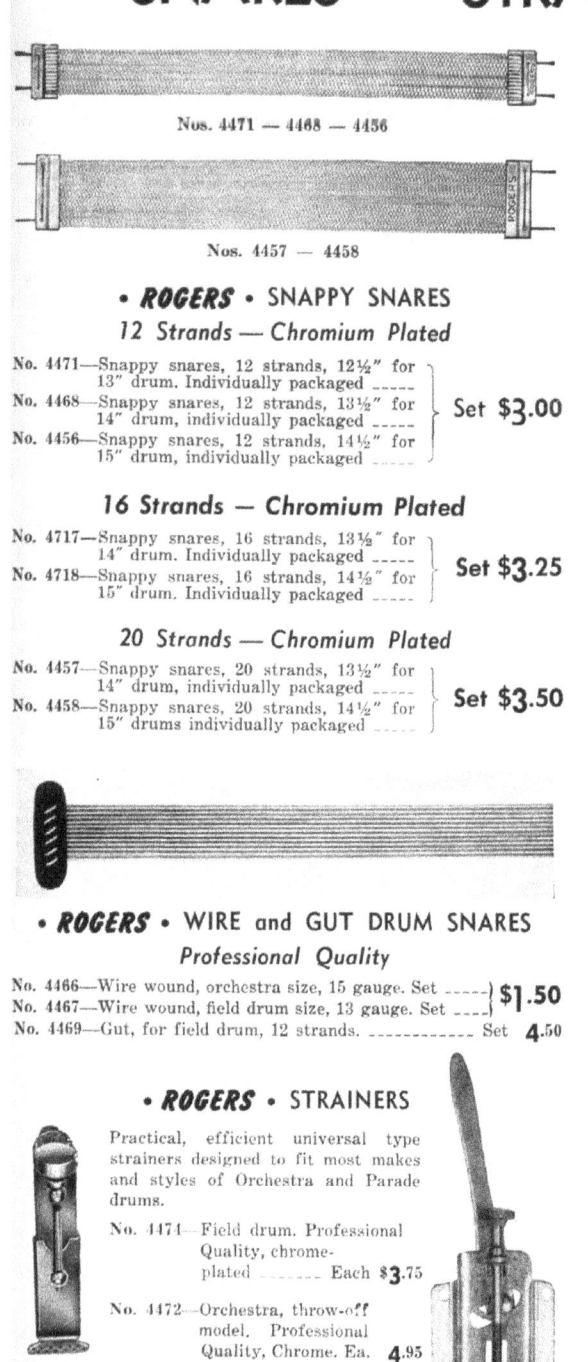

Nos. 4471 — 4468 — 4456

Nos. 4457 — 4458

• ROGERS • SNAPPY SNARES

12 Strands — Chromium Plated

No. 4471—Snappy snares, 12 strands, 12½" for 13" drum. Individually packaged
No. 4468—Snappy snares, 12 strands, 13½" for 14" drum, individually packaged
No. 4456—Snappy snares, 12 strands, 14½" for 15" drum, individually packaged

Set $3.00

16 Strands — Chromium Plated

No. 4717—Snappy snares, 16 strands, 13½" for 14" drum. Individually packaged
No. 4718—Snappy snares, 16 strands, 14½" for 15" drum. Individually packaged

Set $3.25

20 Strands — Chromium Plated

No. 4457—Snappy snares, 20 strands, 13½" for 14" drum. Individually packaged
No. 4458—Snappy snares, 20 strands, 14½" for 15" drums individually packaged

Set $3.50

• ROGERS • WIRE and GUT DRUM SNARES
Professional Quality

No. 4466—Wire wound, orchestra size, 15 gauge. Set ⎫ $1.50
No. 4467—Wire wound, field drum size, 13 gauge. Set ⎭
No. 4469—Gut, for field drum, 12 strands. Set 4.50

• ROGERS • STRAINERS

Practical, efficient universal type strainers designed to fit most makes and styles of Orchestra and Parade drums.

No. 4474—Field drum. Professional Quality, chrome-plated ...... Each $3.75

No. 4472—Orchestra, throw-off model. Professional Quality, Chrome. Ea. 4.95

No. 4475—Back plate for above, Chrome ...... Ea. .75

No. 4474

No. 4472

4476 - 4482

THROW-OFF STRAINERS

Chromium-plated finish. A small, yet highly efficient strainer, suitable for any drum.
No. 4476—Orchestra Model ...... Each $3.75
No. 4482—Back Plate to fit ...... Each .60

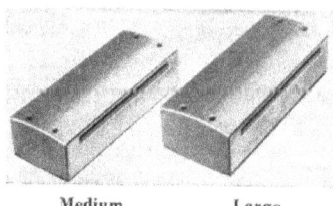

Medium Large

• ROGERS • WOOD BLOCKS-Professional Quality

Made of selected wood, especially adapted for authentic wood block tone. Slotted top and bottom. Carefully shaped and neatly bevelled. Attractive reddish brown or natural finish. Fit standard holders.

No. 4816R—Medium, 6¾", shaded reddish brown ⎫ Each
No. 4898R—Medium, 6¾", natural blond finish ⎭ $2.50
No. 4817R—Large, 7½", shaded reddish brown ⎫
No. 4899R—Large, 7½", natural blond finish ⎭ 2.75

STANDARD COW BELLS
(Height includes loop)

No. 4786—Tuned Cowbell, 3⅜" ...... Each $1.75
No. 4787—Tuned Cowbell, 4½" ...... Each 1.95
No. 4788—Tuned Cowbell, 5⅛" ...... Each 2.25
No. 4789—Tuned Cowbell, 5¾" ...... Each 2.50
No. 4790—Tuned Cowbell, 6⅞" ...... Each 2.95

• ROGERS • WOOD BLOCK HOLDER

No. 4805—Clamps to bass drum. Holds any size wood block. Nickel-plated .. Each $ .90
No. 4805C—Same, polished, Chrome-plated 1.20

Nos. 4805 4805C

• ROGERS • COW BELL HOLDERS
Chromium Plated Each

No. 4814—Single, Chrome Plated, has 2" Post $1.95
No. 4846—With 4" post, 1 "U" clamp. Chrome-plated .. 2.25
No. 4815—For 4 Cow Bells, with 4 "U" Clamps, chrome, has 7¼" post 3.30
No. 4796—"U" Clamp, Separate, Chrome, with wing nut ...... .45

No. 4814

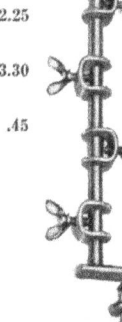

No. 4815

QUICK-HITCH TRIADS

Block holder adjustable to any size block, bells to any angle.
No. 1502 ...... Each $3.75

HALF MOON TRIAD HOLDERS

No. 1722—For small bass drums. Holds wood block and cow bells high, within easy reach. Nickel-plated ...Each $4.50

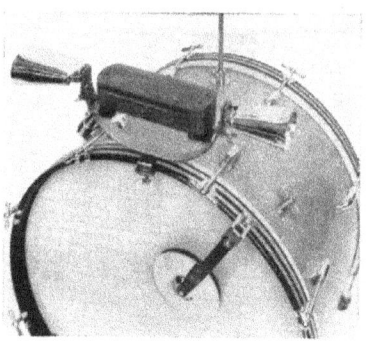

ROGERS PARTS

Catalog 62R, 1962

PEDAL PARTS

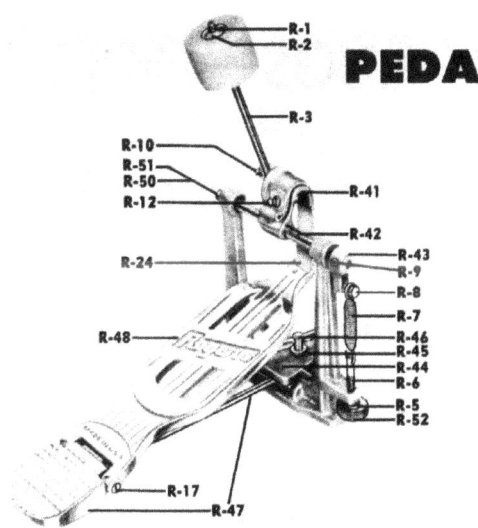

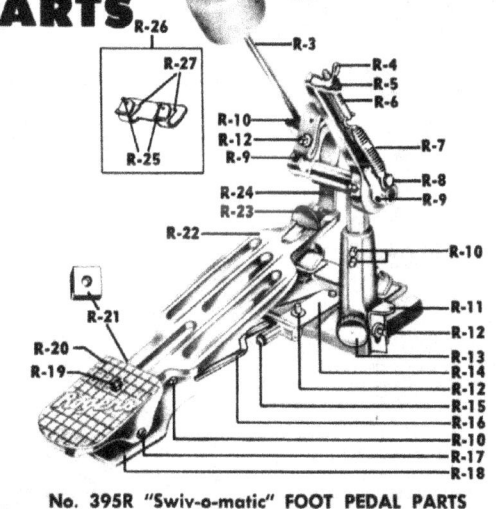

No. 398 "Rocket" FOOT PEDAL PARTS

No.		Each	No.		Each
R-1	Pedal Ball Hex Nut	.15	R-41	Beater Cam, with set screw (R10)	3.50
R-2	Pedal Ball Washer	.05	R-42	Rocker Shaft Rod	1.00
R-3	Pedal Beater, complete	2.50	R-43	Rocker Cam	1.25
R-5	Lock Washer	.05	R-44	Toe Hoop Clamp	1.00
R-6	Spring Adjustment Screw	.35	R-45	Toe Clamp Washer	.05
R-7	Spring Assembly, with hooks and bushing	1.20	R-46	Thumb Screw	.50
R-8	Cam Bolt	.50	R-47	Heel, with "T" Rod	3.50
R-9	Allen Screw	.15	R-48	Footboard	5.50
R-10	Set Screw, 5/16" thread length	.15	R-49	Footboard Assembly, (R47—R48) complete	9.00
R-12	Pull Set Screw, 3/8" thread length	.20	R-50	Rocker Shaft Locking Nut	.15
R-17	Heel Bearing Screw	.50	R-51	Rocker Shaft Locking Screw	.50
R-24	Leather Strap, with screw	.75	R-52	Tension Spring Adjusting Nut	.40

No. 395R "Swiv-o-matic" FOOT PEDAL PARTS

No.		Each	No.		Each
R-1	Pedal Ball Hex Nut	.15	R-16	"T" Rod	2.00
R-2	Pedal Ball Washer	.05	R-17	Heel Bearing Screw	.50
R-3	Pedal Beater, complete	2.50	R-18	Heel Base	1.50
R-4	Wing Nut	.15	R-19	Heel Pull Set Screw	.20
R-5	Lock Washer	.05	R-20	Heel	2.00
R-6	Spring Adjustment Screw	.35	R-21	Threaded Heel Plate, (underneath heel)	.50
R-7	Spring Assembly, with hooks and bushing	1.20	R-22	Footboard	6.00
R-8	Cam Bolt	.50	R-23	Toe Stop, with screw	1.00
R-9	Allen Screw	.15	R-24	Leather Strap, with screw	.75
R-10	Set Screw, 5/16" thread length	.15	R-25	Set Screw, 7/16" thread length	.20
R-11	Pedal Spur (specify right or left)	.75	R-26	Pedal Hoop Clamp complete	6.00
R-12	Pull Set Screw, 3/8" thread length	.20	R-27	Clamp Pressure Plate, (Specify right or left)	.50
R-13	Locking Screw	1.00	R-28	Footboard Assembly, complete (R10—R16—R17(2)—R-18—R-19—R20—R21—R22—R23)	12.50
R-14	Swivel Unit	2.00			
R-15	Spring Pin Assembly	.75			

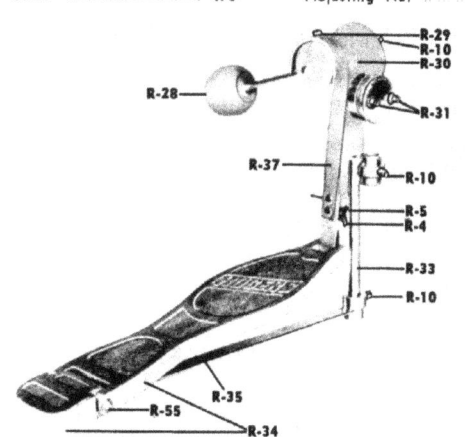

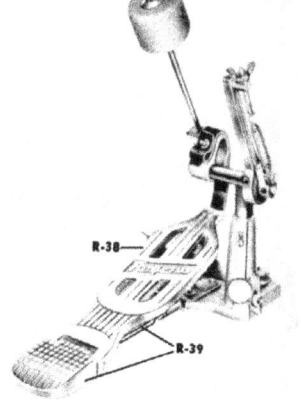

No. 396R "Swiv-o-matic" FOOT PEDAL PARTS

Same as on No. 395R, except Footboard, Heel & "T" Rod

No.		Each
R-38	Footboard	5.50
R-39	Heel, with "T" Rod	3.50
R-40	Footboard Assembly, (R38—R39—R17(2)) complete	10.00

No. 205R "Cocktail" FOOT PEDAL PARTS

No.		Each	No.		Each
R-4	Wing Nut	.15	R-31	Pull Set Screw, 5/8" thread length	.25
R-5	Lock Washer	.05	R-32	Spring Adjustment Screw (not shown)	.35
R-6	Spring Adjustment Screw	.35	R-33	Pedal Adapter, complete with set screw (R10)	2.00
R-7	Spring Assembly, with hooks and bushing (not shown)	1.20	R-34	Footboard and Heel	4.25
R-10	Set Screw, 5/16" thread length	.15	R-35	Metal Footboard Strap, with collar	1.50
R-28	Wood Pedal Beater	2.50	R-36	Footboard Assembly, complete (R34—R35—R55)	5.75
R-29	Slotted Set Screw	.25	R-37	Leather Strap, with metal hinge	1.00
R-30	Pedal Housing Assembly	10.50	R-55	Rivet	.10

No. 399 "Jet" FOOT PEDAL PARTS

Same as No. 398, except Footboard, Heel & "T" Rod.

No.		Each
R-53	Footboard	3.00
R-54	Heel & "T" Rod	2.50
R-55	Rivet	.10
R-56	Footboard Assy. (R53—R54—R55) complete	5.50

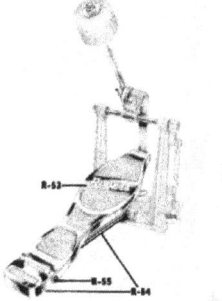

ROGERS PARTS

Catalog 62R, 1962

DRUM RODS—HOOKS—LUGS—HOLDERS

•ROGERS• DRUM KEYS
No. 4409—Chrome-plated per dozen **$4.80**

Full gross ....per dozen $4.32
Made of hard tool steel, specially designed to fit triple flange hoops as well as "L" hoops. Will fit all SWIV-O-MATIC and KNOBBY holders, spurs, tilters, etc.

•ROGERS• KEY HOLDERS
No. 4414—Chrome Finish, with screws and washers. ......Dozen **$6.00**

•ROGERS• KEY TENSION RODS
Key Tension Rods, square head, triple-plated. Specify size. (Length from under collar to threaded end)

No. 4930—1½"		No. 4936—4½"	
No. 4931—2"	**$4.80** Doz.	No. 4937—5"	**$6.00** Doz.
No. 4932—2½"		No. 4929—5½"	
No. 4933—3"		No. 4938—6"	
No. 4934—3½"	**$6.00** Doz.	No. 4939—8"	**$7.20** Doz.
No. 4935—4"		No. 4940—10"	
		No. 4942—13"	

•ROGERS• PARADE or SCOTCH DRUM RODS
Professional Quality — Chrome Plated
Square head, key tension, triple-plated, with 2 Scotch claw hooks.
No. 4493—For 8 inch drum, Chrome-plated ....
No. 4480—For 10 inch drum, Chrome-plated .... } Each **$2.70**
No. 4481—For 12 inch drum, Chrome-plated ....

•ROGERS• "T" HANDLE RODS ONLY—With Collar
For Double Claw Hooks
No. 4943—Size 3¾ inch, Chrome-plated .... Each $ .90
No. 4944—Size 7½ inch, Chrome-plated .... Each 1.00
No. 4911—Size 13¼ inch, Chrome-plated .... Each 1.10
No. 4912—Size 15½ inch, Chrome-plated .... Each 1.20

With 2 Double Claw, Hooks and Collar Under "T" Handle
No. 4297—For 12 inch drum, Chrome-plated .... Each } **$3.15**
No. 4298—For 14 inch drum, Chrome-plated .... Each }

HOW TO ORDER DRUM RODS
Give Shell Measurements Only, Without Counter Hoops.

•ROGERS• DRUM CENTER SUPPORTS
No. 4477—For use with drum rods, complete with screws, washers, etc. Chrome-plated. For snare drum. .... Each $ **.50**
No. 4470—Same as above. For bass drum .... Each **.50**

•ROGERS• DRUM HOOKS — CHROME PLATED
No. 4406 —Collar hooks, double claw .... Each $ .50
No. 4406P—Collar hooks, double claw, threaded insert Each .70
No. 4407 —Collar hooks, single claw .... Each .40
No. 4478 —Scotch type, double claw, plain .... Dozen 9.60
No. 4479 —Scotch type, double claw, threaded .... Dozen 10.80
No. 4483 —Washers for drum rods .... Dozen .35

•ROGERS• LUGS - LUG NUTS - LUG SPRINGS
Drawn Brass—Mirror Finish Chrome-Plated

PLEASE SPECIFY for which type of drum desired

No. 4945R—Lug, 2⅝" long, 2 holes for single tension rod to go through lugs (without lug nut or springs). Mounting holes spaced 2⅛" apart .... Each **$1.20**

No. 4946R—Lug, 2⅝" long, with 1 self-aligning nut and spring. For separate tension. Mounting holes spaced 2⅛" apart .... Each **$1.35**
No. 4948R—Lug Spring, for above .... Each .06
No. 4949R—Lug Nut, for above .... Each .25

No. 4947R—Lug, 2⅝" long, with 2 self-aligning nuts and springs. For separate sension. Mounting holes spaced 2⅛" apart .... Each **$1.35**
No. 4948R—Lug Spring, for above .... Each .06
No. 4949R—Lug Nut, for above .... Each .25

No. 3915R—Lug, 2¼" long. 2 holes for single tension (without lug nut or spring). Mounting holes 1¾" apart .... Each **$1.20**

No. 3916R—Lug, 2¼" long, with 1 self-aligning lug nut and spring. For separate tension. Mounting holes spaced 1¾" apart .... Each **$1.35**
No. 3918R—Lug Spring, for above .... Each .06
No. 4949R—Lug Nut, for above .... Each .25

No. 3917R—Lug, 2¼" long, with 2 self-aligning lug nuts and springs. For separate tension. Mounting holes spaced 1¾" apart .... Each **$1.35**
No. 3918R—Lug Spring, for above .... Each .06
No. 4949R—Lug Nut, for above .... Each .25

No. 3920R—Lug, 1¾" long, with 1 self-aligning lug nut and spring. For separate tension. Mounting holes spaced 1¼" apart .... Each **$1.35**
No. 3921R—Lug Spring, for above .... Each .06
No. 4949R—Lug Nut, for above .... Each .25

ROGERS PARTS

Catalog 64R, 1964

ROGERS · SNARES and STRAINERS

SNAPPY SNARES

Made of special quality coiled steel wire. Trenched butt plates provide for better response. Chrome-plated. Individually packaged.

12 STRANDS

No. 4471—For 13" Drum.................
No. 4468—For 14" Drum................. } Each **$3.00**
No. 4456—For 15" Drum.................

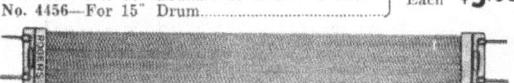

16 STRANDS

No. 4717—For 14" Drum................. } Each **$3.30**
No. 4718—For 15" Drum.................

20 STRANDS

No. 4457—For 14" Drum ....
No. 4458—For 15" Drum .... } Each **$3.50**
No. 4465—For 16" Drum ....

WIRE-WOUND SNARES WITH BUTTS

No. 4466—Wire wound, orchestra size, 15 gauge. Each..... } **$1.50**
No. 4467—Wire wound, field drum size, 13 gauge. Each... }

GUT SNARES WITH BUTTS

No. 4118—12 Strands, light weight .... Each $4.00
No. 4119—12 Strands, heavy weight .... Each   4.50
No. 4709—Fiber Butts .... Each   .10

FIELD DRUM OR MILITARY STRAINER

Carefully engineered to give smooth, easy, positive action. Has holes for wire-wound or gut snares.
No. 4474—Chrome-plated,
(without back-plate) .... Each **$4.50**

No. 4474

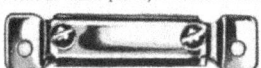
No. 4475 — Back-plate for
4474 Chrome-plated.
Each $1.00

"UNIVERSAL" ➤ THROW-OFF STRAINER

The standard, reliable throw-off strainer. Operates with ease and precision. Used on both orchestra and parade drums.   Each
No. 4472—Chrome,
(without back-plate) **$5.50**

No. 4475 — Back-plate for
above, Chrome ...... Each $1.00

SWIVO-MATIC PERMA-TENSION STRAINER

A Rogers Engineering Triumph

Most practical and most efficient strainer ever designed . . . The special tempered roller mechanism, combined with the precision slide construction, assures smooth, perfect action with a minimum of effort. The spring-loaded cartridge bearing, carrying the tension screw, eliminates constant readjusting of snares by holding tension screw in fixed position, whether snares are on or off . . .

The angular, cut-away base allows strainer to pull snare cord at the proper angle for precise action and alignment . . . the SWIV-O-MATIC Perma-Tension snare strainer renders positive, fool-proof performance. Fits practically all makes and models of Orchestra and Parade Drums.

Patent Pending

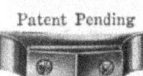
Butt or back plate

No. 390R—SWIV-O-MATIC Perma-Tension Snare Strainer, complete with specially designed butt assembly. **$13.50**

New . . . Rogers STA-TITE STRAINER

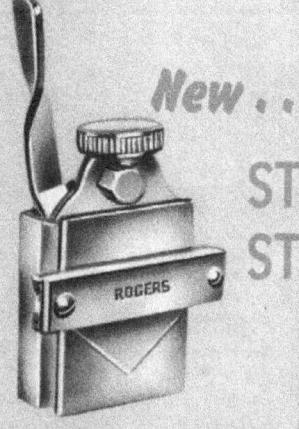

Rogers Scores Again with its New, Sta-Tite Strainer. Designed with a minimum of moving parts for trouble free performance. Spring loading against tension screw eliminates needless adjustment of snares. Fits all types of orchestra and marching drums.

Back-plate

No. 392R—Sta-Tite Strainer,
complete with butt plate **$9.95**

TENSION SCREW

With knob, for field drum strainer. Permits adjustment of snare tension.
No. 3468—Chrome-plated .... Each   **.75**

ROGERS PARTS

Catalog 64R, 1964

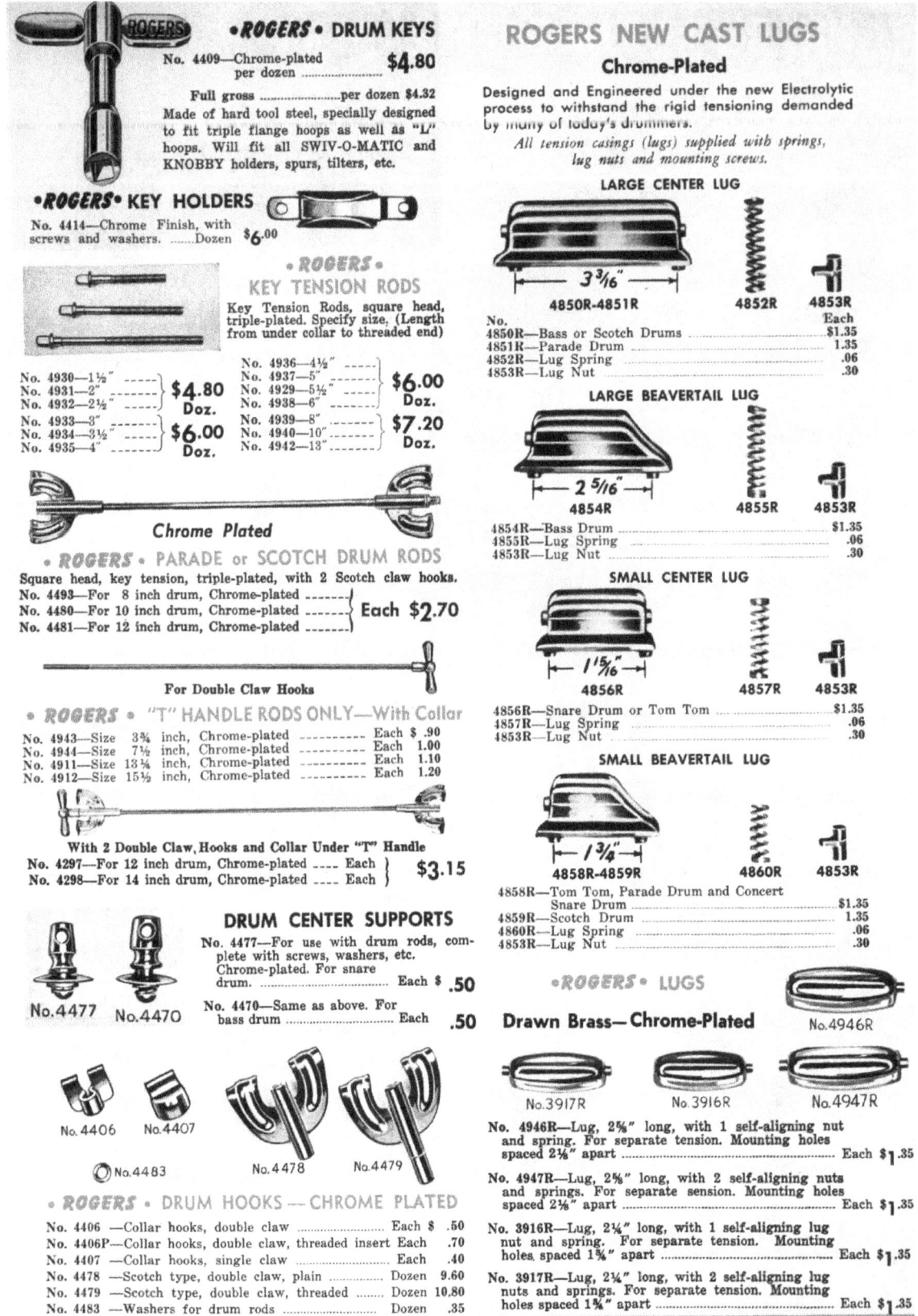

• ROGERS • DRUM KEYS
No. 4409—Chrome-plated per dozen $4.80
Full gross ..... per dozen $4.32
Made of hard tool steel, specially designed to fit triple flange hoops as well as "L" hoops. Will fit all SWIV-O-MATIC and KNOBBY holders, spurs, tilters, etc.

• ROGERS • KEY HOLDERS
No. 4414—Chrome Finish, with screws and washers. ..... Dozen $6.00

• ROGERS • KEY TENSION RODS
Key Tension Rods, square head, triple-plated. Specify size. (Length from under collar to threaded end)

No. 4930—1½"	No. 4936—4½"
No. 4931—2" $4.80	No. 4937—5" $6.00
No. 4932—2½" Doz.	No. 4929—5½" Doz.
No. 4933—3"	No. 4938—6"
No. 4934—3½" $6.00	No. 4939—8" $7.20
No. 4935—4" Doz.	No. 4940—10" Doz.
	No. 4942—13"

Chrome Plated
• ROGERS • PARADE or SCOTCH DRUM RODS
Square head, key tension, triple-plated, with 2 Scotch claw hooks.
No. 4493—For 8 inch drum, Chrome-plated
No. 4480—For 10 inch drum, Chrome-plated } Each $2.70
No. 4481—For 12 inch drum, Chrome-plated

For Double Claw Hooks
• ROGERS • "T" HANDLE RODS ONLY—With Collar
No. 4943—Size 3¾ inch, Chrome-plated ..... Each $ .90
No. 4944—Size 7½ inch, Chrome-plated ..... Each 1.00
No. 4911—Size 13¼ inch, Chrome-plated ..... Each 1.10
No. 4912—Size 15½ inch, Chrome-plated ..... Each 1.20

With 2 Double Claw, Hooks and Collar Under "T" Handle
No. 4297—For 12 inch drum, Chrome-plated ..... Each } $3.15
No. 4298—For 14 inch drum, Chrome-plated ..... Each

DRUM CENTER SUPPORTS
No. 4477—For use with drum rods, complete with screws, washers, etc. Chrome-plated. For snare drum. ..... Each $ .50
No. 4470—Same as above. For bass drum ..... Each .50
No. 4477   No. 4470

No. 4406 No. 4407
No. 4483 No. 4478 No. 4479

• ROGERS • DRUM HOOKS — CHROME PLATED
No. 4406 —Collar hooks, double claw ..... Each $ .50
No. 4406P—Collar hooks, double claw, threaded insert Each .70
No. 4407 —Collar hooks, single claw ..... Each .40
No. 4478 —Scotch type, double claw, plain ..... Dozen 9.60
No. 4479 —Scotch type, double claw, threaded ..... Dozen 10.80
No. 4483 —Washers for drum rods ..... Dozen .35

ROGERS NEW CAST LUGS
Chrome-Plated
Designed and Engineered under the new Electrolytic process to withstand the rigid tensioning demanded by many of today's drummers.
All tension casings (lugs) supplied with springs, lug nuts and mounting screws.

LARGE CENTER LUG
3 3/16"
4850R-4851R   4852R   4853R

No.		Each
4850R—Bass or Scotch Drums		$1.35
4851R—Parade Drum		1.35
4852R—Lug Spring		.06
4853R—Lug Nut		.30

LARGE BEAVERTAIL LUG
2 5/16"
4854R   4855R   4853R

4854R—Bass Drum $1.35
4855R—Lug Spring ..... .06
4853R—Lug Nut ..... .30

SMALL CENTER LUG
1 15/16"
4856R   4857R   4853R

4856R—Snare Drum or Tom Tom $1.35
4857R—Lug Spring ..... .06
4853R—Lug Nut ..... .30

SMALL BEAVERTAIL LUG
1 ¾"
4858R-4859R   4860R   4853R

4858R—Tom Tom, Parade Drum and Concert Snare Drum $1.35
4859R—Scotch Drum 1.35
4860R—Lug Spring ..... .06
4853R—Lug Nut ..... .30

• ROGERS • LUGS
Drawn Brass—Chrome-Plated
No. 3917R   No. 3916R   No. 4946R / No. 4947R

No. 4946R—Lug, 2⅝" long, with 1 self-aligning nut and spring. For separate tension. Mounting holes spaced 2⅛" apart ..... Each $1.35

No. 4947R—Lug, 2⅝" long, with 2 self-aligning nuts and springs. For separate tension. Mounting holes spaced 2⅛" apart ..... Each $1.35

No. 3916R—Lug, 2¼" long, with 1 self-aligning lug nut and spring. For separate tension. Mounting holes spaced 1¾" apart ..... Each $1.35

No. 3917R—Lug, 2¼" long, with 2 self-aligning lug nuts and springs. For separate tension. Mounting holes spaced 1¾" apart ..... Each $1.35

ROGERS PARTS

1971 Parts Catalog

SWIV-O-MATIC PEDAL PARTS

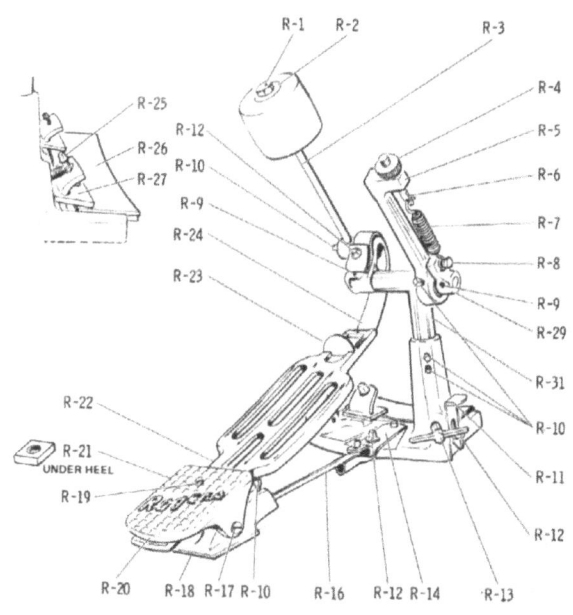

48-0613 PEDAL

Illustration of Stroke Adjustment Arm

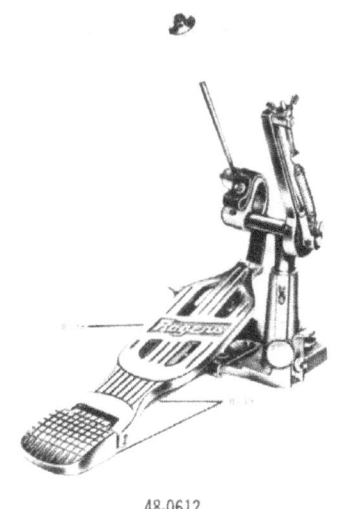

48-0612 PEDAL

FOR 48-0613 PEDAL ONLY

60-9213 (R-16) Connecting rod, each
60-9215 (R-18) Heel base, each
61-0177 (R-19) Heel pull set screw, Pkg. of 6
60-9217 (R-20) Heel, each
60-9218 (R-21) Threaded heel plate (under heel), each
60-9219 (R-22) Footboard, each
60-9220 (R-23) Toe stop with screw, each
60-9225 Footboard assembly complete, each
(R-10, R-16, R-17 (2), R-18, R-19, R-20, R-21, R-22, R-23)

FOR 48-0612 PEDAL ONLY

60-2303 (R-16) Connecting rod, each
60-9226 (R-38) Footboard, each
60-9227 (R-39) Heel with connecting rod, each
60-9228 Footboard assembly complete, each
(R-38, R-39, R-17 (2))

FOR EITHER 48-0612 OR 48-0613 PEDALS

60-9200 (R-1) Pedal ball hex nut, Pkg. of 6
61-0176 (R-2) Pedal ball washer, Pkg. of 12
48-2953 (R-3) Pedal beater complete, each
60-9240 (R-4) Tension spring adjustment nut, Pkg. of 4
61-0158 (R-5) Lock Washer, Pkg. of 12
60-9204 (R-6) Spring adjustment screw, Pkg. of 4
61-0367 (R-7) Spring assy. with hooks & bushing, Pkg. of 4
60-9206 (R-8) Cam bolt, each
60-9207 (R-9) Allen screw, Pkg. of 12
48-2840 (R-10) Set screw $\frac{1}{8}$" thread length, each
60-9208 (R-11) Pedal spur right side
60-9209 (R-11) Pedal spur left side
61-0177 (R-12) Pull set screw $\frac{3}{8}$" thread length, Pkg. of 6
60-9211 (R-13) Locking screw, each
60-9212 (R-14) Swivel Unit, each
60-9214 (R-17) Heel bearing screw, Pkg. of 6
61-0178 (R-24) Leather Strap, Pkg. of 6
48-2841 (R-25) Set screw $\frac{5}{8}$" thread length, each
61-0196 (R-26) Pedal hoop clamp complete, each
60-9224 (R-27) Clamp pressure plate, each
60-5207 (R-29) Rocker Cam
60-5203 (R-30) Pedal Standard
60-7593 (R-31) Bearing housing
60-5204 Stroke adjustment arm
60-5200 Beater Cam

205

ROGERS PARTS

1971 Parts Catalog

ROCKET AND JET PEDAL PARTS

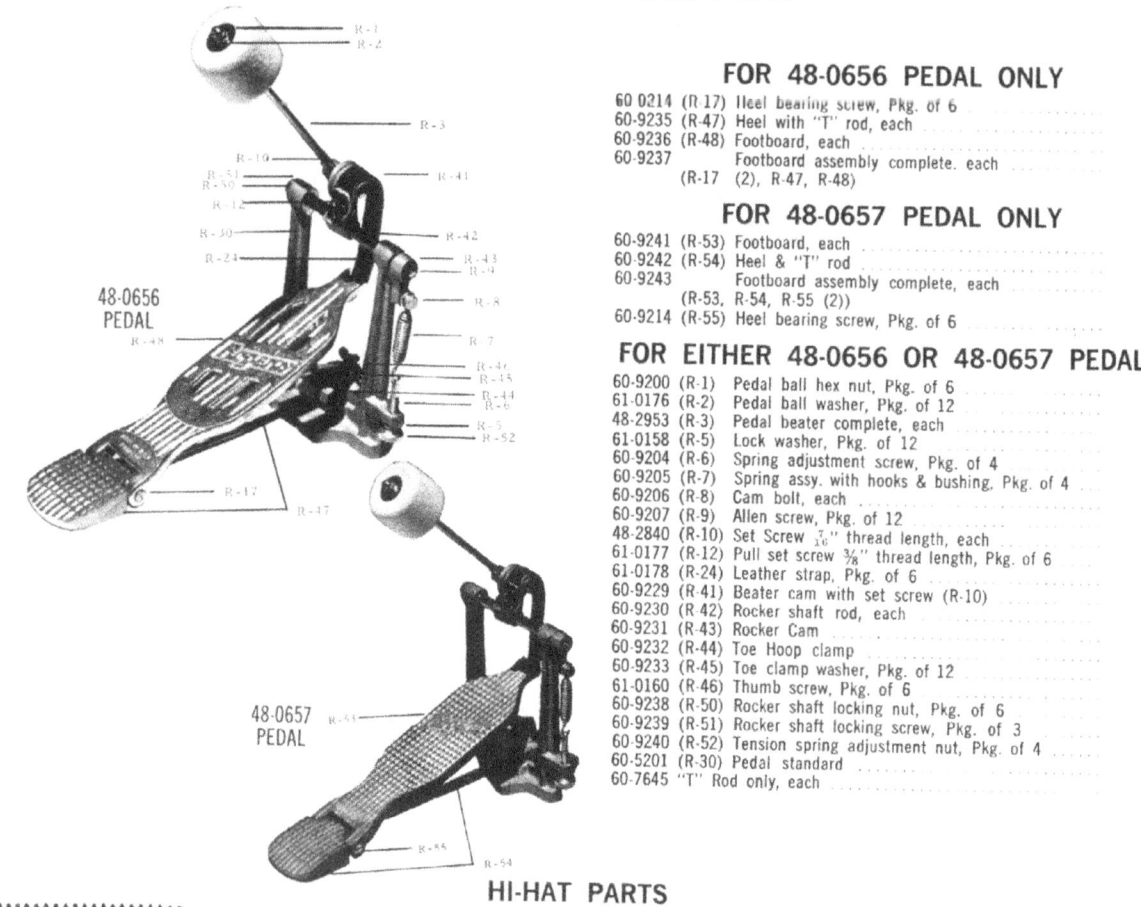

FOR 48-0656 PEDAL ONLY
- 60-0214 (R-17) Heel bearing screw, Pkg. of 6
- 60-9235 (R-47) Heel with "T" rod, each
- 60-9236 (R-48) Footboard, each
- 60-9237 Footboard assembly complete, each (R-17 (2), R-47, R-48)

FOR 48-0657 PEDAL ONLY
- 60-9241 (R-53) Footboard, each
- 60-9242 (R-54) Heel & "T" rod
- 60-9243 Footboard assembly complete, each (R-53, R-54, R-55 (2))
- 60-9214 (R-55) Heel bearing screw, Pkg. of 6

FOR EITHER 48-0656 OR 48-0657 PEDALS
- 60-9200 (R-1) Pedal ball hex nut, Pkg. of 6
- 61-0176 (R-2) Pedal ball washer, Pkg. of 12
- 48-2953 (R-3) Pedal beater complete, each
- 61-0158 (R-5) Lock washer, Pkg. of 12
- 60-9204 (R-6) Spring adjustment screw, Pkg. of 4
- 60-9205 (R-7) Spring assy. with hooks & bushing, Pkg. of 4
- 60-9206 (R-8) Cam bolt, each
- 60-9207 (R-9) Allen screw, Pkg. of 12
- 48-2840 (R-10) Set Screw 7/16" thread length, each
- 61-0177 (R-12) Pull set screw 3/8" thread length, Pkg. of 6
- 61-0178 (R-24) Leather strap, Pkg. of 6
- 60-9229 (R-41) Beater cam with set screw (R-10)
- 60-9230 (R-42) Rocker shaft rod, each
- 60-9231 (R-43) Rocker Cam
- 60-9232 (R-44) Toe Hoop clamp
- 60-9233 (R-45) Toe clamp washer, Pkg. of 12
- 61-0160 (R-46) Thumb screw, Pkg. of 6
- 60-9238 (R-50) Rocker shaft locking nut, Pkg. of 6
- 60-9239 (R-51) Rocker shaft locking screw, Pkg. of 3
- 60-9240 (R-52) Tension spring adjustment nut, Pkg. of 4
- 60-5201 (R-30) Pedal standard
- 60-7645 "T" Rod only, each

HI-HAT PARTS

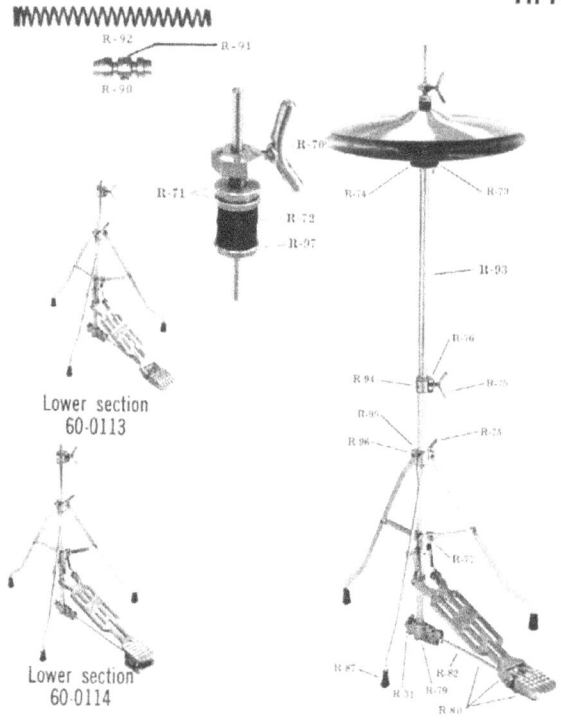

FOR 48-0510 AND 48-0511 HI-HATS
- 48-2841 (R-31) Set screw, each
- 60-9244 (R-70) Wing Screw, Pkg. of 2
- 60-9245 (R-71) Lock Nut, Pkg. of 6
- 60-9246 (R-72) Felt washer, small; Pkg. of 12
- 60-9247 (R-73) Felt washer, large; Pkg. of 6
- 60-9248 (R-74) Fiber washer, large; Pkg. of 6
- 60-9249 (R-75) Wing Screw, Pkg. of 4
- 60-8003 (R-76) Upper "U" Clamp, each
- 60-9251 (R-77) Metal cross-pin with nuts, each
- 60-9252 (R-79) Spur, each
- 60-9253 (R-80) Two-piece footboard (for 48-0510 hi-hat) complete with connecting rod, each
- 60-9254 (R-82) Connecting rod only (for 48-0510 hi-hat), each
- 60-9255 (R-84) One-piece footboard (for 48-0511 hi-hat) complete with connecting rod (not illustrated)
- 60-9256 (R-86) Connecting rod only (for 48-0511 hi-hat, (not illustrated) each
- 60-4418 (R-87) Rubber tips, Pkg. of 12
- 61-0180 (R-88) Upper Pull Rod, Pkg. of 2
- 60-9259 (R-89) Lower Pull Rod, complete with coupler & threaded plug, each
- 60-9260 (R-90) Threaded plug only, each
- 60-9261 (R-91) Allen screw (to fit threaded plug), Pkg. of 12
- 60-9262 (R-92) Compression spring, Pkg. of 3
- 60-9263 (R-93) Upper inside tube with tilter
- 60-9264 (R-94) Metal collar rings, each
- 60-9265 (R-95) Lower "U" clamp, each
- 60-9267 (R-97) Clutch retainer nut, Package of 2
- 60-9268 (R-96) Sliding leg clamps, set of 3
- 61-0113 Lower section assembly of 48-0510 Hi-Hat
- 61-0114 Lower section assembly of 48-0511 Hi-Hat

ROGERS PARTS

1971 Parts Catalog

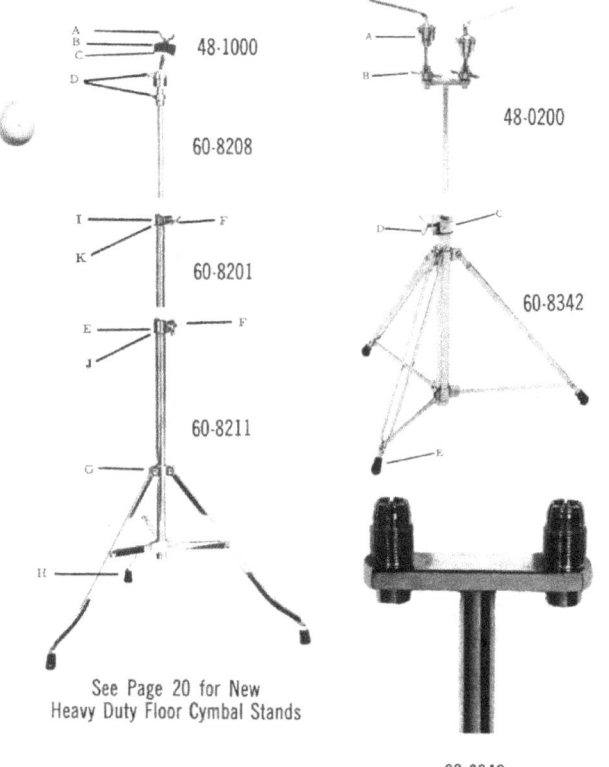

48-0508 FLOOR CYMBAL STAND

- 48-1000 Swiv-o-Matic cymbal tilter
- 60-8208 Upper Rod, each 19⅜" long
- 60-8201 Riser tube assembly with 60-8206 "U" clamp and 60-9249 wing screw, each
- 60-8211 Lower section assembly, each
  (Order by number . . . not letter)
- A — 61-0165 Wing Nut, Pkg. of 12
- B — 61-0166 Felt cymbal washer, Pkg. of 12
- C — 60-5792 Metal cymbal washer, Pkg. of 6
- D — 48-2840 Swivo set screws, each
- E — 60-8003 "U" Clamp, hole sizes ¾" & ⅝"
- F — 60-9249 Wing screw, Pkg. of 4
- G — 60-9268 Sliding leg clamps, set of three
- H — 60-4418 Rubber Tips, Pkg. of 12
- I — 60-8206 "U" Clamp, hole sizes ⅝" & ⅜"
- J — 60-9264 Metal Collar Ring, ¾"
- K — 60-8205 Metal Collar Ring, ⅝"
- — 61-0366 Rubber Sleeve, Pkg. of 24

48-0518 DUAL TOM TOM STAND

- 48-0200 Upper section assembly, each
  Note: This is same as center section of Dual Tom-Tom Holder
- 60-8342 Lower section assembly, each
  (Order by number . . . not letter)
- A — 60-6347 Swivo center section only, each
  Note: This is similar in appearance to the #48-0100 Center Section, but has a shorter riser rod. (To be used only with dual tom tom upper section.)
- B — 48-3400 Collet Nose, each
- C — 60-8290 "U" Clamp, hole sizes 1⅛" & ⅝"
- D — 60-9249 Wing screw, Pkg. of 4
- E — 61-0174 Rubber Tip, Pkg. of 12
- 60-6348 "T" Support Bar

See Page 20 for New Heavy Duty Floor Cymbal Stands

DRUM STANDS

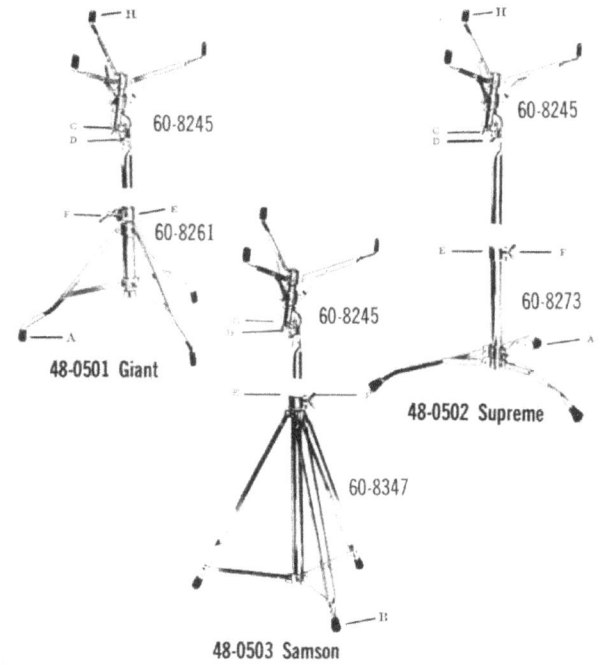

48-0501 Giant
48-0502 Supreme
48-0503 Samson

- 60-8245 Upper section assembly of 48-0501, -0502, & -0503 stands each
- 60-8261 Lower section assembly of 48-0501 stand, each
- 60-8347 Lower section assembly of 48-0503 stand, each
- 60-8273 Lower section assembly of 48-0502 stand, each

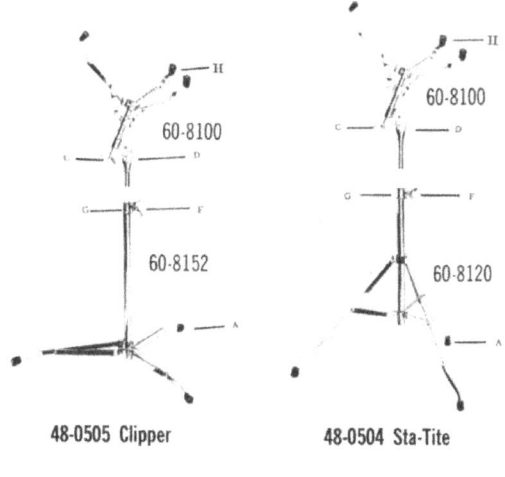

48-0505 Clipper
48-0504 Sta-Tite

- 60-8100 Upper section assembly of 48-0505 & 48-0504 stands
- 60-8120 Lower section assembly of 48-0504 stand, each
- 60-8152 Lower section assembly of 48-0505 stand, each
  (Order by number . . . not letter)
- A — 60-4418 Rubber Tips, Pkg. of 12
- B — 61-0174 Rubber Tips, Pkg. of 12
- C — 61-0173 Thumb screw, Pkg. of 3
- D — 61-0172 Thumb screw, Pkg. of 3
- E — 60-8667 "U" Clamp
- F — 60-9249 Wing screw, Pkg. of 4
- G — 60-9250 "U" Clamp
- H — 60-6433 Plastic Cap for Snare Drum Arms, Pkg. of 12

ROGERS PARTS

1971 Parts Catalog

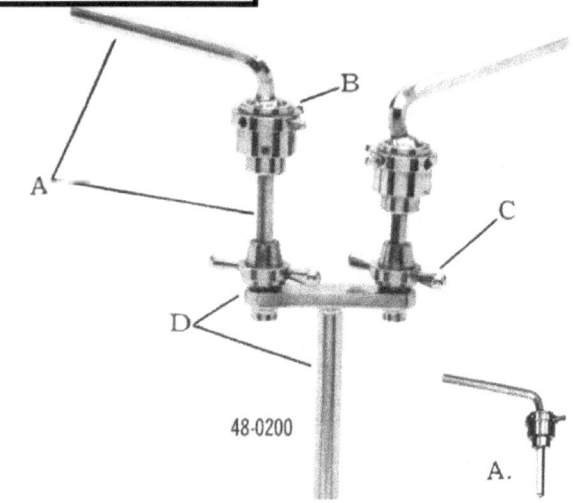

48-0200

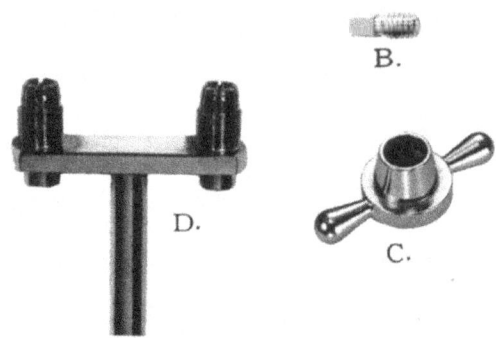

48-2600 DUAL TOM TOM PARTS
48-0200 Swiv-o-Matic Center Assembly (of Dual Tom Tom Holder)

(Order by number . . . not letter)
A. 60-6347 Swivo center section only ....
 Note: This is similar in appearance to the #48-0100 Center Section, but has a shorter riser rod. (To be used only with dual tom tom upper section.)
B. 48-2840 Swiv-o-Matic set screw, each ....
C. 48-3400 Collet nose, each ....
D. 60-6348 "T" Support Bar, each ....

48-2200 Receiving Unit for Dual Tom Tom Holder, each ....
 (Order by number . . . not letter)
E. 60-8003 "U" Clamp, each ....
F. 60-9249 Wing Screw, Pkg. of 4 ....
G. 61-0175 Carriage Bolts (set of 4) Pkg. of 3 sets ....
H. 60-6487 Reinforcing Plate, each ....
I. 61-0170 Hex Nut, Pkg. of 2 ....

48-2200

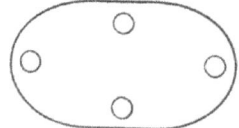

60-9292 Blank Plate with four bolts, washers, & nuts, each ....

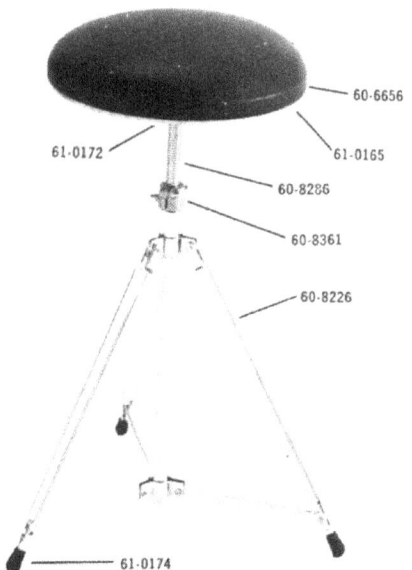

48-4400 SAMSON THRONES
60-6656 Throne Seat Assembly, each ....
 (with reinforcing spider frame)
61-0165 Wing Nut, Pkg. of 12 ....
60-8286 Threaded Rod only, each ....
61-0172 Thumb Screw, Pkg. of 3 ....
60-8361 Clamp Nut only, each ....
60-8226 Throne Base only, each ....
 (tripod with rubber tips)
61-0174 Rubber Tips, Pkg. of 12 ....
60-8293 Reinforced Spider Frame (frame only) ....
48-4600 Back Rest, each ....
48-4500 Heel Rest, each ....

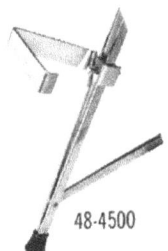
48-4500

48-4600

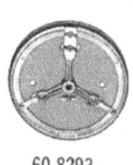
60-8293

ROGERS PARTS

1971 Parts Catalog

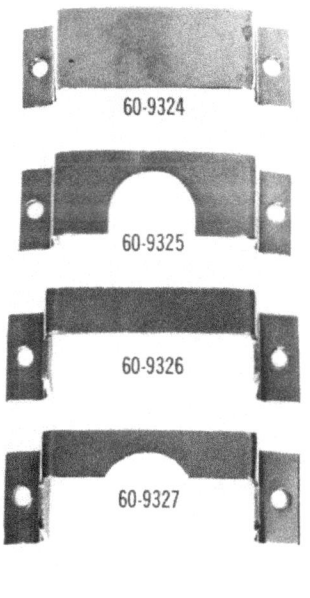

DYNA-SONIC SNARE DRUM and FRAME ASSEMBLY PARTS

- 60-9324 Snare Guard (back plate side), each ....
  (for Dyna-Sonic snare drums with wire snare assembly; with mounting screws and washers)
- 60-9325 Snare Guard (strainer side), each ....
  (for Dyna-Sonic snare drums with wire snare assembly; with mounting screws and washers)
- 60-9326 Snare Guard (back plate side), each ....
  (for Dyna-Sonic snare drums with nylon or gut snare assembly; with mounting screws and washers)
- 60-9327 Snare Guard (strainer side), each ....
  (for Dyna-Sonic snare drums with nylon or gut snare assembly; with mounting screws and washers)
- 60-5678 Back Plate Assembly, each ....
  (with screws and washers)
- 60-5664 Back Plate, each (B) ....
- 60-5663 Back Plate Cover, each (A) ....
- 60-9291 Tension Screw Assembly, each ....
  (tension screw, spring, retainer housing for Dyna-Sonic wire assembly)
- 61-0171 Spring for above tension screw, Pkg. of 4 ....
- 60-7535 Tension Screw, each ....
  (for Dyna-Sonic nylon or gut assembly)
- 60-5271 Threaded Sleeve Insert (for Dyna-Sonic Snare Frame) ....
- 48-8100 Dyna-Sonic Wire Snares (14"), each ....
- 48-8200 Dyna-Sonic Wire Snares (15"), each ....

Nylon and Gut snares for Dyna-Sonic Concert and Marching Drums

Nylon Snares (with slide bar)
61-0109 for 6½x14 concert snare drum
61-0110 for 10x14 Parade Drum
61-0110 for 12x15 Parade Drum

Gut Snares (with slide bar)
61-0111 for 6½x14 concert snare drum
61-0112 for 10x14 Parade Drum
61-0112 for 12x15 Parade Drum

SNARE STRAINERS

- 48-4066 Dyna-Sonic Snare Strainer ....
- 48-4067 PowerTone Snare Strainer ....
  Note: Similar except for the Cam & Tension Assembly.
- 60-6542 Cam & Tension Screw Sub-assembly (for 48-4066) ....
- 60-6540 Cam & Tension Screw Sub-assembly (for 48-4067) ....
- 60-5209 Strainer Housing, each ....
- 61-0163 Boss Screw, Pkg. of 6 ....
- 60-7556 Handle (short for 5x14 snare) ....
- 60-7559 Handle (long for 6½x14 snare) ....
- 60-5210 Face Plate Slide, each ....
- 60-5663 Cover for Face Plate Slide, each ....
- 61-0370 Face Plate Slide Screws (2), Pkg. of 12 ....
- 61-0164 Mounting Screws (to shell, 8/32x⅝), Pkg. of 12 .....
- 61-0167 Lock Washer, Pkg. of 12 ....
- 61-0156 Flat Washer #10, Pkg. of 12 ....
- 61-0169 Nylon Snare Cord, Pkg. of eight 13" lengths, each ....

ROGERS PARTS

1971 Parts Catalog

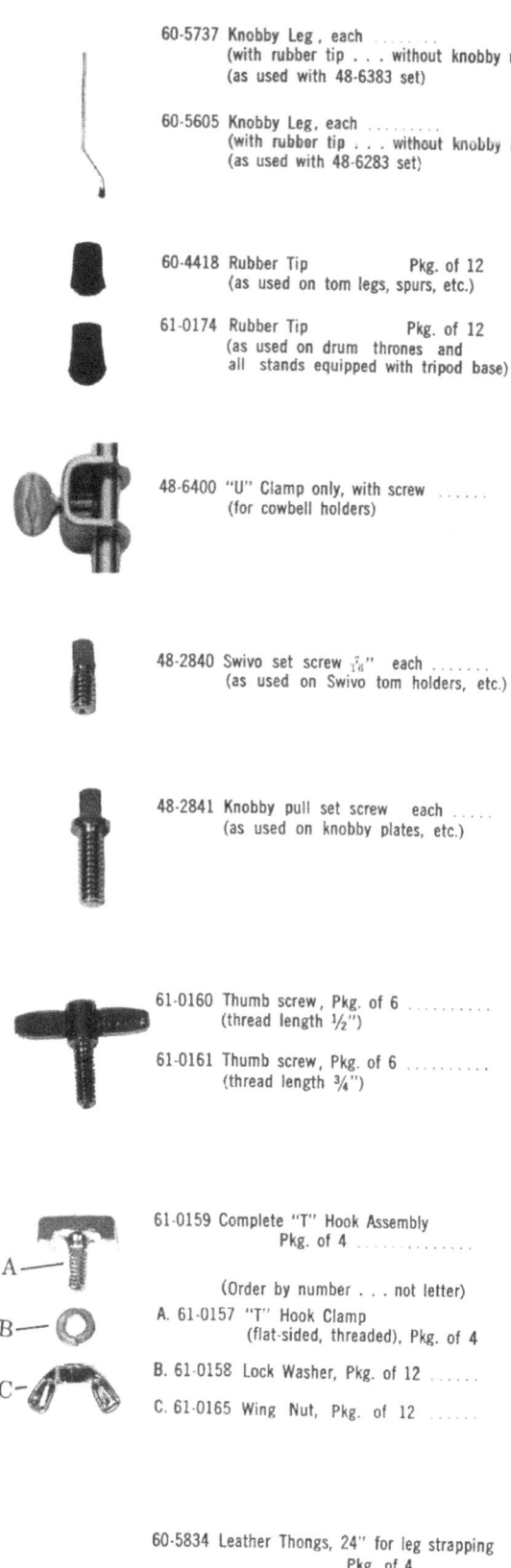

60-5737 Knobby Leg, each ....
(with rubber tip ... without knobby unit)
(as used with 48-6383 set)

60-5605 Knobby Leg, each ....
(with rubber tip ... without knobby unit)
(as used with 48-6283 set)

60-4418 Rubber Tip   Pkg. of 12
(as used on tom legs, spurs, etc.)

61-0174 Rubber Tip   Pkg. of 12
(as used on drum thrones and all stands equipped with tripod base)

48-6400 "U" Clamp only, with screw ......
(for cowbell holders)

48-2840 Swivo set screw 7/16" each ....
(as used on Swivo tom holders, etc.)

48-2841 Knobby pull set screw each .....
(as used on knobby plates, etc.)

61-0160 Thumb screw, Pkg. of 6 ....
(thread length 1/2")

61-0161 Thumb screw, Pkg. of 6 ....
(thread length 3/4")

61-0159 Complete "T" Hook Assembly
Pkg. of 4 ....

(Order by number ... not letter)
A. 61-0157 "T" Hook Clamp
(flat-sided, threaded), Pkg. of 4
B. 61-0158 Lock Washer, Pkg. of 12 ......
C. 61-0165 Wing Nut, Pkg. of 12 ......

60-5834 Leather Thongs, 24" for leg strapping
Pkg. of 4 ......

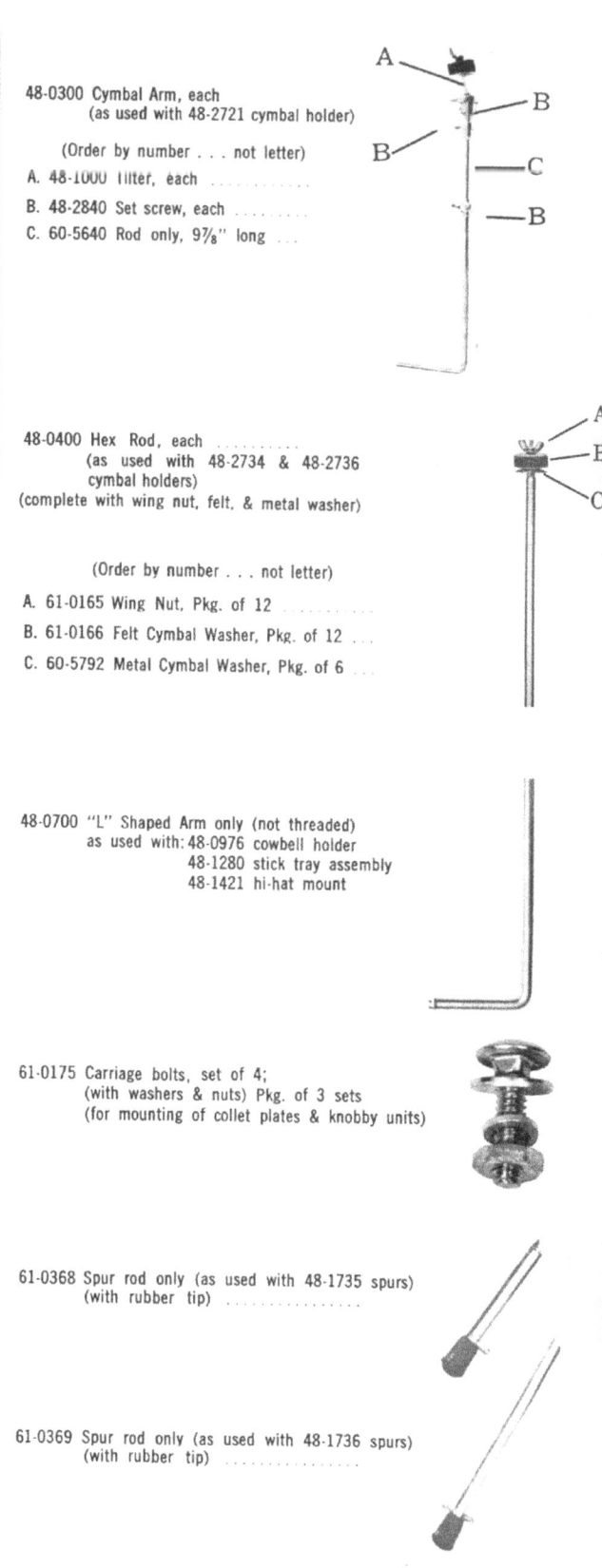

48-0300 Cymbal Arm, each ....
(as used with 48-2721 cymbal holder)

(Order by number ... not letter)
A. 48-1000 Tilter, each
B. 48-2840 Set screw, each ....
C. 60-5640 Rod only, 9 7/8" long ...

48-0400 Hex Rod, each ....
(as used with 48-2734 & 48-2736 cymbal holders)
(complete with wing nut, felt, & metal washer)

(Order by number ... not letter)
A. 61-0165 Wing Nut, Pkg. of 12 ....
B. 61-0166 Felt Cymbal Washer, Pkg. of 12 ...
C. 60-5792 Metal Cymbal Washer, Pkg. of 6 ...

48-0700 "L" Shaped Arm only (not threaded)
as used with: 48-0976 cowbell holder
              48-1280 stick tray assembly
              48-1421 hi-hat mount

61-0175 Carriage bolts, set of 4;
(with washers & nuts) Pkg. of 3 sets
(for mounting of collet plates & knobby units)

61-0368 Spur rod only (as used with 48-1735 spurs)
(with rubber tip) ....

61-0369 Spur rod only (as used with 48-1736 spurs)
(with rubber tip) ....

61-0168 Felt Strip for bass drum, Pkg. of 4

ROGERS PARTS

1971 Parts Catalog

KEY TENSION RODS°

61-0121 1¼" long
60-9356 1½" long
60-9370 2¼" long
60-9360 3½" long
61-0122 5" long

ROGERS DRUM LUGS

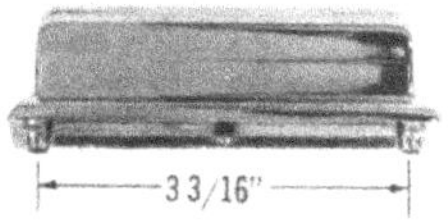

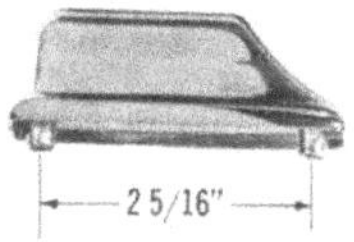

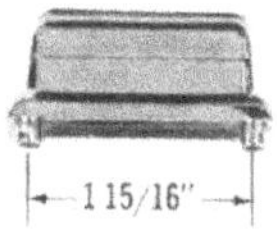

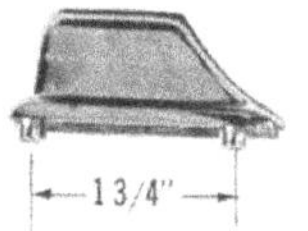

Supplied with springs, lug nuts, and mounting screws.

60-9316 Large Center Lug (Fig. A) each
  (for Cambridge Bass and/or Scotch Drums)
60-9315 Large Center Lug (Fig. A) each
  (for Cambridge and Pageant Parade Drums)
60-9318 Large Beavertail Lugs (Fig. B) each
  (for all dual-row bass drums)
60-9320 Small Center Lug (Fig. C) each
  (for 5 x 14 and 6½ x 14 snare drums)
60-9322 Small Beavertail Lug (Fig. D) each
  (for all dual-row tom toms, Marching
  Drums and Timbales)
60-9321 Small Beavertail Lug (for Bongos) (Fig. D) each

61-0124 LUG SPRING for large center lug (Fig. E) Pkg. of 6
61-0125 LUG SPRING for large beavertail lug (Fig E) Pkg. of 6
61-0126 LUG SPRING for small center lug (Fig. E) Pkg. of 12
61-0127 LUG SPRING for small beavertail lug (Fig. E) Pkg. of 12

61-0128 LUG NUTS (Fig. F) Pkg. of 6

61-0129 LUG MOUNTING SCREWS (Fig. G) Pkg. of 24

TRIPLE FLANGE METAL COUNTER HOOPS
(See chart on page 9-10 for drum size and model usage)

Stock Number	Dia. & Type		Number of Holes (ears)
60-9000	12"	- Batter	6
60-9001	13"	- Batter	6
60-6869	13"	- Snare	6
60-9002	14"	- Batter (for Pageant only)	6
60-9003	14"	- Snare (for Pageant only)	6
60-9004	14"	- Batter	8
60-9005	14"	- Snare	8
60-9006	14"	- Batter (for Dyna only)	10
60-9007	14"	- Snare (for Dyna only)	10
60-9008	15"	- Batter	8
60-9009	15"	- Snare	8
60-9010	15"	- Batter (for Dyna only)	10
60-9011	15"	- Snare (for Dyna only)	10
60-9012	16"	- Batter	8
60-9014	16"	- Batter (for Dyna only)	10
60-9016	18"	- Batter	8
60-9018	20"	- Batter	8

BASS DRUM COUNTER HOOPS

Stock Number	Dia. & Type
60-9050	18" - Plain
60-9048	18" - Pearl Inlay
60-9053	20" - Plain
60-9051	20" - Pearl Inlay
60-9056	22" - Plain
60-9054	22" - Pearl Inlay
60-9059	24" - Plain
60-9057	24" - Pearl Inlay
60-9062	26" - Plain
60-9060	26" - Pearl Inlay
60-9065	28" - Plain
60-9063	28" - Pearl Inlay
60-9068	30" - Plain
60-9066	30" - Pearl Inlay
60-9070	32" - Plain
60-9069	32" - Pearl Inlay
60-9074	34" - Plain
60-9072	34" - Pearl Inlay
60-9077	36" - Plain
60-9075	36" - Pearl Inlay
60-9080	40" - Plain
60-9078	40" - Pearl Inlay

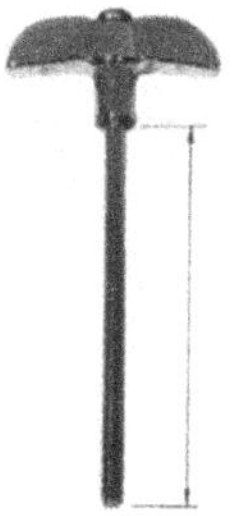

"T" HANDLE RODS°
60-6408 3¾" long, each
  (Measure from shoulder to end of threads)
61-0155 Washers (for all drum rods), package of 48

TIMBALE and BONGO HOOPS

60-2299 Timbale Hoop 13"
60-2300 Timbale Hoop 14"
60-9022 Bongo "L" Hoop 6" (4 ears)
60-9023 Bongo "L" Hoop 8" (4 ears)

° (For information on drum size and model usage, see chart, pages 9-10)

DOUBLE CLAW HOOKS (not threaded)

60-2286 (for all separate tension bass and scotch drums) each

60-6756 Bass Drum Eye Bolts, each
  (Sling hooks for Marching Bass and Scotch Drums)

61-0123 (for Timbales), each

60-4454 Sling hook (for Parade Drums). Package of 2

ROGERS PARTS

1971 Parts Catalog

APPLICATION CHART

CODE:
Quan = denotes quantities used on models and sizes listed.
Pwt = Powertone
Dyna = Dyna Sonic
Camb. = Cambridge

SNARE DRUMS

	KEY TENSION RODS			LUGS			COUNTER HOOPS					
	Stock Number	Length	Quan	Stock Number	Hole Spacing	Quan	Stock Number	Description	Quan	Stock Number	Description	Quan
2½x13 "Skinny"	61-021	1¼"	12	—	none	—	60-9001	Batter (top)	1	60-6869	Snare (bottom)	1
5x14 Pwt	60-9356	1½"	16	60-9320	$1\frac{15}{16}$"	8	60-9004	Batter (top)	1	60-9005	Snare (bottom)	1
5x14 Dyna	60-9356	1½"	20	60-9320	$1\frac{15}{16}$"	10	60-9006	Batter (top)	1	60-9007	Snare (bottom)	1
6½x14 Pwt	60-9370	2¼"	16	60-9320	$1\frac{15}{16}$"	8	60-9004	Batter (top)	1	60-9005	Snare (bottom)	1
6½x14 Dyna	60-9370	2¼"	20	60-9320	$1\frac{15}{16}$"	10	60-9006	Batter (top)	1	60-9007	Snare (bottom)	1

TOM TOMS (DANCE MODELS)

	KEY TENSION RODS			LUGS			COUNTER HOOPS		
	Stock Number	Length	Quan	Stock Number	Hole Spacing	Quan	Stock Number	Description	Quan
8x12 Pwt	60-9356	1½"	12	60-9322	1¾"	12	60-9000	Batter (top and bottom)	2
9x13 Pwt	60-9356	1½"	12	60-9322	1¾"	12	60-9001	Batter (top and bottom)	2
10x14 Pwt	60-9370	2¼"	16	60-9322	1¾"	16	60-9004	Batter (top and bottom)	2
12x15 Pwt	60-9370	2¼"	16	60-9322	1¾"	16	60-9008	Batter (top and bottom)	2
14x14 Pwt	60-9370	2¼"	16	60-9322	1¾"	16	60-9004	Batter (top and bottom)	2
16x16 Pwt	60-9370	2¼"	16	60-9322	1¾"	16	60-9012	Batter (top and bottom)	2
16x18 Pwt	60-9370	2¼"	16	60-9322	1¾"	16	60-9016	Batter (top and bottom)	2
18x20 Pwt	60-9370	2¼"	16	60-9322	1¾"	16	60-9018	Batter (top and bottom)	2

TOM TOMS (CONCERT MODELS - SINGLE HEAD)

	KEY TENSION RODS			LUGS			COUNTER HOOPS		
	Stock Number	Length	Quan	Stock Number	Hole Spacing	Quan	Stock Number	Description	Quan
8x12 Pwt	60-9356	1½"	6	60-9322	1¾"	6	60-9000	Batter (top)	1
9x13 Pwt	60-9356	1½"	6	60-9322	1¾"	6	60-9001	Batter (top)	1
10x14 Pwt	60-9370	2¼"	8	60-9322	1¾"	8	60-9004	Batter (top)	1
12x15 Pwt	60-9370	2¼"	8	60-9322	1¾"	8	60-9008	Batter (top)	1

BASS DRUMS

	"T" HANDLE RODS			LUGS			COUNTER HOOPS			CLAW HOOKS	
	Stock Number	Length	Quan	Stock Number	Hole Spacing	Quan	Stock Number	Description	Quan	Stock Number	Quan
14x18 Pwt	60-6408	3¾"	16	60-9318	$2\frac{5}{16}$"	16	60-9050 60-9048	Plain Pearl Inlay	2 2	60-2286	16
14x20 Pwt	60-6408	3¾"	16	60-9318	$2\frac{5}{16}$"	16	60-9053 60-9051	Plain Pearl Inlay	2 2	60-2286	16
14x22 Pwt	60-6408	3¾"	20	60-9318	$2\frac{5}{16}$"	20	60-9056 60-9054	Plain Pearl Inlay	2 2	60-2286	20
14x24 Pwt	60-6408	3¾"	20	60-9318	$2\frac{5}{16}$"	20	60-9059 60-9057	Plain Pearl Inlay	2 2	60-2286	20
14x26 Pwt	60-6408	3¾"	20	60-9318	$2\frac{5}{16}$"	24	60-9062 60-9060	Plain Pearl Inlay	2 2	60-2286	24
14x28 Pwt	60-6408	3¾"	24	60-9318	$2\frac{5}{16}$"	24	60-9065 60-9063	Plain Pearl Inlay	2 2	60-2286	24
14x30 Pwt	60-6408	3¾"	24	60-9318	$2\frac{5}{16}$"	24	60-9068 60-9066	Plain Pearl Inlay	2 2	60-2286	24
16x32 Pwt	60-6408	3¾"	28	60-9318	$2\frac{5}{16}$"	28	60-9070 60-9069	Plain Pearl Inlay	2 2	60-2286	28
16x34 Pwt	60-6408	3¾"	28	60-9318	$2\frac{5}{16}$"	28	60-9074 60-9072	Plain Pearl Inlay	2 2	60-2286	28
16x36 Pwt	60-6408	3¾"	32	60-9318	$2\frac{5}{16}$"	32	60-9077 60-9075	Plain Pearl Inlay	2 2	60-2286	32
18x40 Pwt	60-6408	3¾"	32	60-9318	$2\frac{5}{16}$"	32	60-9080 60-9078	Plain Pearl Inlay	2 2	60-2286	32

NOTE: If key tension rods are desired on bass drums, use:
60-9360 .... 3½" length

ROGERS PARTS

1971 Parts Catalog

TIMBALES (13" & 14" SET)

	KEY TENSION RODS			LUGS			COUNTER HOOPS			CLAW HOOKS	
	Stock Number	Length	Quan	Stock Number	Hole Spacing	Quan	Stock Number	Description	Quan	Stock Number	Quan
13 inch	60-9370	2¼"	5	60-9322	1¾"	5	60-2299	Batter (top)	1	61-0123	5
14 inch	60-9370	2¼"	5	60-9322	1¾"	5	60-2300	Batter (top)	1	61-0123	5

BONGOS (6" & 8" SET)

	KEY TENSION RODS			LUGS			COUNTER HOOPS		
	Stock Number	Length	Quan	Stock Number	Hole Spacing	Quan	Stock Number	Description	Quan
6 inch	60-9356	1½"	4	60-9321	1¾"	4	60-9022	Batter (top)	1
8 inch	60-9356	1½"	4	60-9321	1¾"	4	60-9023	Batter (top)	1

PARADE DRUMS

	KEY TENSION RODS			LUGS			TRIPLE FLANGE HOOPS					
	Stock Number	Length	Quan	Stock Number	Hole Spacing	Quan	Stock Number	Description	Quan	Stock Number	Description	Quan
10x14 Dyna	60-9370	2¼"	20	60-9322	1¾"	20	60-9006	Batter (top)	1	60-9007	Snare (bottom)	1
10x14 Pwt	60-9370	2¼"	16	60-9322	1¾"	16	60-9004	Batter (top)	1	60-9005	Snare (bottom)	1
10x14 Camb.	60-9360	3½"	16	60-9315	3 3/16"	8	60-9004	Batter (top)	1	60-9005	Snare (bottom)	1
10x14 Pageant	60-9360	3½"	12	60-9315	3 3/16"	6	60-9002	Batter (top)	1	60-9003	Snare (bottom)	1
12x15 Dyna	60-9370	2¼"	20	60-9322	3¾"	20	60-9010	Batter (top)	1	60-9011	Snare (bottom)	1
12x15 Pwt	60-9370	2¼"	16	60-9322	1¾"	16	60-9008	Batter (top)	1	60-9009	Snare (bottom)	1
12x15 Camb.	61-0122	5"	16	60-9315	3 3/16"	8	60-9008	Batter (top)	1	60-9009	Snare (bottom)	1

TENOR DRUMS

	KEY TENSION RODS			LUGS			TRIPLE FLANGE HOOPS		
	Stock Number	Length	Quan	Stock Number	Hole Spacing	Quan	Stock Number	Description	Quan
12x15 Dyna	60-9370	2¼"	20	60-9322	1¾"	20	60-9010	Batter (top and bottom)	2
12x15 Pwt	60-9370	2¼"	16	60-9322	1¾"	16	60-9008	Batter (top and bottom)	2
12x15 Camb.	61-0122	5"	16	60-9315	3 3/16"	8	60-9008	Batter (top and bottom)	2
12x16 Dyna	60-9370	2¼"	20	60-9322	1¾"	20	60-9014	Batter (top and bottom)	2
12x16 Pwt	60-9370	2¼"	16	60-9322	1¾"	16	60-9012	Batter (top and bottom)	2
12x16 Camb.	61-0122	5"	16	60-9315	3 3/16"	8	60-9012	Batter (top and bottom)	2

SCOTCH DRUMS

	KEY TENSION RODS			LUGS			BASS DRUM COUNTER HOOPS			CLAW HOOKS	
	Stock Number	Length	Quan	Stock Number	Hole Spacing	Quan	Stock Number		Quan	Stock Number	Quan
10x26 Dyna	60-9360	3½"	20	60-9322	1¾"	20	60-9060	Pearl Inlay	2	60-2286	20
10x26 Pwt	60-9360	3½"	20	60-9322	1¾"	20	60-9060	Pearl Inlay	2	60-2286	20
10x26 Camb.	60-9360	3½"	20	60-9316	3 3/16"	10	60-9060	Pearl Inlay	2	60-2286	20
10x28 Dyna	60-9360	3½"	24	60-9322	1¾"	24	60-9063	Pearl Inlay	2	60-2286	24
10x28 Pwt	60-9360	3½"	24	60-9322	1¾"	24	60-9063	Pearl Inlay	2	60-2286	24
10x28 Camb.	60-9360	3½"	24	60-9316	3 3/16"	12	60-9063	Pearl Inlay	2	60-2286	24

RUDIMENTAL BASS DRUMS

	KEY TENSION RODS			LUGS			BASS DRUM COUNTER HOOPS			CLAW HOOKS	
	Stock Number	Length	Quan	Stock Number	Hole Spacing	Quan	Stock Number		Quan	Stock Number	Quan
12x24 Dyna	60-9360	3½"	20	60-9322	1¾"	20	60-9057	Pearl Inlay	2	60-2286	20
12x24 Pwt	60-9360	3½"	20	60-9322	1¾"	20	60-9057	Pearl Inlay	2	60-2286	20
14x26 Dyna	60-9360	3½"	24	60-9318	2 5/16"	24	60-9060	Pearl Inlay	2	60-2286	24
14x26 Pwt	60-9360	3½"	24	60-9318	2 5/16"	24	60-9060	Pearl Inlay	2	60-2286	24
14x28 Dyna	60-9360	3½"	24	60-9318	2 5/16"	24	60-9063	Pearl Inlay	2	60-2286	24
14x28 Pwt	60-9360	3½"	24	60-9318	2 5/16"	24	60-9063	Pearl Inlay	2	60-2286	24

ROGERS PARTS

1973 Parts Catalog

HI-HATS

48-0570 Supreme Hi-Hat
48-0510 Swiv-O-Matic Hi-Hat, hinged heel
48-0511 Swiv-O-Matic Hi-Hat, solid footboard

ASSEMBLIES

(A)	61-0409-049	Lower Base Assy (of 48-0570)
(B)	61-0404-049	Footboard Assy (of 48-0570)
(C)	48-1800	Hi-Hat Clutch, complete
(D)	60-8076-050	Lower Base Assy (of 48-0510)
(E)	60-8088-050	Lower Base Assy (of 48-0511)
(F)	60-8043-049	Footboard Assy (of 48-0510)
(G)	60-8037-036	Footboard Assy (of 48-0511)

PARTS

(2)	60-9247	Felt washers, large, pkg of 6
(3)	60-9248	Fibre washers, large, pkg of 6
(4)	61-0500	Tilter screw with nut, pkg of 2
(5)	61-0414-049	Upper tube assy, each
(6)	60-8267	"U" clamp (1-1/8 x 1" hole sizes), each
(7)	60-9249	Wing screws, pkg of 4
(8)	60-8278	"U" clamp (1-1/8 x 1-1/8" hole sizes), each
(9)	60-8337-052	Sliding leg clamp, each (three to a set)
(10)	60-8156-052	Leg link section, each (takes two per leg)
(11)	61-0395-052	Leg, each
(12)	61-0174	Rubber tips, pkg of 12
(13)	61-0382-032	Stirrup, each
(14)	61-0492	Pull set screws, pkg of 6
(15)	61-0390-052	Double self-aligning spur, each
(16)	61-0397	Connecting hinge rod, each
(17)	61-0427	Heel pivot shaft screw, each
(18)	61-0432-066	Heel, each
(19)	61-0428-066	Footboard, each
(20)	61-0499	Spring adjusting block nut, pkg of 2
(21)	60-8284-052	Metal collar ring (1-1/8" I.D.), each
(22)	61-0383-015	Flange tilter bushing, each
(23)	61-0519	Allen screws, pkg of 6
(24)	61-0391	Pivot shaft, each
(25)	61-0496	Pedal links, pkg of 2
(26)	61-0433	Pedal link screw, each
(27)	61-0495	Nut (for pdl. link screw), pkg of 2
(28)	60-9261	Allen screws, pkg of 12
(29)	60-9244	Wing screws, pkg of 2
(30)	60-9245	Lock nuts, pkg of 6
(31)	60-9246	Felt washers, small, pkg of 12
(32)	60-9267	Clutch retainer nuts, pkg of 2
(33)	61-0486-049	Upper tube assy, each
(34)	60-8003	"U" clamp (3/4 x 5/8" hole sizes), each
(35)	60-8091-035	Sliding leg clamp, each (three to a set)
(36)	60-8002	"U" clamp (3/4 x 3/4" hole sizes), each
(37)	60-8054-053	Metal cross-pin, each
(38)	60-5214-035	Footboard, each
(39)	60-8084-035	Heel, each
(40)	60-8038	Heel pivot shaft bearing, each
(41)	60-8066-052	Connecting hinge rod, each
(42)	60-4418	Rubber tips, pkg of 12
(43)	60-8006-052	Spur, each
(44)	60-8011-052	Metal pedal link, each
(45)	60-8008-052	Leg link, each
(46)	60-8012-052	Leg, each
(47)	60-8062-052	Metal collar ring (3/4" I.D.)
(48)	60-5213-035	Footboard, each
(49)	60-8037-066	Heel base, each
(50)	60-9214	Heel bearing screws, pkg of 6
(51)	60-8067-052	Connecting rod, each

ITEMS NOT REFERENCED	for 48-0570	for 48-0510 & 48-0511
Upper pull rod, each	61-0400 W/nylon bushing	61-0180 Pkg of 2
Lower pull rod Assy, each	61-0401-049	60-9259
Compression springs, Pkg of 3	60-9262	60-9262
Rubber sleeve, each	61-0402	
Nylon heel bearings, Pkg of 2	61-0494	
Heat Shrink tubing, Pkg of 4	61-0497	
Rubber bumpers, Pkg of 6	61-0493	
Rivets (3/16 x 1/2") Pkg of 24	61-0490	61-0490
Rivets (3/16 x 11/16") Pkg of 24	61-0488	61-0488
Rivets (3/16 x 13/16") Pkg of 24	61-0489	61-0489

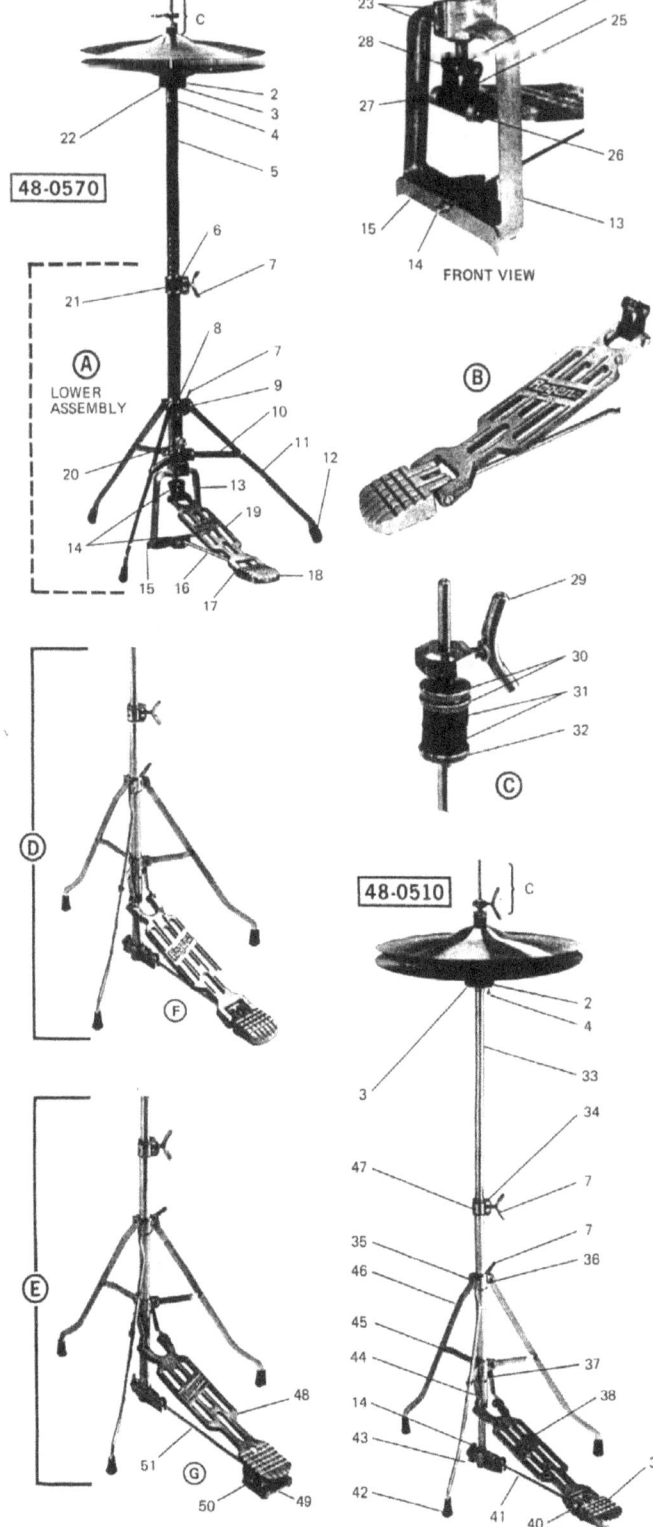

214

ROGERS PARTS

1973 Parts Catalog

DUAL TOM HOLDERS AND STANDS

48-2601 Dual Tom Tom Holder
48-0518 Dual Tom Tom Stand
48-0521 Samson Dual Tom Tom Stand
48-0522 Supreme Dual Tom Tom Stand

ASSEMBLIES
(Reference)
- (A) 48-0200   Swiv-O-Matic Center Assy, each
- (B) 48-2200   Receiving Unit, each
- (C) 60-8342-049   Lower Section Assy, each
- (D) 61-0143   Lower Riser Tube Assy, each
- (E) 61-0147   Lower Section Assy, each
- (F) 60-8273-049   Lower Section Assy, each
- (G) 60-6348-052   "T" Support Bar, each

PARTS
- (1) 60-6347-049   Short center section, each
- (2) 61-0491   Set screws, pkg of 12
- (3) 60-0313   Collet nose, each
- (4) 60-8130   "U" clamp (3/4 x 5/8" hole sizes), each
- (5) 60-9249   Wing screws, pkg of 4
- (6) 61-0175   Carriage bolts, pkg of 12
- (7) 60-6487-053   Reinforcing plate, each
- (8) 61-0170   Hex nut, pkg of 2
- (9) 60-8062-052   Metal collar ring (3/4" I.D.)
- (10) 60-8280-052   Leg section, each (takes two sections for a leg)
- (11) 60-8297-052   Leg link, each
- (12) 61-0174   Rubber tips, pkg of 12
- (13) 60-8338-052   Sliding leg clamp, each (three to a set)
- (14) 60-8290   "U" clamp (1-1/8 x 5/8" hole sizes), each
- (15) 61-0135   "U" clamp (1 x 5/8" hole sizes), each
- (16) 60-8205-052   Metal collar ring (5/8" I.D.), each
- (17) 60-8267   "U" clamp (1-1/8 x 1" hole sizes), each
- (18) 60-8266-052   Metal collar ring (1-1/8" I.D.), each
- (19) 60-8155-052   Leg, each
- (20) 60-8156-052   Leg link section, each (takes two sections for a link)
- (21) 60-4418   Rubber tips, pkg of 12
-      61-0490   Rivets (3/16 x 1/2), pkg of 24
-      61-0488   Rivets (3/16 x 11/16), pkg of 24
-      61-0489   Rivets (3/16 x 13/16), pkg of 24

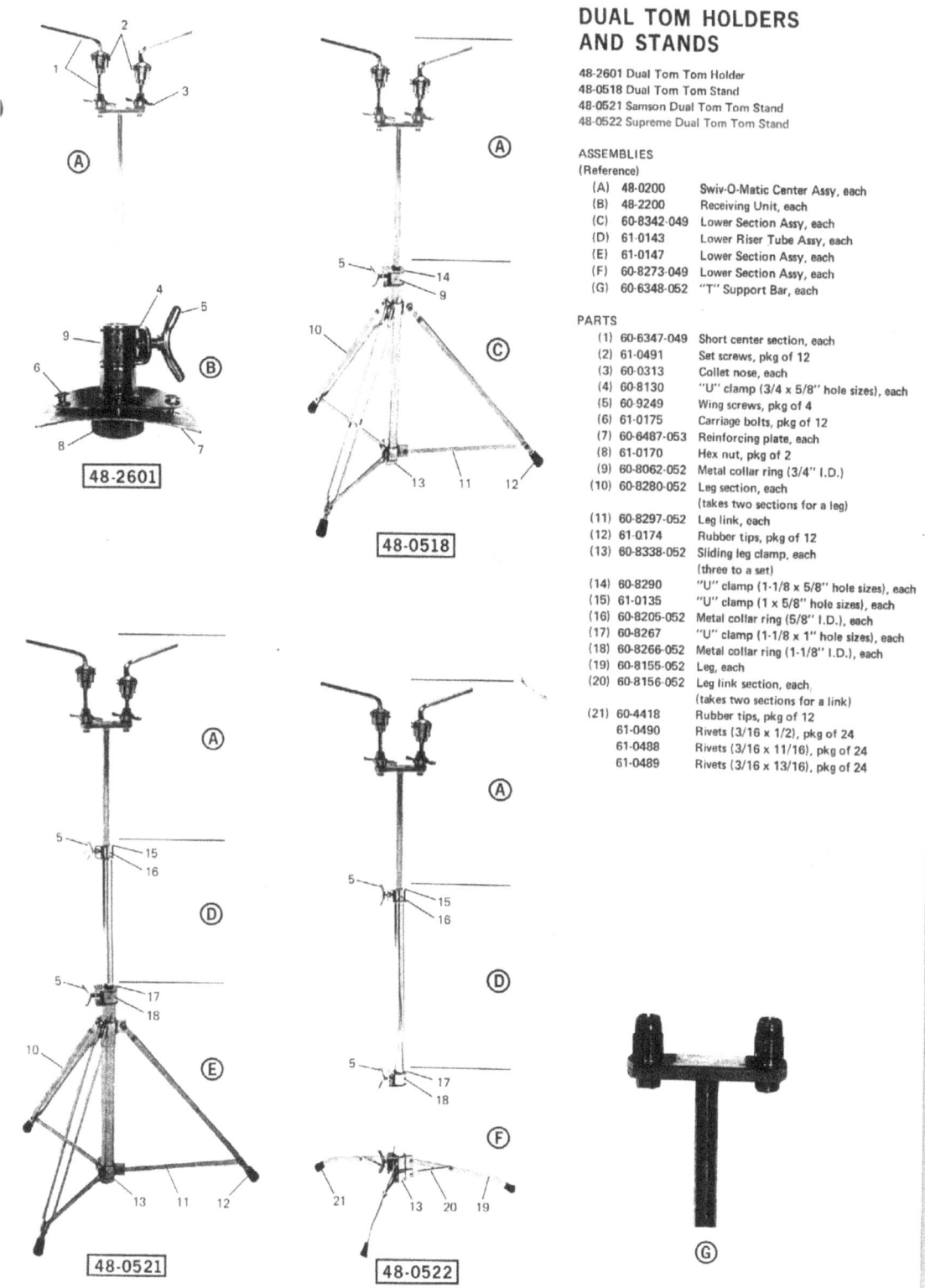

ROGERS PARTS

1973 Parts Catalog

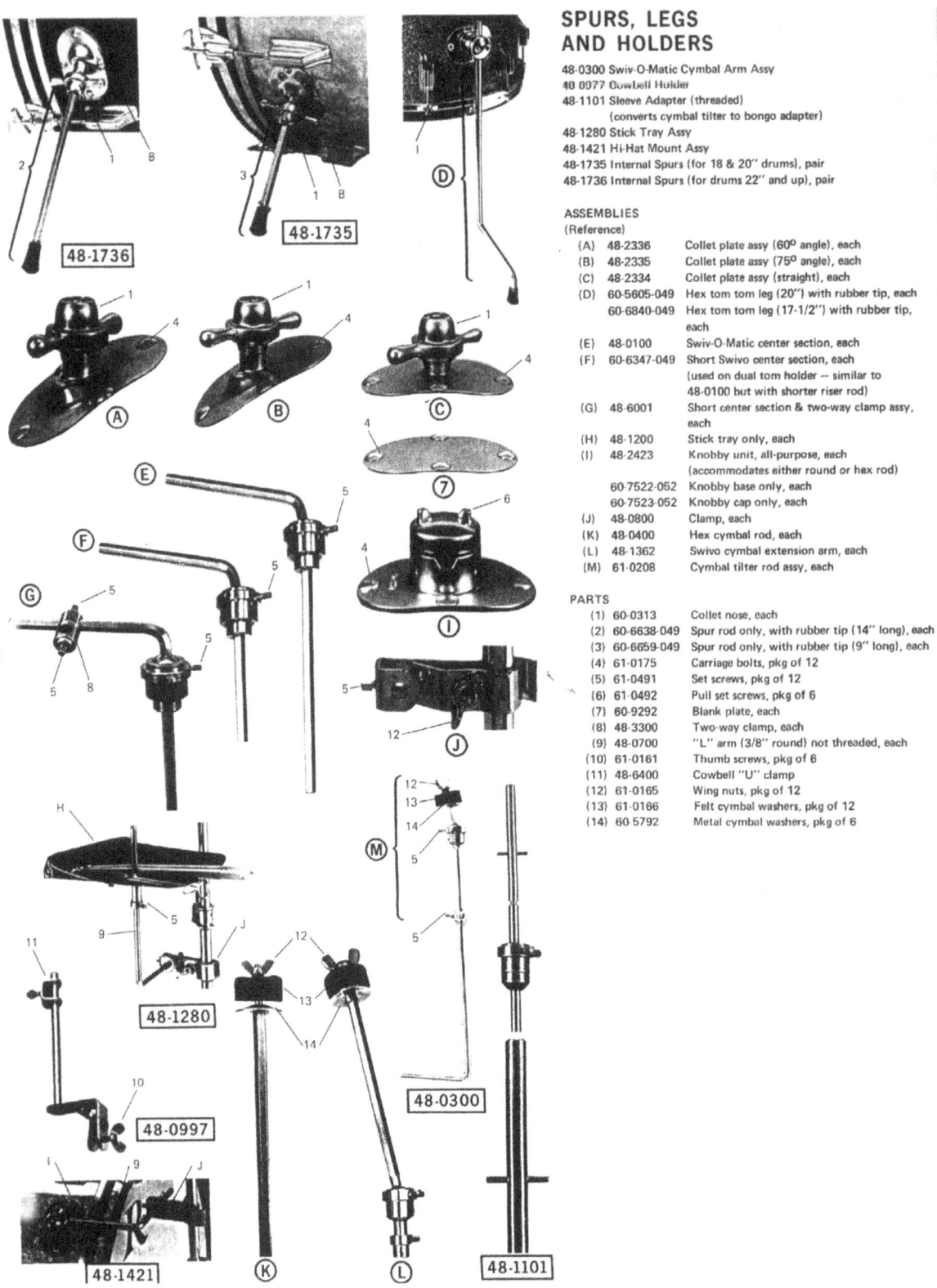

SPURS, LEGS AND HOLDERS

- 48-0300 Swiv-O-Matic Cymbal Arm Assy
- 48-0077 Cowbell Holder
- 48-1101 Sleeve Adapter (threaded)
  (converts cymbal tilter to bongo adapter)
- 48-1280 Stick Tray Assy
- 48-1421 Hi-Hat Mount Assy
- 48-1735 Internal Spurs (for 18 & 20" drums), pair
- 48-1736 Internal Spurs (for drums 22" and up), pair

ASSEMBLIES
(Reference)

(A)	48-2336	Collet plate assy (60° angle), each
(B)	48-2335	Collet plate assy (75° angle), each
(C)	48-2334	Collet plate assy (straight), each
(D)	60-5605-049	Hex tom tom leg (20") with rubber tip, each
	60-6840-049	Hex tom tom leg (17-1/2") with rubber tip, each
(E)	48-0100	Swiv-O-Matic center section, each
(F)	60-6347-049	Short Swivo center section, each (used on dual tom holder -- similar to 48-0100 but with shorter riser rod)
(G)	48-6001	Short center section & two-way clamp assy, each
(H)	48-1200	Stick tray only, each
(I)	48-2423	Knobby unit, all-purpose, each (accommodates either round or hex rod)
	60-7522-052	Knobby base only, each
	60-7523-052	Knobby cap only, each
(J)	48-0800	Clamp, each
(K)	48-0400	Hex cymbal rod, each
(L)	48-1362	Swivo cymbal extension arm, each
(M)	61-0208	Cymbal tilter rod assy, each

PARTS

(1)	60-0313	Collet nose, each
(2)	60-6638-049	Spur rod only, with rubber tip (14" long), each
(3)	60-6659-049	Spur rod only, with rubber tip (9" long), each
(4)	61-0175	Carriage bolts, pkg of 12
(5)	61-0491	Set screws, pkg of 12
(6)	61-0492	Pull set screws, pkg of 6
(7)	60-9292	Blank plate, each
(8)	48-3300	Two-way clamp, each
(9)	48-0700	"L" arm (3/8" round) not threaded, each
(10)	61-0161	Thumb screws, pkg of 6
(11)	48-6400	Cowbell "U" clamp
(12)	61-0165	Wing nuts, pkg of 12
(13)	61-0166	Felt cymbal washers, pkg of 12
(14)	60-5792	Metal cymbal washers, pkg of 6

ROGERS PARTS

1973 Parts Catalog

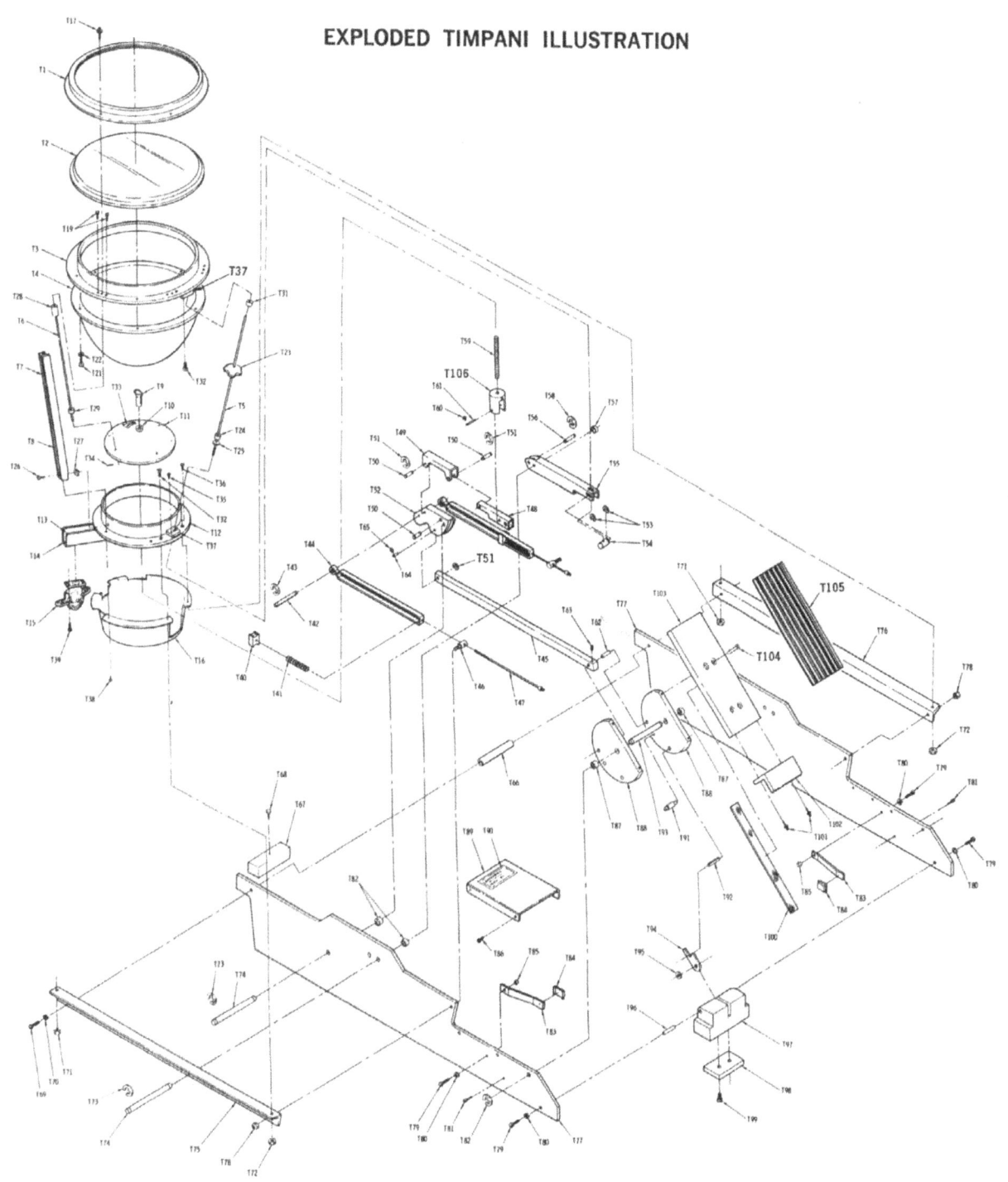

ROGERS PARTS

1973 Parts Catalog

ROGERS ACCU-SONIC TIMPANI PARTS

T#	Part #	Description
T1		Counterhoop
	60-9516	20 inch
	60-9517	23 inch
	60-9518	26 inch
	60-9519	29 inch
T2		ACT Timpani Head (Inside Diameter – Outside Diameter)
	50-6121	20 inch, 21 in., 22 in.
	50-6124	23 inch, 24 in., 25 in.
	50-6127	26 inch, 27 in., 28 in.
	50-6130	29 inch, 30 in., 31 in.
T3		Resonator Ring
	60-9566-090	20 inch
	60-9567-090	23 inch
	60-9568-090	26 inch
	60-9569-090	29 inch
T4		Bowl
	60-9562-090	20 inch
	60-9563-090	23 inch
	60-9564-090	26 inch
	60-9565-090	29 inch
T5		Fine Tuning Rod (Length)
	60-9668-052	20/26 (27-5/16 in.)
	60-9669-052	23/29 (27-5/8 in.)
T6		Rod Tension Tube (Length)
	60-9680-052	20/26 (24-13/16 in.)
	60-9681-052	23/29 (25-3/16 in.)
T7		Strut (Length)
	60-9524-090	20/26 (25-7/16 in.)
	60-9525-090	23/29 (25-11/16 in.)
T8	60-9527	Tape, Walnut grain – 18 ft
T9	60-9600-052	Master Tuning Nut
T10	61-0254	Master Tuning Grommet, Pkg of 4
T11		Spider
	60-9532-090	20/23
	60-9533-090	26/29
T12		Basic Ring
	60-9521-090	20/23
	60-9522-090	26/29
T13	61-0255	Insert, Walnut Grain, Pkg of 2
T14	60-9627-090	Channel Leg, 1/4 x 5-5/16 in.
T15	60-9561	Caster
T16		Bottom Enclosure
	60-9597-090	20/23
	60-9598-090	26/29
T17	61-0492	Tension Set Screw w/collar, Pkg of 6
T18	61-0155	Washers for Tension Rods, Pkg of 48
T19	60-9535	Screw, Flat head
T21	60-9541	Screw 1/4-20 x 5/8
T22	61-0363	Fibre Washer 1/4 x 1/2 x 1/16, Pkg of 8
T23	60-9670	Fine Tuning Knob
T24	60-9671-052	Collar
T25	60-9591	Washer Grommet 3/8
T26	61-0256	Screw 10-32 x 12 Allen, Pkg of 8
T27	61-0257	Retainer Plate, Pkg of 8
T28	61-0258	Bushing, Gum Rubber 3/16 x 1/8, Pkg of 8
T29	61-0259	Bushing, Gum Rubber – Pkg of 8
T31	60-9662	Bushing, Nylon
T32	61-0260	Screw, 8-32 x 1/2 Allen, Pkg of 8
T33	60-2448-052	Name Plate
T34	61-0364	Tension Rod Pin 1/8 x 7/8, Pkg of 8
T35	60-9546	Screw 1/4-20 x 3/4 Allen
T36	61-0260	Screw 8-32 x 1/2 Allen, Pkg of 8
T37	60-9665-090	Bearing Plate for Fine Tuning Rod
T38	61-0361	Screw 10-32 x 1/2, Pkg of 8
T39	61-0362	Screw 1/4-20 x 1/2 Truss Head, Pkg of 8
T40	60-9637	Tension Nut
T41	60-9638	Spring Paragon 33-7
T42	60-9643	Lever Pin
T43	60-3467	E Snap Ring
T44	60-9755-053	Spring Housing
T45		Pedal Link
	60-9640-053	20/23
	60-9679-053	26/29
T46	60-6906-053	Bracket Link
T47		Spring Tension Adjustment Rod
	60-9639-053	20/23, 10-1/8 in. long
	60-9678-053	26/29, 12-7/8 in. long
T48	60-9633-053	Lever
T49	60-9634-053	Link Toggle
T50	60-9040-053	Link Toggle Pin
T51	60-3467	E Ring
T52	60-9635-053	Toggle
T53	60-3464	C Ring
T54	60-9672-053	Trunnion Nut for Fine Tuning Lever
T55		Fine Tuning Lever
	60-9676-053	20/23
	60-9703-053	26/29
T56	60-9673-053	Pivot
T57	60-9656-053	Bushing
T58	60-3465	E Ring
T59		Stud
	60-9615-053	20/23, 3-7/8 in. long
	60-9616-053	26/29, 4-9/16 in. long
T60	60-3467	E Snap Ring
T61	60-9644-053	Clevis Pin
T62	60-9655-053	Pivot Pedal Pin, 3/8 dia x 2-7/8
T63	60-9550	Allen Set Screw 8-32 x 3/8
T64	60-9546	Link Toggle Pin
T65	60-3465	E Ring
T66	60-9601-053	Rod Spacer
T67	60-9684-090	Block Spacer
T68	60-5830	Wood Screw Oval Head, 6 x 1
T69	60-9551	Screw 1/4-20 x 3/4 Truss Head
T70	60-9594	Shakeproof Spring Washer
T71	60-9544	Stop Nut 1/4-20
T72	60-9536	Allen Screw 10-32 x 1-1/4
T73	60-3464	C Ring
T74	60-9645-053	Toggle Rod
T75		Angle Bracket, Left-hand Housing
	60-9613-090	20/23, 15 in. long
	60-9611-090	26/29, 21 in. long
T76		Angle Bracket, Right-hand Housing
	60-9612-090	20/23, 15 in. long
	60-9620-090	26/29, 21 in. long
T77		Side Plate for Pedal Assembly
	60-9608-090	20/23
	60-9609-090	26/29
T78	60-9548	Stop Nut 5/16-18
T79	60-9551	Screw 1/4-20 x 3/4 Truss Head
T80	60-5372	Washer, 1/4 Lock
T81	61-0491	Heel Brake Screw 1/4-20 x 7/16, Pkg of 12
T82	60-9656-053	Spacer
T83	60-9658-053	Brake Spring
T84	60-9659-040	Brake Shoe
T85	60-9544	Stop Nut 1/4-20
T86	60-9699	Cover Screw
T87	60-9656-053	Pedal Support Spacer
T88	60-9651-090	Pedal Support
T89	60-9693-090	Pedal Housing Cover
T91	60-9654-053	Pedal Support Pin
T92	60-9552	Pedal Support Pin
T93	60-9649-053	Pedal Support Spacer Rod
T94	60-9603-053	Pedal Lock
T95	60-9594	Shakeproof Spring Washer
T96	60-9605	Heel Block Pin
T97	60-9607-090	Heel Block Spacer
T98	60-9592	Rubber Pad for Heel Block
T99	60-9547	Allen Screw 10-32 x 1/2
T100	60-9727	Rubber Strip for Footboard Side
T101	61-0492	Set Screw w/collar 5/8 in. length, Pkg of 6
T102	60-9708-090	Pedal Heel Rest
T103	60-9650-090	Foot Plate
T104	60-9546	Foot Plate Allen Screws 1/4-20 x 3/4
T105	60-9726	Footboard Rubber Pad
T106	60-9687-053	Clevis

COMPLETE PEDAL ASSEMBLY
(T40 through T106)

60-9827-049	For 20/23 Timpani with fine tuning
60-9828-049	For 26/29 Timpani with fine tuning
60-9829-049	For 20/23 Timpani without fine tuning
60-9830-049	For 26/29 Timpani without fine tuning

ROGERS PARTS

1973 Parts Catalog

FOOT PEDALS

54-7000 Supreme foot pedal
54-7006 Swiv-O-matic foot pedal, hinged heel
54-7007 Swiv-O-matic foot pedal, adjustable footboard

ASSEMBLIES & PARTS

(A)	61-0685-049	Riser assembly for Supreme model
(B)	61-0919-049	Riser assembly for Swiv-O-matic models
(C)	61-0194-052	Pedal hoop clamp for Swiv-O-matic models
(D)	61-0918-049	Footboard assembly for 54-7007 model
(E)	61-0921-049	Footboard assembly for 54-7006 model
(1)	60-0261	Pull set screw (1/4-20 x 5/8" thread) each
(2)	61-0939-038	Stroke adjustment arm (Supreme Pedal) each
(2-1)	60-5204-066	Stroke adjustment arm (Swivo Pedal) each
(3)	60-2295	Lock washer, each
(4)	61-0749	Wing nut, with nylon insert, each (1/4-20 thread)
(5)	60-6193	Spring adjustment screw, each
(6)	61-0690-049	Spring assembly with hooks & bushing, each
(7)	60-9206-052	Hex head cam bolt (10-24 x 1/2" thread) each
(8)	60-5207-038	Rocker arm, each
(9)	60-5269	Allen screw (1/4-20 x 3/8" thread) each
(10)	60-9222	Swivo set screw (1/4-20 x 1/2" thread) each
(11)	60-9208-052	Right hand spur, each
(12)	60-9210	Pull set screw (1/4-20 x 3/8" thread) each
(13)	61-0681	Heel, for Supreme model, each
(14)	60-9209-052	Left hand spur, each
(15)	61-0684	Toe stop, for Supreme model, each
(16)	61-0697	Pedal strap, each
(17)	61-0747-038	Pedal beater cam, for Supreme model, each
(18)	60-5200-066	Pedal beater cam, for Swivo models, each
(19)	61-0674-049	Black Jack pedal beater, (5/16" shaft for Supreme model) each
(20)	61-0797-049	Black Jack, Jr. pedal beater (1/4" shaft for Swiv-O-matic models) each
(21)	61-0683	Connecting hinge rod, for Supreme model, each
(22)	61-0658-049	Swivel unit assembly, each
(23)	61-0588	Rubber bumper, each
(25)	61-0942	Oval head screw (10-32 x 3/8" thread) each
(26)	61-0130	Slotted hex head screw, each (8-32 x 7/16" thread)
(27)	60-5414	Flat washer (3/16 x 1") each
(29)	61-0590	Nylon bearing bushing, each
(30)	61-0645	Pivot rod, each
(31)	60-5261	Round head screw, for toe stop, each (10-24 x 9/16" thread)
(32)	60-9211-052	Locking screw (5/16" dia. x 3" long) each
(33)	61-0920	Connecting hinge rod, each (for 54-7006 model)
(34)	60-8060	Pivot rod, each
(35)	61-0689	Needle bearing, each (inside fitting, not illustrated)
(36)	60-8084-066	Heel, for 54-7006 model, each
(37)	60-5426	Roll pin, each
(38)	60-5267	Slotted head screw, each (10-24 x 3/8" thread)
(39)	61-0628-066	Toe stop, for 54-7007 model, each
(40)	61-0916	Connecting hinge rod, each (for 54-7007 model)
(41)	60-8037-066	Heel base, for 54-7007 model, each
(42)	60-5189-066	Heel, for 54-7007 model, each
(43)	60-9218-053	Plate (underneath—not illustrated) each
(44)	60-9224-052	Pressure plate, each

Side view of Supreme Pedal
Note: Footboard raised above normal position to expose underneath parts.

54-7000 SUPREME

Ⓐ and Ⓑ

2 and/or 2-1

SWIV-O-MATIC

Copyright © 1970-1973-1974-1975, Rogers Drums, CBS Musical Instruments, a Division of CBS Inc.

ROGERS PARTS

1975 Parts Catalog

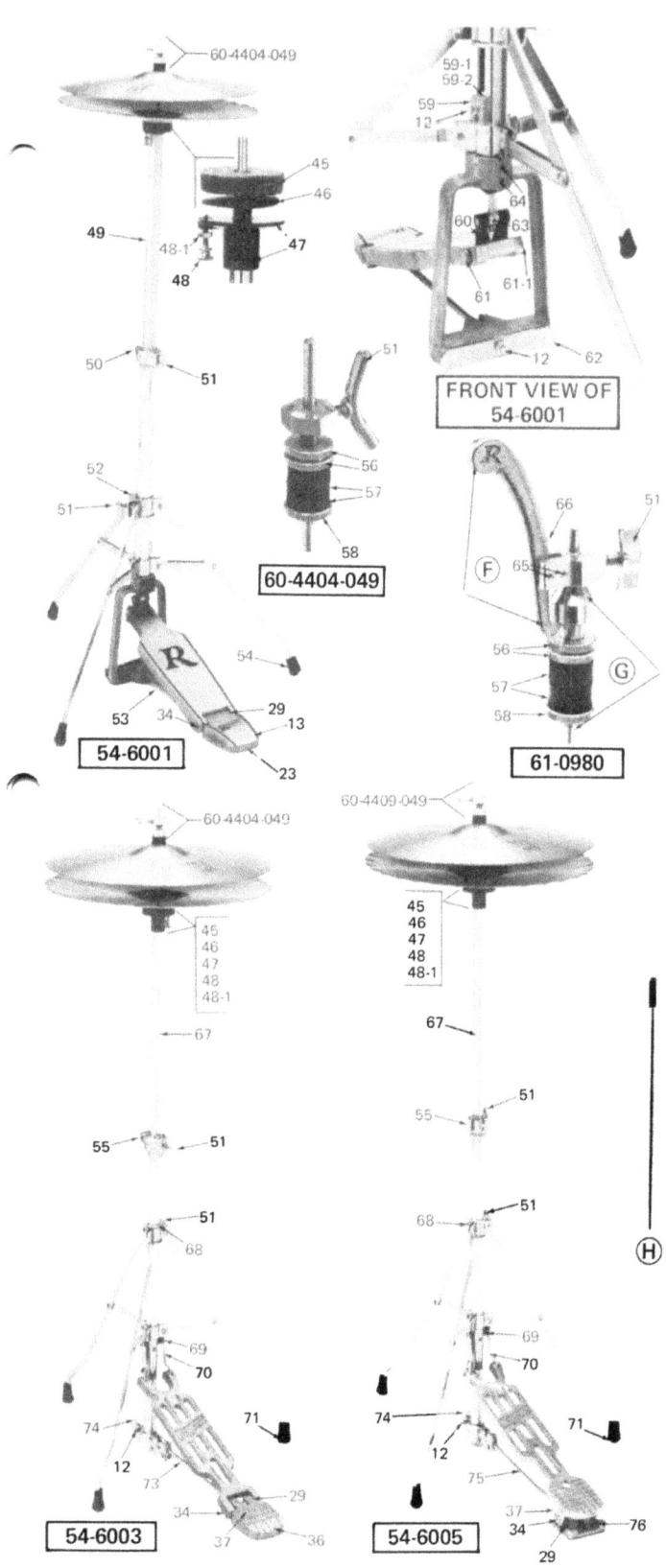

HI-HATS & ACCESSORIES

54-6001 Supreme Hi-Hat
54-6003 Swiv-O-matic Hi-Hat, hinged heel
54-6005 Swiv-O-matic Hi-Hat, 1 pce. footboard
60-4404-049 Hi-Hat clutch
61-0980 Dual-matic Hi-Hat clutch

ASSEMBLIES & PARTS

- (F) 61-0523 Upper section of Dual-matic hi-hat clutch
- (G) 61-0528 Lower section of Dual-matic hi-hat clutch
- (H) 61-0790-049 Hi-Hat extension rod (1/4-20 x 7" thread)
- (12) 60-9210 Pull set screw, each (1/4-20 x 3/8" thread)
- (13) 61-0681 Heel, for Supreme model, each
- (23) 61-0588 Rubber bumper, each
- (29) 61-0590 Nylon bearing bushing, each
- (34) 60-8060 Pivot rod, each
- (36) 60-8084-066 Heel, for 54-6003 model, each
- (37) 60-5426 Roll pin, each
- (45) 60-8057 Large felt washer, each
- (46) 60-8056 Large fibre washer, each
- (47) 61-0383-015 Flange tilter adapter, each
- (48) 61-0951 Tilter screw, each (8-32 x 3/4" thread)
- (48-1) 60-5381 Nut only, each (8-32 thread)
- (49) 61-0848-052 Upper tube of Supreme model, each
- (50) 61-0803-049 MemriLoc clamp (1 in. I.D.) each
- (51) 61-0878 Thumb screw, each (1/4-20 x 3/4" thread)
- (52) 61-0930-037 "U" clamp (1-1/8" holes) each
- (53) 61-0714 Connecting hinge rod, each (for Supreme model)
- (54) 60-8340 Rubber tip (No. 16) each
- (55) 61-0805-049 MemriLoc clamp (3/4 in. I.D.) each
- (56) 60-8040 Lock nut (3/8" thread) each
- (57) 60-8042 Small felt washer, each
- (58) 60-8041-052 Clutch retainer nut, each (3/8" thread)
- (59) 61-0392 Nut (1/4-20 thread) each (for Supreme spring tension)
- (59-1) 61-0484 Nylon bushing, each (f/spring tension assy) (inside fitting—not illustrated)
- (59-2) 60-8049-053 Hex coupling, each (f/spring tension assy) (inside fitting—not illustrated)
- (60) 61-0388 Pedal link (f/Supr. model) each
- (61) 61-0391 Hex head shoulder screw, each (1/4-20 x 3/8" thread)
- (61-1) 61-0434 Hex nut (1/4-20 thread) each
- (62) 61-0390-052 Double self-aligning spur, each
- (63) 60-5274 Allen screw, each (1/4-20 x 3/8" thread)
- (64) 60-5270 Allen screw, each (1/4-20 x 1/4" thread)
- (65) 60-5425 Roll pin, each
- (66) 61-0527 Lever spring, each
- (67) 61-0853-052 Upper tube (Swivo model) each
- (68) 61-0931-037 "U" clamp (3/4" holes) each
- (69) 60-8054-053 Cross pin only, each
- (70) 60-8011-052 Pedal link (Swivo model) each
- (71) 60-2427 Rubber tip (No. 15) each
- (73) 60-8066-052 Connecting rod (54-6003 mdl.) each
- (74) 60-8006-052 Hi-hat spur (Swivo models) each
- (75) 60-8067-052 Connecting rod (54-6005 mdl.) each
- (76) 60-8037-066 Heel base (54-6005 model) each

ITEMS NOT REFERENCED	for model 54-6001	for models 54-6003 54-6005
Upper pull rod, each	61-0400-049 w/nylon bushing	60-8047-052
Lower pull rod assy., each	61-0401-049	60-9259
Compression springs, each	60-8052	60-8052
Silencer sleeve, each	61-0402	
Heat shrink tubing, each	61-0459	

ROGERS PARTS

1975 Parts Catalog

TOM TOM HOLDERS — STANDS

54-3001 Dual tom tom stand
54-3003 Extended Dual tom tom stand
54-5001 Drum throne
56-1100 Single tom tom holder
  (Part number does not include bass or tom tom receiver mounts).
56-1200 Dual tom tom holder
  (Part number does not include bass or tom tom receiver mounts).
56-1300 Triple tom tom holder
  (Part number does not include bass or tom tom receiver mounts).
61-0983-049 Mini-dual tom tom holder
  (Part number does not include tom tom receiver mounts).

ASSEMBLIES & PARTS

(J)	61-0892-049	Ratchet Arm Assembly (8") each
(K)	61-0891-049	Multiple tom center assy, each
(L)	61-0800-049	Shell mount receiver, each (complete with mounting screws & thumb screw)
(M)	61-0880-049	MemriLoc tripod base, each
(N)	61-0868-049	Extension tube with MemriLoc clamp (14" length) each (Fits into 1-1/8" tube and accommodates a 1" tube)
(10)	60-9222	Set screw, each (1/4-20 x 1/2" thread)
(24)	61-0841-052	Pull set screw, each (1/4-20 x 1" thread)
(50)	61-0803-049	MemriLoc clamp (1" I.D.) each
(51)	61-0878	Thumb screw, each (1/4-20 x 3/4" thread)
(51-1)	61-0972	Hex head mounting screw, each
(51-2)	61-0973	Washer, each
(77)	61-0832	"T" handle wing nut, each (1/4-20 thread)
(78)	60-6919	Carriage bolt, each (1/4-20 x 2" thread)
(79)	61-0915-049	Seat assy. (of drum throne) each
(80)	61-0910-049	Upper tube assy. w/insert, each w/MemriLoc clamp (f/throne)
(81-8)	61-0850-037	Ratchet arm (8") each
(81-12)	61-0740-037	Ratchet arm (12") each
(81-19)	61-0895-037	Ratchet arm (19") each
(82)	61-0828	Heavy duty ratchet casting, each
(83)	61-0831	Coil spring, each
(83-1)	60-5366	Washer (1/4 x 9/16") each
	61-0979-049	BD adapter
	61-0978-049	TT adapter

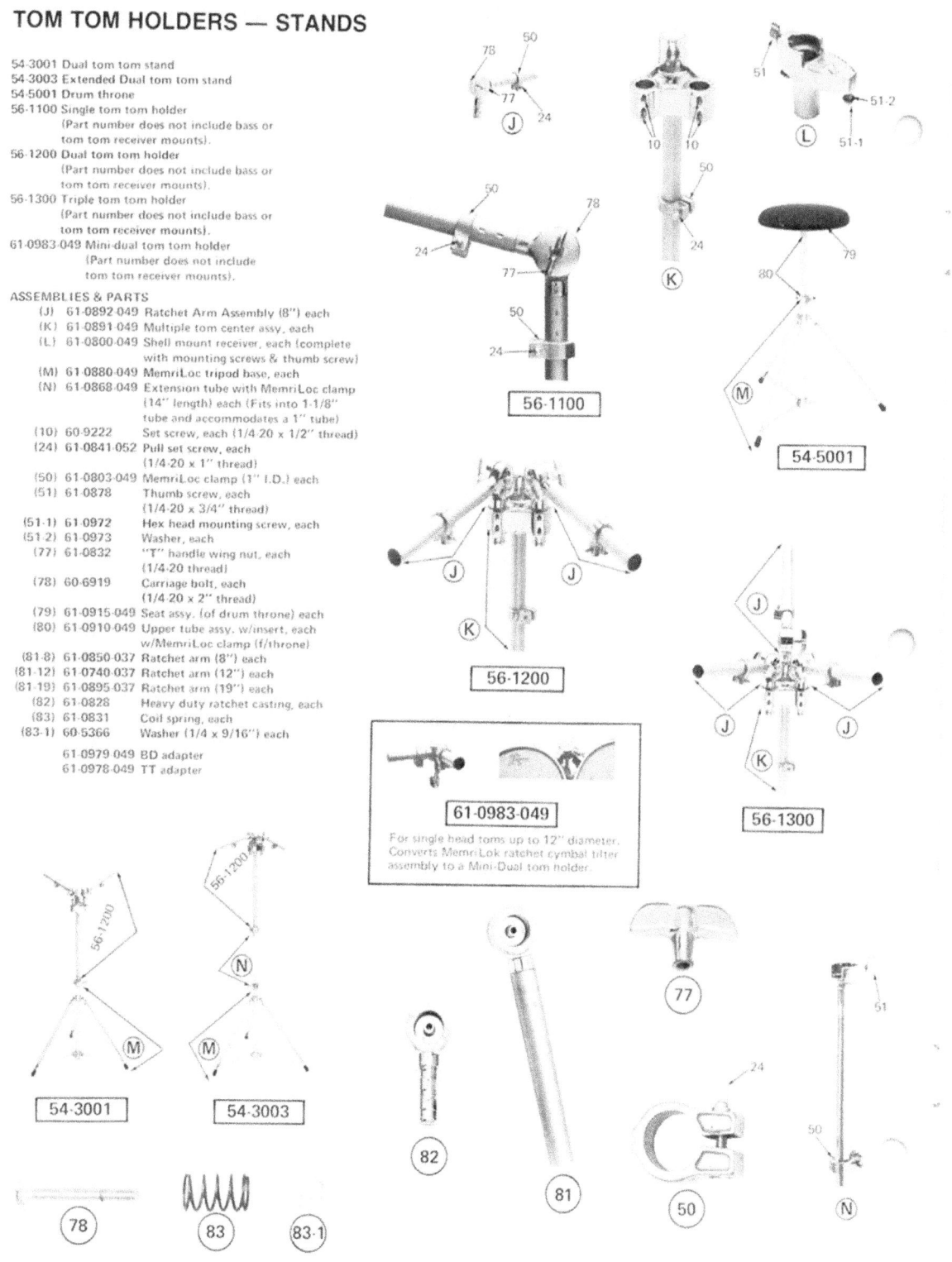

For single head toms up to 12" diameter. Converts MemriLok ratchet cymbal tilter assembly to a Mini-Dual tom holder.

ROGERS PARTS

1975 Parts Catalog

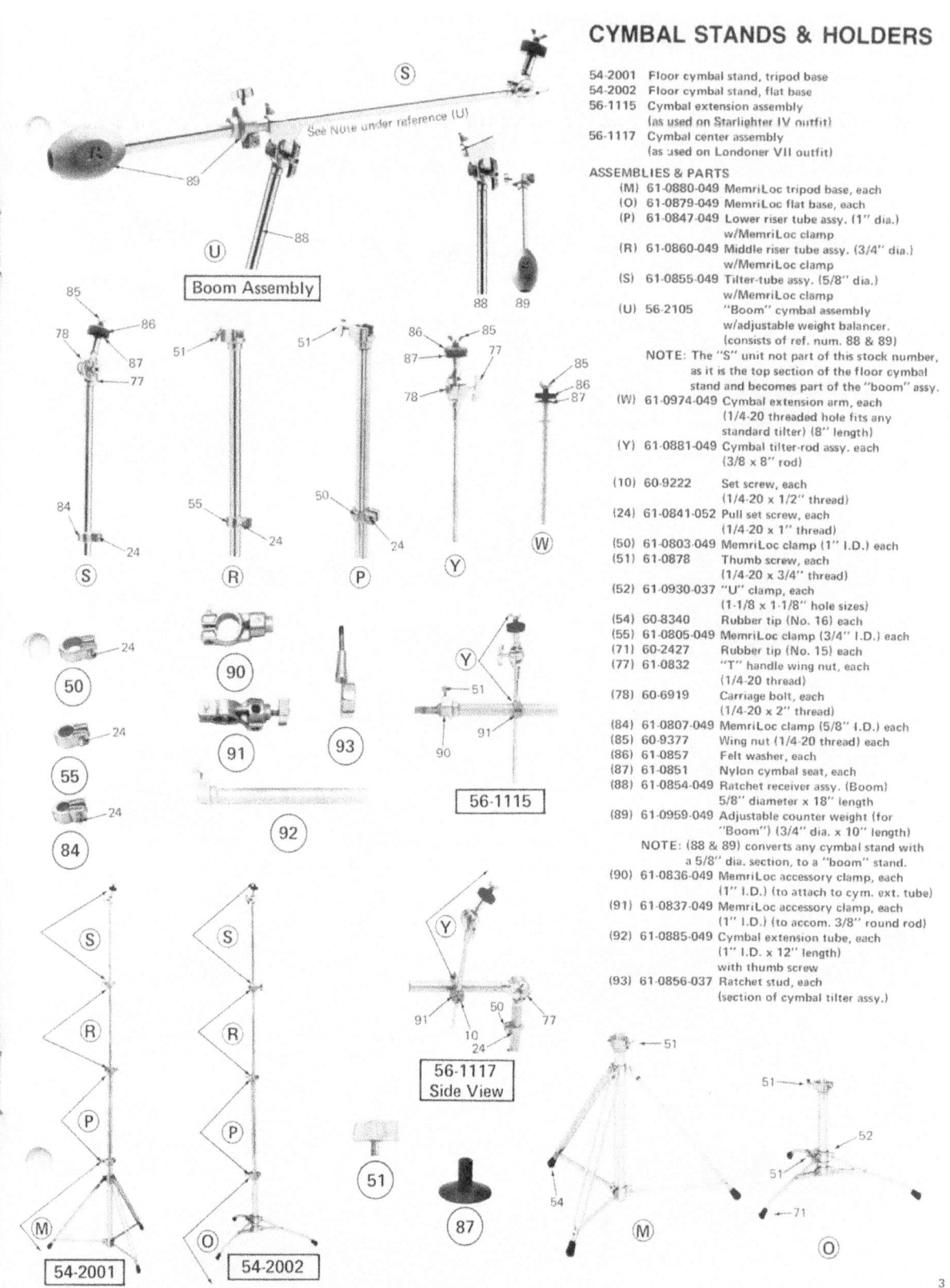

CYMBAL STANDS & HOLDERS

54-2001		Floor cymbal stand, tripod base
54-2002		Floor cymbal stand, flat base
56-1115		Cymbal extension assembly (as used on Starlighter IV outfit)
56-1117		Cymbal center assembly (as used on Londoner VII outfit)

ASSEMBLIES & PARTS

Ref	Part No.	Description
(M)	61-0880-049	MemriLoc tripod base, each
(O)	61-0879-049	MemriLoc flat base, each
(P)	61-0847-049	Lower riser tube assy. (1" dia.) w/MemriLoc clamp
(R)	61-0860-049	Middle riser tube assy. (3/4" dia.) w/MemriLoc clamp
(S)	61-0855-049	Tilter-tube assy. (5/8" dia.) w/MemriLoc clamp
(U)	56-2105	"Boom" cymbal assembly w/adjustable weight balancer. (consists of ref. num. 88 & 89)

NOTE: The "S" unit not part of this stock number, as it is the top section of the floor cymbal stand and becomes part of the "boom" assy.

Ref	Part No.	Description
(W)	61-0974-049	Cymbal extension arm, each (1/4-20 threaded hole fits any standard tilter) (8" length)
(Y)	61-0881-049	Cymbal tilter-rod assy. each (3/8 x 8" rod)
(10)	60-9222	Set screw, each (1/4-20 x 1/2" thread)
(24)	61-0841-052	Pull set screw, each (1/4-20 x 1" thread)
(50)	61-0803-049	MemriLoc clamp (1" I.D.) each
(51)	61-0878	Thumb screw, each (1/4-20 x 3/4" thread)
(52)	61-0930-037	"U" clamp, each (1-1/8 x 1-1/8" hole sizes)
(54)	60-8340	Rubber tip (No. 16) each
(55)	61-0805-049	MemriLoc clamp (3/4" I.D.) each
(71)	60-2427	Rubber tip (No. 15) each
(77)	61-0832	"T" handle wing nut, each (1/4-20 thread)
(78)	60-6919	Carriage bolt, each (1/4-20 x 2" thread)
(84)	61-0807-049	MemriLoc clamp (5/8" I.D.) each
(85)	60-9377	Wing nut (1/4-20 thread) each
(86)	61-0857	Felt washer, each
(87)	61-0851	Nylon cymbal seat, each
(88)	61-0854-049	Ratchet receiver assy. (Boom) 5/8" diameter x 18" length
(89)	61-0959-049	Adjustable counter weight (for "Boom") (3/4" dia. x 10" length)

NOTE: (88 & 89) converts any cymbal stand with a 5/8" dia. section, to a "boom" stand.

Ref	Part No.	Description
(90)	61-0836-049	MemriLoc accessory clamp, each (1" I.D.) (to attach to cym. ext. tube)
(91)	61-0837-049	MemriLoc accessory clamp, each (1" I.D.) (to accom. 3/8" round rod)
(92)	61-0885-049	Cymbal extension tube, each (1" I.D. x 12" length) with thumb screw
(93)	61-0856-037	Ratchet stud, each (section of cymbal tilter assy.)

ROGERS PARTS

1975 Parts Catalog

DRUM STANDS — TIMBALE STAND and ACCESSORIES

	48-3700	Bass Drum Rack
	54-1000	Drum Stand
	54-1001	Concert drum stand
	54-4001	Timbale stand
	61-0521-049	Hoop Spacers, pkg. of 6
	61-0640-049	Super X Muffler
	61-0936-049	Leg rest
	61-0975-049	Stick Tray assembly
	61-0976-049	Hi-Hat mount assembly

ASSEMBLIES & PARTS

(L)	61-0800-049	Shell mount receiver, each (complete with mounting screws and thumb screw)
(M)	61-0880-049	MemriLoc tripod base
(O)	61-0879-049	MemriLoc flat base
(T)	61-0725-049	Upper section of 54-1000 drum stand (12" length riser tube)
(V)	61-0894-049	Upper section of 54-1001 drum stand (19" length riser tube)
(AA)	61-0902-049	Upper section of timbale stand (19" length riser tube)
(BB)	61-0963-049	Cowbell holder assy. of timbale stand
(CC)	61-0673-049	Timbale bracket w/mounting screws
(DD)	60-0221-049	Knobby unit w/mounting bolts
(EE)	60-0284-049	Clamp for stick tray and hi-hat mount assemblies
(10)	60-9222	Set screw (1/4-20 x 1/2" thread) each
(50)	61-0803-049	MemriLoc clamp (1" I.D.) each
(77)	61-0832	"T" handle wing nut, each (1/4-20 thread)
(78)	60-6919	Carriage bolt, each (1/4-20 x 2" thread)
(85)	60-9377	Wing nut (1/4-20 thread) each
(94)	61-0759	Adjustable arm clamp support, each (as used on snare drum stands)
(95)	61-0731	Slotted fillister head screw, each (10-32 x 9/16" thread)
(96)	61-0912	Felt strip (4" length) each (as used on timbale stand)
(97)	61-0977-049	Cowbell "U" clamp, each with wing screw
(98)	60-5951-052	Round rod (3/8 x 10") each
(99)	60-7452-049	Two-way clamp, each
(100)	60-2360-052	Hex "L" rod, each
(101)	60-6169	Large heavy crutch tip, each
(102)	61-0893-049	Spur tube (1" dia.) each with clamp and crutch tip
(103)	61-0641	Wing nut (8-32 thread) each
(104)	61-0794	Internal lock washer, each
(105)	61-0869-037	3/8" ratchet rod, each (8" rod length)
(106)	60-5629-052	"L" rod (3/8" dia. rod) each
(107)	61-0901-049	Timbale stand square receiver, each with ratchet portion attached
(108)	61-0968	Stick tray only, each

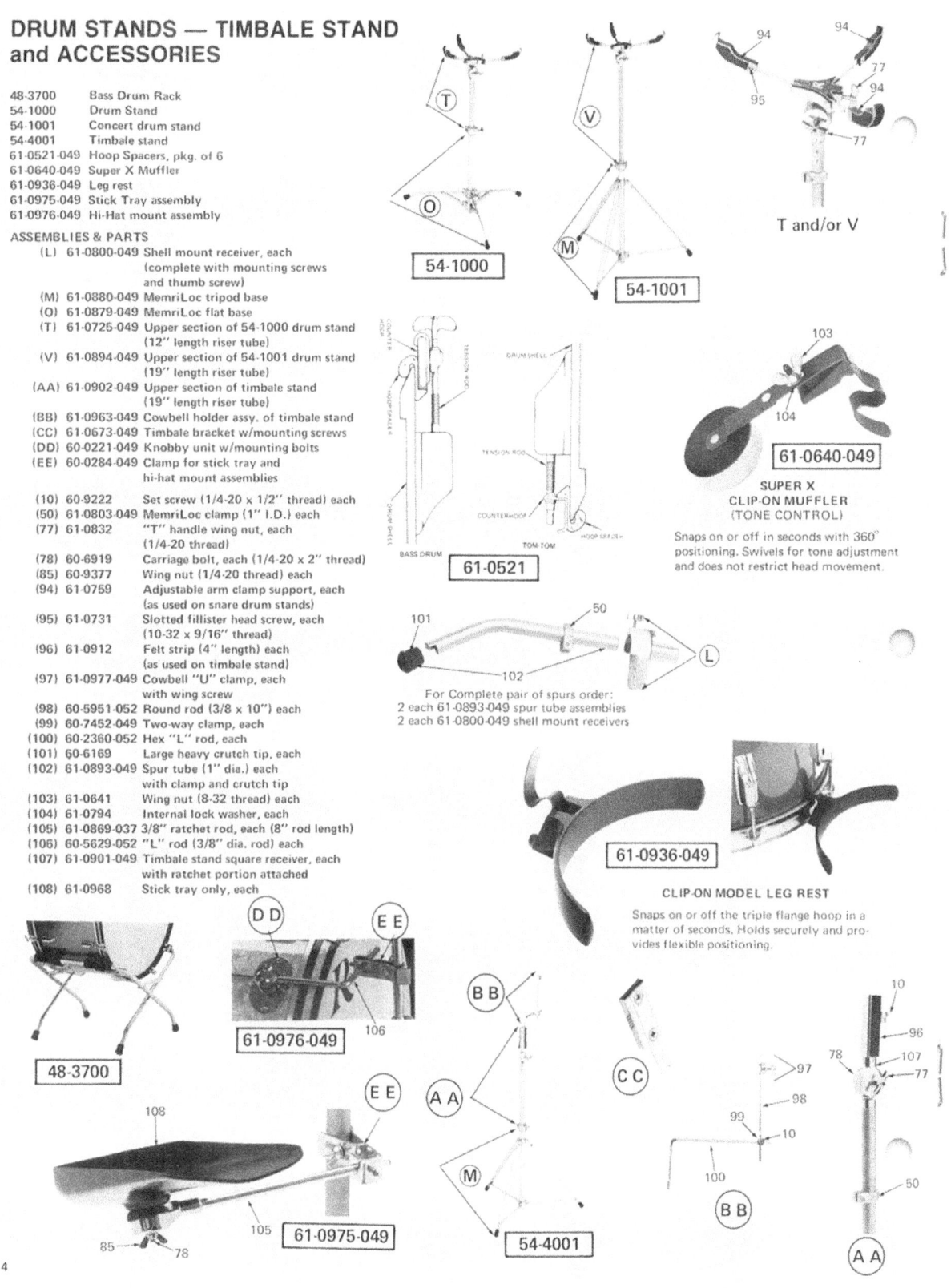

SUPER X CLIP-ON MUFFLER (TONE CONTROL)

Snaps on or off in seconds with 360° positioning. Swivels for tone adjustment and does not restrict head movement.

For Complete pair of spurs order:
2 each 61-0893-049 spur tube assemblies
2 each 61-0800-049 shell mount receivers

CLIP-ON MODEL LEG REST

Snaps on or off the triple flange hoop in a matter of seconds. Holds securely and provides flexible positioning.

INDEX

Arbiter autotune 38
Bashore, Joyce 31, 45
Badges 127
Bass drum logos 129
Beireis, Helen 31
Bellson, Louis 71, 76, 77
Burns, Roy 57–59, 87
CBS acquires Rogers 40
CBS sells Rogers 63
Calfskin heads 1, 7, 8
Catalogs 85–88
Cermenaro, John 52, 60–62
Chiasson, Bobby 84
Clark, Dave 35, 36, 37
Collett, Sam 29
Colors 89-94
Covington 9
Covington factory 24, 25
Covington factory fire 41
Covington personnel 26–29
Curtner, Bob 28
Cymbal stands 131
Dating Rogers products
    Badges 127
    Bass drum logos 129
        Catalogs 85
    Cymbal stands 131
    Hi-Hats 134
    Lugs 112-115
    Outfits 157
    Pedals 140
    Snare drums 149
    Snare stands 137
    Spurs 126
    Strainers 123
    Tom holders 143
Davidson, Peewee 34
Dayton 42, 44
Donahoe, Dave 147, 178
Dyna-sonic 179–194
Endorsees 65–77
English Rogers 35
Etter, Biddy 13, 14
Farmingdale 1–5
Fullerton production 50-52
Flutophone 15
Glass glitter 105
Gordon, Dave 60, 61, 61
Grossman, H.S. 9, 12, 18, 19, 21
Grossman acquires Rogers 19

Holmes, Ray 31
Hoops 148
Krampf, Craig 78–83, 54–55
Lugs 119
Malletron 172
Martin, Don 26
Martin, George 30
Martin, Les 30
Memriloc 46, 147
Minnich, Luellen
.... 29
Nicholas, Bill 30
Outfits 157–171
Parts 198–223
Platt, Dorothy 31
R-340, 360, 380 .... 176, 177
Rack system 47
Rich, Buddy 71, 76
Rogers factory moves 56, 61
Rogers, Joseph H. 1
Rogers, Joseph B. 1–4
Rogers, Cleveland S. 1, 3, 4
Sales of Rogers 1971–1980 59
Schultz, Bill 59, 64
Series II 178
Shells 117, 118
Skinny drum 191, 192
Snare drums 143–150
Snare machine 48, 49
Snare stands 137–139
Sparkle finishes 105
Spitzer, Matt 64
Spurs 126
Strainers 123–125
Strait, Byron 30
Strauss, Ben 20–23
Swivomatic 146
Thompson, Helen 14
Thompson, Joe 11, 14–18, 16–20, 34, 86
Timpani 173–175
Tom holders 143–147
Trostle, Kay 31
Way, George 32, 33
Wildwood 44, 90
XP-8 118

225

REBEATS PUBLICATIONS
visit the Rebeats website or contact us for details

THE GRETSCH DRUM BOOK
by Rob Cook
with John Sheridan
Business history, dating guide

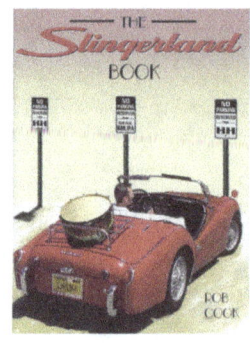

THE SLINGERLAND BOOK
by Rob Cook
Business history, dating guide

THE ROGERS BOOK
by Rob Cook
Business history, dating guide

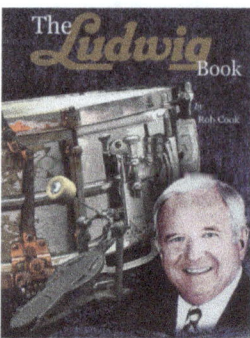

THE LUDWIG BOOK
by Rob Cook
Business history, dating guide

THE MAKING OF A DRUM COMPANY
The autobiography of Wm. F. Ludwig II, with Rob Cook

LEEDY DRUM TOPICS

THE LEEDY WAY
Biography of George Way, History of Leedy, Camco, Conn, L&S

MY LIFE IN PERCUSSION
Five Decades In The Music Products Industry
Karl Dustman memoir

Franks For The Memories

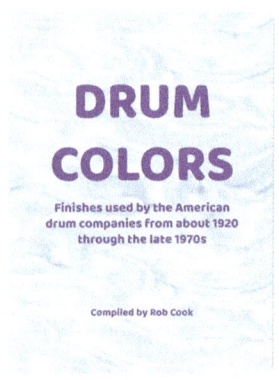

DRUM COLORS

George Way mini-biography, vendor directory

GENE KRUPA, HIS LIFE AND TIMES
biography of Gene Krupa, by Bruce Crowther

THE BABY DODDS STORY

Gretsch 1941 Catalog Reprint

The Rebeats Calfskin Head Book

Best Seat In The House

HAL BLAINE & THE WRECKING CREW

P.O. Box 6, Alma, Michigan 48801
989 463 4757
www.Rebeats.com   rob@rebeats.com

www.ingramcontent.com/pod-product-compliance
Lightning Source LLC
Chambersburg PA
CBHW081107080526
44587CB00021B/3488